READER'S DIGEST
THE GLORIOUS AGE OF
STEAM

Reader's
Digest

PUBLISHED BY THE READER'S DIGEST ASSOCIATION LIMITED
LONDON • NEW YORK • MONTREAL • SYDNEY • CAPE TOWN

A READER'S DIGEST BOOK

Published by The Reader's Digest Association Limited
11 Westferry Circus
Canary Wharf
London E14 4HE

Front cover: Mike Esau
Back cover: (top left) Millbrook House/P. Harris;
(top right) Millbrook House/Chemins de Fer de Provence;
(bottom) David C. Rodgers

ISBN 0 276 42335 6

British Library Cataloguing in Publication Data
for this book may be obtained from the British Library

This book was designed, edited and produced by Eaglemoss Publications Ltd,
based on the partwork *The World of Trains*
Consultant: David Johnson
Foreword by: Anthony Lambert

Printed in Dubai

10 9 8 7 6 5 4 3 2

Throughout the book, dimensions, speeds, pulling power and gauges
are given in their original form only, whether that is imperial or metric.
Other measurements are given in both forms.

CONTENTS

FOREWORD

It would be a dull soul who is not impressed by the sight of a steam locomotive working a heavy train, whether it is roaring a stentorian bark and sending skyward a volcanic column of smoke, or sizzling gently in repose with delicate wafts of steam and the hiss of hot oil.

The locomotive is at the centre of most people's love of railways, but a better understanding of them must be underscored by an appreciation of the railway as a complex organisation, numerous disciplines working harmoniously together. That doyen of writers on the machine age, L.T.C. Rolt, saw in railways a resolution of 'the conflict between the Romantic and Classical ideals, between the desire for individual freedom and the desire for order'.

The chapters of this book also appeal to these different desires. The story of great railway journeys the world over, with all the romantic connotations of travel and adventure it evokes, is balanced by the story of how signalling and carriages were developed. Safety was as important a factor as speed, pulling power and gauges; when systems failed, or human error defeated every safeguard, the results could be awful. The chapter on railway accidents shows how tragedies occurred and what lessons were learned.

Thankfully there are still places where the skills of the professional and the enthusiasm of the volunteer combine to give us an idea of how previous generations did things. Specially maintained steam railways, whether in north Wales or Colorado, are dedicated to imparting an understanding of the past as well as giving pleasure to those who operate and visit them. The focus of this activity is of course the steam locomotive itself, and the story of its evolution from Stephenson's *Rocket* to the goliaths of the Union Pacific appropriately opens this look at the colourful age of steam.

ANTHONY LAMBERT

CHAPTER ONE

THE HEYDAY OF THE STEAM LOCOMOTIVE

Brighton Station

Liverpool & Manchester Railway (LMR) *Rocket* 0-2-2
Designer: Robert Stephenson
Built: Robert Stephenson & Co, Forth Street, Newcastle-upon-Tyne, 1829
Service: built to compete in the Rainhill Trials, 1829. After winning the competition it was bought by the LMR and modified within 12 months. It later became a ballast engine until sold for use in the Midgeholm Colliery of Lord Carlisle
Livery: as built – white chimney, yellow boiler barrel and wheels, black frames, cylinder and boiler ends
Performance: it was recorded that 40 tons were pulled at 14mph on the level, 18 tons up a slope of 1 in 96 and 35mph as a light engine
Withdrawn from service: LMR 1835 and by Midgeholm Colliery 1844

Claiming credit

There have been many suggestions and emphatic statements that George Stephenson designed *Rocket*, but this was not so. It was solely the work of his son, Robert.

George did not see the locomotive once until it was delivered to Liverpool but he did frequently claim credit for his son's work. He was reprimanded in later years at a Parliamentary inquiry for doing just that.

A letter written by Robert and kept in the Devon County Record office, states 'I think it perfectly needless to go into the absurd and ridiculous stories which some writers have hatched up about my Father's conduct with *Rocket*. I had charge of the engine myself – whatever was done to the engine was done under my own eye and direction'.

▶ In 1979, a fully working reproduction *Rocket* was built to take part in the 150th anniversary celebration of the Rainhill Trials. It has run at speeds of up to 27mph. When built, it had a gauge of 8ft 4in, the same as the original LMR, but this was later changed to 4ft 8½in.

Previous page: picture postcard of Brighton Station in the early 1920s.

Rocket and *Planet*

LIVERPOOL & MANCHESTER RAILWAY

Two of the most important events in the history of railway engineering are the development of Robert Stephenson's locomotives *Rocket* and *Planet*. These two designs contained the essential elements used in the majority of steam locomotives built after 1830.

In 1829, locomotive trials took place at Rainhill, Lancashire, to enable the directors of the Liverpool & Manchester Railway (LMR) to decide on two points – whether locomotives or stationary engines should provide the motive power for their railway; and, if it was to be a locomotive, what was the most suitable type. The trial was won by a locomotive called *Rocket*, which had been designed and built by Robert Stephenson at Newcastle-upon-Tyne.

Robert Stephenson returned to England from a trip to South America at the end of November 1827. His father, George, was busy with the construction of the LMR and this left Robert to concentrate on a new type of locomotive. This was needed, as up until then steam engines had only been designed for use within the confines of a colliery or to a canal or river wharf – not hauling freight and passengers between two cities. So the task facing Robert was to build the world's first intercity locomotive.

From the beginning of 1828, Robert became the managing partner at his father's factory at Newcastle-upon-Tyne. He engaged the services of a draughtsman, George Phipps, and a works manager, William Hutchinson. Work soon began on a series of prototypes and once sold to a customer,

usually a colliery, the locomotive's performance was carefully monitored so that later designs could be improved. This was partly because there was no test track at the Stephensons' factory.

Rocket was one such prototype and was built with the forthcoming Rainhill Trials in mind. Work started on the locomotive around May 1829 and it underwent its first tests between 1 and 5 September; it was the nineteenth engine built by Robert Stephenson & Co. *Rocket* was light, fast and powerful and was the logical development of the locomotives Robert had designed and built in 1827 and 1828 when his stated aims were firstly to simplify the design of the steam locomotive and secondly to increase its power.

Essential elements

As early as 1803, Richard Trevithick, a close friend of Robert Stephenson, had introduced the essential elements for a successful steam locomotive, but *Rocket* was the first to combine them all. The most important feature of the locomotive was its use of the tubular boiler, a type which had been used on road locomotives for some time. Patents for railway locomotives using such boilers were taken out by Trevithick in 1815, W H James in 1821 and Marc Seguin in 1828.

TECHNICAL FILE

Rocket*
2 cylinders: (outside) 8in diameter x 17in stroke
Driving wheels: 4ft 8½in diameter
Carrying wheels: 2ft 6in diameter (as built)
Boiler diameter: 3ft 4in
Boiler length: 6ft
Pressure: 50lb psi pressure
Number of tubes: 25
Diameter: 3in
Grate area: 5.16sq ft
Overall length: 11ft
Weight: 4 tons 3cwt
*engine was later modified

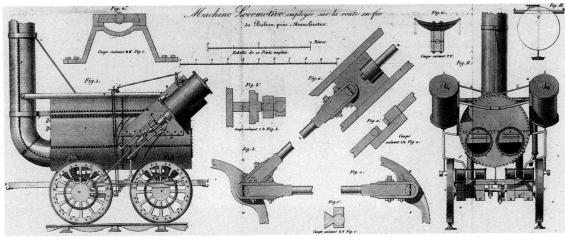

▼ **By combining a number of successful ideas in one design for the first time, *Rocket* was an enormous advance over previous locomotive types. Although the key to its success was the multi-tube boiler, another vital factor was a water jacket around the firebox, which gave a greater heating area for the water. This was supplied from a tender built by Nathaniel Worsdell, a noted English coach builder.**

Early Stephenson engines carried boilers with only a single flue. In 1828, some of these locomotives had been supplied to the St Etienne-Lyon Railway in France, but were unable to produce sufficient steam. The railway's engineer, Marc Seguin, then designed the multi-tubular boiler with its vastly increased surface area. The patent drawing of Seguin's boiler shows it to be identical to that used on *Rocket*, but with a different firebox.

The boiler on *Rocket* contained 25 copper tubes, 3in in diameter, and the firebox had spaces for water on the top and sides. The blast of the exhaust steam in the chimney helped increase the draw on the fire and its temperature. These features improved the boiler's ability to boil water and so produce more steam.

The boiler was supported, as on a previous Robert Stephenson-designed engine *Lancashire Witch*, on a wrought-iron frame made up of flat bars riveted and welded together with steel springs to each wheel. The two cylinders were mounted, again like *Lancashire Witch*, on the side of the

▲ ***Rocket*** **was developed from previous Robert Stephenson designs. These included *Lancashire Witch*, built in 1828 for freight haulage on the Bolton & Leigh Railway. Unlike previous designs which had a single or return flue, this locomotive had two furnace-flues side by side leading into a common chimney. Although an inefficient arrangement, it produced sufficient power for the type of tasks demanded at collieries. The angle of the cylinders was also new, as previously they had been positioned vertically, causing the engine to shake considerably.**

boiler at an angle of about 35° and drove the front wheels through a crosshead, supported by slide bars, directly. The bar frames and outside cylinders became a standard feature of American steam locomotives.

The availability of adequate steam with the light direct drive changed the speed of the locomotive from that of a cart horse to a race horse.

After a short time in service, *Rocket* was modified by the replacement of the original chimney, fixed directly over the tube ends at the front of the

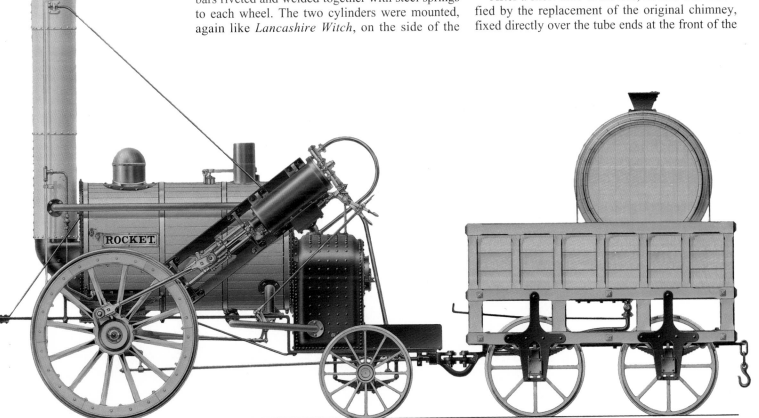

▶ On 26 February 1993, the reproduction *Planet* strolls across Swithland Viaduct, while undergoing trials on the preserved Great Central Railway in Leicestershire. In early locomotives, the boilers were usually fed with water by pumps driven by the engines themselves and it was necessary for the engine to be moving to work the pumps. To avoid this, the reproduction is fitted with an injector as well as a pump and this necessitates a boiler pressure of 100lb psi, rather than the original 50lb psi. The higher boiler pressure would, in turn, make the engine much more powerful and so the cylinder sizes are reduced to compensate. Steel has been used in the boiler and has replaced most of the other wrought-iron components. To conform with the modern safety requirements, this *Planet* has compressed air brakes, and modern buffers and couplings. Gauges and a device assist in reversing.

boiler, with a smokebox and the chimney on the top in the now familiar position. This allowed a more even suction through the tubes and the ashes could be cleared away more easily.

The cylinders were lowered to a nearly horizontal position, providing a steadier ride at speed, since the original position tended to cause considerable deflection of the driving wheel springs, making the engine shoulder and swing up and down and from side to side.

Rocket made the intercity passenger railway possible. There were six more engines built to the same basic design and then two bigger and more powerful Northumbrian types. These had different frames and the fireboxes were inside the boiler shell rather than attached at the back, as on *Rocket*.

The next stage

'Not content with what he had achieved, Robert Stephenson resolved on effecting further improvements and the *Planet* was the result of his renewed exertions', reported the proceedings of the Institute of Chartered Engineers.

While the Stephensons' factory at Newcastle-upon-Tyne was producing the earlier types of engines for the LMR, Robert Stephenson was working on the design for a more efficient machine called *Planet*. Trevithick had told him that the efficiency of a stationary engine he had re-built had been greatly increased by including a steam jacket which heated the cylinder on the outside. In *Planet*, Robert put his cylinders almost horizontally inside the smokebox to keep them hot and reduce condensation. This meant he then had to use a crank axle to drive the wheels.

Some years earlier in 1815, George Stephenson and his partner, Ralph Dodds, took out a patent which included rods to couple the driving wheels.

The rods were worked on cranks inside the wheels. This presented the unwelcome possibility of a crank failing in service. Although metallurgy and production methods had improved, they were not up to those of today. Robert had to design his new engine so that the risk of a crankshaft breaking was greatly reduced and if one did break then the wheels would remain in place and the safety of the engine and train would not be endangered.

The frames were designed and built with six timber members. The outside pair was strengthened with iron plates and each member carried a bearing for the crank axle. In this way, each wheel and each crank had a bearing on both sides. Although *Planet* had the same sized cylinders and boiler as *Northumbrian*, an earlier locomotive with outside cylinders, it was smoother running and the heated cylinders ensured that it was more economical to run.

In 1830, *Planet* and *Rocket* contained all the essential basic features that could still be found in new steam locomotives being built in China in the 1990s. New features included a firebox within the boiler shell. Between the frames, horizontal cylinders, with crossheads and slide bars, supplied power to a cranked driving axle. Horns, horn-guides and leaf springs helped to absorb the vertical forces and the effects of track inequalities.

Planet was completed at the Newcastle works on 3 September 1830 and missed the opening of the LMR by a few days only. On 4 December, it hauled its first train. This consisted of 18 wagons, carrying oatmeal and malt and 15 passengers, totalling 80 tons gross. The journey took just under three hours at an average speed of 12.5mph, and a top speed of 15.5mph. A month after delivery, *Planet* ran as a light engine from Liverpool to Manchester in one hour.

It proved to be far more economical than earlier

Where to see them
In 1844, *Rocket* was returned to Robert Stephenson & Co, Newcastle, for restoration and exhibited at the Great Exhibition in London. It was partly dismantled but no other work was done. Robert died in 1859 and, in accordance with his stated wish, the remains of *Rocket* were presented to the Patent Museum, the forerunner of the Science Museum, in London in 1862 where it can be seen today.

The original *Planet* was not preserved but *John Bull*, built for the Camden & Amboy Railway in America in 1831, has survived. It was a four-coupled engine similar in many ways to *Samson* and *Goliath* but has been much modified to suit American conditions. It is preserved at the Smithsonian Institute, Washington, USA.

TECHNICAL FILE

Planet
2 cylinders: 11in diameter x 16in stroke
Driving wheels: 5ft diameter
Carrying wheels: 3ft 1in diameter (as built)
Boiler diameter: 3ft
Boiler length: 6ft 6in
Pressure: 50lb psi
Number of tubes: 129
Diameter: 1⅝in
Total heating service: 407.66sq ft
Grate area: 6.5sq ft
Overall length: 12ft 9in
Weight: approx 8 tons

prototypes in terms of fuel consumption. When hauling four coaches, *Planet* consumed an average 19lb of coke per mile over 16 trips compared with the 27-28lb of previous engines.

Where steep gradients were found, it was necessary to provide more adhesion than *Planet*'s single driving wheels and so the small leading wheels were replaced by a second pair, the same size as the driving wheels, and coupled to them by outside coupling rods. Two of these engines, named *Samson* and *Goliath*, were delivered to the Liverpool & Manchester Railway in 1831.

The firebox of the Planet-type overhung the driving axle at the back and this caused the engines to swing from side to side at speed. This, together with the increased weights, caused concern. In later designs, an additional pair of wheels was positioned behind the firebox. After 10 years of service, *Planet* was withdrawn. A locomotive called *John Bull*, based on *Planet*, can be seen at the Smithsonian Institute, Washington, USA.

▲ The invention of the multi-tube boiler has often been attributed to Henry Booth, secretary of the Liverpool & Manchester Railway and co-owner of *Rocket* with George and Robert Stephenson. However, the boiler used on *Rocket* was similar to that designed by a Frenchman, Marc Seguin, who had developed it after becoming dissatisfied with the steam produced by two engines he had bought from the Stephensons for the St Etienne-Lyon Railway in 1828.

▼ The Planet-design was the prototype for the majority of locomotives built for British railways in the 19th century and the GWR used the same basic ideas on their City class of 1903. It is recorded in the proceedings of the Institution of Civil Engineers that the chairman, Rennie, stated 'Mr Stephenson has brought his engines to such perfection in construction that all questions appeared to be now a mere matter of detail arrangements'.

Midland Spinners

MIDLAND RAILWAY

The Midland Spinners were an essay in design and elegance. With enormous driving wheels to whisk express trains between London and the Midlands at speeds over 80mph, the class was one of the grand sights of the Edwardian railway.

In the early years of railways in Britain, the single driver locomotive was widely adopted for passenger work – perhaps taking a lead from Stephenson's famous *Rocket* – and by 1840, several engine builders had adopted the 2-2-2 arrangement with inside cylinders and outside frames. The term single driver comes from the use of a single pair of large driving wheels – as opposed to smaller coupled wheels. These designs had proved very successful and the Midland Railway (MR) bought, or built, 2-2-2s with 6ft 8in driving wheels until 1866. A few railways used outside cylinders with this wheel arrangement, but this brought problems with stability at speed.

Different trends

As train weights and scheduled speeds increased, single driver engines became outclassed. New trends evolved, firstly towards the 2-4-0 and then to the 4-4-0 with a leading bogie. In 1858, the MR joined in this change and built 2-4-0s to work its express trains to London.

But there were lingering doubts about the suitability of coupled wheels for fast passenger duties. The limiting factor for single driver engines was adhesion. The limit of the axleload was usually about 18 tons, making them prone to slipping, and heavy trains soon proved difficult for the locomo-

◀ The designer of the MR 4-2-2 singles intended that the class would be ideal for trains south of Derby and Nottingham. Around the turn of the century, No 170 waits at Bedford with a train to St Pancras, while the fireman breaks up some large lumps of coal on the tender.

◄Out of a class of 95 locomotives, 43 survived to be taken into LMS ownership in 1923. They were usually employed on lightweight or pilot duties. Soon after Grouping, No 679 pilots an LMS Class 2P 4-4-0 with a train of clerestory coaches up the Lickey incline south of Birmingham. The smokebox and chimney have replaced the more elegant MR originals.

LOCO LIST

Under the MR renumbering scheme of 1907, the 95 Midland Spinners were numbered between 600 and 694. The 43 which survived into LMS days were renumbered between 600 and 684. Only one of the class received a name – MR No 2601 (later LMS No 685) was called *Princess of Wales*, which was painted on the driving splasher above the Midland crest.

tives, compelling the use of a second engine.

But as so often happens, the need produced at least a partial solution. The MR was one of the first railways to use continuous brakes for its passenger trains, favouring the Westinghouse compressed air brake. The works manager at Derby, Mr Holt, produced a sanding system using air from the brake pump to blow sand under the wheels. This system was highly successful during trials in 1886. However, Westinghouse objected to the use of 'their' air for ancillary purposes – in case it affected the integrity of the air brake. The sanding system was modified to use steam instead and this proved satisfactory. From 1889, the MR standardised on the vacuum brake.

Second wind

Steam sanding gave the single driver locomotives a new lease of life, particularly on the MR, whose operating philosophy was to run frequent passenger trains seldom reaching 200 tons in weight. After a gap of 21 years, 1887 saw a resumption of building single driver engines, now with a front bogie and a 4-2-2 wheel arrangement. This programme continued until 1900, alongside 4-4-0s for the more arduous duties. Five groups of 4-2-2s were built under the direction of the MR Locomotive Superintendent, Samuel Johnson, totalling 95 engines which were broadly similar, but differing in detail.

A common feature of locomotive building at

Where to see them
Only one Midland Spinner survives today. No 673 can be seen at the National Railway Museum, York.

Scots' quip
In the mid-19th century, many railway engineers had some doubts as to the suitability of locomotives with coupled wheels for fast passenger work. One eminent Scottish engineer likened them to 'a laddie trying to run wi' his breeks down'. What he would have thought of BR Standard 2-10-0s, with wheels only 5ft diameter, reaching speeds of 90mph is a matter of conjecture.

◄The MR started building singles after a gap of 21 years, because it was felt that locomotives with coupled wheels were not ideal for express passenger work. The diameter of the driving wheels on the Spinners varied between 7ft 4in and 7ft 9^{1}/₂in. Unusually for MR locomotives, the class had smokeboxes which were flush with the boiler cladding.

Design specifications MIDLAND 2601 CLASS

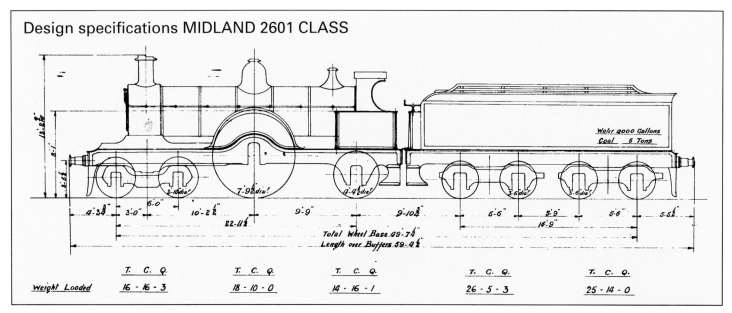

	T. C. Q.	T. C. Q.	T. C. Q.	T. C. Q.	T. C. Q.
Weight Loaded	16 - 16 - 3	18 - 10 - 0	14 - 16 - 1	26 - 5 - 3	25 - 14 - 0

▲The Midland Spinners were produced in five distinct classes which included variations in the size of driving wheels, cylinders, firebox length and driving wheel springing. The last 10 locomotives were given large boilers and rated 2P. In 1906, there was a proposal to rebuild all the Spinners as 4-4-0s, but this idea was later cancelled.

this period was the use of double frames. These provided four bearings on the crank axle, but only outside bearings on the trailing axle. The shape of the frames varied somewhat at the front end. The first engines had either 7ft 4in or 7ft 6in diameter driving wheels, with underhung leaf springs. But from 1890, 7ft 6in wheels were adopted.

The first 60 engines had slide valves in a vertical steam chest between the 18in by 26in cylinders, but for later builds, piston valves below the cylinders were adopted. This was an arrangement widely used on MR express locomotives but it gave a rather restricted steam circuit. The weight on the driving wheels was nominally kept down to 18.5 tons.

It was necessary for the boiler barrel to fit between the large driving wheels and this limited its diameter to about 4ft 1½in. All the boilers had round topped fireboxes surmounted by a lock-up safety valve in a brass casing, while two spring-balance type safety valves were fitted on the dome. The grate area increased progressively from 19.7sq ft on the first examples, to 24.5sq ft on the final engines.

With the boiler gradually enlarged, the Johnson cab began to look skimpy, though one, No 600, was given a more protective Deeley cab and was used to haul the directors' saloon. A standard six-

TECHNICAL FILE

Nos 620-659
2 cylinders: 18½in diameter x 26in stroke
Driving wheels: 7ft 6½in diameter
Boiler diameter: 4ft 1in
Grate area: 19.7sq ft
Boiler pressure: 160lb psi
Tractive effort: 13,372lb
Coal capacity: 4 tons
Water capacity: 3250 gallons
Weight in working order:
Engine: 43.5 tons
Tender: 33.5 tons

Prize comfort
In 1889, No 1853 and a Midland 12-wheeled pressed steel bogie composite coach were sent new to the Paris Exhibition as examples of fine British workmanship. The locomotive won a gold medal and the coach was given the Grand Prix. The French judges were very impressed at the comfort lavished on third class passengers – they even had toilet facilities.

◄The Spinners proved to be popular with the crews for their low fuel consumption and the public for their fast running and good looks. No 16 presents an immaculate appearance at Bedford locomotive depot about 1904. It was said that if an engine had not been cleaned to the foreman's satisfaction it was not released to traffic – and the cleaner responsible sacked.

wheeled 3250 or 3500 gallon tender was provided.

The Spinners were allocated to several depots and worked trains between Leeds, Derby, Nottingham and London, as well as on the West of England line between Birmingham and Bristol. Schedules were not unduly demanding, but on the longer falling gradients, such as from Luton to Bedford, they regularly reached speeds in the 80s and were timed at up to 90mph. There were those who insisted that over the years the Spinners became faster and more powerful.

Final batch

The last Spinners, the very elegant 2601 class of which 10 were built, were turned out from Derby works in 1900. The driving wheels of 7ft 9½in diameter were the largest ever used on the Midland Railway. Twin-coil springs were also adopted. The cylinders were increased to 19½ x 26in and the 8ft long firebox contributed 147sq ft to a total heating surface of 1217sq ft. Working pressure was set at 180lb psi.

As at this time there were no water troughs on the Midland Railway, the class came out with bogie tenders of 4000 gallon capacity. Many enginemen thought that these spoiled the symme-try of the Spinners and disparagingly dubbed them water carts.

In 1900, No 2601 *Princess of Wales* went to Paris and won a gold medal. It was the only Spinner, and only the second Midland Railway locomotive, to be named. This was painted in serif letters in a curve on the driving wheel splashers. The letters M R appeared in serif on the buffer beam – matching those on the sides of the tender.

At first, numbering of the class was rather random, but in 1907 a more logical system was adopted and the bogie singles became Nos 600-694. The 43 surviving examples retained their MR numbers when taken over by the London Midland & Scottish Railway (LMS) in 1923. However, by then all the 2601 class had been withdrawn.

Gradually the Spinners were displaced by larger 4-4-0s and found themselves on less important services or acting as pilot engines. This even extended to coal trains, which on the Toton – Brent run invariably needed two engines. The last one was withdrawn in 1928. One Spinner, No 673 built in 1897, has been preserved and ran in the Liverpool & Manchester cavalcades at Rainhill in 1930 and 1980. The locomotive has been restored to its 1909 condition.

▲ In May 1980, MR 4-2-2 No 673 was present at the locomotive cavalcade for the 150th anniversary of the Liverpool & Manchester Railway. Built in 1897 and withdrawn in 1928, this locomotive is the only one to be preserved.

Careful studies
In 1875, during the Newark brake trials, Samuel Johnson was greatly impressed by the London Brighton & South Coast Railway's single driver No 326 *Grosvenor*. In 1884-85, Johnson carefully monitored the performance of an old single, based at Leicester, which was specially put on London services. Following these observations, Johnson decided that the single would be ideal for lightweight express trains over the less hilly sections of the MR.

Valve working

In a steam locomotive, steam has to be admitted to, and exhausted from, the cylinders at the right moment in the cycle. This is achieved by a valve arrangement inside the steam chest, which is located next to each cylinder.

Typically the cylinder has an aperture (port) at each end, and the function of the valve is to admit fresh steam under pressure at one end, while allowing used steam to escape at the other. The later main line engines were fitted with piston valves, in which the cylindrical steam chest contains two heads on a piston that cover and uncover the ports in sequence.

Laps and leads

The amount of overlap between the valve and the port is known as the **lap**. In slow moving locomotives a long lap on the exhaust port is common. The delayed opening of the port gives time for the steam trapped in the cylinder to make best use of its stored energy and expand fully, pushing against the piston.

On fast running locomotives, exhaust clearance (allowing the port to open early when the valve is in mid-position) helps the steam to escape faster, so reducing back pressure.

Higher speed locomotives also have **long lead**, meaning that the admission port is already open when the piston is at the end of its movement (sweep) to the front or back of the cylinder, so assuring good steam pressure immediately it begins its next movement.

Cut-off

This is the term used to denote the position of the piston in its path, at the moment the valve is closing the port to stop steam being admitted to the cylinder.

When the locomotive is working hard and slowly, long cut-off can admit steam

for most of the stroke of the piston, but at higher speeds this overtaxes the boiler and leads to back pressure. To prevent this, cut-off can be reduced at high speeds until steam is admitted for only 15% of the stroke, its expansive properties being used to push the piston for the remainder of the stroke.

▲ Most steam engines have between two and four sets of valve gear and cylinders. These are usually placed at the front of the locomotive, ahead of the driving wheels and under the smokebox. They are either visible on the side of the engine, as shown here, or hidden between the frames behind the wheels.

The working cycle of valve and piston

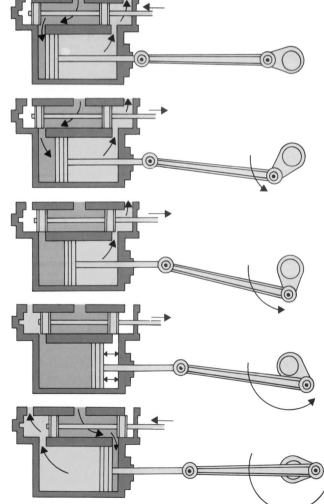

1 The valve head is in front of the forward port, allowing steam under pressure into the cylinder to push the piston back.

2 As the piston continues to move backwards, used steam from the previous stroke is exhausted through the back port at the rear of the cylinder.

3 After about 30% of the piston's full stroke the valve head cuts off the steam supply. The steam continues to expand and pushes the piston back.

4 The front port opens to exhaust the steam while the back port is closed, creating some back pressure before the next stroke is made.

5 Fresh steam under pressure enters by the back port and the process begins again. The piston and valve move forward to begin a new sweep.

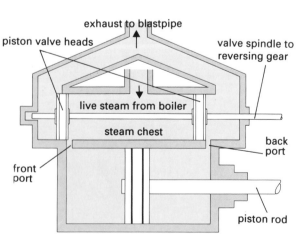

exhaust to blastpipe

piston valve heads

valve spindle to reversing gear

live steam from boiler

steam chest

back port

front port

piston rod

D class 4-4-0

SOUTH EASTERN & CHATHAM RAILWAY

Often hailed as the most elegant British locomotive of all time, the D class 4-4-0 embodied all the dash and style typical of a turn of the century express passenger locomotive. Later successfully rebuilt, some of the class gave 60 years' service.

Despite the increasing numbers of 4-4-2s and 4-6-0s, for the first quarter of the 20th century at least, passenger services on many of Britain's railways were dominated by modestly proportioned 4-4-0 engines. In 1922, for example, there were almost 3200 4-4-0s at work, or rather more than one in eight of the then peaking main line stock of around 24,000 engines.

Weight restrictions

The vast majority of 4-4-0s had inside cylinders and, with their external simplicity of outline, were raised to an art form by several railways; in particular, the Midland Railway (MR) and South Eastern & Chatham Railway (SECR), whose locomotives shared similar features. Alone amongst the dozen or so leading railways, largely on account of stringent weight restrictions, the MR and SECR persevered with the 4-4-0 to handle their most prestigious services until the end of their independent existences in 1922.

The SECR came into being in 1899 as a result of a confederation, rather than an amalgamation, with the establishment of a joint management committee, of two former bitter and impoverished rivals, the South Eastern Railway (SER) and London, Chatham & Dover Railway (LCDR), each of which had its own route between London and Dover, served many of the same towns, and kept its own board of directors.

The SER was the larger of the two, with its locomotive headquarters at Ashford (Kent), while the LCDR had a distinctly cramped locomotive works at Longhedge (Battersea). In 1899, their respective Locomotive, Carriage & Wagon Superintendents, James Stirling and William Kirtley, retired and a former South Eastern man, Harry Wainwright, was placed in overall charge.

▼ The D class was certainly an elegant design. What has sometimes been mistaken for a Westinghouse pump on the right-hand side was in fact the vertical Stirling-type steam reverser. D class 4-4-0, No 729, waits at Charing Cross.

KEY FACTS

SECR Class D 4-4-0
Designer: H S Wainwright/ R Surtees. Later rebuilt to the designs of James Clayton
Built: 1901-07 Ashford works; Sharp, Stewart & Co, Glasgow; Robert Stephenson & Co, Darlington; Vulcan Foundry, Newton-le-Willows and Dubbs & Co, Scotland
Service: express passenger trains, especially boat trains, between London and Folkestone and Dover. Later, secondary duties
Livery: 1901-10 – Brunswick green, lined red and yellow, with red frames, polished brass dome. 1910-14 – Brunswick green, lined yellow, with red frames, dome painted in Brunswick green. 1915 – plain unvarnished green. 1915-22 – battleship grey with white numerals. 1923-40 – lined olive green. 1940-47 – plain black. 1948-56 – plain and lined black
Rebuilt: (21 engines) 1921-27; 30 engines unrebuilt
Performance: 1913, from London Bridge and passing Dover Tunnel, 74.6 miles at an average speed of 56mph with 200 ton trains
Withdrawn: (unrebuilt engines) 1947-56. (Rebuilt engines) 1950-61 (one war casualty, 1944)

▶ Before the final D class entered service, the E class was introduced. This was a slightly larger development of the D, with a Belpaire firebox. In early 1917, the E class was completely redesigned, with superheater, long-travel piston valves and larger Belpaire firebox. In this form, the class continued to give valued service until final withdrawal in 1961. Class E No 1275 hauls a Hastings-bound service near Tonbridge in 1940.

LOCO LIST

From 1923, the SR added the prefix A to each number, indicating that the engine was maintained at Ashford works. The A was replaced in 1931 by 1000 being added to the running numbers. With nationalisation, in 1948 BR added the prefix 3.

Where to see them
No 737 is restored to its as new condition at the National Railway Museum, York.

Elaborate paint scheme
The painting instructions for the D class were quite specific: engine boiler, cab, splashers and wheels given three coats of Brunswick green, fine lined with red and yellow, the wheels fine lined with red only; engine frames deep red, fine lined with red and yellow; the tender, tank and wheels given three coats of Brunswick green, fine lined with red and yellow, wheels fine lined with red only; the frames to be painted deep red, fine lined with red and yellow; the front of buffer plates, inside of frame, motion plate and stay in front of firebox to be painted vermilion (bright red).

▶ Although the last unsuperheated D class was withdrawn in 1961, happily the penultimate survivor, No 737, latterly BR No 31737, was elected for official complete external restoration at Ashford works in 1960, as an example of a Wainwright locomotive in its prime. In its heyday, it had regularly worked Royal Specials between London and Dover. After a spell at Clapham museum in London it was moved to York in 1975.

On seniority, however, a Chatham man, Robert Surtees, became Chief Draughtsman with his younger SER opposite number, Basil Field, serving under him.

Having gained wide experience in carriage as well as locomotive design and building during his time on the MR, Wainwright took a particular interest in the locomotives' styling and embellishment, especially livery. The detailed design devolved upon Surtees, who almost immediately began to scheme an express passenger 4-4-0, Class D, a goods 0-6-0, Class C and an 0-4-4 passenger tank engine, Class H. These were all to be adorned in a particularly elaborate livery, by early 20th century standards, and the new 4-4-0s, in addition to polished brass dome covers, were also to carry copper-capped chimneys, which would earn them the nickname of 'Coppertops'.

This large brass dome was also to be an eye-catching feature on the Wainwright D class. It must have contrasted strongly to contemporary eyes with the austere lined black of the erstwhile LCDR, and the domeless boilers of the SER engines.

The D class was descended from the LCDR Class M3 4-4-0 of 1877, designed by William Kirtley, which had strong leanings towards the earliest S W Johnson 4-4-0s of the MR. William Kirtley was a nephew of Matthew Kirtley, Johnson's predecessor and had left the MR to become Locomotive, Carriage & Wagon Superintendent of the LCDR.

New locomotives
The first 20 D class 4-4-0s were ordered in September 1899 and a total of 51 entered traffic between February 1901 and March 1907, with prices ranging from £2950 to £3575 each. Construction was divided between four private builders and the SECR itself at Ashford works. When new, the class was mainly employed on Continental boat trains between the two SER London termini of Cannon Street and Charing Cross, and Folkestone and Dover.

Midland influence

Before joining the SECR, Wainwright had served on the MR in the carriage department at Derby under Thomas Clayton. There is a similarity in style between Wainwright's D class 4-4-0 built for the SECR and the MR 4-4-0s, designed by Samuel Johnson. Both types were distinguished by sweeping coupled wheel splashers abounding in reverse curves and embellished with polished brass beading. Both had separate numerals cut from brass sheet, rather than the more usual cast numberplates or transfers. What with its flush smokebox door, a Wainwright D class painted crimson lake and with an all black chimney could almost have passed as a 'well fed' Johnson 4-4-0, one of which, No 2202, stands outside Bedford shed in 1904.

A few months after the first engines had been in service, severe problems with leaking tubes due to the hard Kent water were encountered but soon overcome. The boilers steamed freely, and the installation of patent basket type spark arresters in the short smokeboxes checked their habit of fire-throwing on the climb over the North Downs.

Even a year before the final D class entered service, the E class made its debut, of which 26 were built between 1906 and 1909. These had a Belpaire firebox having 6ft more grate area and 6ft 6in driving wheels in place of 6ft of the D class. Like the D class, the E class was initially turned out in the full glory of the Wainwright livery, but the 'Golden Age' began to fade in 1911 in response to economic recession. Shorter plain cast-iron chimneys began to be fitted, reducing the maximum height from 13ft 4in to 13ft in order to facilitate through working over neighbouring companies' lines, especially the London, Brighton &

South Coast Railway (LBSCR).

In late 1913, beset by professional and matrimonial problems, Wainwright resigned officially on health grounds, by which time his 4-4-0s were already no longer quite so resplendent as of yore. A simpler livery incorporating only yellow lining was instituted, and the brass dome covers painted over. Tender side plates were angled outwards over the top, partly to increase their fuel capacity, but also to prevent waiting passengers on suburban station platforms from being struck by flying coal from expresses passing through at speed. Early in World War I, plain unvarnished green was briefly applied to a few engines, before wartime battleship grey with large white numerals on the tenders became the norm until the end of the SECR's independent existence.

At the time of Wainwright's departure at the early age of only 48, designs were well advanced for a large superheated Belpaire 4-4-0, the Class

True engineer

It is often said that the designer, Harry Wainwright, had little knowledge of mechanical matters and concerned himself mainly with styling. However, in 1901, in an interview with the *Railway Magazine*, Wainwright gave a detailed account of his locomotive design policy. He said that for nine of his 22 years in railway mechanical engineering, he had been intimately connected with locomotive departments, including time as a draughtsman and works manager. Of his locomotive policy, Wainwright said his idea was to use larger boilers with a much greater heating surface and grate area, and cylinders giving unrestricted steam and exhaust passages.

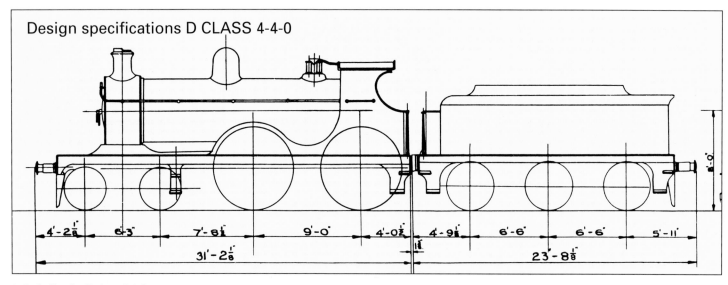

Design specifications D CLASS 4-4-0

▲ As built, the D class 4-4-0s were given round-topped fireboxes, short-travel valves and used saturated steam. When superheating was later fitted to some members of the class, the smokebox was extended to accommodate the superheater header. Dimensionally, especially with regard to the boiler, the D class was modelled on the contemporary Caledonian Railway 'Dunalastair II' 4-4-0.

TECHNICAL FILE

2 inside cylinders: 19in diameter x 26in stroke
Grate area: 20.25sq ft
Maximum boiler diameter: 4ft 9in
Driving wheels: 6ft 7⁷/₈in diameter
Tractive effort: 17,950lb
Boiler pressure: 180lb psi
Length over buffers: 54ft 10³/₄in
Coal capacity: 4/4.5 tons
Water capacity: 3300/3450 gallons
Weight in working order:
Engine: 50 tons
Tender: 38.25/39.1 tons

▶ Between 1921 and 1927, following the rebuilding of the E class, 21 D class 4-4-0s were similarly treated. This left 30 unrebuilt, none of which was later even fitted with superheaters. The D1 and E1 rebuilds were excellent performers, initially working the 300 ton boat trains single handed, until bridge strengthening allowed 4-6-0s to be introduced. In later years the D1s and E1s worked on lighter Kent Coast expresses and semi-fasts. In the 1950s, D1 No 31727 passes with a three-coach local service.

L, which had not yet entered service. By the time World War I had began, of the 22 ordered and built in 1914, 10 had been supplied by German builders. Continental services then virtually ceased for the duration – apart from heavy troop train traffic.

The restoration of Continental services was anticipated well before the Armistice and they were routed into Victoria station (LCDR), using inter-connecting spurs at Chislehurst, leaving Cannon Street and Charing Cross (SER) free for the increasingly heavy suburban traffic. Although it was intended to increase boat train loadings to 300 tons, the 57¹/₂ ton L class was precluded from Victoria on account of excessive weight over the station's approaches.

Locomotive redesign

Wainwright's successor, an Irishman, Richard Maunsell, who had swiftly recruited an outstanding design team, selected as his Chief Draughtsman James Clayton from the MR at Derby where he had worked on Cecil Paget's unique eight-cylinder sleeve valve 2-6-2. Originally a Beyer, Peacock & Co apprentice,

Clayton had worked in the Ashford Drawing Office around the turn of the century and had participated in the original design of the Wainwright D class.

In early 1917, Clayton directed a complete redesign of the E class with superheater, long-travel, long-lap piston valves and larger Belpaire firebox sloped back to increase the grate area. Work resulted in only a 4% increase in weight over the original despite the heavier boiler – a masterly piece of design work. The prototype conversion, which despite appearances retained much of the original engine, emerged from Ashford works in February 1919. It closely resembled the MR 483 class 4-4-0s, with which Clayton had been involved, but with greatly improved performance capacity due to its more economical use of steam.

In 1920, 10 further Es were rebuilt by Beyer, Peacock & Co and this was followed by 10 D class 4-4-0s on similar lines during 1921, becoming D1s. Two more Ds were rebuilt at Ashford in 1922, followed by nine more in 1926-27.

The remaining D 4-4-0s were left unaltered, and condemnation did not begin until 1947, with the last not being retired until December 1956.

Compound Atlantics

NORD RAILWAY

The du Bousquet Atlantics, introduced by the Nord Railway in 1899, were a benchmark in locomotive development and performance. Their four-cylinder divided drive layout was later adopted by Churchward and featured on many GWR express engines.

KEY FACTS

Nord 4-4-2
SNCF Nos: 2641-2675
Designer: Gaston du Bousquet/ J Koechlin
Built: Alsacienne locomotive works 1899-1905
Service: main line express passenger trains
Livery: chocolate brown, yellow lining
Performance: 89km/h (55mph) up 1 in 200 grade with 400 tons. Brussels – Paris, 309km (192.2 miles) at average speed of 110km/h (68mph) with 350 tons (as rebuilt with Lemaître exhaust and superheated)
Withdrawn: 1940-47

At the beginning of the 20th century, the fastest passenger services in Europe, in terms of scheduled average speed, were achieved by the Northern (Nord) Railway of France. A major factor in this was the outstanding success of four-cylinder compound 4-4-0s and 4-4-2s of progressively increasing performance capacity.

Divided drive

The use of compound locomotives in France started in 1876, with Anatole Mallet's little 0-4-2 tanks on the Bayonne – Biarritz line. Tests showed fuel savings of up to 35% compared with simple expansion types. The first application of compounding to main line express locomotives took place 10 years later.

As a result of frequent crank axle failures with the Nord's fleet of powerful inside-cylindered Outrance class 4-4-0s, Alfred de Glehn, technical director of the Alsacienne locomotive works, suggested to Gaston du Bousquet, the Chief Mechanical Engineer (CME) of the Nord, that the crank axle stresses could be greatly reduced by dividing the drive between two axles. His idea was for the two inside cylinders to be mounted well

forward and connected to the leading driving axle, with two cylinders located further back outside the frames, driving the second axle.

A prototype was built in the Alsacienne workshops and numbered 701. Compound drive was proposed by de Glehn with du Bousquet's agreement; he had previously obtained useful fuel economies with compounding, when Nord 0-8-0 freight engines had been converted from two-cylinder simple machines to four-cylinder tandem compounds. On No 701, the low pressure (LP) cylinders were outside and the high pressure (HP) inside the frames.

Originally, the driving axles were uncoupled, as in Webb's three-cylinder express compounds of the London & North Western Railway (LNWR), but differential wheelslip problems between the two uncoupled driving groups resulted in coupling rods being fitted. The leading radial axle was later replaced by a two-axle bogie, which gave greater stability. In express service, 4-4-0 No 701 eliminated the crank axle problem and showed a 20% economy in fuel over the Outrance class.

Meanwhile, express trains were being accelerated and from 1890 du Bousquet introduced pro-

▼At the turn of the century, the performance capacity of the Nord Atlantics was legendary. In 1903, Churchward, the CME of the GWR, ordered one to test against his simple expansion two-cylinder machines. He was impressed by the much smoother riding of the well-balanced four-cylinder locomotive and adopted the divided drive and other features in his Star class four-cylinder simple expansion 4-6-0s.

In 1904, No 102 *La France* passes Subway Junction, Westbourne Park with a train from Paddington. The locomotive was withdrawn in 1926.

The 4-6-0 derivative

With the ever increasing weight of the heavier express trains making more frequent stops, du Bousquet realised that greater adhesive weight was required than that of the Atlantics. A 4-6-0 derivative of the 4-4-2 was designed, with 50% greater adhesive weight and driving wheels of 1.75m (5ft 9in) diameter, compared with 2.04m (6ft 8¼in), to reduce total weight. The steam flow circuit was further enlarged so that they could run as freely as the Atlantics at speed, despite their smaller driving wheels.

A total of 125 highly successful 3513 class 4-6-0s were built. From 1910, superheating was applied to both types, giving further increases in power (by 16%) and efficiency. On 30 July 1964, No 230.D.109, fitted with a Lemaître exhaust and large chimney, departs from Boulogne Ville with an evening train to Desvres. One of these engines is preserved on the Nene Valley Railway.

Pullman performance

Performance of the Lemaître equipped Nord Atlantics on the Brussels Pullman workings was outstanding – on one occasion 110km/h (68mph) was sustained up a long 1 in 200 gradient with 347 tons. No 2659 made up a 10 minute late start from Brussels with the 350-ton Blue Bird Pullman, covering the 309km (192 miles) to Paris in 170 minutes at an average of 110km/h (68mph), without exceeding 125km/h (77mph). This locomotive made 74 consecutive trips without any mechanical incident.

gressively more powerful four-cylinder compound 4-4-0s. In these, the cylinder layout of No 701 was reversed, with the HP cylinders positioned on the outside of the frames and the LP cylinders placed between the frames facilitating the flow of exhaust steam to the blastpipe. The working pressure was also increased, from 156lb psi in No 701, to 199 and later 213lb psi.

Increasing the pace

Successful as these classes were, du Bousquet, his chief designer Jean Koechlin and test engineer Barbier, were dissatisfied with the falling away in cylinder power output at higher speeds. Tests showed that there was severe throttling of steam passing through restricted areas in steam pipes, ports and passages (the steam circuit) when running at speed. This was also a design defect which

handicapped the Midland and London Midland & Scottish Railway compound 4-4-0s in Britain. To overcome this, the cross sectional areas of the steam circuit were greatly enlarged. The lessons from these tests were applied to later Nord locomotives, including du Bousquet's compound 4-4-2s (Atlantics).

Introduced in 1899, the elegant du Bousquet Atlantics, painted in the Nord's chocolate livery, created quite a sensation and one was shown at the Paris Exhibition of 1900. Their boiler pressure was increased to 227lb psi and, like the preceding 4-4-0s, the boiler barrel housed Serve type tubes with four internal ribs. Tests carried out by Adolph Henry, the equally outstanding Chief Mechanical Engineer of the Paris Lyon & Méditerranée Railway, had shown substantially increased heat transfer from a given length of tube.

◄Nord Atlantic No 2.648 stands in original condition before being rebuilt in 1912. It was then fitted with superheater, larger HP cylinders, and piston valves (in place of slide valves) to the LP cylinders. The du Bousquet compound Atlantics weighed several tons less than Stanier Class 5 4-6-0s and as built, could a haul 300-ton train up 1 in 200 grades at 100km/h (62mph).

LOCO LIST

Thirty-five 4-4-2 compounds were built for the Nord Railway and 170 of basically similar, or slightly enlarged, design for other railways in France and abroad – out of a total of over 3000 du Bousquet/de Glehn types.

The HP and LP cylinders were each provided with individual sets of Walschaerts valve gear, regulated from a dual control reversing wheel in the cab. This enabled HP and LP cut-offs (the extent of live steam admission during each piston stroke) to be adjusted together or independently. This gave greater flexibility in controlling the power developed in the two cylinder groups.

Twin regulator controls

Two regulators were provided. The HP regulator controlled steam admission to the HP cylinders. When required, the LP regulator admitted steam from the boiler into the intermediate receiver (the pipework between the HP and LP steam chests), and then to the LP cylinders at reduced pressure. This enabled the pressure of steam passing from the HP to the LP cylinders to be increased and

boosted the power developed in the LP cylinders.

A compound/simple changeover valve allowed steam from the HP cylinders to pass directly to the blastpipe when in the simple position. This made it possible to start heavy trains as a four-cylinder simple locomotive, with the LP cylinders taking steam from the LP regulator. Also the engine could be worked as a two-cylinder simple, by-passing the LP cylinders which was useful when descending gradients when little power was required.

The du Bousquet control system enabled the

▼Often referred to as the de Glehn Atlantics, because of his work in pioneering the four-cylinder compound with divided drive, the Nord Atlantics were the design concept of Gaston du Bousquet, the Belgian-born Chief Mechanical Engineer of the Nord. Alfred de Glehn was born in Sydenham, near London and was the son of a Scottish mother and a father from the Baltic states.

Where to see them
One Nord compound 4-4-2, No 2.670, is preserved in the French National Railway Museum at Mulhouse, Alsace, France. A 4-6-0 derivative, No 3.628, can be seen on the Nene Valley Railway near Peterborough.

Speed limit
When the Nord Compound Atlantics were introduced, maximum speeds on French railways were limited to 120km/h (74.5mph) in service – a limit set by a government edict 50 years earlier. High average speeds required high sustained speeds uphill and on level track. Speeds up to 154km/h (96mph) were attained by the Atlantics, as originally built, on test runs.

Design specifications NORD COMPOUND ATLANTIC

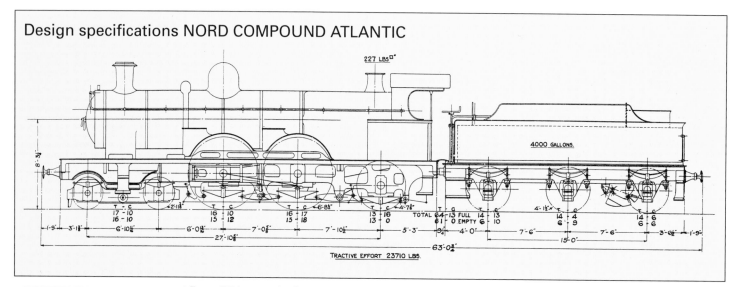

227 LBS □"

4000 GALLONS.

TRACTIVE EFFORT 23710 LBS.

TECHNICAL FILE

2 high pressure cylinders:
15³/₈in diameter* x 25¹/₄in stroke
2 low pressure cylinders:
22in diameter x 25¹/₄in stroke
Grate area: 29.5sq ft
Boiler diameter: 4ft 9¹/₄in
Driving wheels: 6ft 8¹/₄in
Length over buffers: 62ft 6in
Maximum tractive effort:*
Compound: 21,200lb psi
Simple: 28,250lb psi
Coal capacity: 5 tons
Water capacity: 4400 gallons
Weight in working order:
Engine: 63 tons (as originally built); 69 tons (superheated with lengthened boiler barrel)
Tender: 45 tons
*When superheated

Technical advantage
The alternative driving methods possible with du Bousquet four-cylinder compounds sound complicated, but were used most effectively by French locomotive drivers, almost all of whom were workshop trained. British drivers were not given the same degree of technical training as their French counterparts. This was a major factor in the reluctance of British railways to introduce compound locomotives on a large scale.
   The Midland/LMS three-cylinder 4-4-0s had driving controls which were greatly simplified, with some loss of flexibility, to deal with exceptional loading conditions and power demands brought on by traffic requirements.

▲From 1891 onwards, Gaston du Bousquet introduced 60 four-cylinder compound 4-4-0s of progressively increasing performance capacity. The 4-4-2 (Atlantic) type of 1899 represented a major development. Its larger boiler, firebox and grate areas were combined with a larger steam flow circuit to minimise power loss due to the throttling of steam.

Nord Atlantics and other types to develop very high power outputs in relation to their dimensions when this was required and on occasion to handle trains normally worked by more powerful machines without loss of time. On one occasion, a 515-ton train was run from St Quentin to Paris, 153km (95 miles), at an average speed of 95km/h (59mph).

Successful machines

From the time of their construction until the building of the Nord Super Pacifics in 1923, the du Bousquet Atlantics successfully handled many of the fastest and most prestigious trains of the Nord from Paris to Calais, Lille, Brussels and Liège.

In the mid-1930s, the Lemaître multiple jet exhaust system was fitted to the principal Nord locomotive types. This system reduced exhaust back pressure and increased cylinder power. The maximum power of the Nord compound Atlantics and 3513 class 4-6-0s was increased to about 2000 cylinder hp – in locomotives of 70 tons or less.

The Nord Atlantics responded fully to the challenge of the great Paul Javary, the Nord's operating manager: 'My trains run to time because they are timed hard.'

▼ Following trials with No 102 *La France*, Churchward obtained two slightly larger French Atlantics, numbered 103 and 104. He wanted to evaluate their performance and to gain more experience on the use of divided drive. Entering service in 1904, No 104 was later named *Alliance*, after the signing of the Entente Cordiale. It is seen standing at Birmingham Snow Hill around 1910.

How a steam engine works

The heart of the steam locomotive is its boiler. Working under strong induced draught it is the most compact of all types of boiler in relation to the amount of steam produced. Its traditional form of construction is suitable for pressures up to about 300lb per sq in. It is usually fired by coal, though oil has been widely used and in special circumstances wood, sugar cane waste and even peat have been burned.

Solid fuel is burned on the grate (1) within the inner firebox (2). This is surrounded by **water**, in the outer firebox shell, to absorb radiant heat from the fire. To resist the pressure in the boiler the inner and outer fireboxes are joined by many hundreds of stays.

Air to support combustion is of two kinds. Primary air is admitted below the grate, controlled by damper doors (3) in the ashpan, and is drawn through the firebed. This makes the fuel incandescent but is not sufficient to burn all the constituents of the coal. Secondary air is admitted above the firebed, usually through the firehole

door (4) but sometimes also through tubes or hollow stays through the side water spaces.

The brick arch (5), constructed of firebrick or refractory concrete, serves three purposes: being incandescent it encourages combustion of gas distilled from the firebed; it lengthens the path of those gases to give more time for combustion; and it prevents cool secondary air reaching the tubes.

The hot gases are drawn through long tubes (6), surrounded by water in the barrel of the boiler, to the smokebox (7). In a modern boiler these tubes are of two types, small ones about $1^3/_4-2^1/_4$in (43-57mm) diameter and large flues about $5-5^1/_2$in (127-140mm) diameter.

The **saturated steam** generated collects above the water in the boiler (8). Its passage to the cylinders is controlled by the regulator valve (9), operated from the cab and usually placed in a dome (10) at the highest point of the boiler. It travels via the main steam pipe (11) to the superheater header (12), which is a box divided into two separate spaces. The saturated steam (at 250lb per sq in

pressure its temperature is about 405°F/207°C) flows through superheater element pipes (13) fitted inside the large flues to the superheated side of the header.

By this time it has become **superheated steam** and its temperature may have been raised to 600-700°F (316-371°C). From the header it flows via steam pipes (14) through the valves to the cylinders (15).

The **hot gases** from the fire, now much cooler after giving up heat to the water and steam, are ejected through the chimney (16). This is done by the **exhaust steam** from the cylinders, which passes to the chimney through the reduced orifice of the blastpipe (17) at high speed, entraining the gases on the way. Thus the smokebox maintains a partial vacuum which provides the draw on the fire.

Replacement water is forced into the boiler by injectors or pumps to maintain a safe level above the top of the firebox. Safety valves (18) on top of the boiler open to release steam if the pressure tends to rise above a safe level.

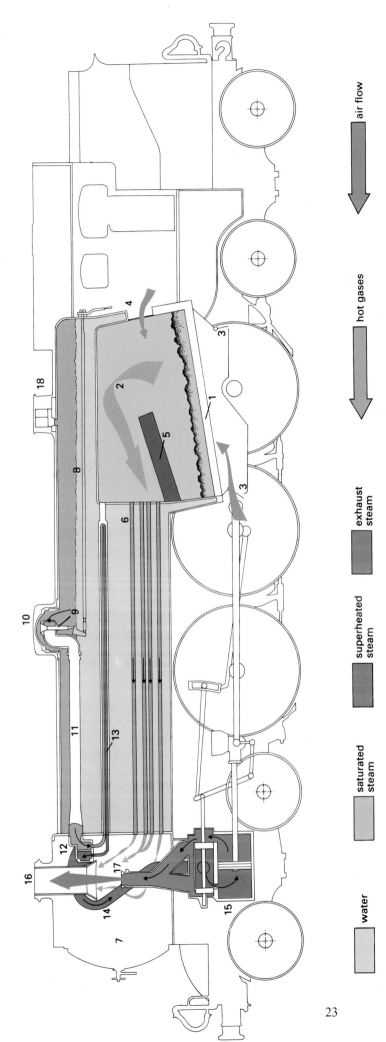

water	saturated steam	superheated steam	exhaust steam

hot gases

air flow

23

Star class 4-6-0

GREAT WESTERN RAILWAY

The GWR Star class was the most advanced British express passenger type of its time, hailed by Sir William Stanier as the cornerstone of British locomotive design. This class was the basis for the later Castles and Kings.

KEY FACTS

GWR Star class 4-6-0
GWR and BR Nos: 4000 (formerly No 40) and 4001-4072. Nos 4000, 4009, 4016, 4032, 4037 and 4063-4072 later rebuilt to Castle class
Designer: George Jackson Churchward
Built: 1906-23
Service: main line express passenger
Livery: Brunswick green, copper capped chimney, polished brass safety valve cover and beading on coupled wheel splashers
Performance: Swindon – Paddington, 77.3 miles at average of 73.6mph with eight coach, 265-ton train. Paddington – Exeter, 173.5 miles at average of 58.7mph with 13 coach, 470-ton train
Withdrawn: 1932-57

The first two 4-6-0s of the Great Western Railway (GWR) were built in 1896 and 1899. They were powerful freight engines with inside cylinders and double frames, whose heavy piston thrusts resulted in crank axle failures. Studies of American practice prompted Churchward, the Locomotive Carriage and Wagon Superintendent of the GWR, to use two outside cylinders in his early 4-6-0s.

Churchward's first two-cylinder 4-6-0, No 100, was built in 1902 and later named *William Dean*, after his predecessor who had retired in that year. In 1903, it was followed by a second 4-6-0, No 98, which had a domeless boiler. In this, steam for the cylinders was collected from the highest point in the steam space, between the inner and outer fire-boxes, instead of the dome in the middle of the boiler. This was made possible by the Belpaire (square topped) firebox which, together with the tapered rear half of the boiler barrel, provided more steam space than the round-top type with a parallel boiler barrel.

Large diameter piston valves with long-travel and steam lap were fitted. These made it possible to obtain relatively high power outputs at short cut-offs with a high degree of steam expansion and, therefore, increased efficiency.

French lessons

In 1899 Gaston du Bousquet, Chief Mechanical Engineer of the Nord railway in France, had introduced his four-cylinder compound Atlantic (4-4-2) type locomotives which rapidly achieved a

◄ Fifteen members of the Star class were given larger boilers, cylinders and side window cabs and converted into Castles. Other Stars received only outside steam pipes similar to those of the larger 4-6-0s. One of these, No 4062 *Malmesbury Abbey* hauls the 16.07 Swindon – Bristol near Chippenham, in the early 1950s.

▲ From 1911, top-feed was applied to the Stars to reduce scale formation, and to provide a measure of feed water heating, by delivering water into the steam space in the top of the boiler. Locomotives fitted with this device could be identified by the pipes running up the side of the boiler to the safety valve cover – shown on 4007 *Rising Star*.

remarkable reputation for performance and economy. This was fully appreciated by Churchward, but he considered that he could achieve equally good results with his latest two-cylinder simple expansion engines working at short cut-offs, in which the overall degree of steam expansion was of the same order as in the French compounds.

To confirm this assessment, in 1903 Churchward persuaded the GWR board to purchase a Nord type four-cylinder compound Atlantic for comparative trials. Meanwhile a third 4-6-0, No 171, had its working pressure raised from 200 to 225lb psi and its wheel arrangement changed to 4-4-2 for closer comparability with the French Atlantics. Two more of these, with slightly larger cylinders, grates and fireboxes, had been

delivered in 1905.

Churchward was greatly impressed by the much smoother riding of the compound Atlantics, with four-cylinder drive and much lighter motion parts. The reciprocating masses of the pistons and driving rods were virtually self-balancing, compared with the much heavier and partially balanced motion parts of his own two-cylinder 4-4-2.

Churchward decided to build a four-cylinder version of his two-cylinder engines. However, in view of the marginal economy offered by compounding in GWR operating conditions and the more complicated mechanism of the du Bousquet type, he chose to use simple expansion drive. Churchward's first four-cylinder locomotive, 4-4-2 No 40, was delivered in June 1906.

▼ Churchward four-cylinder engines embodied other French features including the extended slidebars. These were used to accommodate the vertical forces exerted through the piston crosshead. Another feature was the de Glehn type bogie with side bearers spaced at maximum distance apart to minimise any rolling tendency.

▼Churchward's first four-cylinder locomotive, No 40, was built as a 4-4-2 to give closer comparability with the French compounds. It was later converted to a 4-6-0 for greater adhesion. The American-style bogie was eventually replaced. After criticism, a certain amount of external re-styling also took place. The later members of the class were given downward curving ends to the running plate and the cab sides were lowered.

The boiler of No 40 was generally similar to that on No 98, his second 4-6-0, but was tapered at the top over the whole barrel length, instead of the rear half only. The sides and top of the Belpaire firebox were curved slightly and the backplate was reduced in width and height, so that the sides tapered towards the rear.

This shape, combined with the tapered boiler barrel, gave a greater cross-sectional area at the firebox tubeplate and the first few feet of the boiler – where the steam generation was most rapid. Churchward's jumper top blastpipe provided increased orificial area when working hard and reduced the exhaust back pressure.

Cylinders and valve gear

The cylinder layout and divided drive of No 40 followed that of the French four-cylinder compound Atlantics. The inside cylinders drove the leading coupled axle and the outside pair drove the second axle. However, to allow the use of inside and outside connecting rods of equal length, the inside cylinders were placed above the leading bogie wheels and further forward than on the French locomotives.

Compared with both the French compound 4-4-2s and Churchward's earlier two-cylinder 4-6-0s, the valve gear used on No 40 was simpler. The French 4-4-2s had four sets of Walschaerts gear (two inside the frames and two outside) and Churchward fitted his two-cylinder 4-6-0s with Stephenson's link motion with four inside eccentrics.

No 40 had only two sets of simplified gear. The outside valve spindles were driven through simple rocking levers from two sets of modified Walschaerts gear (housed rather inaccessibly between the frames). In these, the radius rods were moved by links from the opposite inside crossheads and so eliminated the use of inside eccentrics.

This (scissors) valve gear, designed by W H Pearce, functioned perfectly, but it took 10 days of adjustments to set the valves correctly. Churchward realised that this could cause lengthy delays during main works overhauls with a large class of locomotives using this type of valve gear. He therefore decided that in later four-cylinder engines the radius rods of their Walschaerts gear would be driven conventionally from two inside eccentrics on the leading coupled axle. The first production batch of 10 Stars was delivered in February 1907, having been built as 4-6-0s to give greater adhesive weight. No 40 itself was converted to a 4-6-0 in 1909, though retaining its scissors valve gear.

In 1908, dynamometer car trials between Exeter and Paddington were carried out with Star 4-6-0 No 4013 *Knight of the Grand Cross*. Hauling a 390-ton train of older lighter coaches, equivalent in rolling resistance to about 450 tons of GWR modern heavier stock, a net average speed of 57mph was achieved over the 174 mile run.

Maximum horsepower at the drawbar was 1050 at 53mph. Specific fuel consumption averaged about 3.5lb per drawbar hp/hour, which was one half of that for the large four-cylinder 4-6-0s of the Lancashire & Yorkshire Railway (LYR) in their original 1908 form.

Superheating introduction

In 1906, Churchward and George Hughes of the LYR were the first British engineers to apply superheating apparatus to their locomotives. This overcame heat losses through condensation in the cylinders and achieved increased power due to the

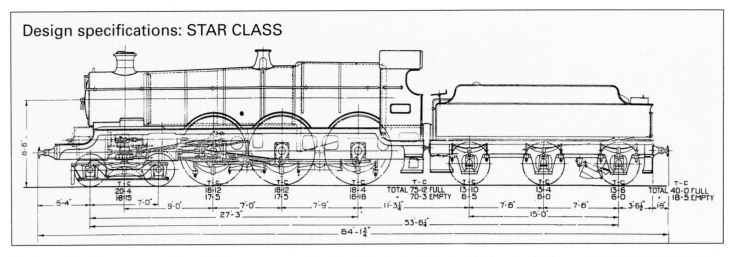

Design specifications: STAR CLASS

▲ In terms of performance capacity and fuel economy, the outstanding British express locomotives in the 20 years from 1903 were Churchward's two- and four-cylinder 4-6-0s of the Saint and Star classes. Their design features greatly influenced British locomotive practice until the end of the steam era.

greater volume of steam at higher temperatures.

Churchward realised, from his own tests and the experience of others, that the cylinder and valve lubricants of the period were unable to withstand very high steam temperatures. Such temperatures could cause carbonisation, resulting in the steam ports and passages becoming partially blocked. Churchward contented himself with maximum steam temperatures of around 550°F (287°C), which avoided this trouble and enabled the power of his locomotives to be increased by 10-15% and fuel consumption reduced for a given power output.

The first Star to be fitted with the standard Swindon No 3 triple element type was No 4021 *King Edward*, later named *British Monarch*, in 1909, earlier engines being fitted retrospectively. By 1913, 750 GWR locomotives had been superheated, saving 60,000 tons of coal per year.

The increased power of the superheated Stars, with cylinder diameter increased to 15in, enabled them to handle steadily increasing express train loadings. In 1914, No 4045 *Prince John* hauled the Cornish Riviera Express from Paddington to Exeter, 174 miles, at an average speed of 59mph with a 470-ton train throughout.

During the 1920s, the maximum axleloading on some principal GWR routes was increased further to between 20 and 22.5 tons. This allowed the introduction of the Castle class from 1923 and the larger King class from 1927. Both designs were based on rationally enlarged boiler and cylinder dimensions from the Stars. Some Stars worked the Paddington – Bristol route until the mid-1950s.

TECHNICAL FILE

4 cylinders: originally 14¼in diameter, later enlarged to 15in with superheating from 1913
Stroke: 26in
Maximum boiler diameter: tapering from 5ft 6in to 4ft 10¹³/₁₆in
Tractive effort: 27,800lb at 85% boiler pressure*
Grate area: 27sq ft
Water capacity: 3500 – 4000 gallons
Coal capacity: 6 tons
Weight in working order:
Engine : 75.6 tons
Tender: 40.4 – 46.7 tons
*15in cylinder diameter

The design of the Star class laid the foundations for all future GWR express locomotives. After a working life of 44 years, No 4003 *Lode Star* was withdrawn from service in 1951 and after a period in store, was returned to its 1932 condition.

Bigger Stars
In 1919, a new two-cylinder mixed traffic 2-8-0, the 47XX class, was produced with an enlarged version of the No 1 boiler used on the 4-6-0s and freight 2-8-0s. It was designated No 7 with grate area increased by 12%. Churchward intended to apply this boiler to the Star and Saint classes, but the additional weight would have restricted their route availability, and the proposal was deferred.

Where to see them
Only one member of the Star class, No 4003 *Lode Star*, has been preserved. After being reconditioned at Swindon works in 1962, it spent many years in the GWR Museum there, before being moved to the National Railway Museum at York in 1992.

A3 class 4-6-2

LONDON & NORTH EASTERN RAILWAY

The Gresley A3 Pacifics were a development on his earlier A1s and bore the brunt of express passenger working on the East Coast main line. In the 1930s these elegant and powerful race horses paved the way for the glamorous streamlined series that followed.

KEY FACTS

A3 Class 4-6-2
BR Nos: 60035-112 including rebuilds from original A1 class. 78 locomotives
Designer: Nigel Gresley
Built: 1922-35, A1 conversions from 1927-48
Service: express passenger and fitted freight trains
Livery: LNER apple green; wartime black; BR lined blue and later dark green
Performance: Newcastle – King's Cross, 268½ miles, at a net average of 72½mph with 290-ton train. 1939, Grantham – King's Cross 105½mph average of 63mph with 510-ton train
Withdrawn: 1959-66

In 1922, Gresley introduced his A1 Pacific. It had a boiler pressure of 180lb psi and relatively short-travel valves. The locomotives were capable performers and, if called on, could haul loads of 600 tons – a tonnage virtually unknown in Britain at that time for express passenger trains.

At the British Empire Exhibition in 1924, the London & North Eastern Railway's (LNER) A1 Pacific No 4472 *Flying Scotsman* was shown back to back with the Great Western Railway's (GWR) four-cylinder 4-6-0 No 4073 *Caerphilly Castle*, a slightly enlarged version of Churchward's earlier Star class. Although the maximum boiler capacity of the Castle was less than the Pacific, the GWR claimed that the Castle was the most powerful express locomotive in the country on the basis of its slightly higher nominal tractive effort.

Valve gear

A locomotive exchange between the two types on each other's home ground was suggested and took place in 1925 between King's Cross and Doncaster for a Castle, and between Paddington and Plymouth for an A1. In this, the smaller GWR locomotive generally showed better performance and greater fuel economy, due primarily to its lower rate of steam consumption with long-travel valves and steam lap. This feature allowed a greater volume of steam to be delivered to the

◄ In June 1962, No 60067 *Ladas* rolls into King's Cross with an express from the north. Late on in their lives, the A3s were rejuvenated by installation of Kylchap double blastpipes and chimneys. Because the new arrangement gave rise to a softer exhaust, German-style smoke deflectors were fitted. This type was chosen because it was a proven and inexpensive solution.

BLAIR ATHOL

LOCO LIST

All of Gresley's Pacifics, built new as A3s, were named after race horses. Originally numbered under the LNER scheme, they were renumbered after nationalisation. The list is in order of construction.

2743 **Felstead**
2744 **Grand Parade**
2745 **Captain Cuttle**
2746 **Fairway**
2747 **Coronach**
2748 **Colorado**
2749 **Flamingo**
2750 **Papyrus**
2751 **Humorist**
2752 **Spion Kop**
2595 **Trigo**
2596 **Manna**
2597 **Gainsborough**
2598 **Blenheim**
2599 **Book Law**
2795 **Call Boy**
2796 **Spearmint**
2797 **Cicero**
2500 **Windsor Lad**
2501 **Colombo**
2502 **Hyperion**
2503 **Firdaussi**
2504 **Sandwich**
2505 **Cameronian**
2506 **Salmon Trout**
2507 **Singapore**
2508 **Brown Jack**

cylinders at short cut-offs. In this, the piston travelled only a small part of its stroke before the supply of boiler-steam was cut off; the steam doing its work by expansion for the remainder of the stroke.

Gresley had previously fitted long-lap, long-travel valves to his K3 class 2-6-0s with excellent results. But there had been problems. A lack of rigidity in the mounting of the bracket providing the main pivot point of the valve gear conjugating levers, meant that the valve spindles could over travel at speed and cause damage to the inside steam chest covers.

While tests and redesign work to provide a more rigid centre pivot mounting were being carried out, the steam lap and valve travel of the K3s were reduced, with the Pacifics fitted similarly. After the 1925 trials, the design modifications

▲ **On 18 February 1961, No 60056 *Centenary* raises steam at Grantham shed. The A3s continued to haul top rank East Coast expresses right up to final withdrawal in 1966. In their last years, the class often replaced 2000hp diesels during their early teething troubles, working for up to 10 days on intensive diesel schedules.**

were completed quickly to the proposals of Bert Spencer and Eric Windle, two members of Gresley's design team. After the Pacifics were equipped with longer travel and lap valves, the power required could be obtained at appreciably shorter cut-offs and their fuel consumption was reduced by about 20%.

However, during the 1925 trials Gresley's contention that ample boiler capacity was essential to

▼ **The A3s were first built new in 1928 and closely resembled the earlier A1s in external appearance. The A3s could be distinguished by a shallow curved casing on each side of the smokebox behind the chimney, which covered the ends of the larger superheater header.**

Exhaustive trials

One of the results of fitting long-travel valves to the A1s and A3s was a softer exhaust which tended to obscure the driver's view. The LNER's attempts to cure this problem included this modification to No 2751 *Humorist* in March 1933. This locomotive was the first A3 Pacific to be given a double Kylchap exhaust system in 1937. Although all of the class eventually received them – often only a few years before they were scrapped – had Gresley's intentions been carried out, this device would have been applied from 1941.

Where to see them

There is only one surviving A3, No 4472 *Flying Scotsman*. It is stationed at Southall and has often hauled excursions over BR.

Overheating problem

A myth has often been circulated that the A3s were constantly plagued by cases of overheated connecting rod middle big end bearings. In almost every case – and these were rare as in LNER days these locomotives averaged 75,000 miles (120,700 km) between failures – this was caused by excessive tightening of the securing nuts and bolts for the two halves of the marine type big end which deformed the spacing piece (glut) between them. In the 1950s, harder metal was used for the spacing piece, which completely overcame the deformation problem and any associated overheating troubles.

rebuilt with higher pressure boilers, although the excellent design and long life of the 180lb psi boilers was such that the last replacement, No 2567 *Sir Visto*, was not made until 1948.

From 1928-30, following the rebuilding of five A1s, 18 new A3s were built and the final nine A3s were built from 1934-35. This batch of locomotives included some features Gresley used on his express passenger P2 class 2-8-2s. The main steam pipes from the dome to the superheater header were almost doubled in area, and the area of the branch pipes from superheater header to cylinders was increased by 23%. This followed Chapelon's practice, by improving the freedom of steam flow and reducing pressure drop losses; these features were incorporated in the boilers used in the later A4 Pacifics built in 1935. Also, like the P2s, perforated steam collectors, housed under a banjo-shaped cover, were also provided.

In service the A3s, and their 180lb psi forerunners, locomotive performance capacity was borne out during the 1926 coal strike. His Pacifics were capable of near normal performance with low grade imported coal while the GWR 4-6-0s, with their small fireboxes and grates designed for high grade Welsh coal, were severely handicapped in performance.

Increased pressure

In 1927, Gresley was looking into ways of achieving greater improvements in the performance and efficiency of his locomotives. These were achieved in the A3s by using 43 element superheaters in place of 32 in the A1s, to take advantage of the greater volume of steam at higher temperatures and increasing the working pressure in the boiler from 180 to 220lb psi. Previously, Gresley had been reluctant to do this because his experience elsewhere with boilers working at higher pressures, where there was no effective chemical water treatment, had led to greater scale formation.

In the A3-type boiler, with 220lb psi pressure, the cylinder diameter was reduced to 19in compared with 20in for the previous 180lb psi engines, but nominal tractive effort was increased by 10%. The greater width of the header for the enlarged superheater in the A3s projected slightly through the smokebox sides just behind the chimney. This made the fitting of cover plates necessary – giving the class an obvious visual difference from the earlier A1s. The 180lb psi A1s were progressively

Conjugating mechanism

In the Gresley Pacifics, the actuating levers (equal motion and 2 to 1 levers) of the Gresley conjugating mechanism driving the inside valve spindle were located in front of the valves. Expansion took place in the outside valve spindles from which the drive was taken and an allowance was made for this when setting the middle valve. However, when starting cold before expansion had taken place, the exhaust beats were slightly irregular until the valve spindles expanded.

During the war, when it was impossible to obtain roller bearings for the two main pivots of the conjugating mechanism, these had to be replaced by plain bushes which wore rapidly. This resulted in irregular valve events and highly syncopated exhaust beats when severe wear occurred.

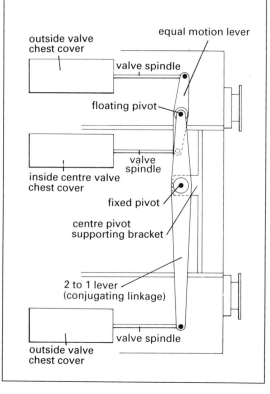

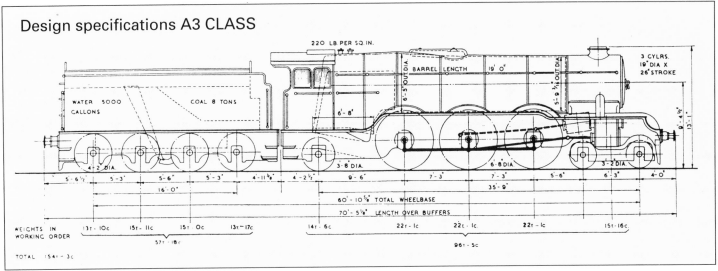

Design specifications A3 CLASS

ners, did remarkable work against a background of continual acceleration of heavy express trains in the 1930s. The Anglo-Scottish Flying Scotsman express schedule of 1938-39 demanded an average speed of 60mph from Grantham to King's Cross with a load of up to 550 tons. In April 1935, No 2750 *Papyrus*, one of the 1929-built A3s, attained 108mph on a high speed run which proved the feasibility of a four hour London – Newcastle schedule for the Silver Jubilee express with an average speed of 67mph. Even more notable was the achievement in 1939 of No 2507 *Singapore*, with enlarged steam pipes, in hauling the 290-ton Coronation streamliner express from Newcastle to London, 268 miles (431km) in 222 minutes *net* – 15 minutes under the A4 worked schedule, at an average speed of 72^1/$_2$mph. During

World War II, the Gresley A1, A3 and A4 Pacifics worked expresses regularly of 20 coaches (700 tons gross) at average speeds of 50mph or more within a nominal 60mph speed limit.

Post-war service

In their final years, equipped with Kylchap double exhaust, the A3s did much notable work. In the late 1950s, during a period of 11 days, one of the class covered 4000 miles (6,437km) after making six return trips from London to Newcastle and two to Leeds – mainly on the fastest trains.

The development of the Gresley Pacifics was an important chapter in British locomotive history. It confirmed the necessity for large boilers and fireboxes to provide an ample margin of steam production capacity.

▲The A3s went through a number of changes and modifications throughout their lives. All of the class were eventually provided with perforated steam collectors, housed under a banjo-shaped cover. This meant that steam could be taken from the highest point above the water line in the boiler, passing to the dome through a number of slots in the boiler barrel to minimise the intake of moisture in the steam.

TECHNICAL FILE

3 cylinders: 19in x 26in
Coupled wheels: 6ft 8in diameter
Maximum boiler diameter: 6ft 5in
Grate area: 41^1/$_4$sq ft
Boiler pressure: 220lb psi
Tractive effort: 32,909lb
Coal capacity: 8 or 9 tons
Water capacity: 5000 gallons
Length over buffers: 70ft 5^1/$_8$in
Weight in working order:
Engine: 96^1/$_4$ tons
Tender: 57.9 tons or 62.4 tons for corridor variety

◄By 1948, there were 78 A3 Pacifics in service on BR. Most of them, however, were converted from A1s. In August 1946, A3 Pacific No 2582 *Sir Hugo* waits at Grantham to take over a northbound express on its journey from London. In 1925, this locomotive was the last Gresley Pacific to be built as an A1 and was given its A3 boiler in 1941.

Class 57XX pannier tank

GREAT WESTERN RAILWAY

The 0-6-0 pannier tank was a classic Great Western engine, accounting for a third of its fleet. Based on a turn of the century design, it could be found on almost any duty from shunting trucks in the local goods yard to marshalling coaches at Paddington station.

Carrying its water supply in tanks on the locomotive itself, the tank engine has the virtues of compactness and of not needing to be turned at its journey's end. Its range depends mainly on the amount of water carried and is normally restricted to about 50 miles (80km) before requiring more.

Until the turn of the century the GWR used saddle tanks on the great majority of its shunting tank locomotives, which numbered about 1100. Most tanks extended from the smokebox front to the cab. But the number of boiler types and variations in the position of the dome caused difficulties at overhaul.

In the early years of the century a programme of boiler standardisation was agreed, using Belpaire fireboxes with their square profile. This would have demanded widespread alterations to the saddle tanks to clear the firebox and caused further reduction in water capacity. The Great Western therefore decided that along with the new

▶ **The legendary days of the Great Western are recalled on the Severn Valley Railway as 0-6-0PT No 5764 waits with a passenger train at Arley. This engine is one of 16 57XXs that survived the cutter's torch. Now in preservation, many of these locomotives are once again doing a job for which they were built – hauling passenger trains on branch lines.**

▼ **The Class 57XX, the first of eight variations of modern panniers, was almost a repeat of the rebuilt Class 2721 of 1897 with Belpaire firebox, dome and full cab. Unlike the later Class 54XX and 64XX the 57XX was not fitted for auto-train working, but occasionally hauled auto-coaches as ordinary passenger stock.**

863 Class 57XXs were built at Swindon works and private builders between 1929 and 1950.

During that time seven other classes of pannier tank were also built. Four classes were introduced before World War II:

54XX: (25 locomotives) Built 1931-35. 5ft 2in wheels; push-pull fitted.
64XX: (40) Built 1932-37. 4ft 7½in wheels; push-pull fitted.
1366: (6) Built 1934. Outside cylinders and short wheelbase for dock working.
74XX: (50) Built 1936-50. Similar to 64XX but not push-pull fitted.

From 1945 three further pannier tank classes were introduced:
94XX: (210) Built 1947-56. 4ft 7½in wheels; larger tapered boilers.
15XX: (10) Built 1949. Outside cylinders and Walschaerts valve gear.
16XX: (70) Built 1949-55. 4ft 1½in wheels; restricted overall height and weight.

boilers their 0-6-0 shunting tanks would be fitted with new pannier tanks.

Virtually a unique GWR design, the tanks were of uniform rectangular cross-section with rounded outer corners, extending from smokebox front to cab. The tops were almost flush with the top of the boiler, leaving the driver a good forward view, while the bottoms were about 18 inches above the footplating, allowing reasonable access to the inside motion. The tanks were carried on outrigger brackets fixed to the smokebox and firebox sides.

The rebuilding programme, running from 1910 to about 1930 (there were a few engines outside these limits), was carried out on engines which were already 15-50 years old. It provided modernised engines for relatively undemanding duties and deferred the need to build new shunting engines from 1905 to 1929 other than six small tanks for dock work.

They may have been modernised in some respects but this did not extend to the cab; half

▲ **In the late 1950s, 863 examples of the Class 57XX pannier tank were in service on BR – making them one of the largest classes of locomotive in the UK. These doughty little panniers could be found at most steam sheds on the Western Region. At Stafford Road depot, Wolverhampton, on 3 March 1957 0-6-0PT No 3725 waits for its next turn of duty.**

cabs were the norm, in some cases supplemented by the luxury of a rear weatherboard. But in 1927 scrapping of these elderly shunters began in earnest; some of them were over 60 years old by this time.

The GWR had a seemingly insatiable appetite, however, for 0-6-0 tanks. In 1927 there were 1195 of them, almost 30% of the locomotive fleet and more than twice the proportion of the LNER and LMS. They were used not only for yard and station shunting but also for empty coaching stock movements, branch line passenger trains and freight trip work. This utilisation continued right through to the 1950s. Where others, particularly

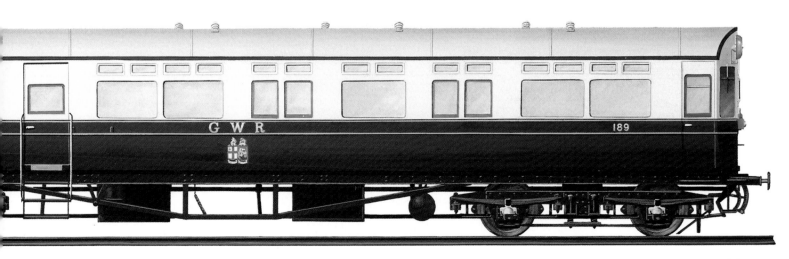

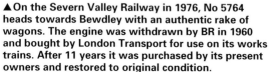

▲**On the Severn Valley Railway in 1976, No 5764 heads towards Bewdley with an authentic rake of wagons. The engine was withdrawn by BR in 1960 and bought by London Transport for use on its works trains. After 11 years it was purchased by its present owners and restored to original condition.**

▼**Until 1957 the railway was defined as a common carrier and required by law to carry almost any load that was asked of it. Because of this, the railways hauled freight on a greater scale and over shorter distances than is normal on today's cost effective network. On 16 July 1952 a typically mixed freight of the period is hauled by Class 57XX No 8783 through the Wiltshire countryside on the branch from Calne to Chippenham.**

the LMS, gladly accepted diesel shunters, the GWR and Western Region cherished pannier tank locomotives.

The renewal of the shunting fleet started in 1929 and continued until 1956, by which time no fewer than 1274 had been put into service. First was the Class 57XX with 4ft 7½in wheels, intended for heavy shunting work in yards. Their introduction coincided with the onset of the Depression, and 250 of them were constructed in 1929-31 by private building firms, using cheap government loans. Incredibly, production continued until the end of 1950 – only in 1932 was none built – by which time the enormous total of 863 was in service.

Design details

Apart from the pannier tanks the design of the locomotives was thoroughly conventional. They had saturated parallel boilers with Belpaire fireboxes and domes. Later boilers were built with topfeeds. A distinctive cast-iron chimney was fitted. The pannier tanks were now supported by brackets from the smokebox and a stool from the footplating – and so from the frames – just behind the driving wheels; the earlier support from the firebox was recognised as undesirable.

Two sets of Stephenson valve gear operated slide valves in a vertical steam chest between the cylinders, reversing being by lever in the cab. All but 50 engines were fitted with vacuum brakes and most had provision for steam heating coaches. Engines built from 1933 had an improved cab and were sometimes known as a separate Class 8750.

Class variations

In 1932-3, 11 of the class were turned out as condensing engines for working freight through London Transport's Metropolitan line tunnels to Smithfield Market, adjacent to Farringdon station. The tanks were shortened at the smokebox end and formed into deep side tanks at the back end. Two large exhaust steam pipes ran from the smokebox to the centre of the tank tops. A vertical feed pump alongside the smokebox dealt with hot water.

A curious application of pannier tanks took place during World War II – 108 GWR 0-6-0 tender engines (Dean Goods) were requisitioned by

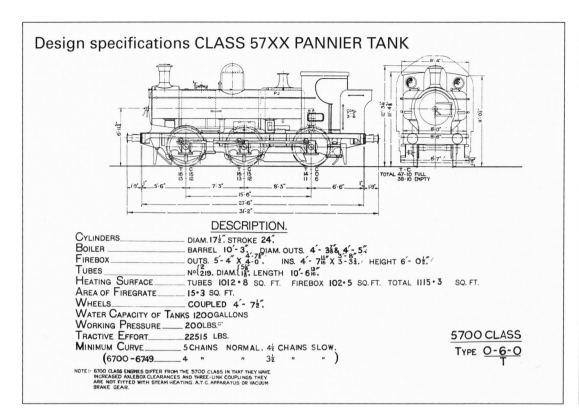

Design specifications CLASS 57XX PANNIER TANK

DESCRIPTION.

CYLINDERS _____ DIAM. 17½". STROKE 24".
BOILER _____ BARREL 10'-3". DIAM. OUTS. 4'-3⅜ & 4'-5⅞"
FIREBOX _____ OUTS. 5'-4" X 4'-0". INS. 4'-7¹¹⁄₁₆" X 3-3¼". HEIGHT 6'-0½"
TUBES _____ N°{2 219. DIAM.{5½ 1⅞". LENGTH 10'-6¹³⁄₁₆".
HEATING SURFACE _____ TUBES 1012·8 SQ. FT. FIREBOX 102·5 SQ. FT. TOTAL 1115·3 SQ. FT.
AREA OF FIREGRATE _____ 15·3 SQ. FT.
WHEELS _____ COUPLED 4'-7½".
WATER CAPACITY OF TANKS 1200 GALLONS
WORKING PRESSURE _____ 200 LBS.☐"
TRACTIVE EFFORT _____ 22515 LBS.
MINIMUM CURVE _____ 5 CHAINS NORMAL. 4½ CHAINS SLOW.
(6700 – 6749 _____ 4 " " 3½ " ")

NOTE:- 6700 CLASS ENGINES DIFFER FROM THE 5700 CLASS IN THAT THEY HAVE INCREASED AXLEBOX CLEARANCES AND THREE-LINK COUPLINGS. THEY ARE NOT FITTED WITH STEAM HEATING, A.T.C. APPARATUS OR VACUUM BRAKE GEAR.

5700 CLASS
TYPE **0-6-0**
T

◀ **The Class 57XX was designed as a standard engine, capable of mass production, to replace a wide range of older and more diverse classes of similar capacity.**

Final operations
Members of the Class 57XX became the last ex-BR steam locomotives to operate regularly on a main line in the UK – London Transport (LT) bought 13 for use on its works trains. The last of these panniers was withdrawn from service from LT on 6 June 1971. Ironically the very first trains on the underground, in 1863, were also of GW design – 7ft gauge 2-4-0 condensing tank locomotives.

TECHNICAL FILE

2 cylinders: 17½in diameter x 24in stroke
Coupled wheels: 4ft 7½in diameter
Boiler diameter: 4ft 5in maximum
Grate area: 15.3sq ft
Boiler pressure: 200lb psi
Tractive effort: 22,515lb
Coal capacity: 3.3 tons
Water capacity: 1200 gallons*
Length over buffers: 31ft 2in
Weight in working order: 47.5-49 tons*
Condensing engines 1230 galls; weight in working order 50.75 tons

the War Department for overseas service, and 10 were fitted with pannier tanks and condensing gear in addition to their normal tenders. The fall of France in 1940 prevented their dispatch, but they were not returned to the GWR.

Last rites
Four other classes of 0-6-0 pannier tank were introduced before the war to meet specific needs. These were the 54XX, 64XX, 1366 and 74XX. Three further pannier tank classes – 94XX, 15XX, 16XX – were introduced postwar for heavy shunt-

ing and empty carriage trains, tasks which demanded stronger locomotives.

Sadly, many of these postwar engines had very short lives – in at least one case only six years. The rundown of wagon load freight and the closure of branch lines took away many of their lighter duties, while the BR Class 08 diesel shunter was more economic in major yards. By 1966 the last pannier tank had gone from BR.

The pannier tanks have proved very suitable for many preserved lines, however, and 16 57XX and 8 of other classes have been saved.

▶ **Some of the most common duties performed by pannier tank locomotives were on local branch line trains serving small communities. No 9628 makes a delightful picture as it arrives at Shepton Mallet station on 24 February 1962 with the 3.17pm Frome to Yatton.**

Blastpipes

Steam production in a locomotive boiler is self regulating. The exhaust steam from the cylinders, in passing through the smokebox to the chimney, creates a draught which draws the smoke and gases along the boiler tubes and pulls fresh air through the firegrate. The harder the engine works the more steam is used, which means a bigger draught, hotter fire, and faster steam production.

Ejecting the steam

The steam from the cylinders is ejected from the blastpipe, which is a vertical nozzle at the bottom of the smokebox facing the chimney exit. Up to a point, the narrower the nozzle the greater the steam velocity and the stronger the draught.

However, although a high velocity steam jet may create a strong draught, it is uneven and tends to draw out lumps of half burned coal with the smoke from the fire. These lumps may make picturesque sparks when the locomotive is working hard at night, but are the outward sign of inefficient combustion.

While a constricting nozzle increases steam velocity, it also creates back pressure in the cylinder because the used steam cannot escape fast enough. An ideal blast is strong but slow and steady, and provides a fast passage for the steam leaving the cylinders.

Improving the draught

Because the strength of the draught is directly related to both the steam velocity and the total area of the steam jet in contact with the gases in the smokebox, it is possible to improve the draught by changing the configuration of the steam jet. Around the turn of the century there were several experiments to this end, but it was not until the 1930s that good arrangements were achieved.

The simplest and easiest method to improve the draught is to have two blastpipes, each exhausting through a different orifice in a double chimney. This method was favoured by the LMS Railway, where it produced a startling improvement in the performance of the Royal Scot class locomotives. After nationalisation it was also applied to GWR Castle and King locomotives, making similar improvements.

Another method, favoured by the Southern Railway, was the Lemaître exhaust, whose outward sign was a very large diameter chimney. Beneath the chimney was a blastpipe, divided into five nozzles, producing five steam jets. This doubled the area of steam in contact with the gases, whereas the double blastpipe only improved the ratio by approximately 50%.

The Kylchap

Probably the most advanced method of draught improvement was the Kylchap, perfected by the French engineer Andre Chapelon. This had two blastpipes, but each nozzle had a cross-section formed of four circles joining in the centre, so steam emerged in the form of four jets that met in the middle. Beneath each chimney were two extra petticoat pipes, shaped to split the four jets and then combine them again into a single jet which was exhausted through the chimney.

Engines fitted with Kylchap exhausts were exceptionally free running. The exhaust from the chimney was so soft that the non-streamlined engines needed deflector plates to lift the smoke into the air away from the cab windows. The ultimate development of the Kylchap exhaust was Chapelon's last locomotive, a SNCF 4-8-4, with a unique triple chimney.

Three stages in blastpipe development

In the last decade of steam, three types of blastpipe arrangements were common: single, double and Kylchap. The choice of blastpipe depended on the tasks the locomotive was designed to perform.

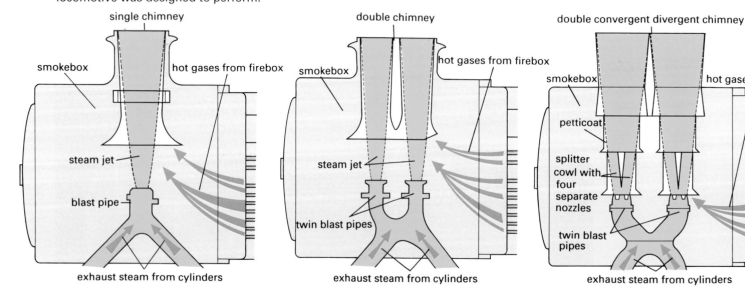

The **single blastpipe** combined exhaust steam from the cylinders to form a powerful jet. This drew hot gases through the boiler and air across the firegrate which assisted the fire in boiling water to produce steam.

The **double blastpipe and chimney** arrangement was favoured for large engines designed to haul heavy loads. It produced more steam in the boiler by improving the draught across the firegrate.

The **Kylchap** was usually given to fast express engines which travelled long distances at high speeds. Designed to have an even effect on the fire, it produced a soft, steady exhaust and improved coal consumption.

Duchess class 4-6-2

LONDON MIDLAND & SCOTTISH RAILWAY

On a summer's morning in 1937, a new streamlined locomotive left London for Crewe on a test run. Just over two hours later, it had gained the British speed record for a steam locomotive. The Duchesses were set for a year's reign as record holders.

The 1930s placed great pressure on railway companies. As the worldwide depression bit, railways found it increasingly difficult to compete with road transport. Railway publicity departments fought hard to keep their companies in the public eye. One of the surest ways to achieve this was by breaking performance records with streamlined trains pulled by ever more powerful locomotives.

Record rivals

In Britain two companies found themselves in informal competition. From 1932, the London Midland & Scottish Railway (LMS) and the London & North Eastern Railway (LNER) had introduced faster services on their competing routes to Scotland in the scramble for prestige. By the summer of 1936, the LMS was running 29 trains a day at start to stop average speeds of 60mph or more, while the LNER had only 15.

However, the far-sighted management of the LNER had encouraged the company's Chief Mechanical Engineer, Nigel Gresley, to build a sizeable fleet of large engines with a 4-6-2 wheel arrangement to handle these more demanding jobs. Their opposite numbers at the LMS, on the other hand, were slow to appreciate the need for more powerful locomotives. By 1935 they had only 13 locomotives of the Princess Royal class to do the toughest jobs.

The introduction of the LNER's streamlined Silver Jubilee express train service between King's Cross and Newcastle in 1935 – and their plans to bring in a similar six hour, London to Edinburgh service in 1937 – brought matters to a head. The

▼ No 46229 *Duchess of Hamilton* is one of the three Duchesses to be preserved – it is based at York. Here the locomotive works hard to pull a 14 coach excursion north over Lunds Viaduct on the long climb up to Ais Gill summit on the Settle to Carlisle line in October 1983.

KEY FACTS

LMS Princess Coronation (Duchess) class 4-6-2
BR nos: 46220-46257, 38 locomotives
Designer: William Stanier
Built: 1937-48, Crewe works
Service: West Coast main line services
Livery: streamlined engines – mid blue, four silver stripes. Later engines crimson lake with four gold stripes. Non-streamlined engines – crimson lake with gold lining. Black during war. Post war – successively lined black, blue, Brunswick green, crimson lake.
Performance: June 1937 – British speed record of 113mph between Stafford–Crewe (No 6220); Feb 1939 – 3333hp (in cylinders) and 2511hp (at drawbar) No 6234
Special features: heaviest express passenger engines built to work in Britain. 24 were streamlined; casing removed 1946-49
Withdrawn: displaced by diesel traction 1962-64

LOCO LIST

A complete list of the 38 Princess Coronation (Duchess) class locomotives built between 1937 and 1948:

6220 **Coronation**
6221 **Queen Elizabeth**
6222 **Queen Mary**
6223 **Princess Alice**
6224 **Princess Alexandra**
6225 **Duchess of Gloucester**
6226 **Duchess of Norfolk**
6227 **Duchess of Devonshire**
6228 **Duchess of Rutland**
6229 **Duchess of Hamilton**
6230 **Duchess of Buccleuch**
6231 **Duchess of Atholl**
6232 **Duchess of Montrose**
6233 **Duchess of Sutherland**
6234 **Duchess of Abercorn**
6235 *City of Birmingham*
6236 *City of Bradford*
6237 *City of Bristol*
6238 *City of Carlisle*
6239 *City of Chester*
6240 *City of Coventry*
6241 *City of Edinburgh*
6242 *City of Glasgow*
6243 *City of Lancaster*
6244 *King George VI*
6245 *City of London*
6246 *City of Manchester*
6247 *City of Liverpool*
6248 *City of Leeds*
6249 *City of Sheffield*
6250 *City of Lichfield*
6251 *City of Nottingham*
6252 *City of Leicester*
6253 *City of St. Albans*
6254 *City of Stoke-on-Trent*
6255 *City of Hereford*
6256 **Sir William A. Stanier, F.R.S.**
6257 *City of Salford*

rival Anglo-Scottish route of the LMS from Euston to Glasgow was eight miles longer and included steeper and longer climbs.

Tests in November 1936 with an LMS Princess Royal class engine pulling a seven coach train showed that a six hour schedule was possible under ideal conditions. But it was hardly a practical proposition on a day to day basis, while commercial pressures dictated that heavier trains of at least nine coaches would be necessary to make any service a financial success.

A Duchess is born

The demand for extra power led the Chief Mechanical Engineer at the LMS, William Stanier, to develop the Princess Royal class by enlarging the boiler and modifying the chassis. A total of 38 Duchess class engines were built at Crewe between 1937 and 1948, with Nos 6220-6229 and 6235-6248 being streamlined.

The first five of the new engines were painted in mid blue with four silver stripes to match the coach livery of the Coronation Scot train. Later streamlined engines continued with this style but used gold stripes on crimson lake to match the normal red painted LMS coaches. All were named: after *Coronation*, five were named after royalty, ten after duchesses, 21 after cities served by the LMS and one after their designer, William Stanier.

Stanier's new locomotives were officially called the Princess Coronation class because they were developed from the Princess Royal class in

▲The streamlined Duchesses were state of the art technology in June 1938 and attracted engineers from all over the world. Delegates to the meeting of the Institution of Locomotive Engineers leave Euston on the 9.50am to Glasgow pulled by No 6225 *Duchess of Gloucester*.

▼*Duchess of Hamilton* was built at Crewe in 1938. It was selected for a Coronation Scot train tour of North America during 1939-40 and temporarily became No 6220 *Coronation* for this trip. The Duchess covered 3121 miles (5,023km) of American railroads and visited 38 towns and cities, ending at the World Fair in New York. The outbreak of war prevented a return to Britain – the Duchess arrived back in 1943 and resumed its original identity. After nationalisation, *Duchess of Hamilton* served on the London Midland Region of British Railways until it was withdrawn in 1964.

1937, the year of George VI's coronation. Unofficially, because of the names of many of the early locomotives, they soon became known as Duchesses. But the enginemen who worked with them gave the locomotives the affectionate nickname Big Lizzies because they were a larger version of the Princess Royal class, the second of which was named after the young Princess Elizabeth.

Once the Duchess class engines were in service, the LMS decided to test the limit of their capabilities. In February 1939 No 6234 *Duchess of Abercorn* hauled a 20 coach, 605 ton train from Crewe to Glasgow and back. On the return journey it topped the 1 in 99 gradient to Beattock summit at 63mph and generated 3333 horsepower in the cylinders – the highest output ever recorded by a British steam locomotive and superior to many diesels. An hour later it was producing 2511 horsepower at the drawbar – another British first.

As a result of the 1939 trial the entire class was fitted with double chimneys to increase the steam

▼ **No 6231 *Duchess of Atholl* in its single chimney condition passes some fine LNWR signals at Wavertree Junction, just south of Liverpool, in the years before World War II. The locomotive was one of only 14 Duchesses that were never streamlined.**

Record breaker
After No 6220 *Coronation* passed Stafford in June 1937, the driver, Tom Clarke, piled on the power. Soon the magic 100mph barrier had been broken, but the LMS wanted a record and Clarke was told to keep going.

When the needle finally touched 114mph he shut the regulator, but the momentum was so great that the train thundered into Crewe station, riding through points with a 20mph limit at over 50mph. This damaged the track and threw the crew and passengers off their feet but disaster was avoided and the record had been broken.

Where to see them
Three Duchesses have been preserved – one can still be seen in action.
● **Duchess of Hamilton** is based at the National Railway Museum, York; currently on loan for short periods to Preserved Railways.
● **Duchess of Sutherland** is at the Midland Railway Centre, Butterley.
● **City of Birmingham** is on exhibition at the Birmingham Museum of Science and Industry.

Design specifications DUCHESS CLASS

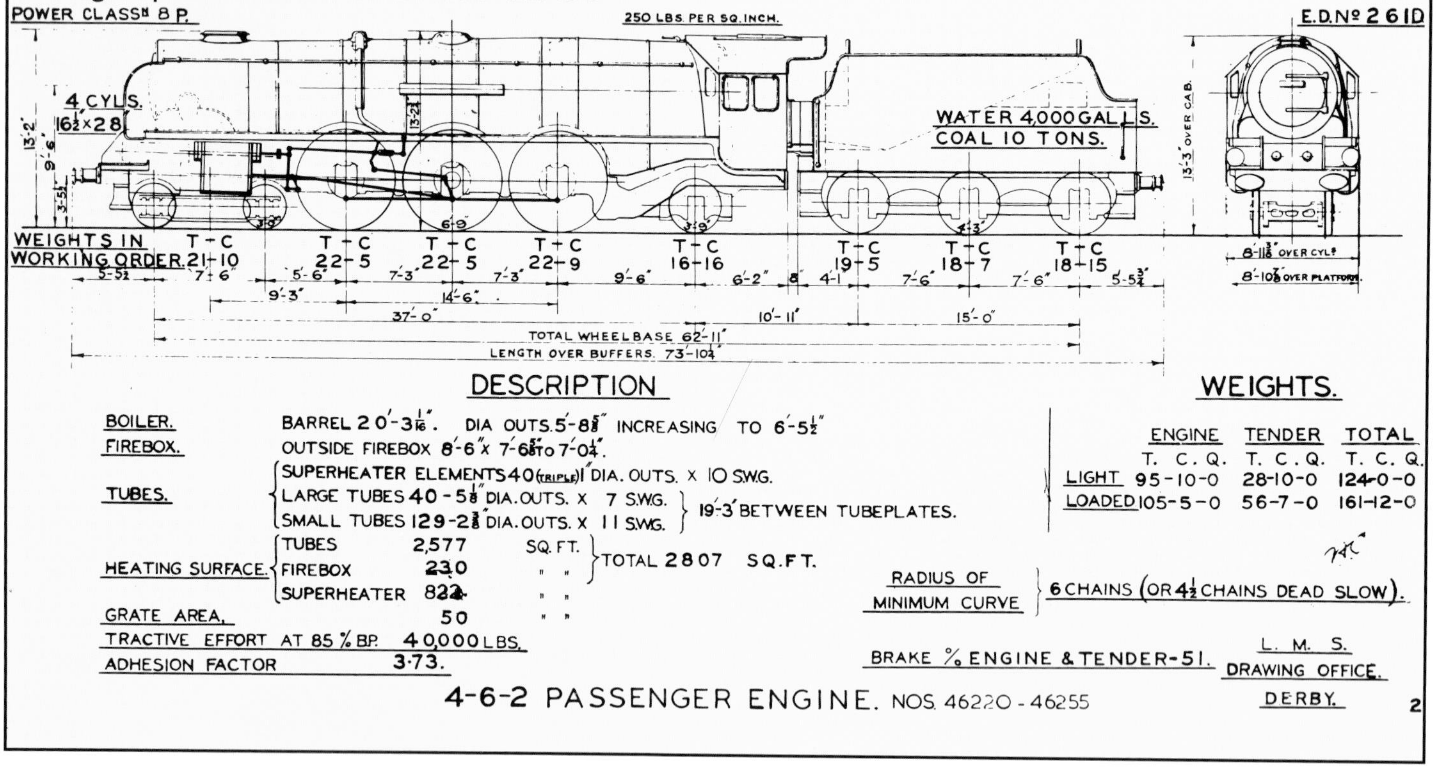
POWER CLASS 8 P.
250 LBS. PER SQ. INCH.
E.D.Nº 261D
4 CYLS.
16½x28
WATER 4,000 GALLS.
COAL 10 TONS.
WEIGHTS IN WORKING ORDER.
T – C 21–10
T – C 22–5
T – C 22–5
T – C 22–9
T – C 16–16
T – C 19–5
T – C 18–7
T – C 18–15
TOTAL WHEELBASE 62'-11"
LENGTH OVER BUFFERS. 73'-10¼"
DESCRIPTION
BOILER. BARREL 20'-3 1/16". DIA OUTS. 5'-8⅝" INCREASING TO 6'-5½"
FIREBOX. OUTSIDE FIREBOX 8'-6" x 7'-6⅝" TO 7'-0¼".
TUBES. SUPERHEATER ELEMENTS 40 (TRIPLE) 1" DIA. OUTS. x 10 S.W.G.
LARGE TUBES 40 - 5⅛" DIA. OUTS. x 7 S.W.G.
SMALL TUBES 129 - 2⅜" DIA. OUTS. x 11 S.W.G.
19'-3" BETWEEN TUBEPLATES.
HEATING SURFACE. TUBES 2,577 SQ. FT.
FIREBOX 230
SUPERHEATER 822
TOTAL 2807 SQ. FT.
GRATE AREA. 50
TRACTIVE EFFORT AT 85 % B.P. 40,000 LBS.
ADHESION FACTOR 3·73.
WEIGHTS.
ENGINE TENDER TOTAL
T. C. Q. T. C. Q. T. C. Q.
LIGHT 95-10-0 28-10-0 124-0-0
LOADED 105-5-0 56-7-0 161-12-0
RADIUS OF MINIMUM CURVE 6 CHAINS (OR 4½ CHAINS DEAD SLOW).
BRAKE % ENGINE & TENDER - 51.
L. M. S. DRAWING OFFICE. DERBY.
4-6-2 PASSENGER ENGINE. NOS. 46220 - 46255

▲ **An original weight diagram for the Duchess class taken from an LMS Standard Locomotives book. Among more technical uses, these diagrams allowed the precise length of royal trains to be calculated. This meant that controllers could position a stop board for the driver and so guarantee the royal saloon arriving exactly in line with the red carpet.**

producing ability. This was so successful that when a Duchess was tested at Rugby in 1956 the wheels lost adhesion and slipped before the limit of the boiler could be measured. Practical tests over the Settle – Carlisle line demonstrated that 27 coaches weighing 900 tons could be pulled up a 1 in 100 gradient at a steady 30mph. But such running was possible only in special circumstances, as the engine consumed a ton of coal every 21 minutes and needed two firemen feeding the firebox to produce the necessary steam.

All streamlining was removed from the Duchesses after World War II as there was no prospect of reintroducing high speed services. The work revealed the way that the smokebox in front of the chimneys had been cut down to clear the rounded front of the casing. This unusual feature was eliminated over the years as each locomotive underwent its regular overhaul.

Without streamlining, and with double chimneys, the driver's view was sometimes obscured, especially in bad weather as steam and smoke drifted down into his line of vision. There was a suspicion that this was a factor in more than one accident in which drivers had passed signals at danger. To prevent the exhaust drifting down, large smoke deflectors were placed alongside the smokebox to create an upward air flow.

Duchesses held their premier position on British Railways' London Midland Region throughout the 1950s. They were based at key depots along the route to Scotland – at Camden in north London, Crewe North, Upperby in Carlisle and Polmadie in Glasgow.

The arrival in the early 1960s of large numbers of powerful diesel locomotives made the Duchesses redundant. All were withdrawn from service between 1962 and 1964.

TECHNICAL FILE

4 cylinders: 16½in diameter, 28in stroke
Coupled wheels: 6ft 9in diam
Boiler diameter: 6ft 5½in max
Grate area: 50sq ft
Boiler pressure: 250lb per sq in
Tractive effort: 40,000lb
Coal capacity: 10 ton
Water capacity: 4000 gallons
Length over buffer: 73ft10¼in
Weight in working order:
Engine: (streamlined) 108.1 ton (non-streamlined) 105.25 ton*
Tender: 56.35 ton*
*(Nos 46256/7 slightly heavier)

▼ **The *Duchess of Hamilton* was withdrawn from service at the end of 1985 for a scheduled overhaul. This was completed early in 1990. Its last duty before withdrawal was to pull a special from Carlisle to York on 26 October when it made good time near Baron Wood tunnels as it headed south towards Lazonby.**

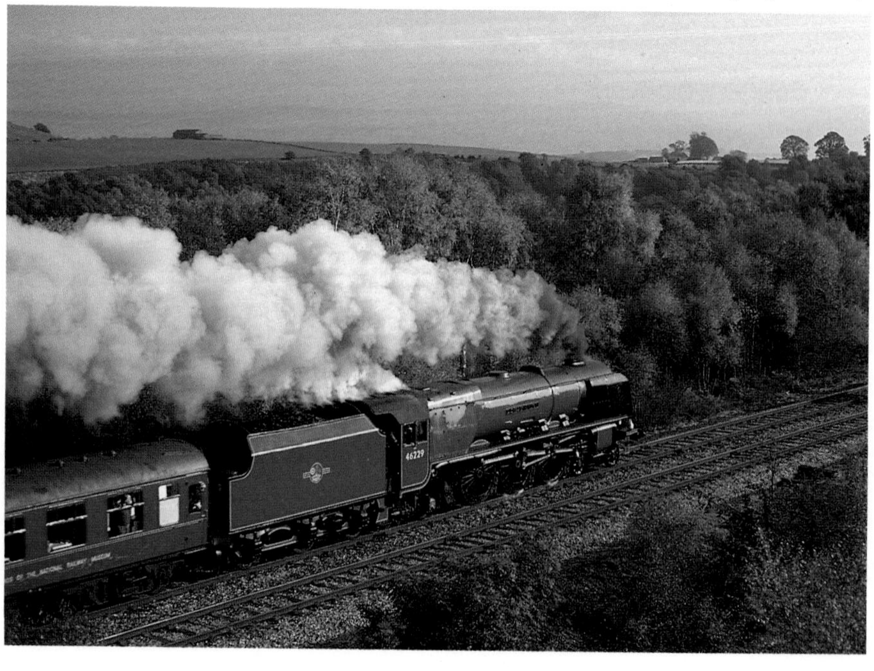

A4 Class 4-6-2

LONDON & NORTH EASTERN RAILWAY

When *Mallard* broke the world rail speed record on 3 July 1938 it set a mark which no steam locomotive is likely to beat. But the world's most famous engine was only one among a great class which hauled the premier trains on the East Coast main line for 25 years.

KEY FACTS

LNER Class A4 4-6-2
BR Nos: 60001-60034
Designer: Nigel Gresley
Built: 1935-1938, Doncaster works
Service: passenger services on the East Coast main line
Livery: 2509-2512 – pale silver grey, side valances in mid grey, nose in charcoal grey, lettering in silver white with dark blue shading, wheels in pale silver grey, external frames and cab roof in mid grey, tender buffer beam in signal red. Some engines painted apple green.

New livery introduced July 1937: Garter blue, nose in black edged with a fine red and a fine white line, cab roof and outside frames black, wheels rich Indian red with polished rims
Performance: 3 July 1938 – 126mph descending Stoke Bank: world speed record for steam traction
Withdrawn: No 4469 Sir Ralph Wedgwood June 1942 – after damage from enemy action. 60001-60034 displaced by diesel traction 1962-1966

The streamlined A4s were the direct descendants of a line of locomotives that started in April 1922 when Nigel Gresley – knighted in 1936 – produced his first 4-6-2 express for the Great Northern Railway, No 1470 *Great Northern*.

Gresley was a devoted advocate of the three-cylinder locomotive with two outside Walschaerts valve gears and a simple conjugated valve gear for the inside cylinder. After trying this arrangement on the Class K3 2-6-0s in 1920, Gresley applied it to his new Class A1 Pacifics (engines with a 4-6-2 wheel arrangement) and was sufficiently satisfied to use it on almost every other locomotive he designed.

All cylinders drove on the centre axle, theoretically improving the balancing of the locomotive. The conjugated valve gear allowed a cylinder layout which gave minimal intrusion into the smokebox bottom. But it created further complications and was abandoned by the LNER on Gresley's death. The large boiler with wide round-topped firebox and 32-element superheater could produce ample steam. But steam temperatures were only

▼ The A4s are known throughout the world as the fastest of all steam engines and No 4468 *Mallard* is the most famous because it holds the world speed record for steam. It can normally be seen at the National Railway Museum, York.

41

LOCO LIST

moderate and Gresley later adopted a larger super-heater.

Learning a lesson

But Gresley did have something to learn from other engineers. Comparative trials in 1925 between the GWR's Castle class No 4079 *Pendennis Castle* and Class A1 No 4474 *Victor Wild* showed the Castle's better fuel economy, attributed largely to its long travel valve gear.

It took Gresley two years of heart searching to apply the lesson, but from 1927 he modified the original valve gear of Class A1 No 2555 *Centenary* to provide freer steam flow. In July 1928 another A1, No 4480 *Enterprise*, was rebuilt to raise the boiler pressure from 180 to 220lb per sq in. Another experiment with No 2544 *Lemberg* raised the number of elements in the superheater from 32 to 43 to raise steam temperatures. All these modifications were incorporated into the first A3, No 2743 *Felstead*, which appeared in August 1928.

By mid 1930 there were 47 class A1 and 23 class A3 locomotives giving sterling service on the East Coast expresses from King's Cross to Leeds, Newcastle and Edinburgh. A further nine A3s were built in 1934-1935.

An interesting feature of some of these Pacifics was the provision for non-stop running between

London and Edinburgh from 1928. As the 8¼ hour journey was too long for a single engine crew, special tenders were built with a corridor connection to the train – it was just 18in wide and 5ft high – so that enginemen could change over at speed between York and Northallerton.

The race for prestige

From 1932 higher speeds and accelerated services were needed to meet mounting competition from the London Midland & Scottish Railway. In 1934 an A1 established the first verified 100mph in

▶ Prestigious express services such as The Elizabethan, which ran non-stop between Edinburgh and London, were pulled by A4s until the introduction of Deltics in the early 1960s. The diesels were little faster than the Gresley Pacifics but they could work more intensive schedules.

▼ No 4468 *Mallard* attained immortality on 3 July 1938 when it touched 126mph and stole the world record for steam traction from the German State Railway. *Mallard*'s double Kylchap blastpipe gave improved steaming and an extra turn of speed that made it faster than single chimney A4s.

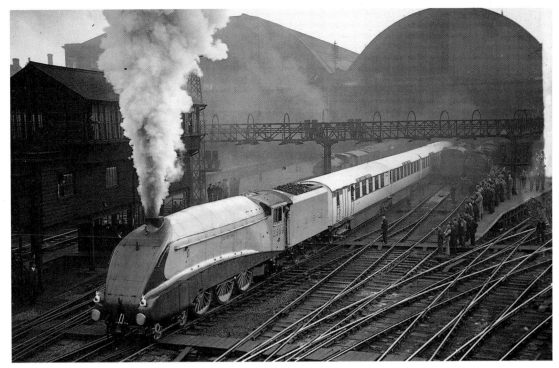

▲ **No 2509 *Silver Link*, seen here leaving King's Cross, was built to haul the Silver Jubilee luxury express between London and Newcastle. The train touched 112¹/₂mph on its first trial run on 27 September 1935 and sometimes topped 100mph while it was in regular service.**

Where to see them
Six A4s have been preserved.
● **Sir Nigel Gresley** is at various depots for main line excursions.
● **Dwight D. Eisenhower** is at the National Railroad Museum, Green Bay, USA.
● **Union of South Africa** is based at Bridgnorth SVR.
● **Dominion of Canada** is at the Montreal Railway Historical Museum, Canada.
● **Bittern** is being restored at Loughborough, Great Central Railway.
● **Mallard** is at the National Railway Museum, York.

Britain. Early in 1935 an A3 pushed the record up to 108mph.

These outstanding performances prepared the ground for the A4s and the LNER's three high speed trains – the Silver Jubilee, Coronation and West Riding Limited – introduced in 1935 and 1937.

The A4 engines were a refined version of the A3s, with a slightly shorter boiler, higher pressure and smaller but improved cylinders. The streamlined casing had a wedge-shaped front end in which a large door opened upwards for access to clean out the smokebox. It soon became known as the cod's mouth.

The A4s quickly showed that 108mph was not the end of the LNER's record-breaking performances. A trial run just before the Silver Jubilee service to Newcastle started in 1935 saw No 2509

Silver Link raise the record to 112¹/₂mph. This was beaten by an LMS Duchess in 1937, only to be recaptured by the 126mph run of No 4468 *Mallard* in 1938.

Mallard was one of four A4s built with double chimneys and Kylchap blastpipes, which improved the draughting. Not until 1957-1958, when coal quality was declining, were the remaining 30 engines similarly fitted.

The first four A4s – 2509-2512 – were painted silver grey to match the Silver Jubilee express,

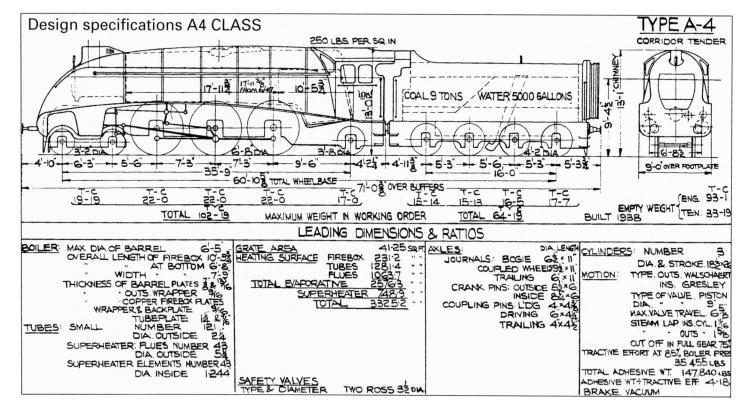

Design specifications A4 CLASS — TYPE A-4 CORRIDOR TENDER

250 LBS. PER SQ.IN — COAL 9 TONS — WATER 5000 GALLONS — BUILT 1938 — EMPTY WEIGHT {ENG. 93·1 / TEN. 33·19}

LEADING DIMENSIONS & RATIOS

BOILER: MAX. DIA. OF BARREL 6·5; OVERALL LENGTH OF FIREBOX 10·5½; AT BOTTOM 6·8; WIDTH 7·9; THICKNESS OF BARREL PLATES; OUTS. WRAPPER 9/16; COPPER FIREBOX PLATES; WRAPPER & BACKPLATE 9/16; TUBEPLATE 14 & 7/8

TUBES: SMALL NUMBER 121; DIA. OUTSIDE 2·4; SUPERHEATER: FLUES NUMBER 43; DIA. OUTSIDE 5·4; SUPERHEATER ELEMENTS NUMBER 43; DIA. INSIDE 1·244

GRATE AREA 41·25 SQ.FT; HEATING SURFACE FIREBOX 231·2; TUBES 1281·4; FLUES 1063·7; TOTAL EVAPORATIVE 2576·3; SUPERHEATER 748·9; TOTAL 3325·2

SAFETY VALVES TYPE & DIAMETER TWO ROSS 3½ DIA.

AXLES: JOURNALS: BOGIE 6½ × 11; COUPLED WHEELS 9½ × 11; TRAILING 6 × 11; CRANK PINS: OUTSIDE 5½ × 6; INSIDE 8¼ × 6; COUPLING PINS: L'DG 4 × 4¾; DRIVING 6 × 4½; TRAILING 4 × 4½

CYLINDERS: NUMBER 3; DIA. & STROKE 18½ × 26

MOTION: TYPE. OUTS. WALSCHAERT; INS. GRESLEY; TYPE OF VALVE. PISTON; DIA. 9·5; MAX. VALVE TRAVEL. 6⅞; STEAM LAP. INS. CYL. 1⅜; OUTS. 1⅝; CUT OFF IN FULL GEAR 75%; TRACTIVE EFFORT AT 85% BOILER PRES 35,455 LBS; TOTAL ADHESIVE WT. 147,840 LBS; ADHESIVE WT ÷ TRACTIVE EFF. 4·18; BRAKE. VACUUM

---

with darker grey fronts and side valances. They were called *Silver Link, Quicksilver, Silver King* and *Silver Fox*.

The following engines were painted in LNER green until June 1937 when seven were turned out in Garter blue for the Coronation workings. All were sporting the Garter blue livery by September 1939.

The wartime workhorse

During the war the A4s handled prodigious loads. Trains of well over 20 coaches were taken out of King's Cross. Some were so long that they had to be loaded at two platforms and joined up for departure, by which time the engine would be out of sight in Gasworks Tunnel.

One A4, No 4469 *Sir Ralph Wedgwood*, was so

▲ The A4s marked the peak of Nigel Gresley's career as chief mechanical engineer at the LNER. His basic design evolved from the A3 Pacific, which first appeared in August 1928. The streamlining was inspired by the Bugatti railcar, which first appeared on French railways in 1934.

badly damaged in an air raid on York in 1942 that it was scrapped.

The modernisation of BR, in particular the introduction of the 3300hp Class 55 (Deltic) in 1961, began to push the A4s off their traditional work.

Scrapping started at the end of 1962, by which time most had run close on 1½ million miles (2½ billion km) each. The survivors were concentrated in Scotland working the three hour Glasgow – Aberdeen expresses. The last A4 was withdrawn in 1966.

3 cylinders: 18 ½in diameter, 26in stroke
Coupled wheels: 6ft 8in diameter
Boiler diameter: 6ft 5in
Grate area: 41.25sq ft
Boiler pressure: 250lb per sq in
Tractive effort: 35,455lb Originally 32,500lb
Coal capacity: 9 tons
Water capacity: 5000 gallons
Length over buffers: 71ft 3/8in
Weight in working order:
Engine: 102.95 tons
Tender: 60.4/65.45 tons

Mallard's record run

No 4468 *Mallard* had been in service only three months when on 3 July 1938 Nigel Gresley approved an attempt on the British rail speed record. The engine was selected because it had already demonstrated that its Kylchap blastpipes gave it extra speed.

Mallard's regular driver Joe Duddington took the train south through Grantham and accelerated up to Stoke summit. The next 20 miles (32km) were downhill, and Duddington gave the engine its head. Four minutes later the British record belonged to *Mallard* but there was still an opportunity to go faster. Eventually the train touched 126mph but then problems developed in the engine and it was replaced at Peterborough. *Mallard* crawled back to Doncaster but no steam engine would ever go faster.

Class 5 4-6-0

LONDON, MIDLAND & SCOTTISH RAILWAY

Sir William Stanier's Black 5 was one of the most successful locomotives of all time, equally at home powering fast express trains or slow coal hauls. Class 5s became the last steam engines in service on BR; 18 examples of this adaptable locomotive are preserved.

The Stanier Class 5 was introduced by the LMSR as a go anywhere and do anything locomotive. Built as a response to the demand for an engine fast enough for passenger trains and strong enough for express freight workings, in service these powerful and capable locomotives did everything that was asked of them.

Stanier arrives

On the LMSR, whose early locomotive policy often verged on the bizarre, the modern mixed traffic engine was introduced only after a lengthy gestation period. Good as it was, the Horwich-designed 2-6-0 of 1926, the Crab, of which 245 were built over the next six years, had its limita-

▼ **On the morning of 4 August 1968, two of Stanier's Class 5s, Nos 44871 and 44894, wait at Manchester Victoria to haul a Stephenson Locomotive Society 'Farewell to Steam' excursion, which originated from Birmingham.**

tions. William Stanier, who took over as Chief Mechanical Engineer in 1932 after moving from the GWR, soon put a 4-6-0 mixed traffic engine on the drawing board.

No doubt because of his Swindon origins, Stanier is usually regarded as having brought the concept of the GWR Hall 4-6-0 to Euston as the prototype for what he intended to build. Perhaps this was because boiler pressure and certain key dimensions were the same. But if he was influenced by other designs (and he was not one to copy practice from elsewhere without very good reason), the Class 5 design probably owed at least as much to the S15 class 4-6-0s of the Southern Railway. These had been built from 1927 with Maunsell's improvements to Urie's design for the London & South Western.

These S15s (several of which have been preserved) were simple, rugged two-cylinder engines with the excellent King Arthur boiler, 5ft 7in coupled wheels and outside Walschaerts valve gear.

KEY FACTS

LMSR Class 5 4-6-0
BR Nos: 44658-45499
Designer: Sir William Stanier
Built: 1934-1951, Crewe, Derby and Horwich works, Vulcan Foundry and Armstrong Whitworth & Co
2 cylinders: 18$\frac{1}{2}$ in diameter x 28in stroke
Coupled wheels: 6ft diameter
Coal capacity: 9 tons
Water capacity: 4000 gallons
Service: passenger and freight over entire LMSR system
Livery: LMSR – black with red lining, LMS on tender. BR – black, lined out in red, grey and cream, BR crest on tender
Performance: 1966, 93mph between Gobowen and Shrewsbury with 7 coaches, 265 tons gross
Withdrawn: 1961-1968

Where to see them
18 Class 5s are preserved; 7 were named in preservation. Some work on the main line, often Fort William – Mallaig.
● **44767** (George Stephenson) – North Yorkshire Moors Rly.
● **44806** (Magpie) – Llangollen Railway.
● **44871** (Sovereign) – Scottish RPS, Bo'ness.
● **44901** – Barry. Not on public view.
● **44932** Midland Rly Centre, Butterley.
● **5000** – National Railway Museum, York.
● **5025** – Strathspey Railway, Aviemore.
● **45110** (RAF Biggin Hill) – Severn Valley Rly, Bridgnorth.
● **45163** – Colne Valley Railway, Castle Hedingham.
● **45212** – Keighley & Worth Valley Rly, Haworth.
● **5231** (3rd Battalion [volunteer], The Worcestershire & Sherwood Foresters Regiment) – GCR, Loughborough.
● **45293** – Colne Valley Railway.
● **5305** (Alderman A E Draper), Loughborough.
● **45337** – East Lancashire Railway, Bury.
● **45379** – Avon Valley Rly, Bristol.
● **5407** – East Lancashire Railway, Bury.
● **45428** (Eric Treacy) – NYMR.
● **45491** – Midland RC.

▲ A number of the early members of the class retained their original domeless boilers until the end of steam. A domeless example, No 45092, waits between duties at Crewe South shed in 1967. Between 1934 and 1951, 842 members of the class were built; the last was not withdrawn until 1968, giving them a service life of up to 34 years.

▼ Though the design was modified over the years, the basic character of the Black 5 remained unchanged. Five of the class, including one of the last to be withdrawn, No 45156 *Ayrshire Yeomanry*, were named in service.

Used predominantly on express freight trains between London yards and the west of England, they were also at home working Southampton ocean liner specials, thanks to a good front end with long lap valve gear.

A popular machine

The first Stanier Class 5 4-6-0 mixed traffic locomotive, No 5020, appeared in August 1934 from the Vulcan Foundry, Newton-le-Willows. The class incorporated the best current practice in a simple machine which proved immensely popular

with enginemen.

Its two outside cylinders and Walschaerts valve gear were of excellent design and fully accessible from the trackside; no pit was necessary for preparation and lubrication. The boiler, with tapered barrel, Belpaire firebox and topfeed, was a splendid steamer. A side window cab gave good weather protection, and the tender held ample coal and water. The Class 5 was also very economical.

The operating department was delighted to get such a versatile machine, with a weight which barred it from very few lines. The Class 5s were quickly employed in express passenger service, particularly on the Midland Division, where they handled some of the fastest trains. They also revolutionised working of the Perth – Inverness route.

The adaptable locomotives lost no time in proving that 6ft wheels were no impediment to high speeds; they could reach, and if necessary exceed, 90mph. They also took over many of the fully braked express freight and perishables trains.

Maids of all work

The Class 5s were in production from 1934 to 1951, during which time a total of 842 was built. Several hundred were built with cheap government loan capital to generate employment during the Depression of the 1930s.

As their numbers increased they could be found from Bournemouth to Wick on a widening range of duties, from express and stopping passenger trains and fast freights to mine workings in the Ayrshire coalfield. Some of these jobs might have been better done by a heavy freight locomotive, but the saving grace was always that at weekends the Black 5s could be used to haul excursions and summer extras, so giving more intensive utilisation. They were also no strangers to Royal trains.

Over the years a number of changes to the original design appeared, without altering their funda-mental character. From 1936 a modified boiler, with sloping throatplate, a separate dome and enlarged superheater, was used. Various devices were introduced to increase their mileage between works repairs. A very visible modification introduced in 1947 moved the topfeed forward towards the front of the boiler.

In 1948 20 new engines were fitted with Caprotti poppet valve gear instead of piston valves, which led to extensive changes in their appearance though the benefits were marginal. One engine was built with outside Stephenson valve gear – a novel layout – for comparison. There were extensive trials of roller bearing axleboxes, and ten engines for use in Scotland (with its soft water) were built with steel inner fireboxes instead of the usual copper. A few engines received double chimneys.

▼ In the typically grimy condition of the class in its last years of service, No 45156 *Ayrshire Yeomanry* waits at Lancaster Castle station in 1963. As mileages increased between overhauls, the class could become quite rough riding, but drivers tolerated this as long as the locomotive steamed well.

Design specifications LMSR CLASS 5

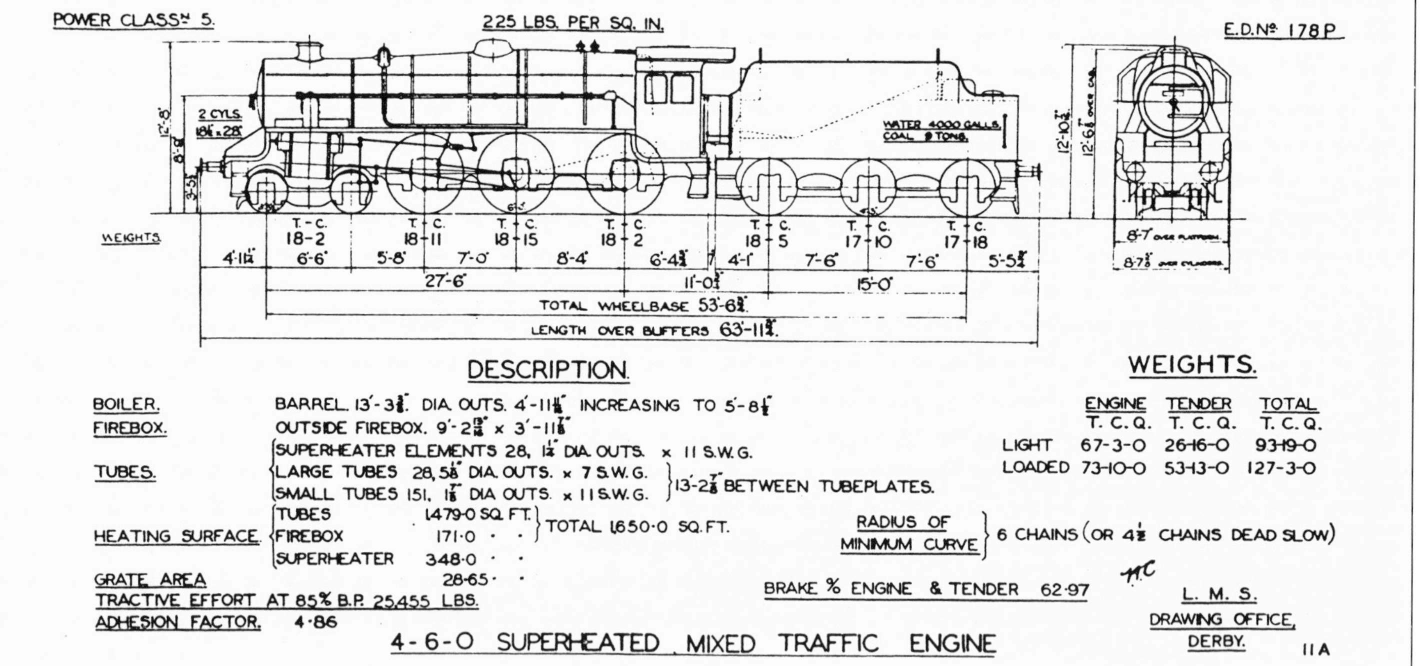
POWER CLASSN 5.
225 LBS. PER SQ. IN.
E.D.Nº 178P
2 CYLS. 18½ x 28
WATER 4000 GALLS.
COAL 9 TONS.
WEIGHTS
T.-C. 18-2
T.C. 18-11
T.C. 18-15
T.C. 18-2
T.C. 18-5
T.C. 17-10
T.C. 17-18
4'-11¼ 6'-6" 5'-8" 7'-0" 8'-4" 6'-4⅜ 4'-1" 7'-6" 7'-6" 5'-5¾
27'-6" 11'-0⅜ 15'-0"
TOTAL WHEELBASE 53'-6¾.
LENGTH OVER BUFFERS 63'-11¾.
8'-7"
8'-7⅜
DESCRIPTION.
BOILER. BARREL 13'-3⅜. DIA. OUTS. 4'-11⅛ INCREASING TO 5'-8½
FIREBOX. OUTSIDE FIREBOX. 9'-2 13/16 x 3'-11⅞
TUBES. SUPERHEATER ELEMENTS 28, 1¼ DIA. OUTS. x 11 S.W.G.
LARGE TUBES 28, 5⅛ DIA. OUTS. x 7 S.W.G.
SMALL TUBES 151, 1⅞ DIA. OUTS. x 11 S.W.G.
13'-2⅞ BETWEEN TUBEPLATES.
HEATING SURFACE. TUBES 1479·0 SQ. FT. FIREBOX 171·0 SUPERHEATER 348·0
TOTAL 1650·0 SQ. FT.
GRATE AREA 28·65
TRACTIVE EFFORT AT 85% B.P. 25,455 LBS.
ADHESION FACTOR. 4·86
WEIGHTS.
ENGINE T. C. Q. TENDER T. C. Q. TOTAL T. C. Q.
LIGHT 67-3-0 26-16-0 93-19-0
LOADED 73-10-0 53-13-0 127-3-0
RADIUS OF MINIMUM CURVE 6 CHAINS (OR 4½ CHAINS DEAD SLOW)
BRAKE % ENGINE & TENDER 62·97
L. M. S.
DRAWING OFFICE, DERBY.
11A
4-6-0 SUPERHEATED MIXED TRAFFIC ENGINE

The last two Class 5s, Nos 44686/7, represented the pinnacle of their development. An improved version of the Caprotti valve gear was fitted, roller bearing axleboxes were used throughout, there was a double chimney and the side platforms were raised very high over the cylinders and valve gear drive shafts. The appearance was very different from the early members of the class, but underneath it all they were still the basic Class 5s, though with added frills. Many drivers reckoned that the improvements had earned the locomotives an upgrading from Class 5 to 6.

Final act

Not even such a versatile engine as the Class 5 could withstand the progressive introduction of diesel and electric locomotives. Withdrawal started late in 1961, and the final 46 engines were withdrawn in August 1968. It fell to two of them, Nos 45212 and 45318, to work the last steam-hauled regular service trains on BR on the night of 3 August.

Eighteen of the class have been preserved and are still as popular as ever with loco crews and enthusiasts.

▲The tapered boiler and Belpaire firebox of the Class 5 was new to the LMSR. Up to that point the parallel boiler designs of Hughes and Fowler were more familiar. The similarity of the class to the Hall 4-6-0s of the GWR has often been noted, but the design probably owed at least as much to the S15 4-6-0 of the Southern Railway.

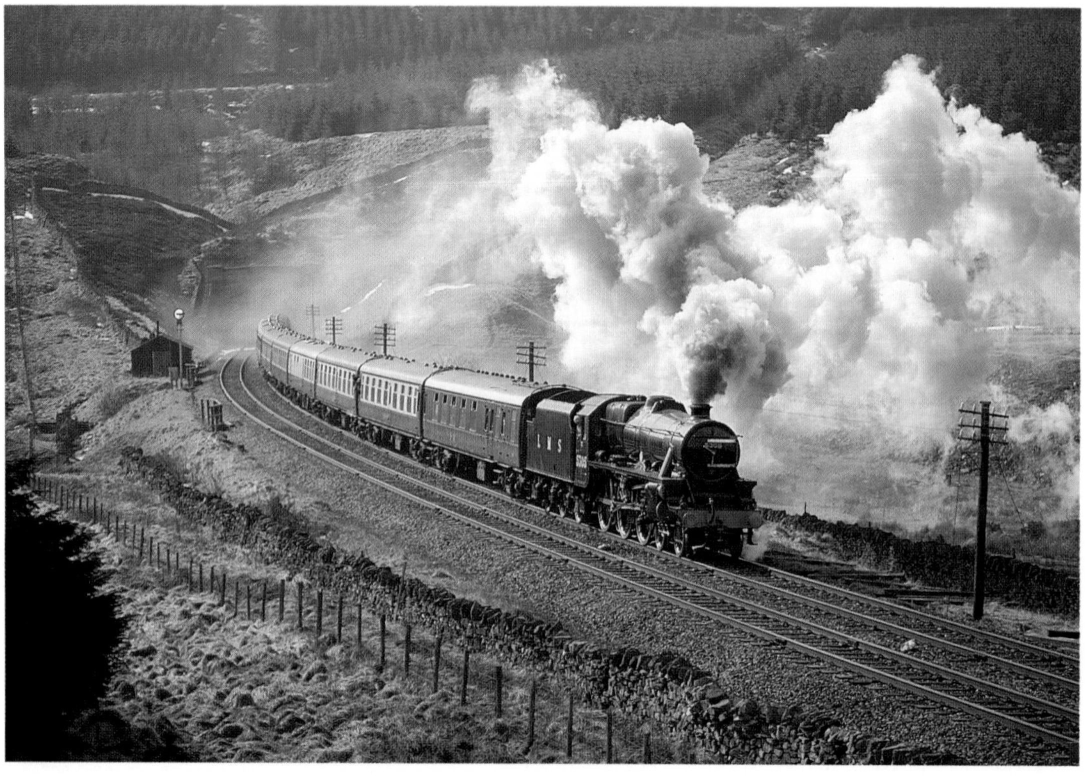
LMS

LOCO LIST

In LMSR and BR days only five Class 5s were named, all Scottish based engines:

45154 Lanarkshire Yeomanry
45155 Queens Edinburgh
45156 Ayrshire Yeomanry
45157 The Glasgow Highlander
45158 Glasgow Yeomanry
No 45155 lost its name within a year

◀Black 5 No 5305 emerges from Blea Moor tunnel en route to Carlisle. In 1968 the locomotive was taken to Draper's scrapyard in Hull, which had cut up hundreds of Black 5s. However, the yard's owner decided to keep it for himself. Later named Alderman A E Draper after the man who saved it, No 5305 is a frequent performer on the main line.

Steam speed records

In 1804, when Richard Trevithick's pioneering locomotive made its journey along the Penydarren tramroad, its inventor operated the controls by walking along the track in front of it. In a letter the following day, Trevithick recorded that 'The engine while working went nearly five miles pr hour' – no more than a brisk walking pace. This was perhaps the first ever steam speed record.

When *Locomotion* ran from Shildon to Stockton 21 years later, it could only out-distance riders on horseback because marshes alongside the line impeded the horses. At full speed the locomotive could just manage 15mph.

At the Rainhill Trials in 1829, Stephenson's *Rocket* achieved 29mph. This was eclipsed in tragic circumstances the following year, when *Northumbrian* reached 36mph as it conveyed the dying MP William Huskisson to Eccles after he had been run over by *Rocket* at Parkside.

The contestants' achievements at Rainhill were carefully recorded. Later, it became difficult to establish accurate claims as speeds increased and railways spread throughout the world.

Unlike world speed records on land and in the air, there are no international standards for railways. For example, the effect of a strong following wind has never been taken into account and on almost every occasion a record-breaking train was appreciably assisted by gravity. This applies equally to the TGV's present world record of 320.2mph (486.4km/h) as to *Mallard*'s 126mph in 1938.

Speed records were usually obtained by stop-watch measurements from mile or kilometre posts. In some cases the speed claimed at the time was later adjusted after the information had been examined further.

The performance of the Milwaukee Road's Hiawatha expresses in the 1930s was accurately measured and the 112mph record by the streamlined Atlantic No 2 in 1925 was adequately proved.

During the 1930s, there was considerable rivalry over maximum speeds between the LNER and the LMS. In 1937, the LMS claimed a maximum of 114mph on the press run of their Coronation Scot streamliner train. This would have beaten *Silver Link*'s record but the figure was not confirmed by a number of experienced recorders on the train. This left *Coronation* sharing the record of 112mph with the LNER A4 and Milwaukee Atlantic.

By 1936 the German Pacific No 05.002 reached 124.5mph and in 1938, *Mallard* achieved an historic all-time record for steam of 126mph.

Date	Wheel arrgt	Name/No	Country	Railway	Speed mph (km)
Feb 1804	0-4-0	Trevithick's Penydarren Locomotive	GB	Merthyr tramroad	5 (8)
Sep 1825	0-4-0	*Locomotion*	GB	Stockton & Darlington	15 (24)
Oct 1829	0-2-2	*Rocket*	GB	Liverpool & Manchester	29 (46)
Sep 1830	0-2-2	*Northumbrian*	GB	Liverpool & Manchester	36 (58)
Nov 1839	2-2-2	*Lucifer*	GB	Grand Junction	57 (92)
June 1845	2-2-2	*Ixion*	GB	Great Western	61 (98)
June 1846	2-2-2	*Great Western*	GB	Great Western	74 (119)
May 1848	4-2-2	*Great Britain*	GB	Great Western	78 (125)
June 1854	4-2-4WT	No 41	GB	Bristol & Exeter	82 (132)
1889	4-2-0	No 604	France	Est	89 (143)
Mar 1897	4-2-2	No 117	GB	Midland	90 (145)
May 1904	4-4-0	*City of Truro*	GB	Great Western	100 (161)
Nov 1934	4-6-2	*Flying Scotsman*	GB	LNER	100 (161)
Mar 1935	4-6-2	*Papyrus*	GB	LNER	108 (174)
May 1935	4-4-2	No 2	USA	Milwaukee	112 (180)
Sep 1935	4-6-2	*Silver Link*	GB	LNER	112 (180)
May 1936	4-6-4	No 05.002	Germany	Deutsche Reichsbahn	124.5 (200)
July 1938	4-6-2	*Mallard*	GB	LNER	126 (202)

▲ All the fully authenticated world records achieved by steam locomotives are the maximum speed attained, rather than averages. Some top speeds, like *Mallard*'s, were sustained only for a few yards.

◀ Although a record of 74mph was achieved by a GWR locomotive in 1846, it was not until 1931 that the company ran trains at such average speeds in everyday service. The Cheltenham Flyer was the first train in the history of railways to average regularly over 70mph. On 14 September 1931, the express sweeps through Tilehurst, Berkshire on its way to London.

Rebuilt Merchant Navy

BRITISH RAILWAYS

**The rebuilt Merchant Navy Pacifics were
the last heavyweight express passenger steam engines
in regular service in the UK. Proving to be as popular
in preservation as it was in service, a third
of this powerful class survives today.**

Appearing in 1941, the Merchant Navy class was the first Pacific built by the Southern Railway. Designed by Oliver Bulleid, formerly personal assistant to Sir Nigel Gresley (Chief Mechanical Engineer of the London & North Eastern Railway), the Merchant Navy Pacifics embodied several important innovations. But although they were impressive performers, problems in service led to the entire class being rebuilt from 1956.

The Merchant Navy class worked express passenger services between London Waterloo and Exeter or Weymouth, where they proved they could pull heavy trains competently and rarely lost any time. The class benefited from the Bulleid designed boiler, which supplied ample steam so long as the fireman was prepared to feed the 48^1/$_2$sq ft firegrate at the necessary rate.

Problems

The Merchant Navy class had a number of faults. The class burned more coal than other Pacifics of similar capacity and in the wrong hands could slip severely. The locomotives vibrated if worked on too short a cut-off, partly owing to the difficulty in adjusting the steam reverser to enable the engine to be worked as economically as possible.

The middle cylinder connecting rod, with its big and small ends, crosshead and slide bar, together with the three sets of Bulleid valve gear, were enclosed in an oilbath which gave continuous lubrication to the working parts. Although overheated connecting rod bearings were virtually unknown on the Merchant Navy Pacifics, the oilbath and its enclosed valve gear gave a good deal of trouble.

The boilers were lagged with a fibreglass mattress, which was often soaked in oil from a leaking

◄The Merchant Navy Pacifics were the last big steam locomotives regularly to haul express passenger trains on BR. In their last few months of service, many Southern Region drivers had a last fling on steam as they pushed their charges to speeds of over 100mph – well above the official speed limit. On 23 March 1967, No 35012 *United States Line* is seen near Nine Elms locomotive depot, south London.

Boiler cleaner
Boiler washouts on the Merchant Navy Pacifics were drastically reduced by use of a French chemical water treatment system, known as TIA (Traitement Integral Armand). It was developed by Louis Armand, Chief Motive Power Running Engineer of the SNCF from 1943-44. During the war Armand was leader of the French railway resistance. In May 1944, he was denounced to the Germans and was to be taken to Germany for imprisonment. His train was cancelled after the Allied landing.

▲ In April 1949, No 35024 *East Asiatic Company* stands in its original condition with the enclosed air-smoothed casing. The class was designed to be easily maintained in wartime conditions, but this did not always prove to be the case. The fitters' work, attending to minor jobs under the casing, involved removing sections of it. These were secured by innumerable small bolts and undoing them often took longer than the job itself.

oilbath. The mattress sometimes caught fire and when this happened, the local fire brigade was called out; they sprayed cold water on the still hot steel boiler and firebox, causing some contraction and inevitable stresses. After such incidents, the boiler would have to be inspected by the leading boilersmith for damage.

Another problem that plagued the class was the poor visibility from the cab. Steam and smoke from the chimney beat down and clung to the air-smoothed boiler casing. This was particularly noticeable when the engine was worked on a light rein, or when the wind was in the wrong quarter.

Although Bulleid had designed the Merchant Navy class with ease of maintenance in mind, some of his novel features actually made life hard-er for the fitters. One of the least sought after chores was working on the oilbath. The class was a heavy user of lubricating oil and at every oil change 45 gallons of fine grade machine oil was put into the oilbath. This was the fitters' job; it was also their responsibility to check the oil level periodically and top it up when necessary. The frequency of oil changes depended on the amount of water that found its way into the oilbath (which was difficult to keep oiltight) causing corrosion of the motion.

Oil from the oilbath would leak through the seals and on to the wheel rims, making the locomotives slip badly. To prevent slipping, sand was used, but when the sandboxes were refilled at the shed, sand often found its way on to the outside-cylinder slide bars, where it caused friction and wear. To stop this happening, the leading sandboxes were closed off – which did not help when starting a train on greasy rails or climbing a steep gradient.

To empty the smokebox ash, the fireman had to stand right over the lubricators – which pumped oil to the cylinders and piston valves – and it was no surprise that ash got into them, causing prob-

LOCO LIST

The Merchant Navy Pacifics were all named after shipping companies whose merchant ships called at the port of Southampton, owned by the Southern Railway.

35001 **Channel Packet**
35002 **Union Castle**
35003 **Royal Mail**
35004 **Cunard White Star**
35005 **Canadian Pacific**
35006 **Peninsular & Oriental S.N.Co**
35007 **Aberdeen Commonwealth**
35008 **Orient Line**
35009 **Shaw Savill**
35010 **Blue Star**
35011 **General Steam Navigation**
35012 **United States Line**
35013 **Blue Funnel**
35014 **Nederland Line**
35015 **Rotterdam Lloyd**
35016 **Elders Fyffes**
35017 **Belgian Marine**
35018 **British India Line**
35019 **French Lines CGT**
35020 **Bibby Line**
35021 **New Zealand Line**
35022 **Holland-America Line**
35023 **Holland-Afrika Line**
35024 **East Asiatic Company**
35025 **Brocklebank Line**
35026 **Lamport & Holt Line**
35027 **Port Line**
35028 **Clan Line**
35029 **Ellerman Lines**
35030 **Elder Dempster Lines**

▼ The Merchant Navy Pacifics were rebuilt using three sets of conventional Walschaerts valve gear. Originally, Bulleid had considered using Caprotti poppet valve gear, but probably because the Southern Railway disliked purchasing equipment which had been built by outside manufacturers, he developed his own type of totally enclosed valve gear. Had Caprotti gear been fitted initially, rebuilding might not have been necessary.

Where to see them
● **Canadian Pacific** – Mid-Hants Railway, Hampshire.
● **Peninsular & Oriental S.N.Co** – Gloucestershire & Warwickshire Railway, Toddington.
● **Shaw Savill** – private site in Brighton.
● **Blue Star** – Colne Valley Railway, Castle Hedingham.
● **General Steam Navigation** – private site in Brighton.
● **British India Line** – Mid-Hants Railway, Hampshire.
● **Holland-America Line** – Swanage Railway, Dorset.
● **Brocklebank Line** – Great Central Railway.
● **Port Line** – Bluebell Railway, West Sussex.
● **Clan Line** – private site in Southall.
● **Ellerman Lines** – sectionalised exhibit, National Railway Museum, York.

lems with the valves and pistons and non-return valves. Later, the lubricators were sealed and fed by gravity from a tank mounted above them.

The frequent disruption of the maintenance schedules did not help matters. Overhauls for the Merchant Navy class were originally intended after every 50,000 miles (80,467km) – quite a low figure – to avoid any risk of mechanical failures after running higher mileages. This plan was upset by ongoing locomotive building and maintenance programmes, some of which were needed to clear the backlog built up during the war.

After nationalisation in 1948, the Southern Region had to adopt the former London Midland & Scottish Railway system for accepting engines into the workshops for repairs. This extended the period from when the leading fitter proposed the locomotive for overhaul to when it was taken into the workshops. In the meantime the condition of the locomotive deteriorated further.

Test bed

In March 1952, Merchant Navy Pacific No 35022, *Holland-America Line* was sent to the Rugby testing station for performance and efficiency tests. These revealed the poor distribution of steam to the cylinders at short cut-offs and slow speeds. Under these conditions, virtually no steam was admitted to the front of the left piston – hardly conducive to a sweet running engine. As speed increased on the rollers, the steam distribution became more even, but was never comparable with locomotives fitted with the conventional Walschaerts or poppet valve gear. Following the tests, the decision to rebuild the Merchant Navy Pacifics was taken and carried out from 1956-59.

The first of the class to be rebuilt, No 35018 *British India Line*, emerged from Eastleigh works in 1956. The design team, led by R G Jarvis, had produced a handsome and capable three-cylinder simple expansion engine.

The air-smoothed casing had been removed, giving the locomotive a more conventional appearance, but the magnificent Bulleid boiler was retained – the pressure had long been reduced from 280 to 250lb psi because suitable firebox stays could not be obtained. The re-designed locomotive

▲ In 1966, No 35030 *Elder Dempster Lines* leaves Southampton Central with the down Bournemouth Belle express. On 9 July 1967, this locomotive became the last Merchant Navy Pacific to work a train into Waterloo. The engine hauled the 14.07 from Weymouth and arrived at the London terminus 10 minutes ahead of schedule.

used steam more efficiently and fuel consumption was reduced by 10-15% for equal work done.

The Bulleid chain-driven valve gear and oilbath were replaced by three sets of conventional Walschaerts valve gear. The driver now had to go underneath to oil the inside drive and motion parts. The mechanical lubricators were transferred to the running plate above the leading coupled wheels and away from the smokebox ash.

Once on the road, the driver reaped some bene-

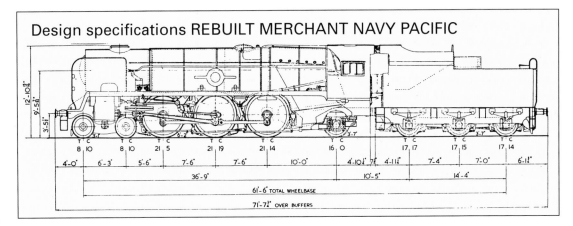

Design specifications REBUILT MERCHANT NAVY PACIFIC

◄ After the class was rebuilt, it retained the most successful features of the original design. These included welded steel fireboxes with thermic water-circulating syphons and a multiple jet blastpipe. Bulleid designed an excellent boiler for the Merchant Navy Pacifics, which proved to be a remarkable steam raiser.

TECHNICAL FILE

3 cylinders: 18in diameter, 24in stroke
Coupled wheels: 6ft 2in diameter
Boiler diameter: 6ft 3½in (maximum)
Grate area: 48½sq ft
Boiler pressure: 250lb psi
Tractive effort: 33,495lb
Coal capacity: 5 tons
Water capacity: 5100 – 6000 gallons
Length over buffers: 71ft 7¾in
Weight in working order:
Engine: 97.9 tons
Tender: 53.3 tons

fit from the rebuilding. Visibility for the crew had improved. The removal of the air-smoothed casing and the addition of smoke deflectors meant that the exhaust no longer beat down and around the cab. A manually operated screw reverser of the drum type was fitted which did not creep from the set position. The drawback was when reversing the locomotive if the train had to be set back slightly to restart. The reversing gear had to be wound back while the steam chest, in which the valve was located, was full of steam. This required considerable strength.

The fireman benefited from a drop grate and hopper ashpan, a smokebox that was easily emp-

tied and accessible sandboxes. The firehole was fitted with a baffle plate to direct secondary air to the fire which, together with control of air admission through damper doors in the ashpan, improved combustion and reduced smoke emission.

All the Merchant Navy Pacifics were rebuilt from 1956-59. They were delightful engines to work on and gave their crews great confidence as they proved more consistently reliable than their air-smoothed predecessors. But the engines were destined to have short lives. By 1964 the first, No 35004 *Cunard White Star*, was withdrawn and by 1967 the last one had gone. Eleven survived.

On 16 May 1992, No 35005 *Canadian Pacific* hurries along a southbound train for Leicester North on the Great Central Railway. This locomotive is one of 11 – over a third of the class – that have survived into preservation. Ten were bought from Woodham's scrapyard in South Wales. The remaining example, No 35028 *Clan Line* was bought by enthusiasts straight from service in 1967.

The locomotive firebox

The steam locomotive firebox is designed to burn fuel efficiently and produce adequate heat to boil water and create steam. The firebox must be large enough to burn sufficient fuel for the heaviest duty without forcing the fire to the point where unburnt fuel is drawn off the firebed in large quantities.

Firebox types

Fireboxes may be wide and extend over the engine frames and wheels, or narrow, waisting in to fit between the frames – this limits their width to about 4ft. The firebox can be round topped and follow the circular profile of the boiler barrel, or Belpaire with the top roughly square. The Belpaire is more costly to produce but makes direct staying simpler and provides more steam space at the top of the firebox where it is needed most.

The locomotive firebox consists of an outer and inner shell. The outer firebox, an integral part of the boiler shell, is made of steel. The inner firebox is either of copper or steel construction. The plates of the two fireboxes need to be stayed together to resist boiler pressure – a large boiler contains well over 1000 stays.

Between the inner and outer fireboxes, boiling water under pressure prevents the inner firebox plates melting in the intense heat from the fire. At their sides and ends these two fireboxes are 3-4in apart but above the inner firebox there is typically a 1½-2ft space to collect steam. At the base is the foundation ring which seals the gap between the two fireboxes.

As a safety feature to protect the firebox, fusible plugs of low melting-point alloy are provided in the crown; these melt and extinguish the fire should it be uncovered by a low water level.

Unburnt fuel drawn off the firebed could produce unwanted smoke and block the boiler tubes, which would impair steaming. To ensure the maximum combustion of gases within the firebox, air from the firehole is guided towards the fire by the deflector (baffle) plate. This air combines with the hot gases whose path to the boiler tubes has been extended by the brick arch, encouraging complete combustion.

Boilers using solid fuel need a grate at the base of the firebox. In order to clear wheels and axles this may be level, sloping or a combination of the two. In general the deeper the firebox the easier it is to fire efficiently, but this is not always practicable.

The amount of air admitted through the grate to the underside of the fire is regulated by dampers, a series of openings cut into the sides and ends of the ashpan and controlled by doors.

The grate consists of cast iron firebars with air spaces between. To clean the fire it is necessary either to remove several bars, using heavy tongs, to give an opening through which the clinker and ashes can be pushed into the ashpan, or to paddle (lift) the remnants out through the firehole door with a long shovel.

To make the task easier, many locomotives are provided with a drop section, manually lowered, or a rocking grate, operated from the cab, allowing ash to be shaken out of the fire during the journey and the remains of the fire dumped during disposal over the ashpit.

Grates over 50sq ft are beyond the capacity of one fireman to handle. This led to the use of mechanical stokers which brought crushed coal by screw conveyor from the tender to a table plate inside the firehole door. Here it was blown by adjustable steam jets on to the fire. This device was particularly popular in the USA.

Function and design

Fuel and air combine in the locomotive firebox to create an intense heat. This heat boils water and creates the steam to give the engine its power. The size and design of a firebox depends on the type of locomotive and the tasks it was intended to perform.

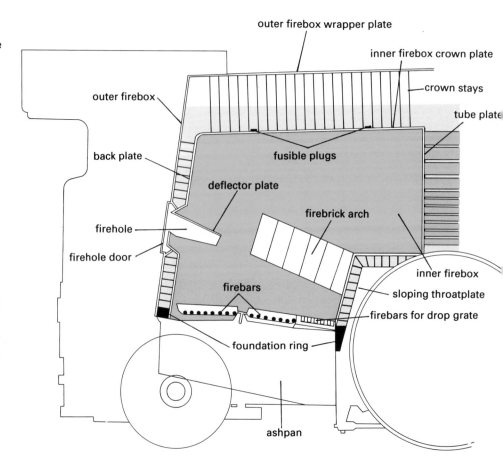

59 Class Garratt

EAST AFRICAN RAILWAYS

The 59 Class Beyer-Garratts were the largest and most powerful locomotives ever built to operate on a metre gauge railway. Designed to haul 1200 ton freight trains over the steep east African mountains, they proved to be as tough as the terrain they conquered.

The 59 Class Beyer-Garratt was the culmination of half a century of experience with articulated locomotives. They were designed and built to answer a desperate need: to haul heavy loads on the tight curves and steep gradients on some of the most difficult terrains in the world – the railways of east Africa.

Railways in east, west and southern Africa are mainly of metre and 3ft 6in gauge, though there are scattered lines of narrower gauge. Many of them were built at the end of the last century, during the grab for colonies, to exploit the natural resources of the continent by carrying them overland to the sea for export.

Building a railway

Kenya and Uganda, British protectorates since 1894/5, were dependent for their external trade on the port of Mombasa. To link the port with the hinterland a metre gauge railway was started in 1896, pushing north-west to reach the site of Nairobi in 1899. Nairobi was then a swampy plain devoid of habitation but destined to become Kenya's capital. The line was extended through mountainous country, to reach Lake Victoria – source of the White Nile – at Kisumu in 1901.

Various branches were built to open up the country and later to link with the system in Tanganyika (now Tanzania), previously a German colony. An extension to Kampala, the capital of Uganda, was not completed until 1931.

Nairobi is reached after a climb of 5750ft (1750m). Beyond, the line climbs a further 7700ft (2347m) to Uplands before descending 6000ft (1830m) to the floor of the Great Rift Valley. A final climb takes the line to its summit at Timbora, 9136ft (2785m) above the sea level.

The terrain through which these lines were built called for heavy, sustained gradients and many curves. Consequently the railways' capacities

KEY FACTS

**East African Railways
59 Class 4-8-2+2-8-4
Nos:** 5901-5934, 34 locomotives
Designer and manufacturer: Beyer-Peacock & Co Ltd
Built: 1955 Gorton, Manchester
Service: mainly freight between Mombasa and Nairobi
Livery: dark red, panels edged black with yellow line; 'EAR' on tanks in raised brass letters
Performance: 1200 tons on 1 in 66 gradient
Withdrawn: 1973-1980

▼ In December 1977 No 5918 *Mount Gelai* hauls the A38 goods eastwards from Samburu over the steep gradient towards Mackinnon Road. The 59 Class was well suited to hauling heavy loads. They had double the tractive effort of any locomotive employed on passenger service in the UK, where they were built in 1955.

LOCO LIST

All 34 of the 59 Class were named after mountains in Kenya, Uganda and Tanjania with the exception of 5928, which took its name from the highest mountain in east Africa.

5901 **Mount Kenya**
5902 **Ruwenzori Mountains**
5903 **Mount Meru**
5904 **Mount Elgon**
5905 **Mount Muhavura**
5906 **Mount Sattima**
5907 **Mount Kinangop**
5908 **Mount Loolmalasin**
5909 **Mount Mgahinga**
5910 **Mount Hanang**
5911 **Mount Skerri**
5912 **Mount Oldeani**
5913 **Mount Debasien**
5914 **Mount Londiani**
5915 **Mount Mtorwi**
5916 **Mount Rungwe**
5917 **Mount Kitumbeine**
5918 **Mount Gelai**
5919 **Mount Lengai**
5920 **Mount Mbeya**
5921 **Mount Nyiru**
5922 **Mount Blackett**
5923 **Mount Longonot**
5924 **Mount Eburu**
5925 **Mount Monduli**
5926 **Mount Kimhandu**
5927 **Mount Tinderet**
5928 **Mount Kilimanjaro**
5929 **Mount Longido**
5930 **Mount Shengena**
5931 **Ulguru Mountains**
5932 **Ol'Donya Sabuk**
5933 **Mount Suswa**
5934 **Menengai Crater**

▼The principal idea of the articulated locomotive was to allow large and powerful engines to run on low-cost lightly laid track and negotiate tight curves. To do this the weight of the engine was spread out as much as possible over many axles. The various sections of the engine were separate units linked by flexible pivots. This enabled them to follow the tight curves of the track independently of each other.

were generally very limited. Much of the line was originally laid with 50lb/yd rail, but by the late 1920s the Mombasa – Nairobi section had been relaid with new, heavier 80lb/yd rail and this was subsequently extended to Kampala. This sort of railway and the Beyer-Garratt articulated locomotive became synonymous.

Enter the Garratt

The Garratt's use of two engine units carrying fuel and water (water in the front, fuel and water in the rear) gave good flexibility on curves, while the boiler cradle was carried on pivots between them. This allowed a very large boiler to be mounted, its firebox completely unobstructed by wheels below it. The spread of weight over many axles – 14 or 16 in the case of the east African machines – kept individual axleloads down while providing ample adhesion and therefore power.

The first Beyer-Garratt, a small locomotive produced for work in Tasmania, Australasia, was built in 1909 and is now in the National Railway Museum, York. The articulated locomotive concept grew steadily into the South African giant

▲ During the 329 mile (529km) journey between Mombasa and Nairobi there would usually be two stops for oil and six to eight stops for water. In the early 1960s No 5901 *Mount Kenya* replenishes its water supply at Tsavo station.

▼An intimate knowledge of the names of the 59 Class would also provide a knowledge of the height of mountains in Kenya, Uganda and Tanjania. The locomotives were named in descending order of height and No 5903 *Mount Meru* was the third highest mountain at 14,979ft (4565m).

built in 1930 which is now preserved in the Museum of Science and Industry, Manchester.

In 1926 the Kenya & Uganda Railway placed its first Garratt order, for four EC Class 4-8-2+2-8-4 wood-burning engines, which were used west of Nairobi and permitted to haul 457 tons on the 1 in 50 gradient. After a satisfactory two year trial the railway decided that its future lay with Garratts f or main line work. Successive orders culminated in the majestic EC class 4-8-4+4-8-4 (later Class 57). These locomotives instituted through running between Nairobi and Kampala.

Different types of Garratt locomotives handled the given loads successfully until the early 1950s when, thanks to continuous traffic growth, the Mombasa – Nairobi section became a bottleneck with exports and imports being seriously delayed. By now the track here had been relaid with 95lb/yd rail and was already supporting the $17\frac{1}{2}$ ton axleload of the EA class 2-8-2s. Careful study of locomotive forces acting on the track showed that axleload up to 21 tons could be borne, provided that the weight tapered off at each end of the locomotive.

Production of the 59s

In 1954 the UK locomotive builder, Beyer-Peacock, was asked to produce a new and much bigger 4-8-2+2-8-4 Garratt, capable of hauling 1200 ton trains on the 1 in 66 gradients and with the enormous tractive effort of 83,350lb. The 34 engines of the 59 Class were delivered in 1955 in an attractive livery of dark red lined out in yellow. Most were given names of mountains in east Africa.

Everything possible was built into the engines to give sustained power and high mileage between overhauls. They had bar frames machined from $4\frac{1}{2}$in thick slabs and roller bearings on all axles and big ends. The boiler was enormous, with a barrel diameter of 7ft 6in – 6in larger than the LNER's solitary 2-8-0+0-8-2 Garratt – and was oil fired. If they had burned coal (and provision was made to fit a mechanical stoker if a change to coal was ever necessary), the grate would have had an area of 72sq ft – half as much again as a Bulleid Merchant Navy Pacific. The front and rear tanks were of Beyer-Peacock's later streamlined form and a power reverser was provided. Air braking

Where to see them
Two 59s are preserved at Nairobi and work occasional excursions to Naivasha, a journey of 65 miles (104km).
● **5918** Mount Gelai.
● **5930** Mount Shengena.

Workers' lunch
Although construction of the Mombasa to Kampala railway posed engineering problems, there were other difficulties too. At one stage, near Tsavo, 130 miles (209km) from Mombasa, work was halted for several months by man-eating lions which killed 28 Indian labourers and an unknown number of natives. Incidents like this helped to give the railway its local name of the 'Lunatic line'.

◀ **The main work of the 59 Class was hauling trains of imports and exports between the port of Mombasa and the towns of Nairobi and Kampala. While the eastbound trains contained exports of tea, coffee and agricultural produce, the westbound trains included imports of farm machinery, fuel and consumer imports. On 21 December 1977, No 5912 *Mount Oldeani* toils uphill with a westbound train of imports to Nairobi.**

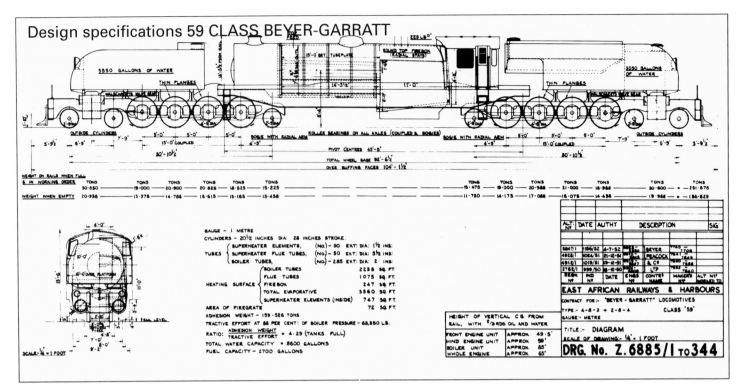

Design specifications 59 CLASS BEYER-GARRATT

EAST AFRICAN RAILWAYS & HARBOURS
CONTRACT FOR:- "BEYER - GARRATT" LOCOMOTIVES
TYPE:- 4-8-2 + 2-8-4   CLASS '59'
GAUGE:- METRE
TITLE:- DIAGRAM
SCALE OF DRAWING:- ⅛" = 1 FOOT
DRG. No. Z.6885/1 TO 344

TECHNICAL FILE

4 cylinders: 20½in diameter, 28in stroke
Coupled wheels: 4ft 6in diameter
Boiler diameter: 7ft 6in
Grate area: 72sq ft
Boiler pressure: 225lb psi
Tractive effort: 83,350lb
Oil capacity: 2700 gall
Water capacity: 8600 gall
Length over buffers: 104ft 1½in
Weight in working order: 251.7 tons

for engine and train was standard.

An interesting feature built into the 59s, like all engines for east Africa since pre-war days, was ease of conversion to 3ft 6in gauge if there was a link with the systems in Rhodesia (now Zambia and Zimbabwe) and South Africa. All wheel rims were just over one inch wider than normal, so that new tyres could be shrunk on to suit the wider gauge.

▼ No 5918 *Mount Gelai* shows off its lines in the evening sun on 19 December 1977. An advantage of the Garratts was the absence of wheels under the centre section. This allowed the inclusion of a larger boiler and deeper firebox than a conventional locomotive to produce more power.

▲The designers at Beyer-Peacock made full use of the permitted axleload of 21 tons and the result was the most powerful locomotive ever to operate on metre gauge metals anywhere in the world. They were originally built for oil firing but provision was made to burn coal.

On test the specified 1200 ton load was handled comfortably and even exceeded. Such was the impact of these remarkable locomotives and their heavier trains (1400 tons permitted between the coast and Nairobi) that within 12 months the main line operation was back to normal and congestion at Mombasa was at an end.

Working days

During normal service the 59s were manned by two regular crews on a caboose basis, one working and one resting in a van with sleeping accommodation, changing over at eight-hour intervals. The engines were kept very clean and the cabs were polished and immaculate.

The performance of the locomotives, if not their appearance, was further enhanced between 1959 and 1967 by the fitting of Giesl ejectors in place of the original single chimneys. This led to separate timings for single chimney and Giesl Garratts, enabling, for instance, several hours to be saved in running between Kampala and the summit at Timboroa.

But, as elsewhere, the diesel locomotive was in the ascendant, even though two were required to do the work of one Garratt. Withdrawal started in 1973 and the fires were doused on the last 59 Class in 1980. Two were saved from the torch and restored to working order.

It was also the end for the locomotive building firm of Beyer-Peacock. In the late 1950s the demand for steam engines collapsed worldwide and the firm's entry into diesel and electric traction came too late. The works closed in 1966.

Valve gear working

The function of locomotive valve gear is to regulate the movement of the valves so that steam is admitted to and exhausted from the correct end of the cylinder at the right time. It enables the driver to choose the duration (cut-off) of steam admission and to reverse the locomotive.

In the Walschaert valve gear, common on UK built locos, fore-and-aft movement of the valve spindle, whose valve heads open and close the steam ports, depends on the movement of both the combination lever (which is worked by the crosshead) and the expansion link. These two sources of fore-and-aft motion are joined at the point where the combination lever and radius rod are pinned together.

The movement of the expansion link is obtained from an eccentric rod attached to the crank axle. The front of the rod is pinned to the bottom of the expansion link, which is made to rock backwards and forwards.

Adjustment to the length of valve travel is obtained by raising or lowering the position of the radius rod in the expansion link. This is done by operation of the reversing rod from the cab.

The length of travel of the radius rod, and hence of the valve spindle, depends on the rod's position in the expansion link. Maximum valve travel (longest cut-off and maximum steam admission) is obtained when the radius rod is positioned furthest from the centre of the expansion link.

Moving the radius rod up and down from one half of the expansion link to the other reverses the movement of the locomotive by admitting steam into what otherwise would have been the exhausting side of the piston at that particular point in the cycle.

In the diagrams opposite, fresh steam under pressure is shown as orange and exhaust steam is coloured yellow.

Cycle of operation

The valve spindle is drawn back as the radius rod is pulled by the oscillating expansion link. This opens the admission and exhaust ports.

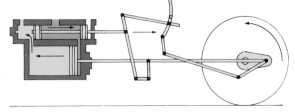

Moderated by the rear-moving radius rod, the advancing combination lever now ensures forward movement of the valve spindle.

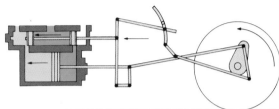

The combination lever continues to push the valve spindle forward, opening the rear port to exhaust.

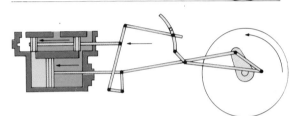

The rear stroke begins, with the radius rod moving the valve spindle further forward to begin steam admission at the front of the cylinder.

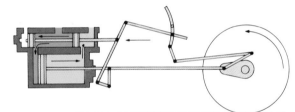

The rear-moving combination lever, regulated by the advancing radius rod, draws back the valve spindle, cutting off admission.

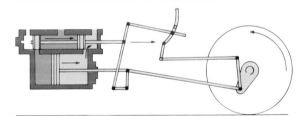

The combination lever continues to draw back the valve spindle, beginning to uncover the forward port for exhaust.

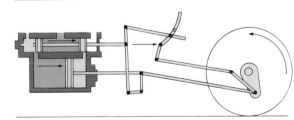

The Walschaert system

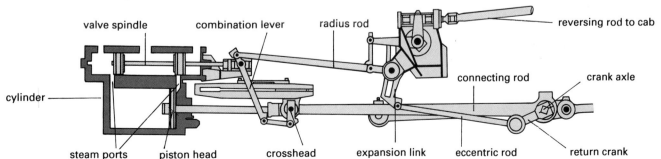

valve spindle · combination lever · radius rod · reversing rod to cab · connecting rod · crank axle · cylinder · steam ports · piston head · crosshead · expansion link · eccentric rod · return crank

Union Pacific Big Boy
4-8-8-4
Nos: 4000-4024
Designer and manufacturer:
American Locomotive Co
Built: 1941-1944, Schenectady,
New York
Service: heavy freight
between Cheyenne, Wyoming
and Ogden, Utah
Livery: black
Performance: 3 April 1943 –
102,000lb drawbar pull up a 1
in 88 gradient
Withdrawn: displaced by
diesel traction in 1961-1962

4-8-8-4 Big Boy

UNION PACIFIC RAILROAD

**Cheyenne, Laramie, Union Pacific – the names
evoke memories of Indian country, the exploits of Butch
Cassidy and cattle rustling. In the 1940s arose another legend –
a fleet of steel leviathans appeared on the scene and
the West became Big Boy country.**

The Union Pacific Railroad formed part of the first transcontinental route across the United States. The final connection was made in April 1869 at a point west of Ogden, Utah. The line has remained one of the most important routes between the Mid West and the Pacific coast ever since.

The main line starts at Council Bluffs, Omaha and runs west through Cheyenne and Ogden to Los Angeles over the Rocky Mountains. It climbs from Cheyenne at just over 6000ft (1829m) above sea level to the top of the Wasatch range at 6799ft (2072m) before dropping to 4298ft (1310m) at Ogden.

The 2501ft (762m) fall into Ogden is 65 miles (105km) long with an average gradient of 1 in 137. A second track for eastbound journeys was added between 1916 and 1923 with 25 miles (40km) of 1 in 88, a formidable challenge.

These gradients made the line over the Wasatch range difficult to operate and a second locomotive was needed on most trains, particularly heavy freight.

From 1909 these helpers were articulated 2-8-8-2s and 2-8-8-0s, which were ponderous and powerful but quite incapable of anything more than moderate speeds. With customers demanding quicker deliveries for their goods, something faster was necessary.

The American Locomotive Company (Alco) was a leader in the development of the most powerful steam locomotives capable of higher speeds. It had pioneered the use of a trailing two-axle truck providing space and support for very large fireboxes. From 1927 Alco introduced machines with 4-6-4, 2-8-4, 4-8-4 and 2-8-8-4 wheel arrangements for many US railways which needed increased power and the ability to move freight at

▼ The extraordinary length of the Big Boys – 132ft 9in (40.5m) – meant that the turntables in the locomotive yards on their route from Cheyenne, Wyoming to Ogden, Utah had to be enlarged to 135ft (41m) diameter. Curved track on the main line was realigned to increase the distance between passing trains because of the amount of overhang on the cab and smokebox.

▶ The massive smokebox of Big Boy was large enough to allow a man to stand upright inside. Union Pacific regulations insisted that the door had to be opened and the interior inspected when the engine reached the shed at the end of each run. Despite its size and weight, the smokebox front could be opened by one man in 30 minutes.

▲The giant 4-8-8-4s were designed to move huge freight trains without assistance over the stiff gradients of the Wasatch range of the Rocky Mountains. Even though the trains frequently weighed more than 3000 tons the locomotives rarely slipped.

60mph (97km/h) or more.

In 1936 the Union Pacific went to Alco for a simple four-cylinder articulated engine, suitable for moving freight tonnage and passenger trains at speeds up to 70mph (113km/h), with good riding qualities. The result was the 4-6-6-4 Challenger with 5ft 9in coupled wheels. By 1944, 105 Challengers had been built.

But with war in Europe and further growth in traffic, even the Challengers could not satisfy the Union Pacific's needs. Alco was approached for an even bigger locomotive, purely for freight haulage but good for 60mph (97km/h) and able to haul 3600 tons unassisted over the Wasatch range.

In 1941 Alco created the first (and only) 4-8-8-4 design. Before the first of the class emerged from the works at Schenectady someone, clearly impressed by the sheer bulk of a locomotive and tender nearly 133 feet (40.5m) long and

LOCO LIST

Twenty Big Boys were built between September 1941 and January 1942. These consisted of Nos 4000-4019. However, because of the increasing demands of war another five were constructed in 1944 (Nos 4020-4024).

There was little difference between the two batches except for the use of heavier wartime materials in the connecting rods and boiler.

Big Boys had an average life of 20 years and saw 1,000,000 miles (1,609,340km) of service. The last Big Boy was withdrawn in July 1962.

Where to see them
Eight Big Boys have been preserved. All are exhibited in the United States.
● **4004** (still owned by the Union Pacific) – Holiday Park, Cheyenne, Wyoming.
● **4005** – Forney Transportation Museum, Denver, Colorado.
● **4006** – National Museum of Transport, St Louis, Missouri.
● **4012** – Steamtown National Historic Site, Scranton, Pennsylvania.
● **4014** – Los Angeles County Fairgrounds, Pomona, California.
● **4017** – National Railroad Museum, Green Bay, Wisconsin.
● **4018** – Texas State Fair Park, Arlington, Dallas, Texas.
● **4023** – Union Pacific's engine sheds, Council Bluffs, Omaha, Nebraska.

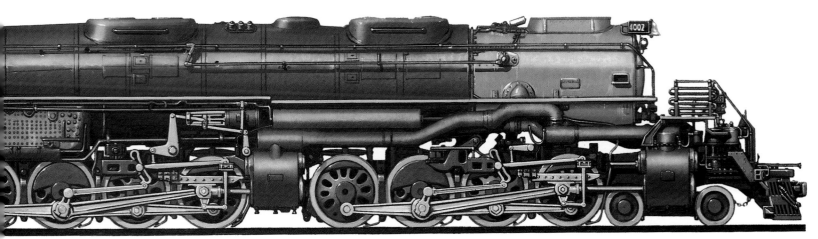

weighing over 530 tons in working order, chalked 'Big Boy' on the smokebox front. The name stuck and quickly became official.

530 tons of power

The name was entirely justified. The boiler worked at 300 pounds per square inch while its barrel had an outside diameter of 8ft 11in (2.72m). Because of the stresses involved in transferring weight on to the leading engine, the barrel plates were 1³/₈in (3.49cm) thick.

The enormous firebox, sitting over the last two coupled axles in the trailing truck, was necessarily shallow. The grate, 8ft (2.44m) wide and 19ft 7in (5.97m) long (bigger than many rooms), had an area of 150sq ft (13.94sq m), while the front of the firebox continued into a combustion chamber more than 8ft (2.44m) long. Seven transverse circulators were fitted which also carried the brick arch.

Coal was fed by a mechanical stoker and a consumption of nine tons per hour was quite normal. Draught was provided by a double multiple-jet blastpipe and double chimney, while a steam operated smoke deflector hood over the double chimney was used when working hard in tunnels to protect the tunnel roofs from the fierce blast.

The two chassis units were one-piece steel castings incorporating the cylinders, a form of construction almost universal in the USA since 1930; they were masterpieces of the steel foundryman's

art. All axles ran in roller bearings. The cab was fully enclosed – the plains of Wyoming in winter can be like the arctic.

The tender alone weighed 191 tons and was carried on seven axles, five rigid and the leading two in a truck – little wonder that the type was called a centipede. It held 24,000 gallons of water (25,000 in later examples) and 25 tons of coal, which was reckoned ample to get a 3600 ton train the 40 miles (64km) from Ogden to Echo before refuelling. Weather affected fuel consumption and the tender was filled close to the top in adverse conditions. In good weather it needed to be only three-quarters full.

Before long the bunkers were extended upwards to hold another 3¹/₂ tons. Soon after World War II, during a mining strike, No 4005 was converted for oil firing but reverted to coal later.

These 25 remarkable locomotives took over most of the freight working between Ogden and Cheyenne. But when traffic peaked they might still be seen with a 2-8-2 or 2-10-2 helper, even though their tonnage rating over Wasatch was

▼ **The clouds of black smoke were a trade mark of the Big Boys because the exhaust contained large quantities of particles of unburnt coal. Water from the tender could be sprayed on to the following cars if red hot cinders threatened to set light to them.**

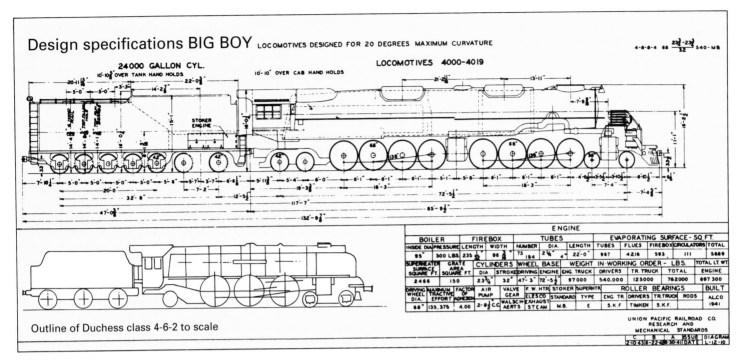

Design specifications BIG BOY LOCOMOTIVES DESIGNED FOR 20 DEGREES MAXIMUM CURVATURE

LOCOMOTIVES 4000-4019

24000 GALLON CYL.

Outline of Duchess class 4-6-2 to scale

	ENGINE										
BOILER		FIREBOX		TUBES			EVAPORATING SURFACE - SQ. FT.				
INSIDE DIA	PRESSURE	LENGTH	WIDTH	NUMBER	DIA.	LENGTH	TUBES	FLUES	FIREBOX	CIRCULATORS	TOTAL
95	300 LBS.	235	96	75 / 184	2¾ / 4	22-0	967	4216	593	111	5889
SUPERHEATER SURFACE SQUARE FT.	GRATE AREA SQUARE FT.	CYLINDERS		WHEEL BASE		WEIGHT IN WORKING ORDER - LBS.					TOTAL LT. WT.
		DIA.	STROKE	DRIVING ENGINE	ENG. TRUCK	DRIVERS	TR. TRUCK	TOTAL			ENGINE
2466	150	23¾	32	47-3 / 72-5	97000	540,000	125000	762000			697 300
DRIVING WHEEL DIA.	MAXIMUM TRACTIVE EFFORT	FACTOR OF ADHESION	AIR PUMP	VALVE GEAR	F.W. HTR	STOKER	SUPERHTR	ROLLER BEARINGS			BUILT
					ELESCO	STANDARD	TYPE	ENG. TR. DRIVERS	TR. TRUCK	RODS	
68	135,375	4.00	2-8½ C.C	WALSCH AERTS	STEAM	M.B.	E	S.K.F. TIMKEN	S.K.F.		ALCO 1941

UNION PACIFIC RAILROAD CO.
RESEARCH AND
MECHANICAL STANDARDS

---

stepped up, first to 4200 then to 4400 tons. During the heavy California fruit season, spare Big Boys arriving at Cheyenne were sometimes sent back westbound as helpers. The sight of a long freight with two Big Boys at its head was impressive indeed.

The cost of power

There was considerable wastage inherent in the performance of Big Boys. The high rate of combustion, combined with the thin fire normal with mechanical stoking, led to prodigious loss of unburnt fuel up the chimneys. There was even provision on the tender back to spray the leading wagons in order to douse burning cinders.

Cinder cutting of superheater flues was so heavy that the firebox ends needed renewal at intervals of 44,000 miles (70,000km). Provision was made for the blastpipe nozzles to be turned regularly to present a new side to the abrasive gas flow. It was a brutal way of producing power.

Before changing completely from steam to diesel, the Union Pacific indulged in a lengthy dalliance with gas turbine locomotives, starting in 1952, as they tried to replace the Big Boys. It was hardly surprising that these newcomers were christened 'Big Blows'. But they were not entirely successful and their availability and economy were not good.

In the 1960s Union Pacific abandoned the gas turbines – but the writing was on the wall for the Big Boys because the company had turned to diesels. Withdrawal started in mid-1961 and by July 1962 all had been withdrawn. The locomo-

▲ **Assisted by staff from Union Pacific, four teams at the American Locomotive Company designed Big Boy. It weighed three times as much as an LMS Duchess and was almost twice as long. Even the tender was enormous and held 24,000 gallons, six times the capacity of a Duchess.**

tives had covered between 818,000-1,064,000 miles (1,316,000-1,712,000km) each.

At maximum firing, the Big Boys in their usual four hour trip up Sherman Hill would consume 20 tons of coal and 12,000-13,000 gallons of water. The engines were restricted to 35mph (56km/h) in general service when new and when after shopping. Although the engines could have quite a turn of speed they were used on passenger trains only in emergencies. This was because of a preference to use the Challenger types which were also available at this time.

TECHNICAL FILE

4 cylinders: 23¾in diameter, 32in stroke
Coupled wheels: 5ft 8in diameter
Boiler diameter: 8ft 11in outside maximum
Grate area: 150 sq ft
Boiler pressure: 300lb psi
Tractive effort: 135,375lb
Coal capacity: 25 tons*
Water capacity: 24,000 gallons. 25,000 gall tenders on Nos 4019-4024
Length over buffers: 132ft 9⁷/₈in
Weight in working order:
Engine: 340-344.8 tons
Tender: 191-195 tons
*Increased to 28½ tons

▶ **Each cylinder had such a large surface area that all four were fitted with lubrication lines on top, at the bottom, back and front and on each valve bush to ensure that they never dried up. The large pipe carried steam from the boiler to the rear cylinder.**

Articulated locomotives

Articulated (jointed) locomotives are those on which the driving wheels are grouped into two, or occasionally three, sets with each set having its own drive. Articulation allows a locomotive with a high number of driving wheels to negotiate tighter curves than one on a rigid frame.

With conventional locomotives, 10 or 12 coupled wheels was the greatest number that could be accommodated without unacceptably hard grinding of the forward and rear coupled wheel flanges against the rail on curves. Articulated locomotives such as the Garratts were built with 16 driving wheels in 2-8-0+0-8-2 configuration for the London & North Eastern (LNER) railway and 4-8-4+4-8-4 configuration for use in Africa and Australia.

The need for articulation developed towards the end of the 19th century, with the quest for greater haulage power, spread so that light track did not suffer. The need was even greater on colonial and narrow gauge lines, where sharp curves and lightly built track were commonplace, once the lines attempted to increase their traffic.

There were several different approaches to articulation, each known by the name of its inventor. Two, the Garratt and the Mallet, grew into massive main line machines. A potential weakness was the steam and exhaust connections to the cylinders but this was overcome by using flexible pipe joints at the cylinders or the pivot centres.

▶ An East African Railways Garratt builds up steam in Nairobi in September 1966. Garratts also saw service in Australia and some were bought by the LNER and LMS in the UK.

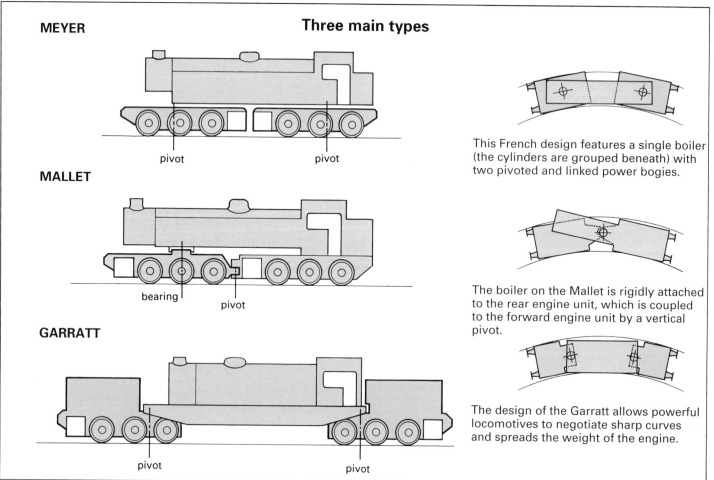

Three main types

MEYER

pivot   pivot

This French design features a single boiler (the cylinders are grouped beneath) with two pivoted and linked power bogies.

MALLET

bearing   pivot

The boiler on the Mallet is rigidly attached to the rear engine unit, which is coupled to the forward engine unit by a vertical pivot.

GARRATT

pivot   pivot

The design of the Garratt allows powerful locomotives to negotiate sharp curves and spreads the weight of the engine.

C38 class 4-6-2

NEW SOUTH WALES GOVERNMENT RAILWAYS

The C38s were the most successful locally designed and built express passenger locomotives in Australia. They incorporated many notable features and gave fast and reliable service. Three have survived into preservation.

The New South Wales Government Railways (NSWGR), built to the 4ft 8½in gauge – unlike the other states, which used either 5ft 3in or 3ft 6in – were more noted for elderly 4-6-0 and 2-8-0 steam engines on rural branches and main lines than for a steady influx of powerful modern locomotives.

Sections of the railway were heavily graded. On the north main line, the southbound climb from the Hawkesbury River was at 1 in 40 to 1 in 50 for five miles (8km), while on the south line grades of 1 in 66 to 1 in 75 abounded, with one 17 mile (27km) section at 1 in 75 with short breaks; train loadings were such that a lot of double-heading was necessary on the severely graded sections.

The problem had been recognised soon after

World War I. In 1921 and 1922, outline schemes had been prepared for 4-6-2s, one having three cylinders, but they were not proceeded with. From 1925, new large two-cylinder 4-6-0s (the C36 class) were constructed for working the heavy express traffic in the coastal belt and on the inter-state south line to Victoria, and ultimately 75 engines of this class were built.

Inadequate power

The C36s were fine, capable engines with an excellent turn of speed, despite their 5ft 9in coupled wheels, but much double-heading was still necessary. There was even a later scheme to rebuild them as Pacifics, but it, too, came to nothing. Four years later came the D57 class 4-8-2s, 25

KEY FACTS

NSWGR C38 class 4-6-2
Nos 3801-3805 streamlined; 3806-3830 non-streamlined; 30 locomotives
Designer: Harold Young
Built: 1943-49. Clyde Engineering Co, Sydney and Eveleigh and Cardiff works
Service: Heavy express passenger trains from Sydney
Livery: wartime – grey. 1947-48 – mid-green with lining. From 1950s – plain black with red lining
Performance: max drawbar hp 2300 at 50mph. Max recorded speed 90mph
Withdrawn: 1961-73

▼ The C38s were noted for their smooth riding characteristics. This was because the rotating masses only were balanced giving less hammer-blow on the track. On 24 October 1988, No 3801 waits for the signal before backing off Seymour shed. Currently, this is the only member of the class preserved in working order.

heavy three-cylinder freight engines with restricted route availability for heavy haul work. Otherwise, NSWGR went into World War II with almost all its engines of pre-1918 provenance.

But the inadequacy of the C36s for traffic needs would not go away, and a locomotive was needed which could work 450 tons unassisted over the south line. After investigating existing modern designs in Europe and North America for a suitable locomotive type, a Beyer-Garratt 4-6-4+4-6-4 based on the Algerian engines of 1936 was recommended because its lighter axleloads and spread of weight gave wide route availability. However, the Chief Commissioner would have none of it, so the Chief Mechanical Engineer was obliged to change tack.

In 1938, work started to design a two-cylinder 4-6-2. For various reasons the design work was prolonged, and an order for five engines, placed

▲ The C38s powered the last steam-hauled express trains in Australia. Their most famous trains were the Newcastle flyers between Sydney and Newcastle – a distance of 104 miles (167km) – which was often completed in 138 minutes. On 24 October 1988, No 3801 glides along the track at Mathiesons siding north of Wandong, with a Melbourne – Seymour excursion.

with Clyde Engineering Co, Sydney in December 1938 at least partly as an unemployment relief measure, was backed by little more than an outline specification.

It was to be four more years before the first engine came from the works – such were the supply difficulties brought about by the war. Even then, a considerable amount of material was manufactured in railway workshops to speed construction. But it was a splendid machine that eventually emerged from Clyde's erecting shop in January

1943. Classed C38, numbered 3801 and painted in wartime grey, it was soon followed by four more.

Much of the design followed North American practice. Plate frames were shunned and a one-piece cast steel bed-frame, complete with cylinders, main air reservoir and all mounting brackets, was adopted. This was designed in detail by the General Steel Castings Corporation in the USA, the only firm producing such castings. The bed-frame weighed 18.7 tons and was reckoned to be four tons lighter than a built-up one – this weight saving was invested in the boiler. The bogie and trailing truck frames were also one piece castings from the same source.

The boiler, of nickel steel, worked at 245lb psi pressure – the highest figure on any Australian railway. It had a tapered barrel and wide Belpaire firebox. The steel inner firebox was rivetted, rather than welded, and contained no less than five arch tubes. A 36-element superheater was provided, with a multiple valve regulator in the header. The smokebox was fitted with baffle plates and mesh screens to be self-cleaning.

The coupled wheels were 5ft 9in diameter, and all axles ran in SKF roller bearings. The 21½in diameter cylinders were fed by 12in piston valves with 6½in travel and the whole steam circuit was generously proportioned to minimise pressure drop. A Franklin power reverser was provided. The bogie tender, weighing 83½ tons loaded, held 14 tons of coal and no less than 8100 gallons of water. A retractable tablet catcher, mounted below the footplate on the left-hand side, was operated from above. A five-chime whistle was, unusually, fixed horizontally to the side of the chimney.

Streamlined styling

An outstanding feature of the C38 was the streamlining and general styling which had overtones of the German Class 05 4-6-4. Grilles in the front of the styling casing admitted air which was deflected upwards behind the single chimney to prevent exhaust drifting to obscure the driver's view.

Hardly had No 3801 proved itself before orders were placed at the railway workshops at Eveleigh and Cardiff for 25 further engines of the class, each plant building alternate numbers. These locomotives were delivered between 1945 and 1949, and differed from the first five mainly in the absence of the skyline casing and conical smoke-

LOCO LIST

Between 1943 and 1949, 30 C38 class Pacifics were built. Nos 3801-3805 were streamlined and 3806-3830 were non-streamlined. None of the class was named.

Where to see them
Three engines escaped the torch. No 3801 is now preserved in running order for steam enthusiasts, while Nos 3820 and 3830 are kept as static exhibits.
● **3801** NSW Transport Museum, Thirlmere.
● **3820** NSW Transport Museum.
● **3830** Museum of Applied Arts & Sciences.

◀ The liveries of the C38s were changed at least twice. The first five locomotives were given wartime plain grey, but in 1947-48 they were painted a medium green livery with horizontal yellow lines.
No 3805 was the first of the streamlined C38s to receive this livery and the locomotive shows off its lines soon after overhaul in May 1946.

High speed finale
The Class C38s were the fastest steam locomotives ever to run in Australia. Although the authorised speed limit on NSWGR was 70mph, some drivers coaxed their charges up to 90mph on occasion – outperforming many contemporary diesel locomotives. Towards the end of their working life many C38s were given a final fling on express passenger work and more than one bowed out with a last run of 70mph.

◀ Some railway historians have said that R A Riddles and E S Cox, who designed the BR Standard Britannia 4-6-2s, were influenced by the look of the C38 class. This may have originated from similarities in styling, but it seems more likely that any foreign influence in the Britannias sprang from E S Cox's visit to the USA in 1945.

Design specifications CLASS C38

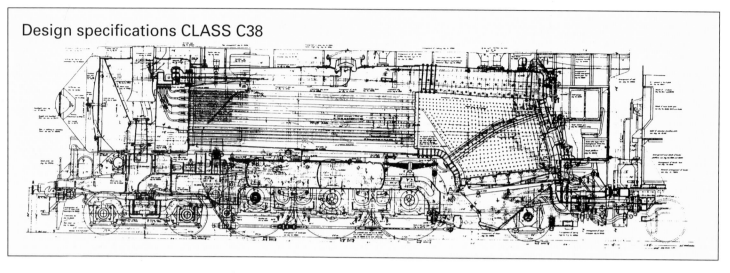

TECHNICAL FILE

2 cylinders: 21½in diameter x 26in stroke
Coupled wheels: 5ft 9in
Boiler diameter: 6ft 6⅛in
Grate area: 47sq ft
Boiler pressure: 245lb psi
Tractive effort: 36,200lb
Coal capacity: 14 tons
Water capacity: 8100 gallons
Length over buffers: 76ft 4⅝in
Weight in working order:
Engine: 111.7 tons
Tender: 83.5 tons

▼ In 1988, NSWGR celebrated Australia's bicentennial by running a number of special steam-hauled excursions using vintage motive power. On 22 October 1988, No 3801, on the 4ft 8½in track, passes Wandong station, while on the 5ft 3in lines Nos R761 and 639 double-head a train on its left. No K153 is seen in the distance.

box outer door.

All members of the class were initially allocated to Eveleigh shed, Sydney, whence they worked north to Newcastle, south to Albury on the Victoria border and west to Dubbo (assisted over the Blue Mountains). Nominally restricted initially to 70mph, this was more honoured in the breach, and at least one maximum of 90mph was recorded. The class could develop more than 2000hp and was light on coal.

Once in service, the authorities were soon to find out what a C38 could do. At first, working south, they ran the 399 miles (642km) to Albury without change – out one day and back the next. In each direction, coal was taken at the Demondrille coaling plant, 158 miles (254km) from Albury, without detaching the engine from the train. But on some workings it proved feasible to change engines at Cootamundra, giving the locomotives a daily out-and-home mileage of 530 (853km).

Smart look

Liveries on the class were changed at least twice. When new, Nos 3801-3805 wore wartime plain grey, but gained the medium green livery with horizontal yellow lines in 1947-48. The remaining

▲ The C38s incorporated many notable features, particularly principles of North American practice employed at Alco. The boiler could produce enough steam to sustain very high cylinder horsepower – when working uphill, or very fast, full boiler pressure could be maintained without excessive firing.

engines carried this colour from new with red and straw lining. From the early 1950s, this changed to all-over black with red lining. A few reverted to green lining in later years.

The inauguration of electrification to Lithgow in 1957 displaced the C38s from the Dubbo route, though they returned to Lithgow later. Diesel traction began to erode their work on the south main line, although they lived on until 1964. Six of the class were transferred to Broadmeadow (Newcastle) in 1960 to continue the express work to Sydney, although in that year the wires reached Gosford, curtailing steam working to only 54 miles (87km). This lasted until 1969, when electric working began throughout.

The general loss of work led to many C38s being put into store from 1963, and withdrawal, which had started in 1961, was completed with No 3813 in 1973.

Class 9F 2-10-0

BRITISH RAILWAYS

The Class 9Fs made a fitting climax to 125 years of main line steam in Britain. No fewer than 251 of these engines were built at Crewe and Swindon works between 1954 and 1960 – they were the last steam locomotives built to run on British tracks.

In 1950 the typical British slow goods train was remarkably little changed from its counterpart of 1900. Largely composed of wooden, loose-coupled wagons without continuous brakes, the train might well be pulled by an elderly 0-6-0 engine – BR inherited almost 4400 of these out of a total of 20,000 locomotives acquired at nationalisation.

At this time BR also owned more than 3000 eight-coupled engines (0-8-0 and 2-8-0). Their starting tractive effort and adhesive weight (the weight resting upon the coupled axles) was sufficient to start and then haul at low speed the longest and heaviest goods trains running on British tracks.

With nationalisation, the prospect of a new fleet of steel wagons fitted with continuous brakes heralded a revolution in BR freight haulage. In locomotive terms this did not necessarily require an increase in adhesive weight, but an enhancement of boiler capacity to give greater sustained horsepower at higher speeds was desirable.

The prospect of these changes underlay the proposal in 1948 to make the future BR standard heavy freight locomotive a 2-8-2, a wheel arrangement common overseas but confined in Britain to the London & North Eastern Railway (LNER) for a comparatively brief period.

Serious discussions about the new freight

▼ **Preserved 9F 2-10-0 No 92220 *Evening Star* stands in York station with a Scarborough Spa Express. *Evening Star* was the only 9F to be finished in lined green livery with copper cap chimney in recognition of its status as the last steam locomotive to be built for British Railways.**

KEY FACTS

British Rail Class 9F 2-10-0
BR Nos: 92000-92250
Designer: Robert A Riddles
Built: 1954-1960, Crewe and Swindon works
Service: primarily freight throughout BR but some passenger work
Livery: unlined black except No 92220 which is middle chrome green, lined in orange and black
Performance: 90mph hauling passenger trains in 1958
Withdrawn: displaced by diesel traction 1964-1968

LOCO LIST

251 Class 9Fs were built at Crewe and Swindon works between 1954 and 1960. They ran until 1968 – many were withdrawn after just a few years' running. Only one of the class, No 92220 *Evening Star*, was named.

engine began in 1950 when Robert Riddles, who was in charge of the locomotive design team on BR, argued for a 2-10-0 wheel configuration. During World War II he had developed a 2-10-0 with a wide firebox for the Ministry of Supply from his own 2-8-0 with a narrow firebox. Of the 150 of these 2-10-0s that were built, 25 were bought by BR which used them in southern Scotland.

The Germans had built literally thousands of 2-10-0s since 1915 and the French several hundred from an earlier date. But the prospect of a British general-purpose ten-coupled engine was something of a novelty, especially as its 5ft diameter driving wheels were 3in larger than almost all

eight-coupled freight engines in Britain.

Argument continued for some time on the design specification for the new engine as the 2-8-2 had the advantage that it could be made from many of the components used to build the Class 7 4-6-2 Britannia which was due in service in 1951. The 2-10-0, first specified in detail in June 1951, needed a slightly smaller, less ideally proportioned, boiler of reduced capacity.

Despite these disadvantages, Riddles opted for the 2-10-0 in July 1951 to take advantage of its increased adhesive weight. This gave the engine greater braking capacity with which to cope with the huge number of wagons without brakes on BR.

Teething troubles

Delayed by a national steel shortage, the first 9F, No 92000, was completed at Crewe Works in January 1954. But the first 20 9Fs were not without teething troubles.

Reports came in from drivers that they occasionally found the regulator difficult or even impossible to close. The potential for a runaway train and consequent disaster was obvious. But tracing the cause of the fault – indeed demonstrating the circumstances in which it occurred – proved difficult.

There was one case coming down from Ebbw Vale when the regulator could not be closed at all. Only after several miles had passed, luckily with

◀ Two freight designs by Robert Riddles at Keighley station on the Keighley & Worth Valley Railway – 9F No 92220 *Evening Star* and former Swedish State Railways Austerity 2-8-0 No 1931 built by Vulcan Foundry in 1945.

▼ Built at Swindon works and handed over to British Railways amid great ceremony, 9F No 92220 *Evening Star* – the last steam engine ever built by BR – was the only one of the 251 class members to be named while owned by the organisation.

▲One of the best known duties of the 9Fs was hauling the iron ore trains from Tyne Dock to Consett. Coal was also taken by rail to the now vanished steel works – here, No 92064 hauls coal for Consett up the grade at Stanley.

not a single signal against them and without mishap, did the regulator function properly.

Design change

When calls from other regions to change the regulator's design were added to the evidence from the Western Region, modification became inevitable. After the design was changed, no further regulator problems were experienced and the 9Fs' success was assured. Repeat orders for the engines contin-

ued to be placed until 1957, well after the decision had been taken to phase out steam on BR.

Batches of 9Fs were built specifically for service on the London Midland, Eastern, Western and North Eastern regions with tender variations to suit. Many of the engines on the London Midland worked the heavy Toton-Brent coal trains which allowed the regional management to scrap the ageing 2-6-0+0-6-2 Beyer Garratts built for the London Midland & Scottish (LMS) Railway in 1927-30.

Some Eastern Region 9Fs worked from Annesley shed in Nottinghamshire over the former Great Central main line, while the small contingent on the North Eastern Region hauled heavy iron ore trains between Tyne Dock and Consett.

The first 2-10-0s were initially received with much reluctance on the Western Region, which experienced their early problems. Later they came to regard them highly and took delivery from Swindon of the last examples to be built.

The 9Fs also did excellent work on passenger services on the Somerset & Dorset Joint line, while a few were stationed on Southern Region for a period around 1961 to work the Fawley (Southampton) to Birmingham oil trains.

The rapid demise of steam on BR in the 1960s was not foreseen in the 1950s when genuine attempts were made to test ideas which might improve the effectiveness of the 2-10-0s. Some of these experiments were made in response to the increasingly poor coal which BR was being forced to use.

Nos 92020-92029 were fitted with Crosti boilers in 1955. These had a second drum under the boiler to preheat the feed water. The hot gases passed through both and were ejected at a chimney on the right-hand side in front of the firebox. The design encountered serious corrosion problems and strong complaints from enginemen. The boil-

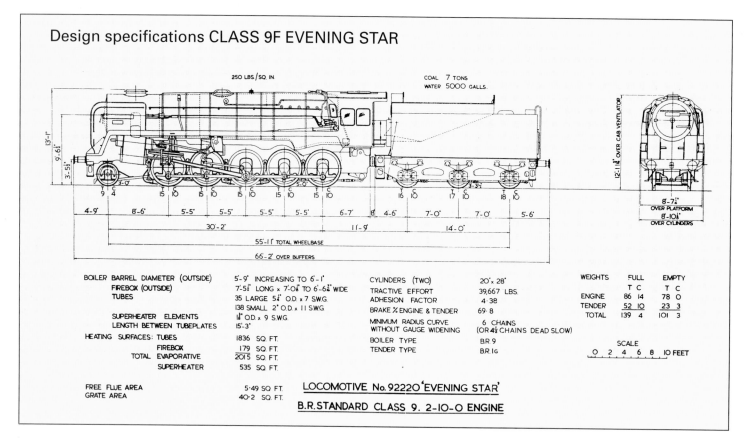

Design specifications CLASS 9F EVENING STAR

250 LBS./SQ. IN.

COAL 7 TONS
WATER 5000 GALLS.

12-1¼" OVER CAB VENTILATOR

13'-1"
9'-6¼"
3'-5¼"

T C T C T C T C T C
9 4 15 10 15 10 15 10 15 10

T C T C T C
16 10 17 10 18 10

4'-9" 8'-6" 5'-5" 5'-5" 5'-5" 5'-5" 6'-7" 8' 4'-6" 7'-0" 7'-0" 5'-6"

30'-2" 11'-9" 14'-0"

55'-11" TOTAL WHEELBASE

66'-2" OVER BUFFERS

8'-7¼"
OVER PLATFORM
8'-10¼"
OVER CYLINDERS

BOILER BARREL DIAMETER (OUTSIDE)	5'-9" INCREASING TO 6'-1"	
FIREBOX (OUTSIDE)	7'-5¾" LONG x 7'-0⅞" TO 6'-6¾" WIDE	
TUBES	35 LARGE 5¼" O.D. x 7 S.W.G.	
	138 SMALL 2" O.D. x 11 S.W.G.	
SUPERHEATER ELEMENTS	1⅜" O.D. x 9 S.W.G.	
LENGTH BETWEEN TUBEPLATES	15'-3"	
HEATING SURFACES: TUBES	1836 SQ. FT.	
FIREBOX	179 SQ. FT.	
TOTAL EVAPORATIVE	2015 SQ. FT.	
SUPERHEATER	535 SQ. FT.	
FREE FLUE AREA	5·49 SQ. FT.	
GRATE AREA	40·2 SQ. FT.	

CYLINDERS (TWO)	20" x 28"	
TRACTIVE EFFORT	39,667 LBS.	
ADHESION FACTOR	4·38	
BRAKE % ENGINE & TENDER	69·8	
MINIMUM RADIUS CURVE WITHOUT GAUGE WIDENING	6 CHAINS (OR 4½ CHAINS DEAD SLOW)	
BOILER TYPE	B.R.9	
TENDER TYPE	B.R.1G	

WEIGHTS	FULL	EMPTY
	T C	T C
ENGINE	86 14	78 0
TENDER	52 10	23 3
TOTAL	139 4	101 3

SCALE
0 2 4 6 8 10 FEET

LOCOMOTIVE No. 92220 'EVENING STAR'

B.R. STANDARD CLASS 9. 2-10-0 ENGINE

▶ **In August 1962 No 92220 *Evening Star* was specially transferred to Bath Motive Power Depot so that it could work the last Pines Express – the express between Manchester and Bournemouth. 9Fs had often hauled the Pines Express after their first trial over the Somerset & Dorset line in March 1960.**

ers were converted back to conventional operation between 1959 and 1962. Nos 92165 to 92167 were fitted with American Berkley mechanical stokers in 1958, but they were removed in 1962. A Giesl oblong ejector was fitted to No 92250 in 1959 and retained until the engine was withdrawn in 1966. This consisted of a line of seven blastpipes exhausting through a long, slender chimney, and was intended to allow lower grades of coal to be burned.

The Crosti boiler and Giesl ejector were thoroughly evaluated at the Rugby Locomotive Testing Station but were found to offer no significant improvement on the basic design, whose boiler proved to be remarkably efficient.

During road tests in southern Scotland in 1955 on a Crosti boilered engine the 9F's abilities at speed were revealed. Due to the excellent balance of the design, the engine was discovered to be safe to run at 80mph. During 1958 conventional 9Fs were timed on passenger services on the former Great Northern and Great Central main lines at 90mph.

The last 9F

Built at Swindon, the last 9F was handed over with a special ceremony on 18 March 1960. No 92220 was also the last steam locomotive to be built by British Railways and was given the name *Evening Star* in recognition of this. It was the only

one of the 251 9Fs named while in service with British Rail. The engine spent its first summer working passenger trains. At the same time an earlier example of the same class was used as a banking engine pushing trains up the 1 in 37.7 Lickey Incline – just one instance illustrating the versatility of the class.

Such virtues counted for little however during the floodtide of dieselisation in the early 1960s. Some 9Fs were withdrawn as early as 1964, with some enjoying working lives of only five years.

At the end of steam on BR in 1968 only two Class 9Fs were preserved. However, seven have since been bought from Woodham's scrapyard in South Wales. In 1990, after 12 years of restoration, No 92240 was returned to service on the Bluebell Railway.

TECHNICAL FILE

Class 9F
2 cylinders: 20in diameter, 28in stroke
Coupled wheels: 5ft diameter
Boiler diameter: 6ft 1in maximum
Grate area: 40.2sq ft
Boiler pressure: 250lb psi
Tractive effort: 39,670lb
Coal capacity: 7-9 tons
Water capacity: 4325-5625 gallons
Length over buffers: 66ft 2in
Weight in working order:
Engine: 86.7 tons
Tender: 52 tons (average)

Scrapyard terminus

At the end of 1958, BR had 16,108 main line
steam locomotives. Ten years later, there were none.
Most of the locomotives had gone to private scrapyards – a few
to be rescued by preservationists, and some
to be cut up and recycled.

As BR changed from steam to diesel and electric from the late 1950s, its works and shed yards throughout the country became clogged with thousands of withdrawn locomotives. As it took at least two men one week to cut up an average sized locomotive, the problem was too large for BR's own works, which had traditionally cut up redundant rolling stock. So BR took the unprecedented step of approaching private scrap dealers.

The demand for steel
In the 1960s, steel furnaces around the world were crying out for scrap steel. It was needed for a whole range of items, from ships to washing machines, and the frames and boilers of BR's locomotives proved to be ideal. They were made from mild steel, which could be hot- or cold-rolled in plate or strip form suitable for cutting into pattern parts. Harder steel from the wheels could be hot-rolled into billets to make nuts and bolts.

The furnaces wanted the steel and the foundries were after the brass and copper fittings. The real prizes were the copper fireboxes, which usually weighed about $2\frac{1}{2}$ tons and represented a scrap value of £1300 in 1966. In that one year alone, the price of copper rose by 75%.

Before a locomotive was officially withdrawn, it was put into store. This usually meant shunting it down one side of a shed with a row of other condemned engines. It was a period of locomotive

▼ A forlorn pile of wheels and boiler tubes is all that remains of Prairie tank 41XX No 4156, a former GWR engine and the last ex-BR main line steam locomotive to be cut up entirely for scrap in Britain. Hauled into Woodham's scrapyard in Barry, south Wales, in 1965, No 4156 was demolished 15 years later. Other engines enjoyed a more benign fate, being snatched from the cutter's oxyacetylene torch by the efforts – and the cash – of the preservationists.

▲ Great Western engines make a melancholy line-up at Woodham's scrapyard in 1970. Both the first and the last steam locomotives to be cut up there were former Great Western engines – Churchward Mogul No 5392 in 1959 and Prairie tank No 4156 in 1980. The last locomotive to leave the yard for preservation was also Great Western – Prairie tank No 5553 – acquired in 1990 by the Dean Forest Railway in Gloucestershire.

limbo in which the engine could be reinstated and put back into traffic if there was a demand, or – as was more often the case – withdrawn and sold to a scrap merchant.

The final journey

After a period in store – which could be anything from days to years – an engine would be prepared for its final journey to the scrapyard. Since working engines were often coaled up again as soon as they arrived back at the shed, the usual prelude to such a run was emptying the tender – in most cases by grab crane.

To improve the chances of a trouble free journey, many engines had their connecting rods removed. Sometimes the motion was dismantled at the shed or works and the rods were tied to the tops of running plates or side tanks.

Occasionally, dismantling was not considered to be worth the trouble and the skilfully crafted rods were cut through by oxyacetylene torch and slung into the empty tender or firebox.

A locomotive that had stood still for too long

ran the risk of an axlebox overheating when moved again over a long distance. To prevent this, the dead engines were usually restricted to a speed limit of 25mph, and stops were made every 25 miles (40km), mainly in order to check that the axleboxes were not overheating. A hot box left unattended could have had serious consequences, causing the wheel to seize in its bearing and bringing the train to a halt so causing chaos to the day's railway operations.

Four engines were considered to be the maximum number in any one scrap convoy. Wagons fitted with vacuum brakes were placed at the front of the procession to give extra braking capacity. If the route took the train over bridges with a weight restriction, spacer wagons were placed between the locomotives to spread the load.

A label bearing the purchaser's name and destination would be tied to the handrail of the locomotive, or daubed in paint on the side of the cab or tender.

Usually the towing was done by a diesel engine or a steam locomotive still in commission, but

The locomotives arrived at the scrapyards encrusted in a coat of dirty black, their ashpans and smokeboxes often still full of the remains of their last run. They were coated in an inflammable mixture of grease, oil and coal dust, which was hazardous to a man wielding an oxyacetylene torch. T W Ward's yard at Killamarsh in south Yorkshire would sometimes set fire to its engines in order to burn off this dangerous mixture before the cutters began their task.

Tools of the trade

The tools of the scrapman were the breaker's hammer and the oxyacetylene torch. Oxygen and acetylene gas produce a white hot flame – hot enough to burn through the $^5/_8$in of a locomotive boiler or the $1^1/_4$in mild steel plate of a locomotive frame.

Many British steel furnaces used the Bessemer open hearth process, which could accept cold scrap only in relatively small pieces. Sometimes engines were cut up at a BR works, loaded into wagons and cut up again at a private scrapyard before being reloaded into wagons and taken to the steel works.

The working conditions for the cutters in some scrapyards would probably contravene most of the current health and safety regulations. Some yards cut up their engines in a systematic, efficient and safe manner. Others, however, with little experience of handling over 100 tons of steam engine, tackled them in a haphazard, cut what is nearest fashion. To become skilled at the task was simply a case of trial and error.

It was a dangerous job which meant balancing precariously on the high, greasy running plates

occasionally one of the condemned engines was put in steam to haul its dead companions to the scrapyard. Once there, its last job completed, its fire would be dropped and it would await its fate along with the other members of the convoy.

Last convoys

On some engines, enthusiasts wrote inscriptions in the grime on the smokebox door – 'Farewell to steam', 'The last one', 'Please save me'. To most members of the public, these sad convoys probably meant very little. They were simply another sign of the new technological age. What use was the steam engine in a decade when man would walk on the moon?

Occasionally, an engine was sold while under repair, in which case it probably arrived at the yard with the replacement parts neatly laid out in the cab. Ironically, because BR were winding down their production of spare parts, legend has it that they were sometimes forced to buy back from the scrapyards some of the parts they needed to keep their existing engines in service.

> **Back door delights**
> Visitors to the tiny village of South Leverton in the Vale of Trent soon discover that resident Phil Rollin is a steam enthusiast. The evidence is a 59-ton Standard 4MT 2-6-0 and tender parked on his lawn. Rollin, an electrical engineer, purchased the items from Woodham's scrapyard in 1983, intending to restore them for the Peak Railway. However, unforeseen problems held up the refurbishment, and No 76084 and tender are now familiar landmarks.

▼ **To the casual observer, these rusting steam engines stored amidst the grass and weeds of Barry scrapyard in 1980 might have seemed like prime candidates for cutting up. But the preservationists had other ideas and all three were duly rescued. The two Standard 2-6-4T engines – No 80080 (left) and No 80098 (right) – are now based at the Midland Railway Centre in Derbyshire, while the Merchant Navy Pacific No 35010 *Blue Star* is being restored at Castle Hedingham.**

along the side of the locomotive, holding a hot torch with one hand and an oily handrail with the other. Sparks flew, boiler tubes crashed to the ground, cab sides and cladding plates fell away under the blows of the breaker's hammer, and lagging made from blue asbestos – now known to be a serious risk to health – flaked and flew about through the air.

To the scrapmen, it was all in a day's work. To them a once proud express passenger locomotive differed from a humble shunter in terms of size only. A legacy of power, speed and performance was just so much time and money. It was good piece work and there was plenty of it, and the dangers and exertions were easily lived with.

Rescue mission

Enthusiasts were soon knocking at the scrapyard foreman's window asking for permission to go round the yard – just as they used to request to go round the shed of steam locomotive depots. At first, many yard workers were only too pleased to make the occasional back-hander by burning off a number plate and handing it down to a grateful enthusiast.

But the occasional request turned into a deluge as young, and not so young, enthusiasts clamoured to be allowed into what were potentially very dangerous places. Eventually, the foremen, cutters and managers lost patience, and anyone found in their yards without permission was treated as a trespasser and possible thief.

In September 1968, Woodham's yard at Barry in south Wales surprised the railway world by selling one of its engines – an LMS Fowler Class 4F 0-6-0 No 43924 – to the Worth Valley Railway in west Yorkshire. The sale put paid to the conventional wisdom that the preservationists were too poor to provide a viable market for withdrawn steam locomotives, and over the next 20 years a further 212 engines went from Barry to preservation groups throughout the country.

New arrivals

It became clear that a hasty and poorly planned switchover from steam had led to many unproven diesel locomotives being produced. Spare part distribution became a problem for BR as stocks diminished. By the time the parts were needed, the manufacturers had already switched their production to other models. Too often it was a case of, 'Sorry, mate – we haven't got the part.'

Ironically, even before the last steam locomotive was hauled away and dismembered, the process started all over again – this time with many of the early pilot scheme diesels which were brought in to replace them.

▼ **A cutter makes short shrift of dilapidated BR rolling stock. It was yards such as this that became places of regular pilgrimage for steam enthusiasts seeking out souvenirs of their favourite locomotives.**

CHAPTER TWO

GREAT JOURNEYS BY STEAM

The Road to the Isles

GLASGOW · FORT WILLIAM · MALLAIG · KYLE · INVERNESS

A fine piece of railway, the West Highland line rolls by lochs and over wild, wild moors, past ruined castles and through rugged glens. Watch out for wild cats on Rannoch Moor – and, perhaps, a golden eagle riding the air.

TRAVEL FACTS

Journey distance: 246½ track miles (397km).
Travelling time: 9½ hours
Points to note: book steam option well in advance. Good insect repellent advisable. Check timetables carefully – overnight stay may be necessary.
Accommodation: plentiful but advance booking advisable in July and August.

A rail tour of the West Highlands is a heady mix of sea and mountains, soaring viaducts and quiet glens. Take in the highlands and islands by travelling the scenic 165 miles (265km) from Glasgow to Mallaig, then board a ferry up the Sound of Sleat to connect with the Kyle line. Why not hop over the sea to Skye – you should still make Inverness for dinner.

The line from Fort William to Mallaig is particularly spectacular, with views of Skye from Ardthurinish to Armadale Bay. Using privately owned locomotives, British Rail ran one of their very few steam operations over this stretch. What better route to hold steam's heritage in trust than to travel the magnificent 41 miles (66km) hauled by a Black Five, a K1 – or maybe even *The Great Marquess,* a K4?

North to Fort William

You are plunged into fine scenery not long after the main train – the sleeper from Euston – pulls out of Glasgow. And what a start to the journey, as the train winds its way up the single line beyond Garelochead, high above Loch Long, before dropping down to Arrochar where, in steam days, thirsty engines sought the water columns.

Framed in the V of the hills lie the peaks of the Argyll National Forest Park, with the distinctive shape of The Cobbler – a favourite with walkers and mountaineers – in the foreground. Driving through a rock cutting here is one of the most thrilling moments on the journey – you feel you're going over the edge down into the Loch below. Only the narrow strip of land separates the head of Loch Long from Loch Lomond.

▼ With Ben Nevis rearing up in the background, the *West Highlander* is about to cross the Caledonian Canal at Banavie. Telford's famous canal steps down 64 feet (19m) on the eight locks of Neptune's Staircase. The train is generally hauled by an LMS 4-6-0 Class 5.

Previous page: The Durango and Silverton narrow gauge line in Colorado, USA, runs on a shelf cut into the red granite cliffs.

Into the wilds

The train now follows the western slopes above Lomondside, with Ben Lomond prominent across the water, before starting the fierce climb up Glen Falloch – look for the falls on the right – towards Crianlarich. Close to the road the train runs through Strath Fillan to Tyndrum, then north to the great Horseshoe Curve with its two viaducts beneath the slopes of Ben Dorain. In the days of steam you could glance back and see a U-shaped cloud of smoke hanging over the track.

Look left where road and rail part company after Bridge of Orchy for the ruin of Achallader Castle. Then off the line heads into the wilderness of Rannoch Moor, haunt of wild cats. The peat bog is 20 feet (6m) deep in places. Only the railway crosses this vast tract – the line is floated across the moor on a bed of tree roots, brushwood and thousands of tons of earth and ashes. There is little sign of life anywhere except a few railway cottages and the odd covey of grouse wheeling to fresh cover in the heather.

Slowly the train climbs from Rannoch towards the final summit – 1350 feet (411m) above sea level – at Corrour. Here snow fences appear on either side of the track and at Cruach cutting the train enters the only snow shed in Britain – vital protection for when winter snowdrifts pile as high as houses.

▲ The view from the train at Glenfinnan, with the long expanse of mountain-flanked Loch Shiel shimmering off into the distance, is one of the finest in Scotland. The West Highland line follows the route that Bonnie Prince Charlie took to the isles. The Glenfinnan Monument – a round tower with the figure of a Highlander on top – marks the spot where the prince unfurled his red and white silk standard to launch the ill-fated 1745 rebellion.

Then, with a hawk likely to be hovering in the distance, you emerge high above the eastern shore of Loch Treig. By Tulloch the train has descended to the level of the loch and runs by the peaty waters of the Spean. Travel then through Monessie Gorge, where the river roars through the rocks – at the steeper ends the rock has been cut into thousands of individual shapes by the swirling waters from winter rain.

Into Fort William

High on a hill on the right at Spean Bridge there's a distant view of a memorial to the commandos who trained here during World War II. Soon the dramatic bulk of Ben Nevis – the highest mountain in Britain – looms large on the left and there's a fast run into the terminus at Fort William. But the first train to Mallaig – and the only steam connection – could well have left earlier.

In the days of steam it was easy – you took the next train up to Mallaig, almost certainly behind one of the Gresley K2 2-6-0s specially fitted with side window cabs and named after local lochs. The adjacent shed was alive with K2s, Kls, Black Fives and maybe a Bl or a North British 0-6-0 – and possibly, until the mid 1950s, a Glen.

But times have changed. The sleeper is likely to be the only loco-hauled train of the day from the

▲ Based at the Severn Valley Railway but on loan for the holiday season, No 3442 *The Great Marquess* steams over the 21 arches of Glenfinnan Viaduct. A listed structure, the 100ft (30m) high ferroconcrete viaduct was built in the late 1890s by Robert – Concrete Bob – McAlpine. The streamlined rail bridge which curves elegantly across the Finnan Valley was Britain's first mass concrete structure – a Scottish author described it as 'a thing so delicate the fairies might have built it'.

The Skye bogie
A line that combined steep gradients with sharp bends demanded a special engine, and the Skye bogie, designed by David Jones for the Skye (later Kyle) line, became a legend. The characterful, plump little 4-4-0 locomotive was the standard engine on the line from the 1880s to World War I.

south, the rest being Sprinters. But though steam has mostly gone to its long rest there are still sparks of life on the West Highland line.

Steaming to Mallaig

The option of steam haulage over the scenic Fort William–Mallaig leg is often booked up well in advance. Whether you go by steam or not, the track runs alongside Loch Eil to Glenfinnan, with the breathtaking sweep of the 100 feet (30m) high ferro-concrete viaduct. Look towards Loch Shiel for the statue commemorating Bonnie Prince Charlie's landing on the road to the isles.

Then it's alongside the island-studded Loch Eilt, through tunnels, past more lochs and yet more tunnels as you squirm north to Arisaig. On this stretch there are views of the islands of Rhum

▼ The West Highland line opened up some of the most inaccessible terrain in the British Isles. Here two diesel multiple units round Ben Dorain on one of the highest points of the route. The line winds through a great variety of scenery, with dramatic changes of mood as bleak mountain pass leads on to sheltered loch and snow-capped peaks give way to wooded valleys.

and Eigg. Finally you travel on through Morar, with its white sands and loch – at 1000 feet (305m) Britain's deepest – to Mallaig.

Hauled by steam you are likely to arrive at Mallaig only to find that the ship to the Kyle of Lochalsh has already sailed. In this territory you need a calendar as well as a timetable. Check the details carefully – you could well find that the steam train runs on Monday, Tuesday and Thursday whereas the ship to Kyle sails on Tuesday, Thursday and Friday. Morar, just down the coast, is a good choice for an overnight stay.

Highlands and islands

Off on your travels again you find that the cruise along the Sound of Sleat is scarcely Pullman luxury – but if the weather is good who wants to be anywhere but on deck? Arrival at the Kyle should give time to visit Skye via the new toll bridge which has replaced the ferry, before catching the train from Kyle of Lochalsh to Inverness.

Once the Highland Railway's route to Skye, the Kyle line is steeped in local history. Pipers were called in for the official opening. But the whisky flowed, the railway was forgotten and an onlooker described how the pipers 'could neither blow, stand up nor all play the same tune'.

The old Skye line achieved brief notoriety during the Battle of Strome Ferry, when there was rioting over Sunday working. In an area where clocks were sometimes stopped during the Sabbath, devout locals were all the more offended because the Sunday workers were east coast fishermen. Tension grew until, one dark night, the locals swooped as the rival east coasters tried to unload their catch off boats and on to wagons. By

▲ Class K4 2-6-0 No 3442 *The Great Marquess* hauls a train in the original LNER excursion livery of apple green and cream. The train runs alongside island-studded Loch Eilt on its way west to Arisaig, where views of the Inner Hebridean isles of Rhum and Eigg open up.

▼ On the last leg of the Fort William-Mallaig section there are views of loch and mountain as the train heads north along the coast. If you want to break your journey for a day or two, Morar, with its deep loch, silver sands and easy access to the islands via Mallaig, is a good place to stay.

Commando view
High on a hill to the right, just beyond Spean Bridge on the last stretch into Fort William, stands a monument to the Commandos who trained in the area during World War II. There are plans to turn the station at Spean Bridge – the point of disembarkation – into a Commando museum.

daybreak Strome pier was held by 150 protesters. The riot was finally quelled and Sunday working resumed, but bitterness lingered for years – some locals boycotted the line by sending goods on the long, roundabout steamer route.

At first the running of the railway was engagingly free of precise timekeeping. What few clocks there were in that remote region kept their own version of time – in spite of strenuous attempts to introduce uniform time at stations, the early timetables are masterpieces of non-committal approximations.

Heading east

The Kyle line is a magnificent section of railway. For many years the haunt of Black Fives, it ran one of Britain's last true mixed trains – passenger and freight in one – until the early 1960s.

As on the previous stages the line snakes through glens, soars high above toytown villages and plunges down to run by deep lochs. In places the sheer cliffs are netted to contain rock falls. The stretch of line that runs beside Loch Carron is particularly superb, with good views of Skye over the water. Look out for the sheltered white houses and palm trees of the pretty village of Plockton.

The train then heads inland to the lonely hamlet of Achnasheen, past Loch Sgamhain in whose depths lurks a water kelpie. Sit tight in your seat – legend has it that anyone unfortunate enough to fall into the loch is gobbled up whole apart from the lungs which float to the surface.

Journeying on out of harm's way, you travel towards Garve past the salmon leap of the rocky Falls of Rogie. On the left towers Ben Wyvis – from the summit there are views right across

▲ **The freshly painted livery gleams in the sunshine as No 37401** *Queen of Scots* **skirts the west side of Loch Eilt with a rake of refurbished InterCity stock. The first diesels used on the line were the Birmingham RC&W Sulzer Type 2s, later known as Class 26.**

Scotland from the North Sea to the Atlantic.

The line is diverted up 1 in 50 gradients in both directions, climbing steeply to loop around the Victorian spa resort of Strathpeffer. Europe's rich and famous once flocked to take the waters here, but a local landowner wouldn't allow a direct route over his land. Though later a branch line was added, at first the popular resort was bypassed – the nearest station was sited an inconveniently long, hard trek away.

On the last stage to the east coast the line turns to join the Further North from Wick to Inverness at Dingwall. On, finally, to Inverness, the capital of the Highlands.

Journey's end

Inverness station, the headquarters of the old Highland Railway, still retains something of an Edwardian flavour despite its spotless terrazzo floors. On the walls of the concourse are blazoned in full colour the arms of the Highland's oldest constituent company, the Inverness and Nairn of 1855, while adjoining is the splendid station hotel, once railway owned. The massive plumbing in the bathroom looks as if it might have started life in the old Lochgorm locomotive works just down the road.

After you've experienced the splendour of the West Highland line you'll almost certainly be back. Rail options give freedom to break a journey for a few days to fish lochs or rivers, walk hills or simply enjoy at leisure the pleasures of the countryside and the hospitality of the people.

◀ **Winding along the shore of Loch Carron, the pretty village of Plockton benefits from mild Gulf Stream currents. With its white houses and palm trees fringing the bay, and sailing boats bobbing in the salt loch, the Highland village could almost be set in the French Riviera.**

Narrow gauge in Provence

NICE • ANNOT • DIGNE

This sole surviving limb of the once great network of narrow gauge lines, the Chemins de Fer de la Provence climbs up into the foothills of the Alps, twisting its way along gorges, over viaducts and past villages perched high in Provence.

Nice, Côte d'Azur: blue skies, grand hotels, the sweeping curve of the Promenade Anglais, the Flower Market by day, by night a magical scene of tiny restaurants, yachts crowding the small harbour on the road to Monte Carlo. Past encounters would include the Blue Train from Paris with its Wagon-Lits sleepers being met by a carriage and four. Today, travel is more mundane – take your car on the motor rail from Boulogne, to arrive fresh and ready for the delights of Provence. For enthusiasts of train travel there is something extra to savour – a ride on the Chemins de Fer de la Provence.

Once linking the coastal villages – St Tropez, St Raphael, Ste Maxime – to Nice as well as running services northwards, what was once the Chemins de Fer du Sud lives under constant threat of road competition and the removal of its Departmental subsidy. In spite of this precarious existence plenty of trains still run, providing a good service for tourists and seasoned passengers alike, although these days many people travel by road which often runs parallel to the rail track.

Historic route

The metre gauge line climbs to over 3000ft (915m) on its snaking, twisting 95 mile (153km) route to Digne-les-Bains, passing through gorges, over high viaducts and past once fortified villages. Not only that, travellers are taking in a little piece of French history. At one time France had 13,000 miles (20,900km) of secondary railways, almost

▼Over arched, stone viaducts, through dark tunnels and along rocky ledges, the Sunday steam special on the Chemins de Fer de la Provence weaves its way towards the ancient village of Annot, arriving just in time for lunch.

83

all being subsidised by the state or local authorities, but better roads with more efficient transport proved their death knell.

Whether you make the tourist trip out to Annot and back on a Sunday with the joy of steam part of the way or take the leisurely three and a half hour diesel run with 21 stops from Nice to Digne, the journey cannot fail to thrill. Beware if you ride the autorail in the heat of the day as it can be packed and the French have no inclination to open windows.

A journey over the Chemins de Fer de la Provence depends on whether you are a tourist or a traveller. If you choose the Sunday day out (unless you are a backpacker, hardened traveller or a local, most do) it is still a long day, starting after breakfast and returning just in time to have a shower and change before an evening meal in the Flower Market.

Regular steam trains for passengers came to an end here a long time ago, so engines have had to be acquired from elsewhere for this line. The engines are well cared for and the mixture of a modern tourist train linked to the dip into the past is nicely balanced. The leaflets advertise a three and a half hour stop at Annot for lunch, a reminder that the French have one main purpose in mind on a day out – eating.

Starting point

The terminus is impressive for a metre gauge line, though clearly it has seen better days. If you have booked your ticket in advance – a wise move – go

straight to the slightly dingy train shed which lies beyond the large booking hall. Here, amid the hustle and bustle, a modern diesel-hauled tourist train waits alongside the low platform.

The first half hour is spent running through the northern environs of Nice but soon the radio commentary comes to life, pointing out the sparkling River Var as it sweeps over the gravel beds, the scene dominated from time to time by *les villages perchés* clinging to the hillsides. Gattières, Carros, La Roquette, Le Broc and Bonson – there is no question that this is Provence.

Once past Plan-du-Var the river narrows into a gorge where the line runs adjacent to a new motor road under construction, one which may eventually be the railway's undoing. A tunnel, another gorge and the scenery begins to open out past more villages with medieval houses rank on rank – Malaussène, Villars, Touët – while the river flows faster as it narrows. It takes two hours of steady climbing to reach Puget-Theniers where it is all change.

Station activity

There is a 20 minute stop at this pretty two-platformed station and for a few moments it is a mini Crewe with railcars passing and the steam train backing down to replace the modern entourage which brought its passengers up from Nice. The rake of wooden-seated coaches dates back to the turn of the century; somehow the whole scene goes back with it.

The engine is a tank with an odd wheel arrange-

▼Composed of a Henschel 2-4-6-0 tank locomotive built in 1923, and pulling carriages dating as far back as 1892, CP E211 first saw service running out of Portugal's Douro Valley before being acquired by the Chemins de Fer de la Provence.

▶ **The historic stone buildings and winding, narrow alleyways of Entrevaux epitomise the Haute Provence style. With its imposing ramparts, fortified bridge and ancient cathedral the town is well worth a visit.**

ment, 2-4-6-0. It carries the letters CP and the number E211 on its red buffer beam, telling the enthusiast that this German built engine once saw service in Portugal on the little railways that run up into the hills from the Douro valley. It was built in Germany in 1923.

Like many metre gauge engines in Europe this is a Mallet – a design which evolved in response to the need for greater power on sharply curved and steeply graded lines. It is also a four cylinder compound – a usual Mallet combination.

Another steam tank engine is kept here, an ex-Brittany Reseau Breton 4-6-0 tank which is under overhaul. Volunteers come up every weekend from Nice to help with the steam running and restoration.

Full steam ahead

Heads are out of the windows now and the train leaves under a pall of black smoke, the engine's copper dome and chimney catching the morning sun.

Over the level crossing, with the river on the right, the train follows the road moving out of old Pièmont and into France proper, clipping along at about 25mph (40km/h) to Entrevaux. Here it stops for a few minutes for passengers to glimpse this once frontier village, perched on a hill overlooking the river and entered by a fortified bridge.

Over the road again, through a couple of tunnels and the climb really begins with the Mallet tank hard at work. Here the line moves away from the road, twisting up into the forested hills with the Var losing itself eastwards. The River Vair comes up on the left, deep below and through the trees, and cars suddenly become dwarfed. Over a great arched viaduct, along rocky ledges and through a deep cutting the scene widens out and the black tank engine comes to a halt opposite the buffet bar at Annot.

Here it really is all change and lunch beckons – either in the vine-roofed station restaurant, or down the steep road to the small town where you can eat at Le Beausejour, L'Avenue, Le Park or La Cigale. The air is thinner now as Annot lies in

TRAVEL FACTS

Nice-Annot (steam from Puget-Theniers to Annot)
Duration: a full day trip to allow for long lunch break
Frequency: one train each Sunday from May-October
Line length: 54 miles (87km)
Nice-Digne (diesel railcar)
Journey time: 3hr 15mins
Line length: 95 miles (153km)
Frequency: 5 trains a day

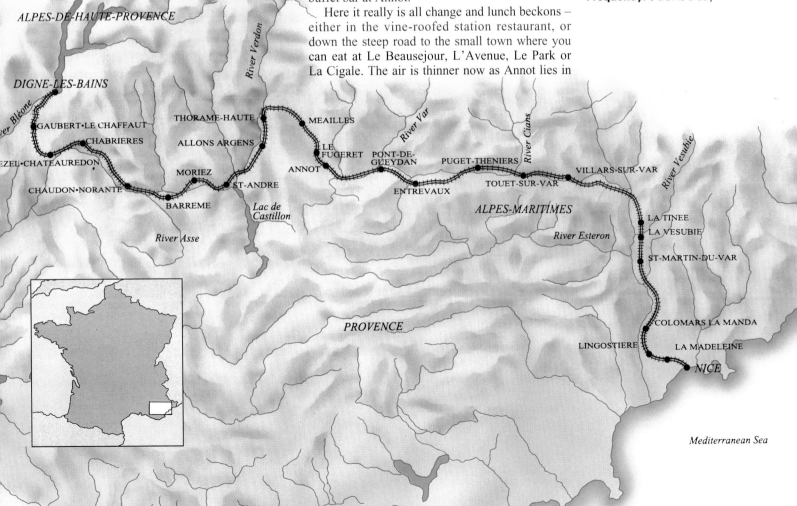

Latecomers
The Chemins de Fer de la Provence was late in appreciating the value of steam as a tourist attraction. By the time the decision was made to introduce steam, little was available in France bar the Reseau Breton 4-6-0 tank. When boiler overhaul became necessary they had to look elsewhere, and the Portuguese 2-4-6-0 tanks became a godsend. Although kept in fairly good condition on the Nice–Digne line, the brasswork does not, sadly, sparkle to the extent that it did in its comparatively recent heyday on the Douro Valley lines.

the foothills at over 2000ft (610m). This makes the appetite keen. The three and a half hour stop is just about right for a leisurely meal, some local wine and a wander around the tortuous alleyways and cool square out of the midday sun.

▲It's all change at Puget-Theniers, where passengers on special steam days move from diesel to steam for the trip to Annot. Apart from this a regular autorail service runs from Nice to Digne five times a day, all year round.

Nice to Digne

To make the railcar journey to Digne be sure that you get to Nice's Gare du Sud a good half hour in advance because there are only five through autorails a day and these are also used by the locals. Backpackers, too, make for Entrevaux so get a seat early. Even with its 21 stops the railcar is faster than the special trains.

The driver sits on the front left of the vehicle separated from the passengers only by a handrail, so there is plenty to see if you can get up in front in good time. Quite often in busy periods there is also a trailer attached. If they are running hard to keep time the swaying, rocking ride can be exciting, especially if you are up by the driver and can see the curves and the vertical drops ahead.

The railcar takes just under two hours to reach Annot where it waits for about 10 minutes to pass a southbound autorail – just enough time for a quick glass at the Buffet de la Gare to steel yourself for the exciting scenery ahead. Beyond the platforms the mountains loom ahead so the line begins to climb steeply.

It takes only a quarter of an hour to reach the great viaduct below Fugeret and you can look down over the hairpin bends of the minor road beneath as the line appears to be hung against the sky. Here too is a great looped tunnel, the only

▲Postcards are used worldwide to extol the virtues of scenery through which trains pass. This view of the Nice–Digne line is a reproduction of one of the old Sud line posters of pre-World War II days.

metre gauge example in Europe outside Switzerland.

Approaching the summit, the line turns sharp left into another tunnel, leaving the larch woods over which loom the 6000ft (1829m) snow capped peaks of the Provencal Alps. Here the Var disappears northwards in the watershed of a sunless valley.

The railcar – horn blaring – bursts out of the southern portal of a tunnel into the valley of the Verdun and drops down towards St André-les-Alpes, descending from over 3500ft (1067m). To the left is the vast Lac de Castillon – if you are on the early morning or evening railcar you are in time to snap up a magnificent picture of light and shade on the mountainside and down over the vast blue waters.

Another tunnel and still at 3000ft (900m) there is Col des Robines. As Barrême approaches, the valley widens out. The railway runs below the modern motor road and above the steel-grey glacial waters of the sluiced and canalised river.

On through Chaudon-Norante and Mézel-Chateauredon to a terminus alongside the SNCF at Digne-les-Bains, where the motor cuts and suddenly the journey is over. A single brand snatched from the burning of the old Chemins de Fer du Sud, the line which now calls itself the Chemins de Fer de la Provence has kept itself alive against all the odds.

The Long Drag

SETTLE · CARLISLE

With its long, deep tunnels, lofty viaducts and wild, sweeping landscape, this is an exhilarating rail experience. Crossing 72 miles of inspiring Pennine countryside, steam locomotives have to work hard over this demanding section of the former Midland Railway route to Scotland.

With its long climb up Ribblesdale into the heart of the Pennines, the Settle – Carlisle line was a real trial of strength and skill in the days of steam. The line as a whole became known as the Long Drag, although travelling in most trains using the line today – such as the Class 156 Super Sprinters – the gradients are hardly noticeable.

Many travellers begin their journey at Leeds, passing the ruined remains of Kirkstall Abbey on the right at Airedale. Along the journey to Skipton the railway plays cat and mouse with the Liverpool – Leeds canal, with its dramatic staircase of five locks at Bingley.

At Keighley, urban West Yorkshire begins to give way to the hills surrounding the Aire valley, and the Keighley and Worth Valley Railway begins the five mile (8km) run to Oakworth. En route is picturesque Haworth, where the Brontë family lived. A little further on is Skipton, a lively and attractive market town with a fine castle and interesting pubs.

Three or four miles (5–6km) from Hellifield, the junction with the Lancashire and Yorkshire line from Blackburn, you reach the Settle and Carlisle line proper. Diverging northwards at Settle Junction from the older line to Lancaster, you immediately start the long climb up Ribblesdale into the Pennines. The 1 in 100 gradient quickly becomes obvious as the other line falls away to the left; the climb is almost continuous for the next 15 miles (24km). Soon, however, your train pulls to a halt in Settle, a charming Dales market town which was a favourite with composer Sir Edward Elgar.

As the climb continues, limestone crags tower above and signs of quarrying appear. Close by the line to the right at Langcliffe is the historic Hoffman continuous burning lime kiln, possible

▼ **West Country class Pacific No 34092 *City of Wells* crosses the 10 arches of Ormside Viaduct with a Cumbrian Mountain Express. It is the first crossing of the River Eden for northbound trains, which then follow the river for much of the route to Carlisle. The viaduct is 200yd (183m) long and 90ft (27m) high.**

TRAVEL FACTS

Length of line: 72 miles 1170yd (117km)
Travelling time: three hours
Frequency: six or seven trains daily
Service: steam trains operate over the line from time to time. Details are advertised in the railway enthusiast press.
Special features:
Number of viaducts: 21
Number of tunnels: 14
Number of bridges: 325
Highest point: Ais Gill – 1169ft (356m)

▲ LMS Pacific No 46229 *Duchess of Hamilton* heads south with a Cumbrian Mountain Express at Baron Wood, where there are two tunnels, No 1 (207yd/189m) and No 2 (251yd/229m).

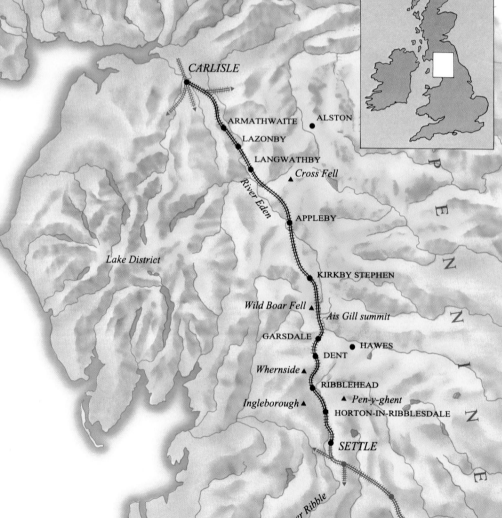

centrepiece of a development to show the history of the Dales limestone industry. By now you have entered the Yorkshire Dales National Park.

Three Peaks of Ribblesdale

Above Stainforth Park the line enters a short gorge, crossing and recrossing the River Ribble, and finally crossing a third time at Helwirth Bridge where there is a short respite from the continuous climb as the line crosses the bed of an old lake. At the same time the looming mass of Pen-y-ghent on the right – at 2273ft (693m) high the first of the Three Peaks of Ribblesdale – heralds the mountainous country to come. More quarries appear to the left before the train draws into Horton-in-Ribblesdale.

Beyond Horton the landscape becomes more open, with the railway gradually edging up the eastern foothills of Ingleborough (2373ft/723m), the second of the Three Peaks but not yet visible itself.

Ribblehead station has no platform for north-bound trains. It was lost to a quarry siding before some smaller stations were reopened in 1986. The station had other claims to fame: for many years it was an official weather station, the stationmaster sending regular reports to the Meteorological Office, and the waiting room, equipped complete with harmonium, served as a meeting place for religious services.

The broad valley of Chapel-le-Dale now opens to the left. The railway heads out to cross it on a high embankment which soon yields to the 24 arches of the 105ft (32m) high Ribblehead Viaduct whose poor condition so nearly led to the line's closure. The characteristic outline of Ingleborough comes into view to the left, and as the line curves eastwards the massive 2419ft (737m) face of Whernside, the third of the Three Peaks, appears on the north side of the dale.

Extremes of weather are far from unusual when south-westerly gales funnel up Chapel-le-Dale. Motor cars were lifted clean off a goods train 30 years ago, and in recent years planks from the scaffolding erected by contractors repairing the viaduct have been scattered like leaves across the hillsides.

Tunnel into Cumbria

Passing the remote signalbox at Blea Moor on the right, you near the summit of the climb from Settle Junction – reached just after entering the 2629yd (2403m) bore of Blea Moor tunnel. The longest on the line, it burrows under the eastern shoulder of Whernside to take you from Yorkshire into Cumbria.

As you emerge into Dentdale and cross Denthead Viaduct, a splendid view opens up to the left as you skirt high around the eastern slopes of the valley. Arten Gill is another great viaduct, crossed on the approach to Dent station.

The next tunnel, Rise Hill, takes you through into Garsdale which opens up on the left 300ft (91m) below the line. On one of the few level

▲ **LMS Class 5 4-6-0 No 5305** *Alderman A. E. Draper* **passes through Shale Cutting north of Blea Moor, one of the worst places on the route for snowdrifts. In 1947 the railway was impassable for eight weeks around Dent. At Kirkby Stephen, snow cutters hung their coats on the tops of telegraph poles.**

▼ **The most famous structure on the line is the 440yd (402m) long Ribblehead Viaduct. LMS Class 5 4-6-0 No 5407 crosses the 24 arches with a northbound Cumbrian Mountain Express. Sometimes the wind here has been so strong that freight trains have been blown to a standstill.**

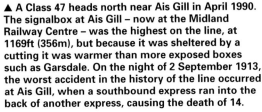

▲ **A Class 47 heads north near Ais Gill in April 1990.** The signalbox at Ais Gill – now at the Midland Railway Centre – was the highest on the line, at 1169ft (356m), but because it was sheltered by a cutting it was warmer than more exposed boxes such as Garsdale. On the night of 2 September 1913, the worst accident in the history of the line occurred at Ais Gill, when a southbound express ran into the back of another express, causing the death of 14.

works of Barrow-in-Furness.

At Ormside the viaduct spans the Eden and you approach Appleby, former county town of Westmorland, still dominated by the Norman keep of its castle where the grounds are home to a fascinating collection of rare breeds of farm animals. Quantities of milk once went daily to London from Appleby where the station is the only one on the line with a real main line atmosphere: long platforms and the only station footbridge on the line.

The building bears a memorial to Bishop Eric Treacy who died here in 1978. Much loved as a churchman and railway photographer, he rated the Settle – Carlisle line as one of the three wonders of the North of England, alongside York Minster and Hadrian's Wall.

The junction north of the station at Appleby links with the one-time Eden Valley line from Kirkby Stephen to Penrith. From here on the landscape becomes gentler, though still with the Pennines high to the right and occasional glimpses of the Lake District fells to the left. The River Eden is frequently in view, and you cross it again at Eden Lacy, north of Langwathby. Close by, great quantities of anhydrite went from Long Meg Mine to feed chemical industries on Merseyside, the heavy trains hauled by BR 9F 2-10-0s.

High points

Dent station, opened in August 1877, is 1150ft (350m) above sea level – a sign above the up platform tells the traveller that this is the highest main line station in the land. The station is four miles (6km) from Dent, a cobbled Dales village which sits in the valley some 400ft (122m) below – the access road from village to station rises at 1 in 4.

lengths of track, water troughs once replenished the tender tanks of steam locomotives at speed. Garsdale station was the junction for a branch to Hawes and Northallerton which closed in 1959. Now a local group is seeking to reconstruct the rail link down Wensleydale, well known for its associations with James Herriot. Wind has been a problem here – legend has it that it once left a locomotive spinning for hours on the turntable.

Wild Boar Fell (2324ft/697m) dominates the scene ahead as you reach the highest point of the line at Ais Gill (1169ft/350m). Look for the summit sign on the right. Shortly after, Hell Gill Force on the same side is a dramatic sight in wet weather. It is your first glimpse of the waters of the River Eden which you follow to Carlisle.

While Mallerstang valley descends to the right, you follow its western slopes, catching sight of the romantic ruins of Pendragon Castle on the right, then it's through Birkett Tunnel and on to Kirkby Stephen, the station again high above and some distance from the little town.

The next 11 miles (18km) to Appleby are marked by two more great viaducts and glorious views on the right to the north Pennines, topped by Cross Fell reaching almost 3000ft (900m). At 130ft (39m) Smardale Viaduct is the highest on the line. It crosses the long closed Barnard Castle – Tebay line which used to feed coke to the iron-

A line is built

Construction of the Settle – Carlisle line was a massive task, without the benefit of mechanised equipment – the railway was one of the last to be built using pick and shovel methods.

An army of navvies toiled for over six years, tunnelling out cuttings and building embankments, to create 72 miles (116km) of high speed railway through some of the most inhospitable country in Britain. Many died. A plaque in the church at Chapel-le-Dale commemorates the 200 men who perished.

The line was opened to passengers on 1 May 1876.

▲ **LMS Class 5 4-6-0 No 5407 and Jubilee class 4-6-0 No 5690 *Leander* work a northbound Cumbrian Mountain Express at Armathwaite, where the Settle – Carlisle crosses Armathwaite Dyke, a band of volcanic rock that stretches from Mull. Armathwaite tunnel (325yd/297m) is the most northerly on the line.**

◀**LMS Class 5 4-6-0 No 5305 *Alderman A. E. Draper* takes a southbound Cumbrian Mountain Express over Dent Head Viaduct. Built of local blue limestone known as Dent marble, the 10-arch viaduct is 190yd (173m) long and 110ft (33m) high. Stone built snow cabins were provided at Dent for gangs of men engaged on snow clearing work.**

Before reaching Long Meg, Langwathby station provides access via a summer weekend bus link to Alston, England's highest market town. Alston is home of the South Tynedale Railway, an attractive narrow gauge line along the trackbed of the former BR branch.

Late autumn is a fine time to see the Eden between Lazonby and Armathwaite – you view the river through a golden screen of birches as it churns and twists through the gorge below on the right.

All too soon, but nearly three hours out from Leeds, you reach the Border City of Carlisle. Citadel station, once the meeting place for seven railway companies, was specially enlarged to accommodate the Midland Railway's Scottish traffic off the Settle and Carlisle line.

There is a fine museum at Carlisle, which tells the story of the city. With so much to explore, both on and off the line, you are likely to be back – the Settle and Carlisle in winter is an unforgettable experience.

By steam to Victoria Falls

BULAWAYO · VICTORIA FALLS

Cecil Rhodes once imagined a great railway linking Cairo to the Cape. Though it was an impossible dream, one of the sections completed was the run from Bulawayo to Victoria Falls in present day Zimbabwe. It remains one of Africa's most dramatic lines.

Bulawayo, second city of Zimbabwe and capital of the Matabeleland region, is one of the main railway crossroads of southern Africa. The city has a spacious, colonial feel to it, and the period atmosphere is heightened by the sight and sound of steam trains. It is one of the last great African strongholds of steam operations.

Around the city are a number of popular tourist sights, chief among them being the Matopos Hills, with Cecil Rhodes's simple grave on one of the peaks and a game reserve near by. However, for the railway enthusiast there is another irresistible attraction – the Bulawayo steam depot.

Although Zimbabwe has a growing fleet of diesels, Bulawayo shed is still home to some 15 or 20 steam locos. All articulated Beyer-Garratts, they have large boilers slung between two sets of driving wheels to provide high power output coupled with flexibility on sharply curved routes.

Several impressive Beyer-Garratt classes worked from Bulawayo. The 15th Class 4-6-4+4-6-4s – the Flying Fifteens – are the world's last surviving passenger Garratts, and the 20th Class 4-8-2+2-8-4s were among the world's largest steam locos. The first of the highly successful 15ths arrived from Beyer, Peacock and Co Ltd of Manchester in 1940, and the 20th Class monsters followed from the same stable in 1954. Both classes measure almost 100ft (30m) and turn the scales at 120 tons (15th class) and 250 tons (20th class). There were few more fascinating sights in Bulawayo than watching them rolling out from the depot at dawn, each locomotive being swung on the huge turntable before heading off to its day's work.

From Bulawayo, the National Railways of Zimbabwe (NRZ) lines (all 3ft 6in/1070mm gauge) spread out in four directions: west to Botswana, south towards South Africa, east to the capital Harare, and north-west towards the Zambezi River. On this north-west route the Victoria Falls marks the border with Zambia, and the service from Bulawayo to the Falls has long been one of southern Africa's most celebrated railway journeys.

▶ **Hwange Colliery Company locomotive No 6, an ex-Rhodesia Railways 19th Class, steams out of the remote Hwange mines with a full complement of coal. The mines are connected by a series of short branch lines to the main line at Thomson Junction.**

▼ **Linking Zambia and Zimbabwe, the great railway bridge crosses the Zambezi gorge just below the Falls and stands 400ft (122m) above the river. Rhodes died three years before the bridge was completed, but he asked that it be built so close to the Falls that the spray would wet the carriage windows.**

TRAVEL FACTS

Journey distance: 295 miles (475km)
Travelling time: 12 hours 30 minutes by NRZ overnight service. Rail Safaris run several tour programmes of different duration.
Points to note: book berths on overnight train well in advance; full bedding sets are provided in first class. River trips and game drives can also be booked in advance.
Accommodation: booking advisable for hotels in Victoria Falls.

The trip covers 295 miles (475km) of single track through forests and savannah grasslands, skirting Hwange National Park, one of Africa's finest game reserves, on the way. Journey's end is only a short walk from the Falls themselves.

You have a choice of two services. The regular NRZ daily (or, more accurately, nightly) working leaves Bulawayo at 7pm and reaches Victoria Falls early next morning. It runs to a dozen or so coaches and is generally hauled by one of Zimbabwe's modern diesels. The handsome passenger stock is painted in teak and cream livery, often with clerestory roofs and wood-panelled interiors, embellished on the side with the NRZ coat of arms.

The other service, organised by the Rail Safaris Company, runs slower paced trips along the Falls line as part of its regular steam train tours programme from Bulawayo. Usually two or three vintage saloons are coupled to the rear of regular goods trains, providing patrons with a leisurely journey behind steam.

Beyond Bulawayo

Whether one takes the evening NRZ departure to Victoria Falls or the Rail Safaris tour, the first feature of the journey is the great engine shed, half a mile out from Bulawayo station. Even in the dusk a smoky cloud hangs above the depot, and there should be a glimpse of the resident Beyer-Garratts as the train goes past.

A little further on comes the junction where the Botswana line branches off to the left, quickly followed by another divide where the Zambian line leaves the double track route to Harare, and swings away on its single line north out of the city.

Once the night train is rolling steadily north through the bush, passengers may be tempted by a visit to the dining car. This is not quite the dining

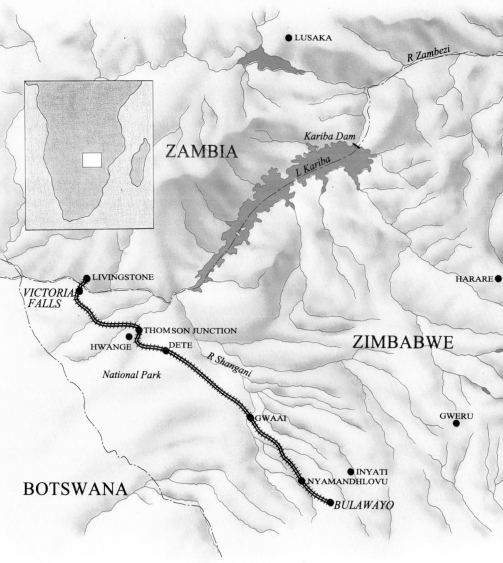

experience the train deserves, and the railway authorities would do well to exploit more fully the tourist potential of the Victoria Falls service. Travelling in daylight, the Rail Safaris passengers do rather better, and are able to survey the passing countryside from the cocktail bar before sitting down in their dining saloon.

During the night the train covers a remarkable section of the line between the towns of Gwaai and Dete. Dete straight, the longest straight piece of track in Africa (70 miles/112km), forms the eastern boundary of Hwange National Park. Even today the animals' antics in these parts can have untoward effects on the timetable. In a recent incident, a steam train even went missing. It had stalled on the line, but a lioness devouring her kill close to the lineside telephone was more than enough reason to prevent the crew reporting the train's predicament for several hours.

Sleeping passengers may wake momentarily at one of the isolated passing stations to hear a southbound steam engine hissing slowly past their compartment window on a parallel track. Night travel offers few more evocative sounds.

African hospitality

An aspect of the railway scene in Zimbabwe which will become quickly apparent to Rail Safaris patrons is the footplate hospitality of NRZ steam drivers and firemen. Indeed, any visitor taking a close interest in steam locomotives is liable to be invited to 'Come on up!' before very long.

▲ **A 20th Class Garratt, No 730, crosses the Victoria Falls bridge hauling a mixed goods train and two vintage saloon coaches. The bridge was built by the Cleveland Bridge & Engineering Company of Darlington in 1903-4.**

On most railways the presence of tourists riding on the engines would be frowned upon, to say the least. However, in Zimbabwe the authorities have bowed to the inevitable, and visitors are issued with footplate indemnity passes which provide official sanction for riding with the driver.

There is plenty of room for a visitor or two in the roomy cab of a Garratt; even on these modern Zimbabwean engines, the unique elemental feel of the traditional steam footplate immediately engulfs the newcomer in heat, coal dust and noise. A footplate trip along a short stretch of the line is not to be missed, and the articulated Garratts provide a comfortable ride, rolling along smoothly on their two separate sets of wheels.

Beyond Hwange National Park the line twists and turns through a range of hills to reach an isolated spot called Thomson Junction. The night train reaches here around dawn and the crews change over during the station stop.

Thomson Junction is where the heavy coal traffic from the collieries at Hwange joins the main line, and as the sleeping cars stand in the bare platform the more wakeful passengers may hear the colliery company's own engines arriving at the junction with their full trains of coal.

Colonial origins
Framed maps of the old rail system are mounted on the panelling in the sleeping compartments of the National Railways of Zimbabwe night train and represent a history lesson in themselves. Labelled Rhodesia Railways, they date back to the days of Sir Roy Welensky and the Central African Federation, when the systems of Northern Rhodesia (now Zambia) and Southern Rhodesia (Zimbabwe) were operated as one.

The Victoria Falls route was then part of Rhodesia Railways' north-south main line. However, it had been opened in 1904 with even greater aspirations – that of one day forming part of Cecil Rhodes's proposed 3ft 6in (1070mm) gauge route through to Cairo from the Cape.

These colliery locomotives, rather surprisingly for such mundane work, are green painted 4-8-2s, built by the North British Locomotive Co Ltd in Glasgow. There are several on the branch lines around Thomson Junction, their smoke blackening the sky as they struggle to get the coal trains on the move. Along with the activities of the NRZ Garratts which take the coal traffic south, the green 4-8-2s have attracted a steady stream of steam enthusiasts even to this remote area. They give the Baobab Hotel nearby an unlikely cosmopolitan clientele.

On this final leg of the journey the line winds through wooded country, seen at its best in the clear light of early morning. In the train, coffee is brought round, and early risers can open their compartment windows and look out for antelope, zebra and other wildlife among the trees.

Arrival at the Falls is heralded by clouds of water vapour billowing high above the Zambezi. The Edwardian atmosphere of Victoria Falls station provides a fitting end to the rail journey from Bulawayo, and when the vintage Rail Safaris coaches make their afternoon arrival, the steam age scene is complete.

The little township spreads out beneath the trees on either side of the railway, which winds on downhill from the station towards the great bridge

▼ An excursion train from South Africa, hauled by 20th Class Garratt No 730, thunders through the bush north of Thomson Junction. At 100ft (30m), the 20th Class 4-8-2+2-8-4s are among the world's longest steam locomotives.

that strides magnificently across the Zambezi gorge and carries the freight traffic over into Zambia. Few of the world's railway bridges have a more dramatic setting than this, arching 400ft (122m) above the churning water.

The Falls themselves are only a short walk from the station. The Zambezi, a mile wide at this point, drops sheer for more than 300ft (92m). The sight of this roaring, thundering curtain of water provides an unforgettable climax to a memorable journey.

▲ The Zambezi gorge below Victoria Falls, with the famous bridge spanning the chasm high up on the horizon, is a popular place for white water rafting. Dr Livingstone, on finding the Falls, said that it was a 'scene so lovely that it must have been gazed on by angels in their flight'.

Bradshaw timetables

One of Britain's foremost bishops was a timetable fanatic. He freely quoted this as one of his relaxing leisure pursuits. A chair by the fireside on a winter's evening with his collection of Bradshaws took him on dreamlike yet real journeys all over the kingdom. He would spend hours working out his best route between two given points.

A Bradshaw was the only satisfactory way of doing this as the timetable was 100% independent, and no railway company in its senses would quote a competitor's route. For example, you could go from, say, Stafford to London direct via the LMS main line or you could take the LNER's old Great Northern train and travel a very long way round via Uttoxeter, Derby, Nottingham and Grantham to King's Cross. Or even worse (or better), go from Swansea (St Thomas) to London (St Pancras) on the Midland via Brecon, Hereford, Birmingham New Street and Leicester.

Bradshaw is railway history. It began as a purely local timetable (for the north of England) in 1838, but the first real Guide came out in two parts, north and south, in 1839. The name of the month (October) was not shown as Bradshaw was a Quaker and the Society of Friends did not approve of pagan names in the calendar. The actual date of the first national guide was shown as 10th Mo. 19th 1839.

The first one-volume Railway Guide came out in December 1841 and despite religious scruples was dated 'For December 1841'. The only known extant copy is in the Bodleian Library, Oxford.

At first only the main stations were listed but, with the increase in the number of lines, from 1856 all stations were shown in the index. Perhaps in an attempt to economise, the size of type was reduced, making it difficult to read; matters did not improve until 1909.

The original price was sixpence, a considerable sum in those early days. But by attracting good advertising within its pages (the advertisements alone are worth collecting) this price was held until 1916 when it became a shilling. By the outbreak of World War II the price was 7s 6d and 10s in 1955.

By 1960 the Bradshaw was dead. BR produced its own standard timetable; there were no minor railways except those in preservation, and the endearing idiosyncrasies were all gone.

Bradshaw's main rival was the ABC or Alphabetical Railway Guide, which began publication in 1853, though others like the Intelligible Railway Guide came close after. Bradshaw also published a Continental Guide, but this was very much outdone by Cook's Continental Timetable, still available today.

Bradshaw had its difficulties – its notes were often confusing, and sometimes it dropped howlers. One of the best was in 1936 when it noted that the 10.45 from Paddington had a 'Buffer Car'.

Bradshaws are pure nostalgia, so if you want to make a journey but into time, choose your period and your Bradshaw and just sit by the fireside with the bishop.

Collecting Bradshaws

These timetables can be obtained in varying degrees of rarity and price from most of the better secondhand specialist railway book dealers (rather than bookshops which usually don't stock them).

Generally the older they are the more expensive they will be. However, you might find editions from 1850–75 are rarer and therefore slightly more valuable than those from the first decade as it seems they had by then lost their novelty value and were discarded more readily.

History at your fingertips – a selection of Bradshaws from 1880, 1914, 1925 and 1961. Note how the earlier two designate the date of issue as, for example, 1st Mo. (January), reflecting the Quaker publisher's reticence at printing pagan calendar months.

The Cambrian line

SHREWSBURY · PWLLHELI

There is much to relish on this journey into the heart of Wales, from rolling green hills to medieval castles which once guarded the shore. And, if you have time, pause to explore some of the fine narrow gauge railways that run in these parts.

Once, not so long ago, the Cambrian Coast Express left Euston in the late afternoon with through coaches for Aberystwyth via Shrewsbury. Before that it was a morning train out of Paddington behind a glistening green King or Castle with coaches not only for Aberystwyth but also for stations to Pwllheli. Today you have to change at Shrewsbury on to a modern Sprinter with radio-controlled signalling all the way.

The Sprinter is comfortable but there is no chance to see ahead in a modern diesel multiple unit (DMU), so you must decide which side to sit as far as Dovey Junction. While there is still time – colour light signalling has yet to be installed at Shrewsbury – watch out for the huge ex-London & North Western Railway (LNWR) signalbox in the triangle of tracks on the left after leaving the station. This has always been a tremendous railway landmark which has recently been listed.

Within minutes the line swings right on to what was once a joint line belonging to the LNWR and the Great Western Railway (GWR), and the multiple unit makes tracks for Welshpool. There are so many interesting possible jumping off points on

▼A steam special makes its way along the mile long Barmouth Bridge which crosses the Mawddach estuary. At the end of the viaduct are two steel spans. At one time the swing bridge allowed shipping up the river. This section of the bridge was used in the making of the film *Ghost Train* where the villains and their train are plunged into the river, although a model was used for the actual drop.

A rare sight
As you travel on the Cambrian line, you may be lucky enough to catch a glimpse of a red kite hanging motionless on the wind. A slim-winged bird of prey, the red kite once thrived throughout Britain, but it was persecuted to the brink of extinction during the last century and as a result is now found only in the oak-wooded hillsides of central Wales. However, numbers are increasing year by year.

TRAVEL FACTS

Line length: 119 miles (191km)
Journey time: 3½ hours
Frequency: seven trains daily, change usually required at Machynlleth.

the way that the journey can be done in one fell swoop or in a series of hops with diversions. This is worth pondering on as the train passes the earthworks of the old Shropshire & Montgomeryshire Light Railway and makes off towards the Breidden Hills which rise 1202ft (366m) to the right.

Half an hour out of Shrewsbury the train reaches Welshpool, whose station building – a lovely old Oswestry & Newtown Railway structure – is still intact. In the good old days you walked out of the station building to find the Welshpool & Llanfair narrow gauge railway, a 2ft 6in gauge line running to Llanfair Caereinion. This was

▲ A locomotive carrying the Cambrian Coast Express nameboard cuts a path through the green hills of the Welsh countryside. Apart from having a good supply of narrow gauge lines to satisfy the railway enthusiast, central Wales is a mecca for the energetic walker.

known as the farmers' line because the trains took coal out to the villages and hamlets and brought back sheep for Welshpool market. Today there is no train in the station square but from Easter to early October passenger trains do run on this preserved line.

From Welshpool the single line track continues beyond the Marches and into Wales proper: past Abermule, scene of a head-on collision of two trains in 1921; through Newtown, which still retains its old Oswestry & Newtown Railway buildings; via Caersws, and then up towards the summit in the hills at Talerddig. From here the line twists down on a steep, wooded embankment towards Cemmaes Road and a first glimpse of the

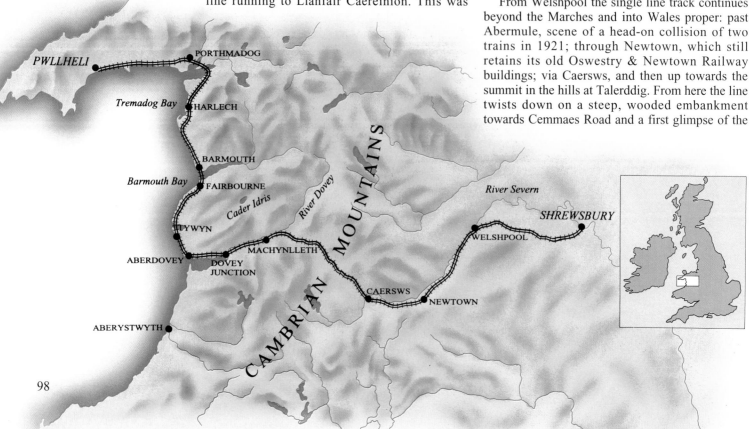

Worm-eaten

In the spring of 1980 some of the wooden piles supporting Barmouth Bridge were found to have been destroyed by the shipworm *Teredo*. About 70 piles among the 117 spans were affected and the structure was weakened so much that the bridge was closed.

Repairs costing £1½ million were started immediately. By the end of 1981 diesel units were allowed back over the bridge, but the heavier locomotive-hauled trains had to wait until 1986.

Further modernisation has included radio signalling and automatic crossings.

▼ The Class 150 DMU winds along the coast near the village of Penhelig. Along much of the route the Cambrian line acts as the sea wall, protecting the coastline from erosion. Though most people make the journey on a modern Sprinter, special steam journeys have been run on the line.

River Dovey. Cemmaes Road is a typical GWR country station name – the railway could not get near enough to the village to call the station by just its name, hence the addition of Road.

Before long you reach Machynlleth – on the left of which are the remains of an old engine shed. Loco crews still book on at Machynlleth, either working back to Shrewsbury, going on to Aberystwyth or travelling along the coastline to Pwllheli via Barmouth. Machynlleth was the seat of Owain Glyndwr's Welsh parliament in the early 15th century and in 1991 the town celebrated the 700th anniversary of its market charter, granted in 1291.

It is only a few minutes over the marshy estuary to Dovey Junction, a bleak, windswept island platform, where the track divides, the DMU taking the right fork for the coastal route. Even in summer this lonely spot at the head of the Dovey estuary can be rather windy.

The Coast line

From here on it is better to sit on the left-hand side of the coach for the Coast line – so named because it never moves far away from the water's edge on its way to Pwllheli. As the Sprinter clacks its way towards the sea the tidal waters of the Dovey widen out. The far bank recedes further and further into the distance with the tiny holiday village of Borth just visible as a series of dark smudges on the landscape. The train twists its way along the northern shore, riding over low stone embankments with the sand and water just below, and stopping at a couple of rural halts as it goes.

Past Picnic Island there is a climb up to Aberdovey – the jewel in the crown of mid Wales

▲The Cambrian line runs past Harlech Castle, which was built to hold down a turbulent Wales. The castle played an important part in numerous battles, including the Wars of the Roses in the 15th century.

holiday resorts, with a forest of masts from small boats and yachts which crowd the harbour and front. There is a steep climb up through a tunnel before emerging at Penhelig Halt, a typical Great Western wooden platform, where passengers alight for the harbour and that end of the small town.

Then it's down through another tunnel to sea level and into Aberdovey station itself. The station is to the north of the town and adjacent to the sand dunes which mask a continuous view of Cardigan Bay. Standing proud on a small cliff is the Treffeddian Hotel, family run for generations, and popular with golfers and holidaymakers who still stop to watch the train go by, even if it is now just a humble multiple unit.

Get ready at Tywyn to see the Wharf terminus of the Talyllyn Railway – there may be a 2ft 3in gauge train in the station waiting to make its slow but charming way up the valley of the Afon Fathew to Dolgoch Falls and Abergynolwyn terminus. You need a full day to explore the Talyllyn Railway – the first in the world to be taken over and run successfully by enthusiasts. This forms the basis of the Skarloey Railway of the Reverend Awdry's Thomas the Tank Engine books and a trundle up the valley at an average speed of around 15mph (24km/h) is a journey when time has almost stood still.

Along the sea's edge

Beyond Tywyn the railway runs beside the edge of the sea where huge rocks piled up as defences against high tides are spread out along the base of the small coastal embankment, a costly but vital piece of civil engineering work. On the right marshlands turn into green fields which in turn lead to green hills with the mountains of the Cader Idris range in the far distance.

A small estuary with an army type Bailey

▶ **The Cambrian Coast Express enters Machynlleth from the east. The engine, 4-6-0 No 7819** *Hinton Manor,* **was taken out of regular service in 1965, and preserved on the Severn Valley Railway, but has operated steam specials over the Cambrian line. Out of 30 Manors built by the Great Western Railway and British Railways, nine are preserved.**

bridge over the river runs parallel to the line and leads to the remains of Tonfanau army camp, once home to thousands of conscripts and territorials. The train climbs up along the cliff edge and drops down to the stone cottages of Llwyngwril, a little inland. There is another climb up the cliff, this time high up above the blue sea with the Lleyn Peninsula and journey's end just visible across the hazy bay.

Down into Fairbourne

High up on the rocky ledge the DMU rattles through the only avalanche tunnel in the British Isles. Before it was built, this was the scene of two nasty accidents when trains were flung down on to the rocks below by bouncing boulders. The train then makes its way to the single-platformed station at Fairbourne.

Here is another small railway, technically a miniature one built originally to the 15in gauge and rebuilt to 12¼in using replica locomotives from famous narrow gauge railways the world over. This line runs along the dunes to Penryn Point opposite Barmouth's small harbour on the other bank of the Mawddach estuary. There is a regular ferry service to meet trains and the trip across the swirling waters of the estuary brings the tang of seaweed to your nostrils.

'Finest sight in all Wales'

On now over more marshland to Morfa Mawddach – once known as Barmouth Junction because from here the Cambrian line branched off to Dolgellau-Dolgelley to meet the GWR's branch from Ruabon head on.

The train swings left as if to drop into the estuary itself. As you travel over a stone embankment to start the long rumble over a superb trestle viaduct crossing the river, look to your right – Cader Idris rises black and forbidding, its summit often covered by cloud – a truly marvellous view. A footpath accompanies the line over the bridge where fishermen sit ever hopeful, and as the DMU moves slowly towards the other side reflect on the words of George Borrow that 'this is the finest sight in all Wales'.

Then it's through a small tunnel, along a concrete trestle overlooking a small harbour on the left, through sand dunes, towards a level crossing and into the two-platformed station. Barmouth is an excellent holiday and sea fishing spot, and well worth a stop-over just to explore the estuary.

The line climbs into the scrubby coastal plain beyond Llanbedr & Pensarn station with Shell Island on the left; myriad pink and white shells lie there just for the collecting. Ten minutes more and Harlech Castle comes into view, again on the left, perched high above the town. The Sprinter moves across the marshy Morfa Harlech, past Talsarnau

Halt with views of Clough Williams-Ellis's Italianate Portmeirion on the left and the Vale of Ffestiniog to the right, the line paralleling a wooden road toll bridge. The train rounds the bend into Penrhyndeudraeth where at one-time trains picked up the empty vans of explosives used in nearby quarries.

Minffordd station

It's a steep climb from here to Minffordd where you can change for the narrow gauge Ffestiniog Railway en route to Blaenau Ffestiniog. The old exchange point for freight between the two railways is on the left as the train leaves the station, though the little railway itself passes over the south end of the platform by an overbridge. Walk up the ramp and you are in another world. Minffordd is also the station for Portmeirion – well worth a few days' stay.

Round the north coast of Traeth Bach, with the high mountains of Snowdonia glowering in the sun or invisible in the Welsh wet, to Porthmadog. This handsome harbour town was developed in the 19th century as a port for the export of slates brought down from the Blaenau quarries deep in the Moelwyn mountains.

The train makes its way over more coastal scrubland to Criccieth and its 13th century castle, through Afon Wen which once made a junction with the London Midland & Scottish line to Bangor, ending up in Pwllheli – gateway to the Lleyn Peninsula, the most westerly stretch of land in north Wales and journey's end.

Talyllyn Railway

The narrow gauge Talyllyn Railway, taken over by preservationists in 1951, is famed for being the first enthusiast-operated railway in the world. First opened in 1865 as a passenger and slate-carrying line, the Talyllyn Railway never prospered.

The company owned two locomotives built by Fletcher-Jennings of Whitehaven. The first was 0-4-2 saddle tank No 1 *Talyllyn* built in 1864, while No 2 *Dolgoch* (1866), shown here, was an 0-4-0 tank with a long wheelbase. This engine was renamed *Pretoria* during the Boer War.

A journey on the Mixto

GUAYAQUIL • ALAUSI • (QUITO)

**The Mixto must be one of the world's most exciting –
and most chaotic – trains to travel on. Running from flat
coastal plains outside Guayaquil and up into the high Andes,
the railway was built against all the odds to connect Ecuador's
capital, Quito, to the teeming sea port of Guayaquil.**

Until recently the Guayaquil & Quito line (G&Q) was the only regular steam-run railway in the Andes. These days it is outpaced by a modern road and, to add insult to injury, the line is frequently severed by landslides. However, being cheaper than the bus, the railway still acts as a lifeline for the mountain people, transporting livestock and goods to and from market, and it is a wonderful journey for those tourists brave enough to take it.

While the rest of the world was slowly but steadily replacing its steam engines with diesels, the G&Q – quite unintentionally – was doing the opposite. On a good day up to seven Baldwin 2-6-0 and 2-8-0 steam locomotives, fired by oil from wells in the upper Amazon, were active and the last of the railway's original diesels rarely rumbled out of its shed.

It was not meant to be like that. In 1970, 12 American-built diesels arrived to lay the G&Q's steam locos to rest and revitalise what was a rather haphazard service. The old Baldwins were shunted into sidings and left to rot under the creeping vegetation. At last it seemed that long delays for frequent engine repairs and replacements would be over. Not a bit of it. Instead of hauling their loads

▼ An American-built Baldwin 2-8-0 steam engine heads the train on its way through the Andes. Although it may start the journey from Duran pulled by a 2-6-0, the stronger 2-8-0 always takes over from Bucay for the mountainous climb.

▶The oil-fired Baldwin 2-8-0 No 44 in grimy red livery wheezes and clanks its way up the high street in the town of Milagro. The Mixto acts as a lifeline to the villages and towns it passes through, transporting oil, animals and produce to and from market.

TRAVEL FACTS

Line length: Duran to Alausi 87 miles (140km); Duran to Quito 276 miles (445km)
Journey time: 6 to 7 hours
Frequency: daily

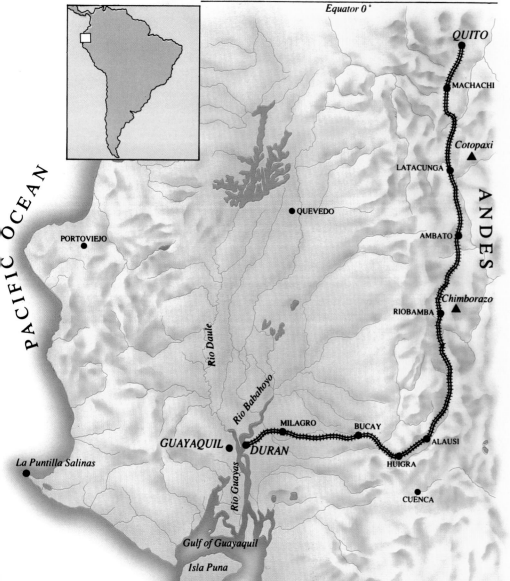

up to heights of 11,500ft (3500m) all the way to Quito, the diesels repeatedly coughed and choked and broke down, and within less than a decade two-thirds of them had given up the ghost. The major problems were lack of power, spare parts and indifferent maintenance.

In 1980 only three were still in operation, and with the cannibalisation of the other seven, now lying useless in the sheds at Duran, two of them made it through the next decade. However, by 1995 the arrival of diesel locomotives from France changed the traction scene again and steam is now only available by special charter.

Steam's swansong

Over the last two decades the Baldwins were literally dug out of retirement and hastily overhauled to tackle once again the 1 in 15 slopes to the plateau at Alausi. The remaining diesel, when operational, stayed on the flat line between the starting point of Duran and the town of Bucay, where the great climb begins.

The railway does not enter the port of Guayaquil – instead the terminus is at nearby Duran on the east bank of the River Guayas. During the steam era of the 1980s, the line to Quito was repeatedly blocked by landslides and part of the journey was undertaken by bus with railcars only in use from Riobamba to the capital city.

The Mixto comprises a haphazard series of up to seven wooden carriages and trucks crammed to the gills with sugar cane, bananas, chickens and pigs, with most of the travellers choosing to ride on the roof.

A gentle start

The first stage of its path from coastal Duran crosses flat, lush farmland where houses are built on blocks – for fear of snakes – amid field upon field of sugar cane and maize. The people wear a mixture of western dress and traditional South American costume, with women in bright red cloaks carrying multi-coloured sacks of wares for market on their backs.

In Bucay, a few hours by train from Duran, the Baldwins are still stabled in open sheds where the couch grass runs wild, pushing the track up and outwards like a fairground switchback. Bucay station is just a large building in a line of shops which opens on to a muddy road of sleeping dogs and arguing farmers. No one worries about the engines hissing laboriously up the high street, often at an angle of 20° on the twisted track.

The engine, with Ferrocarriles Ecuatorianos in large letters on the tender and proudly bearing its brass plate proclaiming 'The Baldwin Locomotive Works, Philadelphia, USA', was red or green or black – or all three. It was usually filthy. It

▲ The train swings round a corner and the famous Devil's Nose – a mountain ending in a perpendicular ridge rising from a deep gorge to a height of 8000ft (2440m) – comes into view. The railway conquers the mountain by a series of switchbacks over the very steep grade.

wheezed and clanked to itself while the villagers loaded the coaches with vegetables, fruit and livestock, often hauling squealing black pigs on to the roof to be tethered for the journey.

In high spirits

On one notable occasion the driver lurched on to the engine, obviously far too overcome by a party the previous night to drive. The whole town was treated to a spirited argument between driver and fireman about who was fit enough to handle the engine over the long and arduous route. The fireman won and the driver spent the whole journey sleeping, cuddling a bunch of bananas like a lost love, or back-seat driving from the tender. It's a mark of the South American's easy-going manner that no one for one moment considered leaving him behind to be spotted and have his pay docked by the authorities.

From Bucay the train immediately lurches into the Andes for two hours of frantic delight, with rooftop passengers ducking down to avoid sweeping branches of trees, choking through the tight, pitch black tunnels where the smoke penetrates every pore, and coughing in the fog and mist which often wreaths the mountains and streams along the way. The line follows the Chanchan river through equatorial rainforest echoing with parrot calls and looped with hanging vines, and up to more barren pastures where the pale coloured scree is dotted with hardy vegetation.

This route is also the villagers' main pathway

◄ Now and again on the journey the engine grinds to a halt where the track gang is at work. Irregular timetables mean that the driver needs to keep a sharp lookout for maintenance crews.

▲The angle of Baldwin 2-8-0 No 43 coming off the shed at Bucay reflects the precarious state of the track on parts of the G&Q. The water tower behind the locomotive was at one time supplemented by a reservoir made from a water tank off one of the two Garratts that once worked on the line.

Slipping and sliding
Ever since the Guayaquil & Quito line opened in 1908 it has been dogged by problems. For example, two American engineers, brothers John and Harman Archer, had to rebuild the line in 1928 after a devastating earthquake.

Apart from the everyday landslides, a more recent disaster to befall the G&Q line was the storms of 1984 which washed away parts of the line between Alausi and Riobamba. The same fate recently befell the Cuenca branch, which is now closed.

into the mountains, and a dangerous walk for those who attempt it. Through tunnels, across lattice bridges and along precipices, there is no room for a pedestrian to stand by and let the train go past. The only way is to flag it down and ride on the front until the next possible passing point.

The length of each halt at tiny stations along the way can vary from a few minutes to half an hour or so, while the engine takes water from wooden water towers constructed beside mountain streams. One of the reasons these sturdy little engines have lasted so long is the lack of corrosion or scaling in their boilers because the water is taken from the clear, pure melted snow which cascades down the hillsides.

At each station the 70 or so travellers, sitting crosslegged on the carriage roofs, can take their choice of pasta, rice, bacon and eggs or buns and fruit from the bustling buffet stalls. Children trot up and down the train, inside and out, delivering and collecting plates to save people from losing their seats. The children even run up and down the line all day to collect plates from the next station up if the stop was too short for the passengers to finish their meal before leaving.

All around are sheer cliffs, occasionally masked by mountain mist, eucalyptus and bamboo, and the calls of strange birds in the distance. The route climbs 10,000ft (3050m) into the hills, with the train chortling and jerking over astonish-

ing bridges of wooden posts, sleepers and track before diving into yet another endless tunnel. At Huigra the Baldwin keeps full speed up the high street, making good use of its chime whistle to clear the path ahead. The gradient is still 1 in 15 and to slow down for pedestrians might mean having to stop altogether.

Conquering the Devil's Nose
It is after Huigra that the Mixto faces its greatest challenge – the Nariz del Diablo or Devil's Nose. This conical mountain blocks the end of the valley floor between Huigra and Alausi with almost sheer cliffsides. The only way of climbing the 1 in 15 slope is for the Mixto to zigzag backwards and forwards up one side of the 8000ft (2440m) mountain. It is a slow, laborious process, with conductor and fireman clambering off and on the engine to change points and supervise the clearances.

It's almost a trundle from the Devil's Nose to journey's end, Alausi, at 10,000ft (3048m), getting colder and more barren by the minute. At last the engine steams into the high street of the little town and stops, wheezing, at the place guaranteed to cause the most chaos for traffic, and occupy pride of place for the night.

This was the inconvenient end of working in the 1980s. Following reversal, the locomotive would return with the same train, starting the long journey south the next morning.

Railway guide books

Railway companies published guide books to the beauty spots which lay within their territory to boost traffic and to increase their share of the holiday trade. An early example is *The Tourist Hand Book For Ireland* published in 1852 by the Chester & Holyhead Railway.

The end of the 19th century saw a great increase in the numbers of such books. The newly built West Highland Railway published *Mountain Moor and Loch* 'Illustrated by Pen and Pencil' in 1894, with a second edition in 1895.

Improvements in photographic reproduction meant that illustrations could be used to much greater effect. In 1895, the Cambrian Railways brought out *A Souvenir. Gems of Picturesque Scenery in Wild Wales. 55 Views.*, priced sixpence. The Great Eastern Railway (GER) published *Photo Pictures in East Anglia.*

At the cheaper end of the market there are the paper-bound booklets, often with very colourful covers, such as the North Eastern Railway's *Summer Resorts* series, including *Teesdale and District* of 1897 and *Tynedale and the Roman Wall District* of 1898, both priced threepence.

Several lines published their own variation of the GER's *Farmhouse and Country Lodgings*, offering accommodation at budget prices.

The London, Brighton & South Coast Railway (LBSCR) published *The South Downs* by The Tramp, a booklet that was to run to many editions. Indeed, the Southern Railway continued to produce it after Grouping. The LBSCR, in true international spirit, also produced *Picturesque Normandy* priced one shilling, as well as a slim paperback, *South Coast Holidays*, which extolled the virtues of England's south coast and was printed in English, German and French.

The most prolific publisher was the Great Western Railway (GWR), beginning in the early 1900s with an admirable series of books by A M Broadley (who first coined the phrase 'Glorious Devon'). Later, the GWR commissioned the redoubtable walker and author S P B Mais to write *The Cornish Riviera* and *Glorious Devon*.

Collecting railway guide books

Secondhand bookshops are probably the best source of railway guide books. Those produced by the Great Western, London Midland & Scottish, London & North Eastern, Southern and BR are quite common, as are the publications of the London Underground companies. Although more scarce, pre-Grouping publications can still be found, including some real bargains.

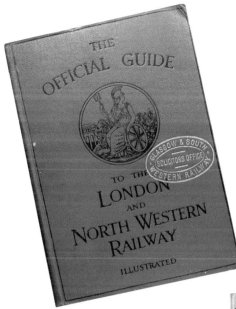

Top left: *The Official Guide to the London and North Western Railway,* first published in 1885, reached its 18th edition in 1912, when this copy was printed.

Top centre: *The North British & Highland Railways' Tourist Guide,* published in 1911, contains many advertisements for hotels.

Top right: The North British Railway's *Fort-William to Mallaig* first appeared in 1901, the year the line opened.

Bottom: The final *Official A.B.C. Tourist Guide to the Highlands of Scotland via the Highland Railway* came out in 1922.

Narrow gauge into the Harz

GERNRODE • ALEXISBAD • HARZGERODE • HASSELFELDE • EISFELDER TALMÜHLE

The narrow gauge lines through the Harz Mountains have a complicated history, with many branches and options for travellers. The scenery is some of the best in Germany and the trains may be diesel or steam hauled.

Quedlinburg, in Germany's eastern Harz, is a town where the spirit of the Middle Ages lingers. Narrow streets with timber-framed houses are overshadowed by a hilltop castle. East of the medieval centre is the railway station, and taking the 09.43 Deutsche Reichsbahn (DR) service to Gernrode, hauled by a maroon B-B diesel of Class 201, is a leisurely start to a day in the hills.

Gernrode's imposing, patterned brick station is reached after a 15 minute journey on to the wooded flanks of the Harz. Situated just across the road is the metre gauge station of the Harzer Schmalspurbahnen (HSB), the new name for the 81 mile (130km) Harz narrow gauge network since the local authorities took over the system from the DR on 1 February 1993 (averting a likely

closure threat). Through booking is no longer possible, and the three-minute connection allows you scant time to buy a ticket from the single-storey building, formerly used as DR staff quarters, that has now been refurbished as the HSB booking office and shop.

Locomotives standing outside the engine shed are visible from the red-and-cream coaches of the narrow gauge train. As well as the 2-10-2Ts and C-C diesels that work most services, there may also be 0-6-0T No 99.6102-0, built by Henschel in 1914, and 2-6-2T No 21 (previously No 99-6001-4), delivered by Krupp in 1939 to the Nordhausen-Wernigeroder Eisenbahn (NWE). Sometimes you can even see the Harz line's most unusual locomotive – 0-4-4-0T tram Fairlie No 99.162, built by

▼ **Bunker first, 0-6-0T No 99.6101 drifts down the steep gradients of the 1⁴/₅ mile (2.9km) Harzgerode branch, opened as an extension from Mägdesprung in 1888.**

The 81 mile (130km) Harzer Schmalspurbahnen (HSB) narrow gauge network was taken over from the Deutsche Reichsbahn (DR) by the local authorities on 1 February 1993, averting possible closure.

◀ This picture of 2-10-2T
No 99.7222-5 at Eisfelder
Talmühle was taken in 1992, so
there are Deutsche Reichsbahn
(DR) plates on the engine. The
2-10-2T was a standard DR
design, with 17 built in the
1950s, based on this 1931
prototype.

> **Steam in the Selketal**
> The first GHE locomotives
> were six 0-6-0Ts, built
> between 1887 and 1890 by
> Henschel, followed by three
> Borsig 0-4-4-0T Mallets in
> 1905. The only GHE engine
> to survive World War II,
> 0-6-0T *Gernrode*, was
> scrapped in 1967.
>   After the war, motive
> power was provided by
> NWE 2-6-2T No 99.6001-4,
> and six 0-4-4-0T Mallets,
> Nos 99.5901-99.5906, the
> earliest built by Jung in
> 1897. These seven engines
> worked all services until the
> 2-10-2Ts and diesels arrived
> in the 1980s. Two Mallets
> and the 2-6-2T are still
> available for special trains,
> while two more Mallets
> await restoration.

Hartmann in 1902 for a metre gauge line in Saxony.

Working the 10.01 to Harzgerode is 2-10-2T No 99.7236-5, from a class of 17 built in the 1950s by Lokomotivbau Karl Marx, Babelsberg. As the train leaves the station and crosses the main road, the red roofs of Gernrode and the twin spires of the 10th century Stiftskirche St Cyriakus stand out against the wooded slopes of the Harz. Gernrode's name commemorates the Margrave Gero, who died in 965 (*rode* referring to the forest clearing where the town was founded).

Skirting the banks

The train winds past orchards and gardens up to the Osterteich, a small lake popular with swimmers in summer, and served by a request stop. The line then enters the woods, a mix of evergreen and deciduous trees, which enclose much of the route. Climbing on a ledge through the valley of the Wellbach, a mountain stream, the train is soon skirting another lake, the Heiligenteich.

Following the stream, the line curves through the woods on 1 in 30 gradients, well away from the nearest road. Sternhaus-Haferfeld is a request stop 3¾ miles (6km) from Gernrode. It was once a passing place with a rustic station building, but now there is just a bare gravel platform by a level crossing where the valley opens out a little. Another kilometre uphill is Sternhaus-Ramberg, at 1355ft (413m) the summit of this section. This stop is 663ft (202m) above Gernrode, and a popular starting point for woodland rambles.

The train now plunges downhill, with the locomotive visible from the carriages round the sharp curves. On a summer evening, standing on the rear balcony of the last train back to Gernrode is quite an experience, as the locomotive attacks the 1 in

25 gradients, with the low sunshine filtering through the trees and swirling smoke. Towards the bottom of the bank, the ruins of the 13th century Heinrichsburg Castle surmount a hill to the left, just before the two crossings over the main road that precede arrival at Mägdesprung.

The big station building here, sited on a curve, was the first terminus of the line from Gernrode. Plans for railways in this part of the Harz date back to 1853, but no progress was made until the standard gauge reached Gernrode in 1885, prompting the founding of the Gernrode Harzgeroder Eisenbahngesellschaft (GHE) in

▼ No 99.5902-4 hauls a train bound for Alexisbad near Drahtzug. Typical of many sections of Continental narrow gauge lines, the line here runs alongside a road. The Mallets are now confined to special trains; before the introduction of the 2-10-2Ts in the 1980s they worked most services.

1886. The opening of the 6⅓ mile (10.2km) Gernrode – Mägdesprung section on 7 August 1887 made it the first metre gauge line in the Harz.

The journey to Mägdesprung takes the train over a ridge into the valley of the River Selke. The railway follows the river all the way to Stiege, giving it the popular name of Selketalbahn (Selke Valley Railway). Leaving Mägdesprung, with the village visible through the trees, the train winds round minimum radius curves along a hillside ledge above the river and road. Drahtzug Halt lies in a narrow wooded valley and the tortuous route goes on through rocky cuttings, climbing gradually as the valley widens. Its bell clanging furiously, the train crosses the road, then runs alongside it into the pleasant resort of Alexisbad.

Waiting in Alexisbad station is the 09.10 Hasselfelde – Gernrode train, hauled by C-C diesel No 199.892-1. This ungainly machine is a standard gauge B-B locomotive, like the ones working between Quedlinburg and Gernrode, but on metre gauge bogies. Ten engines were

▼ ▶ The HSB's only 2-6-2T, No 99.6001-4, on the climb from Alexisbad towards Harzgerode (right), and at Gernrode station (below – the standard gauge station is to the right, out of shot). No 99.6001-4 was delivered to the Nordhausen-Wernigeroder Eisenbahn (NWE) by Krupp in 1939. The outbreak of World War II meant that no more were built. Since these pictures were taken it has been renumbered No 21 and now sports a green livery.

along a wooded ledge above the river and road through attractive low, rolling hills, with watchtowers guarding the pines. Strassberg, with its prominent grey church tower, is a neat village across the Selke. The river here once formed the boundary between Anhalt and Prussia, and until 1952 the station was called Lindenberg after the tiny community on its side of the Selke.

In 1946, most of the GHE was dismantled as war reparations for the USSR. Rebuilt by the surviving workers, it reopened in 1949 from Gernrode to Harzgerode and Strassberg, but the continuation to Stiege was not rebuilt. However, in 1972, when the German Democratic Republic's Transport Ministry gave the Harz narrow gauge a long-term future with protected status, it was accepted that the Strassberg – Stiege link should be rebuilt. This would allow standard gauge wagons to reach Silberhütte from Nordhausen on metre gauge transporters, not possible from Gernrode because of the sharp curves and limited clearances. The DR's surviving narrow gauge goods wagons could then be abandoned, along with costly transhipment at Gernrode. The DR, which had absorbed the GHE in 1949, rebuilt the line. It reopened for goods traffic in 1983 and passengers in 1984.

Beyond Strassberg, the line follows a quiet valley with few signs of human activity bar treeplanting and felling. Little remains of the 1 mile (1.5km) branch to the Herzogschacht fluorspar

TRAVEL FACTS

Line length: Gernrode – Eisfelder Talmühle, 28½ miles (46km); Alexisbad – Harzgerode, 2 miles (3km); Stiege – Hasselfelde 3 miles (5km)
Duration: Gernrode – Harzgerode, about 1hr; Gernrode – Eisfelder Talmühle, 2hr 20min
Frequency: Gernrode – Harzgerode, 5 returns daily (1 involving change at Alexisbad); Gernrode – Stiege, 3 returns daily; Stiege – Hasselfelde, 4 returns daily; Stiege – Eisfelder Talmühle, 3 returns daily
Reservations: groups only; 3-day rover tickets are available for both the Selketalbahn (Gernrode – Harzgerode – Hasselfelde) and the whole HSB

regauged in the late 1980s, out of 30 conversions planned for the full dieselisation of the Harz narrow gauge. Currently, trains are steam or diesel worked at random.

Alexisbad is a junction and, after taking on water, No 99.7236-5 curves left on to the 1 in 30 gradients of the 1⁴/₅ mile (2.9km) branch to Harzgerode, opened as an extension from Mägdesprung in 1888. This attractive little line winds through woods and clearings, curving up the rocky hillside before approaching Harzgerode past a small lake. The terminus has a typical GHE twostorey building just by the 16th century castle. Before the return journey you have nearly an hour in which to explore the town, which for centuries has been the focal point of the Lower Harz.

Through fields and woods

If you take the train back to Alexisbad there is just time for lunch in the station buffet before the 12.01 Gernrode – Eisfelder Talmühle service arrives, hauled by 2-10-2T No 99.7233-2 (built in 1954). Beyond Alexisbad the Selke valley is broader, a gentle climb through fields and woods to Silberhütte, a rural industrial centre with sawmills, a large fireworks factory and several abandoned sidings, reached by the GHE in 1889. From 1887 to 1909 a 750mm gauge industrial railway, worked by a Krauss 0-4-0T, ran 2⁴/₅ miles (4.5km) south to the lead and iron mines at Neudorf, connecting with the GHE by cable incline.

Leaving Silberhütte, the train passes the siding to the disused central boiler house, once the destination of much coal traffic. The track continues

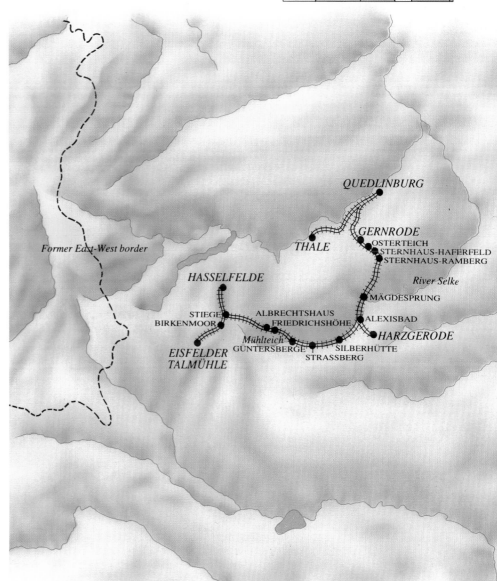

▲ C-C diesel No 199.877-2 climbs away from Alexisbad with a Gernrode – Brocken service. A standard gauge B-B locomotive on metre gauge bogies, it needs 12 wheels on the narrow gauge line, rather than the usual 8. Ten engines were regauged in the late 1980s.

Rocket power

After Fritz von Opel reached 143mph (230km/h) at Berlin's Avus Ring in a car propelled by 24 firework-style dry-powder rockets, the German engineer Max Valier formed a partnership with Herr Meyer-Hellige, proprietor of the Eisfeld firework factory at Silberhütte, to conduct similar experiments.

In June 1928 a rocket-propelled light wooden railcar is said to have briefly touched 130mph (210km/h) on the GHE before crashing. A similar standard gauge vehicle attained 157mph (253km/h) on the nearby Halberstadt – Blankenburg railway before Valier's death in a rocket explosion in 1930.

mine, which replaced a horse-worked tramway.

Güntersberge station opened in 1890 with the extension from Silberhütte. It serves another pleasant village of red-roofed half-timbered houses and Güntersburg Castle ruins are on a hill nearby. Beyond the station the train skirts the Mühlteich, a reservoir formed by damming the Selke, before hurrying through the woods, passing the request stops of Friedrichshöhe and Albrechtshaus in quick succession. After negotiating some low shale cuttings the railway emerges from the forest plantations on to an upland plateau, with extensive views of the undulating moorland and woods ahead.

Cattle graze by the track as the train, with only a few passengers now left on board, drops into a grassy hollow, passing a small lake as it enters Stiege, where the GHE arrived in 1891. A short walk through the town brings you to the castle, dating from 1202 and overlooking another lake, where boats can be hired. Your train changes direction at Stiege, either by running round in the station or by travelling over the circular turning loop, installed when the line was rebuilt.

The track continuing straight ahead, past the turning loop, is the 3 mile (5km) Hasselfelde branch. This was the last section of the original GHE to be built, and it opened in 1892. It climbs to a low ridge just outside Stiege, then descends round sweeping reverse curves through an open, pastoral landscape, approaching the terminus

alongside the main road. Deer can be seen in the fields and there are fine distant views of the Brocken and the main chain of the Harz.

The route to Eisfelder Talmühle follows a $5^2/_3$ mile (9km) link opened in 1905 to connect the GHE and the NWE, though it closed for several months in the economic crisis of the 1920s. From 1946 to the 1980s, when no trains ran between Stiege and Strassberg, Eisfelder Talmühle – Hasselfelde was a branch of the Harzquerbahn.

Leaving Stiege, the train climbs steeply for 2 miles (3km), first past open fields, then on an embankment through the woods, to Birkenmoor, a halt in the forest clearing used mainly by walkers. The summit here is the highest point on the Selketalbahn, at 1716ft (523)m. From Birkenmoor the train drops into the narrow, steep-sided valley of the Behre, running on a ledge high above the stream. Imposing pines darken the landscape as the train cautiously descends the 1 in 27 gradients, crossing two side valleys, the Bartschenkulk and Mosebach, by arched bridges.

As the railway drops towards the stream, a siding on the right serves a ballast quarry. Stone from here should contribute towards a revival of goods traffic, all of which has been lost on the HSB since reunification. The line then follows the quarry road downhill, crosses the stream by a low bridge and, with the Harzquerbahn sweeping in alongside the Tiefenbach, enters the junction station of Eisfelder Talmühle.

Steam hauled to Darjeeling

NEW JALPAIGURI • DARJEELING

The only railway to weave its way into the Himalayan massif, the line to Darjeeling offers travellers one of the most exhilarating railway journeys in the world, still using only steam locomotives.

Darjeeling is, of course, synonymous with tea, but writers from Mark Twain to James Cameron have helped to make this small town almost equally famous for the extraordinary railway that intrepid travellers use to reach it. 'So wild and interesting and exciting and enchanting that it ought to take a week', wrote Mark Twain after his journey over the line in 1896. After the 8-8½ hour journey, most travellers would probably demur from such enthusiasm, but nevertheless it is an experience they would not have missed for all the tea they passed on the way.

The creation of the town and its railway resulted from one factor – its location. Situated at 6500-7500ft (1980-2286m) above sea-level, and almost free from endemic diseases, it was chosen in the 1830s as the site for a sanatorium. Its cool climate, coupled with the breathtaking views it provides of the Himalayas, soon attracted government officials and their families as a refuge from the sweltering heat of Lower Bengal. The consequent need for good transport was increased by the rapid growth of tea cultivation following the success of the first garden, which was set up in 1856.

Rapid development

The agent (general manager) of the Eastern Bengal Railway (EBR), Franklin Prestage, was so convinced of the good economic prospects for a railway that he set up and became chairman of the Darjeeling Steam Tramway Co; his plans were approved in 1879 and work began before the end of the same year. The Northern Bengal Railway (NBR) railhead was then at Siliguri, and the intention was to build from it a 2ft (610mm) gauge line, 50¾ miles (82km) long, to the hill station, largely following the Hill Cart Road, which had been completed in 1869. Construction was pursued with such vigour that in March 1880 the Viceroy of India, Lord Lytton, was able to travel the 20 miles

▼ Ghum is the summit of the line, at 7407ft (2258m), and was reached in April 1881. The section from the double spiral at Batasia loop, seen in this shot, down to Darjeeling provides the most impressive views of the journey.

(32km) as far as Tindharia.

On 4 July 1881, the line was formally opened right through to Darjeeling, with a succession of special trains carrying the customary dignitaries, including the Lieutenant-Governor of the Bengal government, Sir Ashley Eden (grandfather of Anthony). Two lavish breakfasts were followed by a banquet at Darjeeling, where speeches were made and 'loyal and patriotic airs' played by a band. The only setbacks to the day were a series of derailments and a landslide that blocked the line – a problem that has continued to bedevil this route ever since.

Prestage's optimism proved fully justified: the railway cut goods tariffs by a half, and journey time to a fifth of that taken by the trudging bullock carts. The Darjeeling Himalayan Railway Co (DHR), as it was renamed shortly after opening, was soon paying an 8% dividend.

New southern terminus

Until 1964, Siliguri remained the interchange station, with metre gauge trains bringing passengers on the final leg of their journey from Calcutta. However, the disruption to established routes caused by the creation of East Pakistan (now Bangladesh), at partition in 1947, necessitated substantial railway construction and reorganisation to restore good links with Assam. Part of this work was the building of a new broad gauge line to New Jalpaiguri, four miles (six kilometres) south of Siliguri. To speed transfers, both the metre gauge and DHR 2ft (610mm) gauge lines were extended to the new station to connect with trains from Calcutta, and elsewhere.

Most rail travellers coming from the south arrive at New Jalpaiguri on the 3143 Darjeeling Mail, which leaves Calcutta Sealdah daily at 19.00

◄ Loop 3 is called Agony Point. A Government Inspector of 1888 doubted 'the wisdom of calling the attention of timid passengers to their seeming danger by the exhibition of boards with alarming placards such as *Sensation Corner, Agony Point,* etc.'

and arrives at New Jalpaiguri, a distance of 360 miles (577km), at 08.30 to connect with the 09.00 departure for Darjeeling. First class passengers can use a saloon, usually at the back of the train, which seats 11 on each side of a central gangway; a seat on the left side as you face the locomotive affords the best views.

Rather than examine the diminutive 0-4-0ST that will haul your train – there will be time enough later – it may be better to spend the last few minutes before departure looking at any broad gauge steam in the vicinity; New Jalpaiguri is the last broad gauge steam depot on the North East Frontier Railway, and you may be lucky enough to see one of its WP Pacifics or WG 2-8-2s on the few remaining steam passenger trains.

The only viaduct

Unfortunately, the engine shed at New Jalpaiguri is set well back from the line, but the quickening chatter of the locomotive's exhaust as the terminus is left behind turns attention to the only flat open views for the whole journey. As far as Siliguri the gradient is level, and from there on remains easy as far as Sukna, where the train is divided up as necessary into portions of up to four coaches for the serious climbing ahead.

At Siliguri Junction you are unlikely to see any metre gauge steam, as it has been almost eliminated in this area. However, in the park at Siliguri is an 0-4-0ST, thought to have been built by Orenstein & Koppel; named *Baby Sivok*, it was used for miscellaneous duties on the DHR. A mile (1600m) north of Siliguri Junction, the DHR

▼ An 0-4-0T returns to its train at Darjeeling. The town's prosperity dates from the mid-19th century, when Lt Napier (Royal Engineers) built a road from the Bengal plains to the mountain village of Darjeeling. Initially a sanatorium, tea plantations did so well here that Darjeeling tea is now known world-wide.

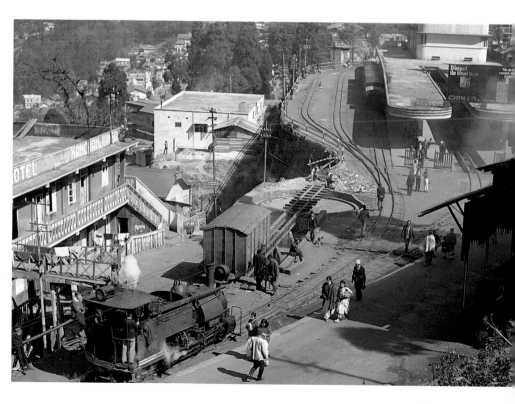

crosses the River Mahanuddy on a seven-span, 690ft (210m) long bridge. For a mountain railway, and to anyone familiar with the lines to Simla or Ootacamund, it is astonishing that this is the only structure of note on the entire line. The ability of the line to follow the Hill Cart Road is one factor, but the principal reason is the way the engineers chose to gain height. They copied the pioneering example of the Semmering line in the eastern Alps, where the line is looped over itself to gain altitude.

The line climbs into a forest of sal and toon trees garlanded with creepers and orchids, through which tea plantations and paddy-fields can be glimpsed. In the early years of the railway, these forests were still home to elephants, tigers, leopards and rhinoceroses; on one occasion a driver pulled up 20yd (18m) from a male elephant stand-

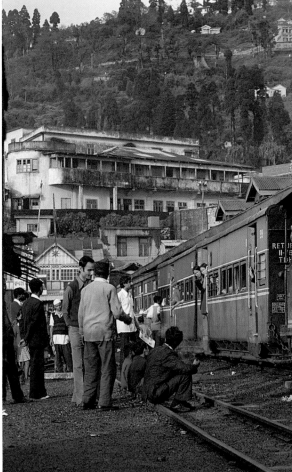

◀ **Locomotive No 779 is seen here on the climb up to Tindharia, 20 miles (32km) from Siliguri. Note the precarious positions of certain passengers. These small engines are labour-intensive, considering their size, and require a crew of five.**

ing four-square on the line, and made a rapid reversal to the previous station.

The splitting of trains at Sukna is a railway photographer's dream, with good opportunities for several bites of the cherry. However, declining traffic has reduced the number of portions from the days when six separate sections would form a procession up the hill, usually keeping just in sight of each other. The stop at Sukna gives passengers an opportunity to stretch their legs and admire the sturdy locomotive that will have to climb 6874ft (2095m) in the next 40 miles (64km) to the summit at Ghum.

Victorian veterans

The oldest of the 17-odd B class 0-4-0ST locomotives still at work on the DHR were built in 1892 by Sharp, Stewart & Co in Glasgow. Later sisters, with differences in detail, were built by the North British Locomotive Co, and three each by Baldwin in Philadelphia, and at the DHR workshops at Tindharia. Despite their small size, weighing only 15 tons, these locomotives have a crew of five: besides the driver and fireman, there is a coal pusher to break up lumps and feed them back to the fireman from the twin bunkers in front of the

◄ Passenger trains no longer stop at Kurseong station for an hour in order for their occupants to enjoy tiffin. Nowadays there is only a 10 minute delay before the engine is reversed out of the station to continue on its journey to the summit at Ghum.

TRAVEL FACTS

Line length: 55 miles (88km)
Duration: 8-8½ hours
Frequency: two trains run each way daily; an additional train, used principally by school children, runs once a day each way between Kurseong and Darjeeling
Reservations: advisable, especially April-May and October-November, which are the most comfortable months in which to travel
Requirements: those travellers visiting Darjeeling by rail (or road) once had to obtain a permit from the Foreigners' Registration Offices at Calcutta, Delhi, Bombay or Madras, although this requirement has now been suspended

washed away by monsoon rains over the years. The frequency and severity of the breaches have increased recently, due to deforestation and to excessive lorry traffic on the adjacent road, which has weakened the structure. Priority is given to mending the road, leading to further loss of traffic from the railway, which is often closed for months on end to through trains.

Now over the 3000ft (914m) level, screw pine, oak and chestnut can be seen on the mountain slopes, soon to be replaced by birch and maple as the line climbs to 4000ft (1219m), the massive scale of the views over the valleys and mountain villages becoming ever more impressive. Another zigzag brings you to a loop known as Agony Point; in the railway's early years passengers were warned not to leave their seats in a rush to enjoy the view here, as this might have pitched the train into the valley. It is easy to see why, since the overhang of the carriages often gives the impression of riding on air, so precipitous is the drop at such points.

Refreshment at Kurseong

After another zigzag you pause at Gayabari station. The line then runs beside the road to a tank filled by the Pagla Jhora (Mad Torrent), where the locomotive's small reserves are replenished. A deep rock-cutting near Mahanadi station opens up a new view of the plains below, before almost incessant whistling accompanies the slow progress through the main street of Kurseong into the terminus platform.

cab, and two men who sit on the buffer beam hand-sanding each rail.

The bark from the engine becomes noticeably fiercer after Sukna. The average gradient to Ghum is 1 in 30½, and the line starts to wind through the forest towards the first loop shortly before the station at Rangtong.

The first giant fir trees appear in the creeper-strewn woods as the railway scales the contour lines of the hills. A water-stop soon after Rangtong precedes the first of five Z-shaped reversing points on the DHR; there was once a tight-radius double loop here, but it was replaced by the zigzag during World War II, when traffic was very heavy. A white-painted board with a large Z heralds the reversing point, at which the locomotive propels its train back up the hill before continuing. This method of scaling mountains is most common in the Andes.

Another loop and zigzag brings the train to Tindharia, where the works can be seen on the left as the line describes a horseshoe bend before passing the large locomotive shed on the right and arriving at Tindharia station. Clamorous calls from the platform vendors tempt hungry passengers to buy tea or snacks before the train leaves to climb to the third loop.

The threat of landslides

Evidence of recent work to stabilise the track formation can be seen beyond Tindharia, though this is but one of many places where the line has been

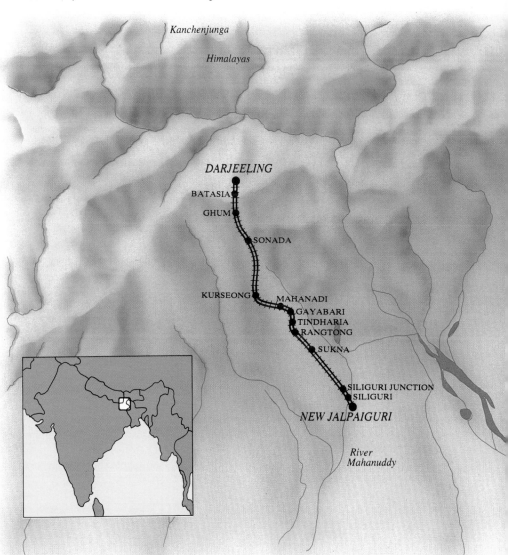

Trains used to stop for an hour at the hill station and former railway headquarters of Kurseong for passengers to take tiffin (lunch) and change into warmer clothes. Now just 10 minutes are allowed for a thorough rake of the fire, yet more water to be taken on and an oil round.

The reversal out of the station and full throttle ascent of the bank out of the town is a bizarre sight, which still arrests the attention of locals, even though they have seen it a thousand times before. The train passes inches from shop fronts through a mêlée of traffic, its whistle and cacophonous exhaust echoing off buildings and the surrounding slopes.

Ghum at the top

Road and railway continue their interlaced ascent, the 132 ungated level crossings on the DHR providing plenty of scope for mishaps, which have been mercifully few. At Sonada there is a siding, which allows two trains to cross by means of one of them reversing into it, and also gives passengers a chance to study the village as the train pauses in the main street.

▲ This Sharp, Stewart & Co 0-4-0, No 779, is one of the oldest locomotives still at work on the DHR. Seen here in 1983, the train is near Ghum, on its way down to Darjeeling. A recently unearthed photograph suggests that at least one of these locomotives was streamlined, although nobody knows why!

Just before the summit at Ghum the train plunges into the town, weaving its way through the wooden buildings to stop in the shadow of a battered corrugated-iron canopy covering the platform. The descent to Darjeeling is no anti-climax, for it is this section that affords the most spectacular views – providing that you are lucky enough to have good visibility.

As you near the celebrated double spiral at Batasia, a panorama of the vast, white Himalayan massif opens up, dominated by Kanchenjunga (28,150ft/8580m) and receding range upon range, as far as the eye can see. Against this pure white backcloth, the fir trees on the promontories around Darjeeling stand out in dark silhouette, as the train descends through the outskirts to the 1930s-style terminus.

Locomotive sales
Amongst the withdrawn DHR B class 0-4-0STs are five that have found new working homes. No 778 was sold to a private railway in the USA after withdrawal in 1960, and four were sold in 1968 to the Assam Railways & Trading Co for use on colliery lines owned by the company.

Unfortunately, the DHR's unique 0-4-0+0-4-0 Beyer Garratt, built in Manchester in 1911, proved unsuccessful and was withdrawn in 1954, and probably scrapped.

Tunnels

Tunnels are slow, expensive and dangerous to construct and railway engineers only build them when there is no other option.

Railway companies have built tunnels in many locations: through coastal headlands, rocky outcrops in valleys and even under rivers and seas. In Switzerland, spiral tunnels are built into the mountain sides to gain height.

Hazards await the tunneller through high mountain ranges. Workers in the 12 mile Simplon Tunnel, between Switzerland and Italy, faced temperatures up to 127°F (53°C), while in one place the pressure of the rock caused the tunnel supports to splinter. The tunnellers remedied this problem by using more beams.

In 1908, when the Lötschberg, another Swiss tunnel, was being built, a blast holed a deep fissure filled with water. The sudden inrush drowned 25 tunnellers and flooded over a mile of the tunnel, which finally had to be diverted round the affected area.

Most tunnels are wet inside because water seeps down from the ground above, making drainage essential. The gradient inside the tunnel must slope gently towards one or both ends. The three

Standedge Tunnels, between Huddersfield and Stalybridge, are exceptions to this rule and are entirely level. This is possible because a canal tunnel runs parallel to the railway and drains off the water. Because the railway tracks are level, there were water troughs inside one tunnel during steam days.

The Channel Tunnel is the most outstanding example of an underwater crossing, but when the GWR built the 4¹/₂ mile (7km) Severn Tunnel, over 100 years ago, it was the longest underwater tunnel in the world. Running below the Bristol Channel, it took more than 13 years to construct and additional difficulties arose when fresh water, from an underground source, frequently flooded the workings.

In recent years, many changes have taken place in tunnelling methods. When materials like soft chalk marl were encountered under the Channel, massive Tunnel Boring Machines (TBMs) cut through the ground easily, positioning the lining segments behind them as they worked. The TBMs advanced as much as a quarter of a mile in a week.

The tunnel lining, made from reinforced concrete, has to resist massive pressure from above, but sometimes there

is also significant pressure from below. To help deflect these forces, most tunnels are circular in cross section or arched top and bottom with curved sides – the track bed built up on the curved floor. Altering the floor when lowering the track in a tunnel to increase clearances can be difficult. It was during such an operation in 1979, that Penmanshiel Tunnel on the East Coast main line collapsed.

Some tunnels are bored through rock so solid that it does not need any lining, but explosives are required to break up the material for removal. To speed up the construction of long tunnels, intermediate shafts are sometimes sunk from the surface to the track level, each of them opening up a new pair of working faces. All the spoil and materials have to travel up and down the shaft, and water has to be pumped out instead of drained.

Simpler tunnels are constructed on the cut and cover principle. A deep cutting is made, lined and then covered over. This was used to prevent a line being seen from a wealthy landowner's house. Nowadays, such is the influence of environmentalists, that German Railways are building much of their Neubaustrecke (new high speed line) in tunnels.

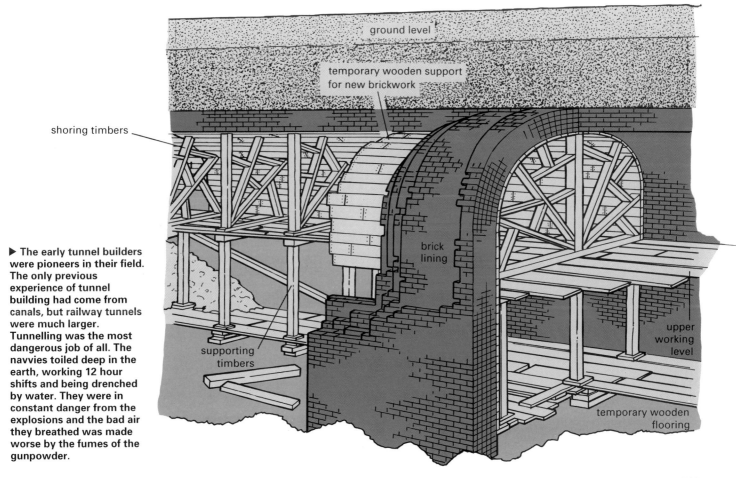

▶ The early tunnel builders were pioneers in their field. The only previous experience of tunnel building had come from canals, but railway tunnels were much larger. Tunnelling was the most dangerous job of all. The navvies toiled deep in the earth, working 12 hour shifts and being drenched by water. They were in constant danger from the explosions and the bad air they breathed was made worse by the fumes of the gunpowder.

ground level

temporary wooden support for new brickwork

shoring timbers

brick lining

supporting timbers

upper working level

temporary wooden flooring

In Xanadu

BEIJING • LANZHOU • JIAYUGUAN

One of the world's most exotic journeys follows the Great Wall of China for its entire length from Beijing into the Gobi Desert and through the fabled lands of Kubla Khan. It was also one of the last great long-distance steam routes.

TRAVEL FACTS

Line length: Beijing – Jiayuguan 1522 miles (2450km)
Journey time: three to five days depending on the number of stops
Frequency: twice a week from Beijing
Reservations: every passenger needs both a ticket and a docket for an allotted seat or bed. There are three standards of travel, first class being termed soft class lying, with four white-sheeted bunks in a compartment. Hard class lying has 60 bunk beds open on to the corridor with a blanket and a hard pillow and compulsory lights-out at 9.30pm. Hard class sitting is just that.

▼ A QJ (for *Qianjin* – Advance Forward) class 2-10-2 hauls a passenger train through the Gobi Desert at Zhongwei on the Beijing – Lanzhou section. The QJs will go down in history as probably the last steam locomotives ever built for regular main line use.

The Great Wall of China is the largest manmade construction on earth – yet most visitors see only the short, rebuilt section outside the capital. They rarely venture beyond Beijing where the Wall (and the railway line) flows for thousands of miles into the desolate Gobi Desert and the tree-less wastes of Inner Mongolia.

This journey to the borders of the Middle Kingdom, and the point where the Wall fades into nothing at the fort of Jiayuguan, is a journey back to the land of Xanadu and Genghis Khan, the Mongol conqueror of north China, and the ancient crossroads between East and West.

It was also one of the world's great steam adventures. For most of the journey the train was hauled by the giant QJ Forward 2-10-2s, often working in pairs. These 135-ton giants have been built in China since 1964, although older versions date back to 1956. When production ceased at Datong in 1989, they passed into posterity as the last steam locos in the world built for use on main line railways. The long 18-carriage trains and the steep, winding track through the Gobi make for spectacular onboard photography.

Departures from Beijing's huge brick main line station are all from upstairs – or, more correctly, up escalator. Even today, these moving staircases are a new and frightening experience for many Chinese. It's not unusual to see a panicking, squealing old man falling over and being helped to his feet by more experienced passengers.

The first stage of this epic four-day journey to the Great Wall's western end is Beijing to Datong in Inner Mongolia, usually pulled by two BJ

hydraulic transmission diesels, and taking about seven hours.

The train crosses the flat, fertile plain surrounding the capital before climbing into the hills guarded by the Great Wall. On a train where the windows open, this is one of the best places to photograph the Wall and marvel at its inaccessibility away from the sections reconstructed for tourists. If the windows don't open, photography is virtually impossible: with thick, badly fitting double glazing, Chinese train windows are almost always grimy.

Under the Great Wall

The diesels haul the train as far as Qing Long Qiao, where Zhan Tianou, the engineer who built the line, is commemorated with a stiffly posed statue. One engine then changes ends, and the train reverses to cope with the gradient, passing under the Great Wall itself and continuing the journey north-west.

The next stop for all but express trains is Badaling, a stone's throw from the most popular part of the Wall. Local trains do regular business bringing international tourists here every day of the year.

The train climbs on along the valley of the Yang Ho River to a broad, semi-desert plateau of scrub and brush which runs into the desert itself. Very little is farmed because of the poor soil, but the train is now deep in the heart of China's main coalmining area, dotted with a series of polluted and drab mining towns.

The landscape dries and withers into the begin-

ning of the Gobi Desert before Datong appears, lying just below the northern arc of the Great Wall and the border with Inner Mongolia. It's a grim, polluted coalmining city, which was briefly capital of all China in the Jin dynasty of the 4th century. All that remains of its 100 years of power are the mysterious Buddha caves where more than 50,000 painted statues are etched into the mountainside.

Datong steam works

For the railway enthusiast, Datong's main claim to fame was the last great steam engine factory in full production in the world. The Datong

▲ No matter what the weather, hundreds of patient travellers lounge around the vast concourse outside Beijing main line station. No one is allowed inside until an hour before a train's scheduled departure time.

Great white elephant

The Great Wall was never much of a success as a defence. At 3107 miles (5000km) it was simply too big to guard successfully, and as each section was built individually by each province, some bits of it do not link up very accurately. Built 2000 years ago at the beginning of the Qin dynasty, on completion the Wall stretched from Shanhaiguan on the eastern coast of China to just beyond Jiayuguan in the western desert. Many thousands of men, mostly convicts or soldiers, worked on it, and those who died were buried within the stone. Only three places have been restored, two near Beijing and a third at Jiayuguan.

◄ At Qing Long Qiao, with the Great Wall snaking across the hills in the background, BJ 3081 runs round NY7 0018 on the 11.01 Beijing to Lanzhou. Most trains out of Beijing are now diesel hauled – steam is used only in remoter parts of the country.

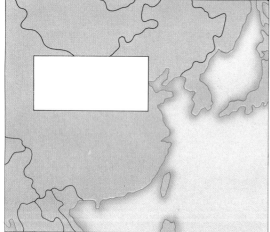

▲ Datong is a foul-smelling, sulphurous coalmining town west of Beijing but it is also home to the Datong Locomotive Works – the last factory in the world to make steam locos. Manufacture ceased in 1989 but maintenance continues on China's ageing fleet. It's a fascinating place, with most operations being carried out by an army of workers scampering among hunks of smoking iron to the tune of *The Anvil Chorus*.

Locomotive Works was built with Soviet help during the 1950s, the first steam locomotive rolling out in 1959.

Up to 1989, it was a steam enthusiast's paradise with much of the works open to visitors. Most of the work was done by hand, hammered skilfully out of iron and brass; it was one vast blacksmith's shop – filthy, noisy and dangerous. Even now, with steam engine repairs still going strong, the site is well worth a visit.

From Datong the route runs north-west for 27 hours through the Gobi Desert to Lanzhou. Only five hours out of Datong comes Hohhot, capital of

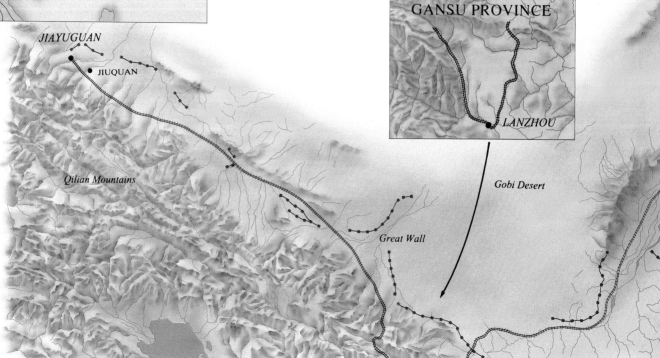

GANSU PROVINCE

LANZHOU

JIAYUGUAN

JIUQUAN

Qilian Mountains

Gobi Desert

Great Wall

Inner Mongolia. It's an ugly, Russian-designed town but once every year its people seem to drop their dour mask and become young and vibrant. The great occasion is the annual summer festival which features dare-devil races and death-defying stunts by Mongol horsemen who come in from the fertile grasslands to the north where they live a wandering, nomadic life.

The beauty of this journey depends completely on the season. Springtime brings fertility even to the Gobi Desert, with artesian wells supplying irrigation along a line of fertile oases, and tapping the beds of dried up rivers. But in summer, autumn and winter the desert looks totally barren, with mile after mile of dust, gravel and swirling sand.

Crossroads at Lanzhou

One of the ancient gateways to China where traders had their last chance to change mounts before heading for the outer limits of the empire, Lanzhou sprawls along the southern bank of the Yellow River. The capital of Gansu Province, it lies in a pall of dusty smog from the petro-chemical industries in the western suburbs.

The Silk Road was the main reason for the city's development, with silk coming north from the fertile lands of Middle China to be allotted to caravans bound for Tibet, Siberia, India and Europe. Incoming goods from the West were dispatched to Beijing, Shanghai and the south.

The Yellow River was used for transporting coal, oil and iron ore from Lanzhou long before the building of the first Chinese railway in 1909. By 1960 there were lines through Lanzhou northwest to Urumqi (two days further on) and west to Xining, but neither is now used to full capacity. The line to Xining was extended to Golmud in 1984, but there it comes to a dead end, while that to Urumqi was pushed towards the USSR in the late 1980s. The demise of the Soviet Union immediately put the line's continued use in doubt. This is particularly ironic as it took great determination for the Chinese to push it through after the Soviets

pulled out of the joint project in 1960 and took all the plans with them. There used to be a slogan for the line, 'This year Urumqi, next year the border'. That was in 1958.

Trains west of Lanzhou are a pleasure to travel. The services are rarely busy so travellers in hard class can stretch out across the seat, and the soft class carriages are virtually empty with the communal washroom offering a degree of privacy.

All the village settlements in the north are walled with mudstone, originally to deter marauders as well as for protection from the harsh winds which tear across the desert. The line follows the

▲ **A QJ 2-10-2 climbs near Chang Lui Shui in the desolate Gobi, on the run from Zhongwei to Lanzhou. A passenger train is often up to 18 carriages long and offers excellent onboard photo opportunities of the locomotive as the train winds through the foothills up to the desert plateau.**

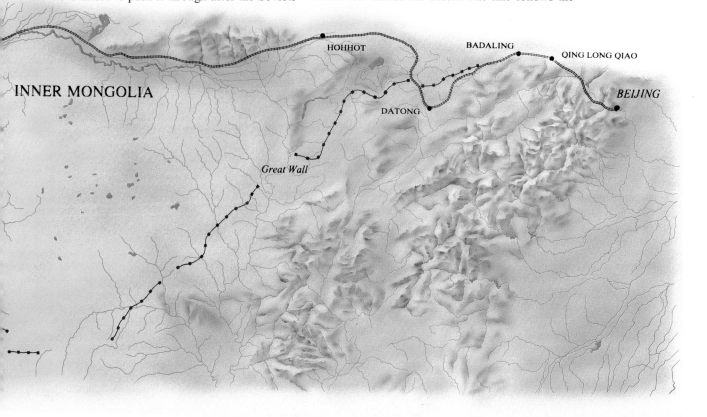

INNER MONGOLIA

HOHHOT   BADALING   QING LONG QIAO

DATONG   BEIJING

Great Wall

Timely reminder
There is no question of China's communist credentials as you wait to start your journey. The clock on Beijing's massive main line station chimes out 'The East is Red' every hour, on the hour.

valley of the Pingfan Ho River on the edge of the Gobi. Motor traffic is rare, with most transport by donkey, horse or camel cart. The animals are allowed to roam free when not working; their only regular food comes from their owners so they rarely stray.

Gansu Province is 80% desert with the snow-capped Qilian Mountains rising to 17,000ft (5200m) in the far west. This is the land of the Uighurs, non-Chinese people of the Asian steppes, and their culture of donkey carts and exotic dancing displays. The region is known as the Chinese Siberia, and the desert's name in local dialect is translated as 'earth's greatest barrier'.

The Great Wall reappears here as it does sporadically along the journey. By now it's broken and sloping and piled up, a muddy-looking heap of brown bricks and rubble.

The Wall's end

The oil and mineral outpost towns of Jiuquan and Jiayuguan mark the end of the Wall. To attract workers, both pay and conditions are much better than in Beijing since most of the young people would prefer to head east to the excitement of the big cities rather than spend their lives looking at the desert.

Travellers often stop at the smaller of the two towns, Jiuquan, and take a bus to the Wall. However, it's easier to continue onwards by train, running parallel to the shattered, dying Wall which looks so insignificant and unimpressive as it limps along outside the grimy window that few people realise what it is.

Its last fanfare is the great fortress of Jiayuguan which was built as the Wall's final outpost in 1372, during the Ming dynasty. The fortress has been rebuilt many times over the centuries, mostly in the original wattle and daub, but sometimes in stone. It features ornamental wooden pavilions on a magnificent monument to a past which must have been lonely and tedious for those forced to maintain and defend the garrison. All that can be seen from the ramparts is the desert, and nowadays the busy steelworks just beyond Jiayuguan, with the railway snaking into the distance, back to the fertile lands of China.

▼ **At Jiayuguan the battered, mudstone hump that remains of the Wall limps on for a mile or so towards the hazy Qilian Mountains. As no one could cross the mountains and survive the desert long enough to reach and attack the Wall, it simply fades away.**

Railway posters

The railway companies' use of advertising posters effectively began in the late 1870s. Before then, the only posters normally seen were those announcing changes in the train services or, occasionally, auction sales of livestock at markets adjoining the stations.

The earliest posters were produced by the letterpress process and did not have any pictorial content, except perhaps for a simple sketch. In these letterpress prints a great variety of different typefaces was used, some of them very attractive. Often, each line would be in a different letter style.

As printing technology progressed, so illustrated posters began to appear. By the mid-1880s there were some fine examples, lithographed in several colours. Initially, these so-called pictorials tended to feature composite illustrations which incorporated part of the text.

The Great Western Railway (GWR) produced just such a poster in 1908. This comprised two pictures of New Quay in Cardiganshire, together with one of their new 'Road Motor Cars', and was captioned, 'Motor service from Llandyssil'.

The passing of the Edwardian era saw a simplification of tastes. For posters advertising holiday resorts, a single picture was generally used. These were often specially commissioned by the railway company from well-known artists. This particular style was to continue right up to the late 1950s.

The next generation of railway posters used more stylised designs, often with the artwork carried right to the edge of the paper. These works typified the fashions of the 1950s and 1960s. Posters were also seen as a good way of advertising the various publications put out by the railway companies. The North Eastern Railway, for example, had a series of six booklets entitled *Historic Monuments in North East England*.

These included sites such as Bamburgh Castle, Rievaulx Abbey and Richmond Castle, and were publicised by six posters, each featuring a sepia pen and ink drawing of a particular monument. The LNER also used posters to promote their series of *Rambles* books.

Occasionally, two or more railway companies combined to produce a joint poster. One of these was for the 'Direct Route Via Cheltenham to and from Southampton and the Isle of Wight', produced by the Midland Railway and the Midland & South Western Junction Railway in 1902.

The GWR and London Midland & Scottish Railway also joined forces on some of the pictorials in the 1930s, a typical example being that for the west coast resort of Weston-super-Mare.

During World War II there was a conscious effort to discourage the general public from travelling by rail, so that more resources would be available for transporting troops and war materials. The Railway Executive Committee, set up to control the railways at this time, published posters bearing such catch-phrases as, 'Is your journey really necessary?' Others underlined the risk of giving away secrets in idle chatter. One warned that 'Careless talk costs lives', another that 'Walls have ears'.

The most common poster size was 25in wide and 40in high, and was known as Double Royal. Some locations could accommodate posters of twice this width, these being known as Quad Royal. A smaller standard size was the Double Crown, measuring 20in by 30in.

Collecting posters

A fair quantity of railway posters is still coming on to the market, with Sheffield Railwayana Auctions being the best source. Most of the other specialist railway auctions usually include some posters. Another possible source is the private advertisements included in specialist publications such as *Railway Antiques Monthly*.

Prices can vary widely, with British Railways pictorials from the 1970s commanding around £20 and late Victorian lithographs selling for anything up to £1000, or even more. A typical 1930s pictorial from the GWR or LNER should cost between £60 and £100.

◀A poster from around 1910 promotes two north Devon resorts that could be – almost – reached by the London & South Western Railway (LSWR). Passengers would travel over the picturesque LSWR line from Exeter to Barnstaple, where they would take the narrow gauge Lynton & Barnstaple Railway to Lynton. To get from here to Lynmouth, it was necessary to travel by road.

Narrow gauge in Colorado

DURANGO • SILVERTON

The narrow gauge track running between Durango and Silverton, USA, was originally built to take ore out and equipment in to the rich silver deposits of the San Juan Mountains; its trains have also starred in films. Today it is a successful and exciting tourist attraction.

The Durango & Silverton Narrow Gauge Railroad (DSNG) is one of the last surviving fragments of what was once an extensive narrow gauge (3ft/914mm) system covering southern Colorado. The biggest operator in the area was the Denver & Rio Grande Railway (DRG), which was founded in 1870 and, only 12 years later, had more than 1000 route miles (1600km) in operation, mostly through very mountainous terrain.

Over one hundred years of history

Silverton lies in the San Juan Mountains and in 1879 the DRG decided to develop a line from Denver, through Alamosa and Durango, towards this remote range, which was known to be rich in silver. The line was built remarkably quickly in the face of great technical difficulties. It reached Durango at the end of July 1881, despite having been still some 18 miles (29km) away on 7 July. The opening ceremony on 5 August was apparent-

ly marred only slightly by the fact that the special train bringing the dignitaries from Denver failed to arrive, due to a washout of the track. The fine station at Durango was opened in January 1882 and today, after careful restoration, it appears much as it did 110 years ago.

Little time was wasted in starting the branch line from Durango north towards Silverton: work began in August 1881 and the first train ran into Silverton in July 1882. Silverton is nearly 500 miles (800km) by rail from Denver, and as far as the DRG wanted to go, but three other companies developed branch lines out of the town, two of which terminated at heights of over 11,000ft (3353m). Mining peaked in this region early in the 20th century, and the last mining operation in the Silverton area closed as recently as 1991. Much of the town survives, and it has been designated a National Historic Landmark.

The fate of the railway mirrored that of the

▼ **It is rare to get such a clear picture of the Silverton – Durango train crossing the Silver Truss Bridge. Usually, as the train crosses the bridge the boiler is blown down, causing the engine to be obscured by clouds of steam. On this occasion the engineer happened to close the right-hand valve first, and the steam dissipated just in time for the photographer to get his shot.**

town. Improvements in the local roads and the closure of the mines led to reductions in demand, and only pressure from residents kept the branch open. In 1962 the then owners, the Denver & Rio Grande Western Railroad (DRGW), sought to close the railway, but were refused permission. They therefore began exploiting its potential as a tourist attraction, but in 1968 the link to the south was severed by the closure of the line from Alamosa to Durango. The DRGW sought a buyer for the now isolated Durango to Silverton line and finally, in March 1981, sold it to Mr Charles Bradshaw, now the President of the DSNG, which is one of the best-known private passenger railways in the United States.

A steady and twisting climb

The scenery through which the railway runs is extraordinarily beautiful and for most of its length the line follows the Animas River. Durango is at an elevation of 6520ft (1987m) – here the river is brown and meanders back and forth across the flat-bottomed valley; at Silverton (alt 9288ft/2831m) the Animas is a small, green mountain stream. For much of its journey between the two towns the river runs through deep canyons.

For a mountain line, the Durango to Silverton maintains a remarkably consistent rate of climb. The first 11 miles (18km), to Hermosa, are generally flat, then the line climbs steadily for virtually all of the remaining 34 miles (55km). The maximum gradient is 1 in 40, which by narrow gauge standards is not steep. The minimum radius of curvature is 191ft (58m), which for 2-8-2 locomotives with an all-up weight – including tender – of 140 tons is tight, and explains the fact that only the wheels on the front and rear driving axles are flanged.

The line has neither tunnels nor avalanche shelters, and few bridges. The majority of the engineering work in the construction consisted of blasting a shelf for the line, most of it close to river level, but part of it teetering more than 400ft (122m) above the water.

The rolling stock

All operations are based at Durango, where the company's maintenance and storage facilities are located. All trains run round trips to Silverton, where there is a two hour stop, and then go back to Durango. Trains consist of a mix of coaches and open observation cars, each painted in 'Rio Grande Gold' with black lettering. Half of the coaches date from the 1880s; the remainder were built either in the 1960s, during the final phase of the DRGW ownership, or in the 1980s by the DSNG. The open cars were originally built as box cars, or stock cars (for carrying animals), in two batches in 1916 and 1937.

The railway has six coal-fired locomotives in running order and four others awaiting refurbishment. The working locomotives are outside-frame 2-8-2s bought from the DRGW. The three 470-Series (K28 class) engines, built in 1925, have a tractive power of 36,200lb (16,420kg) and weigh 143 tons.

There is no fixed signalling installation. Instead, all train movements are carefully preplanned and scheduled so that the whereabouts of each train is known. The engineers (drivers) maintain their speed by accurate timing and reference to mileposts. Flags, lamps and whistle signals are still used and all train movements require the permission of the 'despatcher' at Durango. Each train is shadowed by a small, petrol-driven car, known as a pop-car. These too are historic vehicles, most of them built by Fairmount in the 1940s. In addition, all trains nowadays have radio connections with Durango.

Departure from Durango

As part of the rigid control over timetables, passengers are required to be on board 15 minutes before departure. Dead on time, the engineer sounds two long blasts on the whistle and sets the

▲ **A Durango-bound train reaches the highest point of the High Line. It was impossible to construct a railway through the lower part of the Animas Gorge, so the Rio Grande engineers responded by blasting this 1¼ mile (2km) long shelf out of the rock – one of the greatest-ever feats in American railway engineering.**

About ¾ mile (1200m) further on is Rockwood, a station in the middle of nowhere. This lonely stretch of line is quite awe-inspiring – some 400ft (122m) above the thundering Animas River.

The first train of the day is preceded by a motor-driven trolley to check for fallen boulders on the line.

▲ Locomotive K36 No 481 approaches milepost 495 by the Animas River on a spring day. Engineers keep their trains on schedule by scrupulous timing and reference to these mileposts.

K37s used to operate on this line, but their weight caused problems when negotiating some of the sharper curves, so they were replaced with K36s. These engines are entirely standard products of their day, apart from the exceptional size and power for the slim gauge.

bell ringing, and the train slowly pulls out of the depot, across 6th Street and along Narrow Gauge Avenue, parallel to Main Avenue, its whistle sounding frequently until the train is safely out of the town. Just outside Durango is the first of the river crossings, on a three-span bridge that started life as three different bridges in three different locations. Until Hermosa, the valley is a flat alluvial plain between two cliffs a mile or more apart. The meanders of the river here are so old that oxbow lakes have been formed. The valley is full of willows, which in the morning light are a lovely pale green. Here there are plenty of reminders of the real world, but after Hermosa, where the climbing starts and the engine begins to work hard, the railway is in a world of its own.

For several miles the left wall of the valley closes in on the train, which finally starts to ascend, leaving the river down on the right. The rock wall reflects the roar of the engine along the length of the train. On the right is a view down on to Shalona Lake, after which the line takes a sharp right-hand curve and enters Beaver Creek Canyon. After two more turns the train passes through Rockwood and then descends through several cuttings in the red granite. The gaps between these cuttings afford superb views of the river in the canyon below.

A long way to fall

The train then slows down to a walking pace and, immediately after passing a sign denoting the San Juan National Forest, takes another sharp turn to the left and starts to inch its way along the appropriately named High Line. This is the most spectacular part of the journey. A shelf just wide enough for the train has been blasted out of the rock, leaving a 400ft (122m) sheer drop beneath.

▼ Locomotive No 478 is seen here just leaving Silverton, after a two-hour lunch stop, to make the return trip to Durango. The three K28 class, 470-Series engines operated by the DSNG were built in 1925.

The small creek is a tributary of the Animas River – which the train follows for most of its journey – and a good site to spot beavers at work.

TRAVEL FACTS

Line length: Durango – Silverton 45 miles (72km)
Duration: eight or nine hours for the round trip, including a two-hour stop at Silverton
Frequency: varies from four per day in the peak season, to only one at the beginning and end of the season. There are additional shorter trips in the spring and winter, but no trains at all between January and March, when the snow and consequent avalanches make reliable timetabling impossible
Reservations: advance reservations are strongly recommended

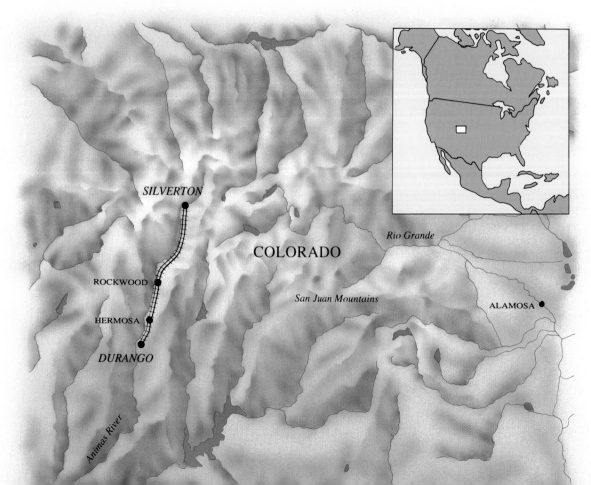

SILVERTON

ROCKWOOD

HERMOSA

DURANGO

COLORADO

Rio Grande

San Juan Mountains

ALAMOSA

Animas River

The engine is now relatively quiet, and the river can be heard clearly below as it thunders through Animas Canyon.

After the High Line the railway resumes its climb. Just how steeply the river falls towards Durango is shown by the fact that about a mile further on the railway is at water level again.

The train passes the Tacoma hydro-electric plant and then stops to take on water at Tank Creek. In places the valley bottom widens out, creating small areas of meadow. Aspen trees appear, their quivering leaves the palest of green in the spring, turning to yellow and red in the autumn. A particularly beautiful stretch follows after Cascade Canyon.

Avalanche country

At many places in the 10 miles (16km) after Needleton the track is subject to avalanches. Many of these occur at the same places each year, leaving permanent scars as they crash down the steep mountain-sides, dragging rocks and trees with them, and creating jumbled piles of debris. It is quite common for such slides to fill the bottom of the valley and bury the track. Before the spring train service can start these slides have to be cleared with snow-ploughs and bulldozers brought in on construction trains.

Most railways, of course, cannot tolerate three-month winter closures, and are therefore obliged, when passing through such terrain, to build long avalanche shelters or to tunnel out of harm's way. It is to the visitors' advantage that the DRGW did not take such measures, as the result is an unimpeded view of the scenery.

The end of the line

The line continues to thread through the Animas Valley until, quite suddenly, the valley opens out into a triangular plain surrounded by mountains, in the middle of which sits Silverton. With its bell ringing, the train slowly runs into the town and stops at Blair Street, one block east of Greene Street, the town's main thoroughfare.

With the final demise of mining in the area, Silverton is now largely dependent on tourism.

▲ Just outside Durango is the first of the river crossings, on a three-span bridge over the Animas. The scenery in this area contains many extraordinary rock formations created by a mixture of mining activities and natural erosion.

The DSNG runs late-afternoon conducted yard tours, enabling visitors to see the disposal of the locomotives, and spend a couple of hours behind the scenes.

A three-span bridge
The first river crossing, outside Durango, is over a three-span bridge. The first span was brought from the Pleasant Valley branch in Utah in 1927; the second is a Pratt truss, built in 1888 and brought from the Conejos River near Antonito in 1917; the third is a wooden open-deck truss built in 1936.

▲ Locomotive K36 No 481 is seen approaching Beaver Creek Overlook through cuttings in the red granite on its way to Silverton. No 481 is a 2-8-2, as are the other locomotives on this line. They are known by the Americans as Mikados.

When the railway was still a working line, rather than a tourist attraction, it was used for transporting sheep to and from their summer pastures, in addition to its main role of transporting ore from over 50 major mines.

Marooned

The travellers who once depended on the line in winter as well as in summer might have welcomed avalanche shelters. The line was frequently closed for days at a time in bad weather, and it was not unknown for passenger trains to be marooned for up to 10 days. In 1886 the line was closed for four weeks, and in 1891 Silverton was cut off for 51 days. It was common practice in those days to tunnel through the worst of the snowslides.

This industry at least appears to be secure, since the DSNG is remarkably successful; in 1992 it carried 213,000 passengers. There is one paved road in Silverton, on which some fine buildings survive; the other streets are still just dirt roads. Most of the horses have gone, to be replaced by pick-ups, and most of the historic buildings are in use either as souvenir shops, or as eating places.

Despite the changes in its economic fortunes, it is still just about possible to imagine how the mining town must have looked a century ago when it first flourished.

After the two-hour break, during which the train is turned round on the wye, the return journey is announced on the whistle and the train starts away. The engine does not have to work so hard on the way back to Durango, since it is nearly all downhill.

A little more than three hours later the train trundles back along Narrow Gauge Avenue in Durango and into the depot, its bell clanging and its whistle sounding. The whistle must be one of the most haunting of any man-made noises, and continues to be heard after passengers have left the depot, as the engine crew assembles its train for the next day's run.

Chapter Three

Life And Times Of The Steam Railway

GWR 4-6-0 No 2920 *Saint David* tackles the climb to Sapperton summit on the Gloucester to Swindon line with the farewell special to the Saint class on 15 June 1952. This was one of over 200 specials organised by W. A. Camwell for members of the Stephenson Locomotive Society from Birmingham.

A day in the life of a steam engine driver

The 1950s were the last of the great years for the long distance engine driver. His recognition was earned on a daily schedule that often took him away from home on overnight trips in all weathers.

On a raw winter's afternoon, a driver in his late 50s, small and dapper, carrying a cheap attache case, is walking down the slope from Dean Lane, Manchester, into Newton Heath engine shed. His boots glow with a shine that relieves some of the gloom from the pall of smoke that hangs in the air. His shiny greasetop cap sits firm and straight on his grey hair.

Seeing him walk into the shed lobby, the foreman's assistant riffles through the plastic-covered work dockets and hands the driver his itinerary: the 4.12pm from Manchester Exchange station to Glasgow, followed by the 10.50am return the next day. It's 2.15 now and the engine is due off shed at 3.30.

The driver is a member of a group known as the Glasgow link, which covers the run from Manchester to Glasgow and other work. Promotion to this link of eight driver/fireman teams is a normal step for senior drivers attached to Newton Heath shed, although they can opt to avoid it. The fireman volunteered to work in this link for two years because the high mileage bonuses are attractive, although the work is hard and may involve overnight stops.

Final checks

Today's journey to Glasgow has two temporary speed restrictions: one caused by mining subsidence south of Wigan, and a 20mph (32km/h) slowing just before the train reaches Penrith. But even that is not the final word, and the 'Late Notice Case' in the lobby is checked for last minute alterations.

Collecting a greasy overall coat from his locker, the driver sees the fireman at the stores counter drawing his firing shovel, bucket full of spanners and a gauge lamp and brush. The two men carry the equipment to the waiting locomotive, then the driver runs a

◀ At the start of another long haul the driver waits, ready for the off. In charge of an express passenger locomotive, a driver in the mid 1950s could expect to earn about £10 12s a week, supplemented by an average of £4 mileage allowance.

Page 129: On a cold winter's day, the fireman of an LMS 4-6-0 locomotive looks back for the 'right of way' signal whilst a guard emerges from the escaping steam carrying rear warning lamps.

practised eye over the engine. Though far from immaculate – she has run 40,000 miles (64,374km) since her last works overhaul – her lined green paint is clean and the 4000 gallon (18,184 litre) tender is piled high with good Yorkshire coal.

Making ready

The crew have an hour to prepare the locomotive. The fireman replenishes the sandboxes and builds up the fire while the driver concentrates on dealing with the brakes and lubrication. The more inaccessible parts are usually covered in oil and dirt, which is why the driver has taken the precaution of wearing the greasy overall coat.

Once both men are satisfied, the fireman hoses down the cab floor while the driver eases the engine down the shed yard and signals to the outside foreman's cabin. The driver then pulls to a halt at the shed outlet so that the fireman can ring off to Thorpes Bridge signalbox. So far they are on time.

At Red Bank sidings they pick up four carriages and drift slowly down to Exchange station. A second section of seven coaches from Liverpool, including the dining car, will be attached at Preston, making up the full permitted load of 365 tons (370,840kg) for their engine.

Over each buffer are the two express headlamps which glint in the gathering, late afternoon gloom. The train leaves Manchester and heads for the junction with the West Coast main line at Springs Branch. It's an easy task with their light load of four coaches and they are able to draw down to the north end of platform three in Preston on time.

The Liverpool section arrives soon after and stops well back on platform two. As the second engine is uncoupled and moved off, the Manchester driver draws his coaches out of the station and reverses back into platform two to couple the sections together. Preston is not well laid out for this manoeuvre and the darkness does not help.

Leaning from his cab window with one hand on the brake, the driver looks down the train. The shunter hangs from the last coach waving his handlamp which forms a pinpoint of light to guide the driver. One bad judgement and the train will buffer up too hard, jolting passengers and spilling the aperitifs being enjoyed in the diner.

After a quick brake test and a glance round the cab to make sure everything is in order, the driver looks back down the platform for the right away signal. Four minutes late, the guard waves his green lamp and the driver feeds high pressure steam to the cylinders – the pistons begin to move

and the train inches forward. Next stop Carlisle.

There is plenty of hard work ahead – 101 minutes are allowed for the 90 mile (145km) journey, which includes the climb from close to sea level at Carnforth to Shap Summit at 915 feet (279km).

A testing time

As he approaches the Lancaster curves, the driver shuts off steam and lets the train coast through the 60mph (97km/h) restriction. With no speedometer in the cab, he must judge how fast he is going from the motion of the engine and the passing landscape.

Now drizzle starts to fall, blown in from Morecambe Bay. The cab windows blur and the reflected glare from the firehole only adds to his difficulties in sighting signal lights. A good knowledge of the route is the key to spotting them.

The driver is constantly wiping the small glass windshield with his sponge cloth. Now and then he glances round to check how his mate is doing and to keep an eye on pressure and water gauges. Hardly a word passes between the two men.

The drizzle adds to the driver's problems by bringing the risk of wheel slip. With hard climbing ahead, he decides to rush the gradients to keep up

▼ The Manchester-Glasgow express speeds through the countryside – during the five to six hour journey the Jubilee class 4-6-0 engine works hard, consuming six tons of coal and thousands of gallons of water.

Banking engine may be needed to push the train up the steep inclines of Shap and Beattock. But it isn't only the engine that feels the strain. By the time the train reaches its destination the driver and fireman will have had a hard day, both mentally and physically.

◄Even an engine driver has to do paperwork. At the beginning of his shift the driver signs on and picks up all the notices for the journey. Later he may have to make out a repair card listing faults with the engine needing attention.

▼ Before they leave the depot the driver and fireman have to satisfy themselves that the engine is fit for the road. An engine such as this one with two outside cylinders was easy to prepare – but in order to oil the inside valve gear of a Jubilee it was necessary to climb up between the frames from the pit.

▲After signing on, the driver examines the Engine Arrangements Board to see which engine is allocated for his trip. No 45642 *Boscawen*, stabled on road 14, is scheduled for the Glasgow journey. Apart from engine provisions for this and the following day, the board lists engines under repair and those needing maintenance.

speed and gives his engine more steam to do so. His hand is poised to release sand on to the track to remedy any wheel slip but he is lucky.

Over the top

The rain is falling harder; the climb to Shap Summit becomes a battle against gravity. The engine is pounding away but only doing 25mph (40km/h). Once it is over the top, the run into Carlisle is mainly downhill and steam can be shut off.

As the train reaches platform three, the driver carefully brakes so that the engine halts with the rear of the tender opposite the water column. While the tender is replenished, he checks all the bearings to ensure that none is running hot.

Despite the mountain of mail at Carlisle, they get away on time and head for the Scottish border. The climb to Beattock is particularly hard with two crests before Lockerbie. But the final ascent for ten miles (16km) to the summit up a 1 in 75 gradient is the toughest test on the line.

Dripping lineside trees increase the likelihood of slipping and the driver errs on the side of

▲ Before leaving the yard the engine has to take on water. The fireman puts the leather bag into the filler hole while his driver turns the water on at the valve. Alongside stands a fire cresset on a stove – a simple but effective way of preventing the water freezing in winter.

The tender holds up to 4000 gallons (18,184 litres) – it needs 8000 gallons (36,368 litres) to complete the journey. There are four water troughs on this route which allow the supply to be replenished on the move.

◀ The journey begins, with the enginemen at work in their traditional greasetop caps and bib-and-brace jackets. Having built up a good fire the fireman maintains the boiler close to maximum pressure, without wasting fuel and water by blowing off at the safety valves.

◀ The correct ordering of engines to take up their duties off shed needs great organisational skills from the running shed foreman. At many depots turntables are used – some are vacuum operated, using the engine as power, others are pushed round by hand.

caution. He crows on the whistle as he passes Ecclefechan signalbox so that the signalman can warn Beattock that they have 20 minutes to provide a banking engine to push them up the hill.

The train seems hardly at a stand before the banking engine buffers up at the rear. The banker crows on the whistle to indicate that it is ready to push. The train driver replies in kind and the two engines start their 20 minute battle to the summit.

Once they are over the top the banking engine drops off. The express rolls down Upper Clydesdale into Carstairs, where the section for Edinburgh is uncoupled from the rear. The final stage is a gentle roll downhill into Scotland's industrial belt with a brief stop at Motherwell. The last short sprint brings them into platform two at Glasgow Central just five minutes late. They have used over 8000 gallons (36,368 litres) of water and six tons (6096kg) of coal since they left Manchester.

A well-earned rest

Local men take charge of the engine and deliver it to Polmadie shed while the tired crew take their ease with a beer apiece in the dining car.

From Larkfield carriage sidings they have a short walk to the railway hostel where they will spend the night. They have earned almost 14 hours' pay on their eight-hour shift, thanks to a bonus scheme in which every 15 miles (24km) over 140 (225) count as an extra hour of pay. Consoled by that and drained by their mental and physical effort, they sleep soundly in their cubicles.

The following day is a mirror image of their journey north. Another crew relieves them on arrival at Newton Heath shed so that the driver can make out a card for any repairs that might be necessary, check his schedule for tomorrow and head home for tea. With a few home comforts on his mind, he is glad to leave the noise and the smoke behind him for another day.

▲ Contact with Control was a regular feature of a driver's day. The graffiti on the wall, with the message 'Control can hear', sums up the rivalry that often existed between footplate staff and those they referred to as 'bank clerks and bureaucrats'. But, while drivers may have resented Control's supervision of operating matters, they were always glad when Control found relief crew at short notice.

Learning the road

When he joined the link, the driver had to learn the route. Until that point he knew the line only as far as Carlisle. Now he had to learn all the signals, gradients and speed restrictions on the 102 miles (164km) from Carlisle to Glasgow. These varied from the formidable climb to Beattock Summit to the complexities of the track on the approach to Glasgow.

To pick up these points, he rode with old hands and worked under their guidance. Then he learned the Sectional Appendix, a book which lists local details such as the location of passing loops of track and their holding capacity and special local whistle codes. It was three weeks before he 'signed the road', certifying that he could handle any type of train on the route, night or day in complete safety. This signed card is kept by the train crew foreman for reference should he need to replace a driver at short notice.

Working on the railway

**The pay was low, the discipline was harsh and
the chances of being killed or injured were greater than
those normally faced by a soldier. Yet a job on
the railway was once a coveted prize.**

Karl Marx was able to influence millions and to set continents ablaze, but he failed to impress the Great Western Railway. When he applied for a job, he was turned down on the grounds of poor handwriting. It was a bitter disappointment. But then, as he later expounded in *The Communist Manifesto*, life could not be expected to give people what they wanted.

He could, however, take consolation from the fact that there were many like him. For every Victorian working man wanted a job on the railway. Not only was steam transport one of the fastest growing, most prosperous and most important sectors of Britain's economy, but it also had a magnetic allure.

Even the lowliest shed sweeper was surrounded by the very latest in technological development, and as for the élite, the locomotive drivers, they were the fastest men in the world – the jet pilots and astronauts of their time.

A high regard for safety and good time-keeping was, of course, paramount for anyone working on the railway. But many other qualities were also demanded, and staff selection methods were remorselessly stringent. An employee was expected to be healthy, literate, courteous, well-dressed, physically strong, sober, vigilant, quick-witted and of impeccable character.

A railwayman safeguarded the national interest as much as a soldier, and initially the two callings had a lot in common. They were both subject to extreme discipline, they both wore uniforms that reflected their sharply differentiated ranks and they were both expected to obey, without question, the precise orders of their superiors. Indeed, many railway managers were men who had served long years as army or naval officers.

Breaking the rules

Infringement of company regulations brought stern retribution. Offences for which employees were dismissed ranged from exercising a dog while on sick leave, to betting on a horse. One man who quit without giving proper notice was prosecuted and sentenced to three weeks' hard labour.

The prevailing attitude was vigorously expressed by E B Ivatts, an official of Ireland's Midland Great Western. In his *Railway Management at Stations*, published in 1885, Ivatts wrote that 'Obedience is gained by fear and respect, and lost by a deficiency of firmness and moral courage...Submission to a leader is given tacitly upon the belief that the leader is able to

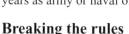

◀ **With his carefully waxed moustache and neat
collar and tie, this Southern Railway driver is the
epitome of the old-time engineman. Note the medal
ribbon, no doubt a legacy of World War I, worn
prominently on his waistcoat. The picture, taken at
Clapham Junction in 1944, also shows No 788 *Sir
Urre of the Mount*, which was to haul American
soldiers to Southampton.**

lead, and on that account is a superior kind of man.'

And then there were the hours. One Victorian guard was told by his superintendent, 'You've got 24 in the day like every other man and they are all ours if we want them.' Often that was an understatement. In 1871, the Board of Trade received a report detailing instances of men working for 37 hours continuously. Days of 16 hours and upwards were commonplace.

Huge casualty rate

On top of – and often because of – the hours, there were the accidents. Men were forever being casually crushed between buffers; collisions lit up rural horizons like a harvest sunset; spilled embers from racing locomotives were constantly starting trackside fires.

Even the simple act of reducing speed could maim – the transmitted jolt of braking a long goods train could toss the guard from one end of his van to the other. As late as the first decade of the 20th century, some 5,000 railwaymen were killed and almost 240,000 injured.

Even so, the railwaymen stuck by the railways.

▼ **Dining car attendants line up at Euston station, the London terminus of the London & North Western Railway (LNWR), in 1906. According to one LNWR manager, the railway service demanded 'a high degree of smartness, alacrity, energy and zeal on the part of every individual engaged in it'.**

Decorating zeal

Pride in their work was the hallmark of the true railwayman. Drivers were particularly devoted and often spent hours of unpaid overtime lovingly grooming their locomotives.

On top of this, they would add their own decorative touches. Some painted the chimney or smokebox, others inscribed their names in gilt script or advertised the insignia of their Masonic lodge.

During the 1870s, a visitor to Carlisle noted of one bright green engine that 'Her driver has further embellished her with a pair of polished-brass antlered stags in her uncompromising stove-pipe chimney and there is a gaudy transfer picture of the Royal Family on her sandbox...'

Occasionally, the zeal for decoration could become excessive, as in the case of the North British Railway whose royal engine was so covered in tapestry, shrubbery, flowers and painted carpentry, that it was virtually impossible to make out its livery.

▲ **The yard inspector looks out from the signalbox at London's Victoria station in 1939. The senior ranks of the railway hierarchy had to be particularly mobile, often uprooting family and home every few years in order to climb further up the promotion ladder.**

The pay was as good as in any other industry, on top of which there was cheap accommodation, free fuel, free uniforms and later free rail travel. Tips for station staff were forbidden at first, but in 1857 the London & North Western Railway permitted them and other companies fell into line. More important than all this, however, was the knowledge that, whatever happened, the 'guv'nors' would look after you.

From early Victorian times, railway companies operated schools, orphanages, banks and friendly societies on behalf of their employees. And when railwaymen became unable to fulfil their duties through such reasons as age, ill-health or injury, posts were usually found for them elsewhere in the organisation.

The all-powerful presence

An observer who visited the new railway town of Wolverton in Buckinghamshire was struck by the 'considerable number of men who have lost a finger, hand, arm or leg. All, however, whether whole or mutilated, look for support to "the Company", and not only their services and their thoughts, but their parts of speech are more or less devoted to it: for instance, the pronoun "she" almost invariably alludes to some locomotive

engine; "he" to "the chairman", "it" to the London Board.'

The price for the security offered by the railway companies was loyalty, and most employees were happy to pay it. The 19th century saw few strikes by railway workers – only 10 are recorded in the 40 years from 1830 to 1870 – and men willingly followed fathers, uncles and brothers into the companies' paternalistic embrace.

Community of the railway

The railwaymen and their families formed a separate, close-knit community, with their own rules, their own traditions and their own strict hierarchy. In his book *Men and Rails*, published in 1913, Rowland Kenney, who had himself worked in a goods yard in the north of England, wrote that 'The man in one of the higher grades was regarded as socially superior to the lower grade man. The goods porter was looked upon as an inferior animal by the shunter. The shunter was tolerated as a necessary evil by the goods guard, who had wild

hopes that some day he might be able to look a passenger guard squarely in the eyes as a man and brother of equal rank.'

Another striking aspect of railway life was its distinctive vocabulary, some of which passed into common usage. 'Light at the end of the tunnel' and 'full steam ahead' were obvious examples of footplate patois. Other phrases, however, remained obscure. Outsiders might possibly have guessed that 'Australian days' and 'birth-control hours' referred to night work. But only initiates could have recognised 'the razor gang' as company auditors, or know that a 'set of Huns' was nothing more alarming than enginemen from another depot.

Company name-calling

There was, in fact, a good deal of rivalry between the different companies, with employees scoffing at competitors' uniforms, facilities, liveries and rolling stock. Derogatory nicknames emerged for different lines. So the Lancashire & Yorkshire became the 'Languish and Yawn', the Somerset & Dorset the 'Slow and Dirty', the London, Chatham & Dover the 'London and Cheetham', and the London, Midland & Scottish the 'Elleva Mess'.

In cities such as Carlisle, which boasted sheds belonging to five different companies, crews would cross the street to avoid each other, and intermarriage between the children of opposing liveries was regarded as outright betrayal.

The early 1900s, however, saw a gradual crum-

▼ Silhouetted against a curtain of steam, a guard carries rear warning lamps along one of the platforms at Liverpool's Lime Street station in 1954. 'It is very doubtful,' wrote one observer of the inter-war rail scene, 'if even in the most unfavourable circumstances anyone has ever seen a guard "rattled" or in any danger of losing his dignity.'

already apparent in the inter-war period became even more marked after 1945. Morale slumped disastrously and the long-awaited nationalisation of 1948, rather than improving the situation, removed much of the partisan pride that had infused the old regional lines. A few years later, the British Railways chairman Richard Beeching removed many of the lines themselves.

Steam trains were soon superseded by diesels and electrics, which were themselves outstripped by jet aircraft. Computerisation and technological advance shrank the workforce still further. Nevertheless, despite all the upheavals the railway workers have faced over the past 75 years, it would be hard to dispute Rowland Kenney's verdict of 1913: 'I do not suggest that railwaymen are better or worse, or more or less necessary than any other section of the national labour forces, they are different, that is all.'

▼ A GWR guard, beard groomed and boots shining, awaits the 'right away' with the 9.15am local service from Solihull to Birmingham Snow Hill in 1899. The early railway managers, many of whom were ex-army men, insisted on station staff presenting a parade ground appearance.

▲ An 0-6-0 tank engine holds centre stage at the opening of the Midland Railway's Barnoldswick line in Yorkshire in the early 1900s. The stationmaster and footplate crew, the latter in their Sunday best, pose on the locomotive itself, while the lowlier staff merely stand in its shadow. The man in mufti with the brass armband is probably a shunter. He is flanked on one side by a porter, and on the other by someone whose appearance suggests that he is the local postman.

bling of company loyalty. The railwaymen, increasingly restive over their low pay, long hours and poor working conditions, turned in increasing numbers to the rail unions.

The reaction of the employers was summed up in the comment of the London & North Western's Sir George Findlay, 'That you might as well have trades unions in Her Majesty's Army as have it in the railway service.'

Discontent came to a head in 1911, with the first ever national rail strike. Two more all-out stoppages followed in 1919 and 1926 – the latter as part of the General Strike called by the TUC.

A further blow to the old style of master-servant relationship was the Grouping of 1923, which combined some 120 privately owned railway companies into just four. Yet loyalties still remained strong in the regions.

At their peak, after World War I, the railways employed more than three-quarters of a million workers. After World War II the payroll still numbered an impressive 635,000. But the decline

The races to Scotland

**Just over a century ago, the rivalry between
the two main rail services to Scotland exploded into
open warfare. Night after night, express trains from Euston
and King's Cross thundered north in the most dramatic
railway racing that the world had ever seen.**

A hundred years ago, two routes carried the bulk of rail traffic from London to Scotland, just as they do today. There was the eastern line from King's Cross, passing through Peterborough, York, Newcastle and Berwick on its way to Edinburgh. The western way, which went from Euston and took in Rugby, Crewe, Carlisle and Carstairs en route to the Scottish capital, was longer, though only by about eight miles (13km).

A fierce rivalry sprang up between the operators of the two services, and the result, over the course of two summers in the closing decades of the 19th century, was the most celebrated railway racing that Britain had ever experienced.

The rivalry had existed ever since the east coast service, operated by the Great Northern Railway (GNR) as far as York, and then by the North Eastern Railway (NER), was established in the 1850s. Although arriving on the scene later than its west coast competitor, it quickly won a reputation as the faster route.

The 10.00am Special Scotch Express – the predecessor of the Flying Scotsman – out of King's Cross took just nine hours to the Scottish capital. By contrast, the trains out of Euston, run by the London & North Western Railway (LNWR) to Carlisle, then onwards by the Caledonian Railway, needed 10 hours.

Until November 1887, however, the King's Cross express had been reserved for first- and second-class passengers only, while the slower Euston trains had a monopoly of third-class traffic. In that month, though, the GNR opened the doors of the 10.00am train to third-class passengers also.

To the LNWR, this was tantamount to a declaration of war, and the following June the company responded by altering its schedules to remove the time differential; now its Edinburgh express would also take a mere nine hours. Two weeks later, the GNR took up the challenge by cutting half an hour off its journey time. Just a fortnight after that, the Euston timetables were again trimmed to match.

wear and tear. The new management's philosophy, however, was to establish their railway as 'the premier line' in Britain. The company already boasted that its track maintenance gave it 'the Finest Permanent Way in the World'. Now it wanted to capitalise on that advantage.

Vital junction

The contestants in the 1895 race, which was to make the 1888 contest seem like a warm-up, were the night expresses that left King's Cross and Euston at 8 o'clock each evening. The two trains followed separate routes through England and the Scottish lowlands as far as Kinnaber Junction, three miles (5km) north of Montrose and 38 miles (61km) south of Aberdeen, their ultimate destination. Thereafter the two routes converged, and since there was no possibility of overtaking, the race depended on being first to the junction.

Like its predecessor seven years earlier, the 1895 contest was set off by an apparently innocent timetable adjustment. The LNWR announced a 10 minute cut in journey times to Aberdeen, ostensibly to ease a tight connection with the popular morning tourist train to Ballater. The problem was that this reduced most of the time advantage enjoyed by the marginally faster east coast service

▼ During the 1888 races, the Caledonian's unique 4-2-2, No 123, later elevated to Royal Train Pilot, worked every Carlisle to Edinburgh train. It was renowned for its 'late braking', on one occasion covering the last 2.2 miles (3.5km) in 2min 35sec.

▲ Stirling 8ft single No 221 stands at the main arrival platform at King's Cross in the 1880s. During the races of 1888, the Great Northern Railway (GNR) entrusted the run from King's Cross to Grantham to sister engines of No 221. By the time of the 1895 races, all the other railways involved were using four-coupled engines, but the GNR persisted with Stirling singles.

By 3 August, the GNR was promising an eight-hour journey, and its partner, the NER, which had at first proved an unwilling competitor, had entered sufficiently into the spirit of things to offer to shave a further 15 minutes off even that time. But the LNWR operators were not to be outdone. They made a supreme effort and sent a train through in 7hr 38min, cutting nearly two and a half hours off the original scheduled time.

Calling a truce

By mid-August, both sides felt that honour had been upheld, and common sense dictated a truce. New timetables restored the time differential between the two routes, but reduced it to a mere 15 minutes. The revised schedules were a considerable benefit to passengers: three-quarters of an hour had been clipped off the journey from King's Cross, while travellers out of Euston gained no less than an hour and a half.

The fragile peace restored in August 1888 was to be shattered by two events at the start of the following decade. One was the opening of the Forth Bridge in 1890. Previously, the Firth of Forth barrier had given the Euston trains an undisputed advantage north of Edinburgh. Now the King's Cross – Aberdeen route was suddenly 16 miles (26km) shorter than the journey from Euston.

The second factor was a change of management at the LNWR. The outgoing chairman had been a reluctant racer who had actively discouraged high speeds because of the expense incurred by extra

◀The famous Precedent class 2-4-0 No 790 *Hardwicke*, of the London & North Western Railway, seen here in the early 1900s heading a Euston-bound express near Kenton in Middlesex, produced the most remarkable performance of any of the engines in the 1895 races. It covered the 141 miles (227km) from Crewe to Carlisle, including the fearsome 30 mile (48km) ascent to Shap Summit, in just 126 minutes – an average speed of 67mph (108km/h).

(a)	First engine, "Shark"	(e)	Carriage in which body of Donald Mavor was found	(k)	Train on Main Line approaching Preston Station,	
(b)	Tender "	(f, g, h)	Carriages		showing the curve	
(c)	Second engine, "Vulcan"	(i)	Rear Guard's van	(l)	No. II. Cabin at north end of Preston Station	
(d)	Tender "	(j)	Point at which the train left the rails	(m)	Messrs. Stevenson and Co.'s Yard—a drop of 20 ft.	

THE ACCIDENT TO THE SCOTCH EXPRESS AT PRESTON

▲The wreckage of the derailed Aberdeen night express out of Euston litters the track near Preston station in 1896. The train was being hauled by two Jumbo 2-4-0s, *Shark* and *Vulcan* – the latter a veteran of the 1888 races – and although only one passenger was killed, the fact that the accident had been caused by excessive speed led to an absolute ban on any further racing.

Dramatic arrival
At the climax of the 1895 races, enthusiastic crowds turned out to see the rival trains thundering through the night to Aberdeen. On 21 August, there was more excitement than the crowd had bargained for.

People had gathered at Berwick at 1am to watch the King's Cross flyer negotiate the station's notorious curves, which then bore a speed limit of just 5mph (8km/h). But the sight of the Worsdell 4-4-0 'Railcrusher', No 1620, charging along the tracks at some 40mph (64km/h) was more than most could stand, and the spectators scattered across the platform in panic.

The train had averaged 58mph (93km/h) over the mile and a quarter (2km) from Tweedmouth Junction to the station.

---

from King's Cross. On 22 July, one week after the LNWR announcement, the GNR advised passengers of a 50 minute cut in its own running times, and it was clear to both parties that another fully fledged race was looming.

Abandoned timetables
This time, the LNWR management adopted a no-holds-barred approach, abandoning from the start any pretence of keeping to published timetables. To avoid problems caused by leaving intermediate stations ahead of schedule, they hit on the device of splitting their trains; a racing section containing only through passengers rushed for Aberdeen, while a slower section loitered behind to pick up connecting traffic.

The GNR, for its part, was hampered by the unwillingness of stationmasters on the line north of Edinburgh, which was operated by yet another eastern route company, the North British Railway (NBR), to allow any deviations from the schedules.

The result was that, for more than a month, the Euston trains consistently outpaced their rivals. This was both an extraordinary achievement in itself and a serious challenge to the GNR.

The battle resumes
At first, the GNR simply refused to accept the LNWR's victories, arguing that its rival's abandonment of the schedules had given it an unfair advantage. By mid-August, however, the GNR had had enough. Convinced that the damage to its reputation could no longer be tolerated, and having finally persuaded the stationmasters of the NBR to co-operate, it tore up its own timetables.

The GNR's chief locomotive superintendent, Patrick Stirling, wrote to one of his lieutenants: 'The L&NW Co have expressed their intention to reach Aberdeen before us. This of course we cannot permit...Please put your men on their mettle!'

But Stirling and his colleagues were to be disappointed. On the night of 15/16 August, the bell in the signalbox at Kinnaber rang to announce the arrival of the west coast train just 60 seconds before it rang to announce the arrival of the east coast train.

The following night, both bells rang together, and the rival footplate crews waited with seething impatience for the signalman to make up his mind. He was an employee of one of the west coast lines, the Caledonian, but in a sporting gesture he gave the right of way to the train from King's Cross.

Neck-and-neck to Kinnaber
There was another epic contest on the night of 20/21 August. The competing trains ran so closely that, as the driver of the east coast express pounded out of Montrose, 40 miles (64km) short of his destination, he could see in the first light of dawn the steam of the rival locomotive racing for Kinnaber away to his left, on the converging western line.

The length of the block sections in this part of the track favoured the trains from the west, and as a result the signalman at the junction accepted the Euston train first, less than 60 seconds before he was offered its eastern rival. So the King's Cross express was forced to a standstill, and the driver and fireman had to watch their competitor surge

▼ The London & North Western's 2-4-0 No 790 *Hardwicke*, which was to distinguish itself in the 1895 races, is pictured in brand new condition at Crewe Works in 1892. The locomotive, built to a design by F W Webb, was first introduced in 1874.

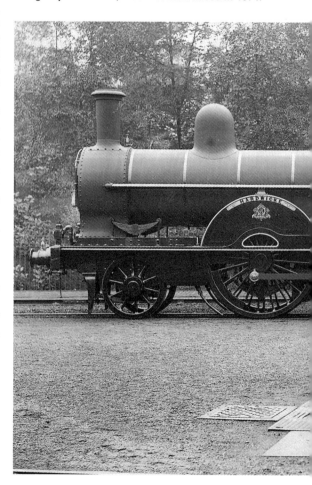

over the points and on to Aberdeen ahead of them.

It was a defeat the GNR was determined to reverse. By now, the press had got wind of what was happening, and the race had become front-page news. Enthusiastic crowds turned out, not merely in London and Aberdeen, but also at intervening stations along the way.

They were rewarded with extraordinary scenes of high speed running, for on 21/22 August, the east coast express reached Aberdeen in a record-breaking 8hr 40min – almost three hours less than the scheduled time. The train from Euston arrived 14½ minutes later.

Terrified passengers

While the rival expresses fought to establish their supremacy in speed, comfort and safety were forced to take a back seat. One alarmed resident of Dundee later gave a passenger's eye-view of travelling in one of the racers: 'Once the carriage lifted a foot from the rails, and my wife, who was vainly trying to snatch a sleep, started up, saying she had the feeling she was falling over a precipice...I never wish to experience the like again. I would rather walk than travel the same route in the same way.'

After a week of racing, it was clear that the risks involved were, indeed, becoming unacceptable. So the King's Cross express reverted to normal running. The LNWR, however, was not prepared to pull out on a losing note. As the company's chairman put it, 'There is no such *thing* as a race. But our company will not be last in it.' On the night of 22/23 August, the LNWR mounted a

▲The heaviest locomotives to take part in the 1895 races were the North Eastern Class M1 4-4-0s, appropriately nicknamed 'Railcrushers'. The drivers of these 50-ton monsters took considerable risks, and one of them is said to have rounded the curve through Portobello station at over 80mph (129km/h).

so-called 'exhibition run', for which its train was reduced to just three coaches.

The 7ft Webb compound *Adriatic* hauled the express from Euston to Crewe, and from here it was taken on to Carlisle by the Precedent class 2-4-0 *Hardwicke*. Although pulling 2.98 times its own weight, *Hardwicke* covered the 141 miles (227km) to Carlisle, including the climb over Shap Summit, in an astonishing 126 minutes.

The final triumph

In Scotland, the locomotives of the Caledonian Railway were equally outstanding – the Drummond 4-4-0 No 90 covering the 150¾ miles (243km) from Carlisle to Perth in 149½ minutes, and the Lambie 4-4-0 No 17 racing the 89¾ miles (144.5km) from Perth to Aberdeen in 80½ minutes, repeating *Hardwicke*'s average of 67.2mph (108km/h).

The express pulled into Aberdeen at 4.32am, eight minutes earlier than its east coast rival had managed the previous night. Its time of 512 minutes for the 540 mile (869km) trip was to remain a record until the introduction of the InterCity 125s more than 80 years later.

Night train derailment

Although, on this occasion, the GNR refused to respond, many believed that the contest would soon resume. But it was not to be. In July 1896, an Aberdeen night express out of Euston came off the rails just north of Preston, and the whole train except for the rearmost brake van was wrecked.

Fortunately, only one passenger was killed, but the accident, caused by excessive speed, gave rise to widespread public concern over safety. Any further record-breaking was ruled out. Thereafter a growing emphasis on passenger comfort encouraged the introduction of heavier and hence slower trains. Not until the 1930s would the lines again echo to the sound of racing expresses out of King's Cross and Euston.

Changing tracks

The point enables trains to change tracks while in motion. Having only two moving parts, it consists basically of the movable **points**, which change the direction of travel of a vehicle's wheels, and the **crossing** (frog) which enables the flanged wheel to cross the intervening rail.

Components

Check rails are placed alongside the outer rails to restrain the flanges of the outer wheels – this prevents the inner wheels shaking themselves out of the correct flangeway in the crossing.

The two **point rails** (switches) move in unison to change the route. Each inner end (blade) is tapered to fit closely alongside the rail when in the engaged position. Only one is held close to the rail, the other being positioned four to five inches from its running rail. The outer ends of the point rails are attached to the fixed **closure rails**, which provide the rail link with the crossing.

For most of their length the point rails rest on planed steel plates which, ideally, are well lubricated because the points are set by swinging the switch rails from one side to the other. To prevent distortion caused by the lateral forces produced when the point is changed, the two blades of the switch rails are held at their fixed distance apart by metal **stretcher bars**.

In Britain, with facing points – points at which trains diverge rather than converge – it became mandatory to provide in one of the stretcher bars two holes, into one of which a metal tongue was inserted when the point was set. This was the **facing point lock**, ensuring that the point was tightly closed and would not shift under a passing train.

Operation

One of the switch rods makes an end-on connection with the **operating rod**, whose lateral motion changes the position of the points. Originally, the operating rod was actuated by a large lever in the hands of a pointman. In Britain, operating rods were usually extended to the nearest signalbox, where the signalman handled levers for the points of his area as well as the signals controlling movement over them. This saved time and labour and, additionally, facilitated mechanical interlocking devices to ensure that signals for a given route could not be cleared until the corresponding points were correctly set.

The rodding between signalbox and point was quite heavy. Despite frequent lubrication point operation was a highly muscular activity. Points could not be located at more than 350 yards (320m) from the signalbox, often necessitating the provision and manning of an extra box. A solution to this problem, appearing in the late 19th century, was the electric or electro-pneumatic point, operated by electric power and actuated not by a lever attached to yards of rodding but by an electric switch. Electric operation of points made possible their setting by an operator many miles distant, and also permitted new – electric – forms of interlocking.

Construction and durability

Points can be made complete on site at the manufacturer's and split up into separate components, or the rails can be taken off, short slave rails put on and the point assembled in small sections. The various segments are craned into position, the slave rails removed and the metal rails laid in their place.

Wooden sleepers are often a more common form of support than concrete ones because of the accuracy involved when laying new points. If the holes for the base plates on the sleepers are more than $1/8$in (3mm) out the rails cannot be fitted correctly.

An express point made for high speed track can be expected to last only a year before replacement if it is placed on a very busy junction. Most of these points last around 25 years. BR has something in the region of 20,000 points on their system.

How points work

The key component of a set of points is the switch rail. Tapered at its leading end, it engages the wheel flanges to transfer the path of locomotive and its train. At one time switched mechanically, many points are now electronically controlled.

Diagram labels: toes and heels of first switches; check rails; wing rail; stock rail; stock rail; switch rails; stock rail; stock rail; toes and heels of second switches; stretcher bar; stock rail; switch rail; slide chair

Birmingham New Street

**With its soaring glass roof and central
position, New Street station – proudly hailed as
Birmingham's Grand Central – was once one of
the finest and busiest in the land.**

The opening to traffic in June 1854 of Birmingham's New Street station was a great event in the history of England's second largest community. Earlier in the same year the *Birmingham Journal* had described the progress of the city during the previous 50 years as having few parallels 'even in the new world'.

The town – Birmingham was not officially recognised as a city until 1889 – had 'almost tripled in magnitude, and every year seems to increase its power of expansion and the energy of the community'. Indeed, within a single year, 1853, its growth was such that building plans had been registered for no fewer than 2784 houses, 22 factories, 38 workshops, 23 workhouses, three foundries and 37 'shop fronts', not to speak of five schools, three chapels and a synagogue.

The 19th century growth of England's greatest centre of industry had depended on railways, and six lines from New Street station – including a new Stour Valley line – radiated to 'every part of the kingdom'. No fewer than 254 trains went through the station on 'ordinary days'.

A triumph of iron and glass

The Victorians loved statistics and dwelt also on the fact that the arched roof of the new station, 840ft (256m) long and 'the largest in the world', contained upwards of 130,000sq ft (12,077m²) of glass, weighing nearly 120 tons. Over 1400 tons of iron had been used and there were 93,000sq ft (8640m²) of corrugated iron sheeting.

Like the Crystal Palace, opened only three years earlier, New Street was a triumph of iron and glass. But it took far longer to build than the Crystal Palace – nearly eight years instead of the

▼ First opened in 1854, Birmingham's New Street station played a central role in the growth from what was then a town into a city. Until 1922 two railway companies used the station – the London & North Western and the Midland. The Midland occupied the smaller curved section, completed in 1885.

The station's magnificent glass roof was eventually spoiled by smoke and steam and part of it had to be removed altogether after sustaining bomb damage in World War II. Birmingham New Street was rebuilt completely in 1964.

three contemplated when five Acts of Parliament were passed in 1846 dealing with Birmingham's railways. The station cost the then huge sum of half a million pounds.

The new station strengthened the link between Birmingham's businessmen and their sources of materials and markets, but the building of it caused much disturbance to local property.

A burial ground had to go, along with two chapels and a school, and a central footbridge was erected, at the expense of the railway companies, to link two now divided parts of the town. If New Street station had not been built where it was, the commercial centre of Birmingham might have been further to the east.

Fortunately, among the 'immense number of houses' that were pulled down, many were squalid and dilapidated so that the rebuilding enterprise has rightly been described as Birmingham's first slum clearance scheme.

Early days

The New Street station of 1854 was not Birmingham's first or only railway station. Following the opening of the Birmingham to Manchester line, the Grand Junction, Curzon Street station was opened for passengers in 1837. The Birmingham to London line was opened soon afterwards, bringing Birmingham within six if not five hours of the

capital. Curzon Street now linked London and Manchester. A little later the line was established between Birmingham and Derby.

Not everyone was happy about the new developments. As one observer indignantly reported in 1838, 'So much has the opening of the London & Birmingham Railway increased the number of travellers through this town that the principal inns often have their beds engaged two days deep; and last week so great was the difficulty of procuring accommodation that the Countess of Chesterfield was obliged to sleep at the Acorn, in Temple Street.'

Out of the tangled railway politics of the 1840s emerged the London & North Western Railway, led by the piratical Captain Mark Huish, and the Midland Railway, controlled by the equally piratical and far more notorious George Hudson. Meanwhile, the Great Western Railway, linking Birmingham with Oxford in the south and Wolverhampton in the north, had its own station, 'Brunel's station', at what came to be Snow Hill.

Curzon Street station had been endowed with an Ionic portico which contemporaries believed compared in quality with the triumphal arch at Euston. Yet, after 1854, Curzon Street was reserved for goods only. New Street itself proved too small by the 1880s, when Birmingham's population had increased over 30 years from 233,000 to 401,000 and the town had spread far out into the countryside, pulling in villages which now became suburbs. Within this huge complex, suburban railways were a necessary new development.

The new section, completed in 1885, cost about as much as the whole station of 1854 and made New Street the largest station in the British Isles at the time. There also had to be further track widen-

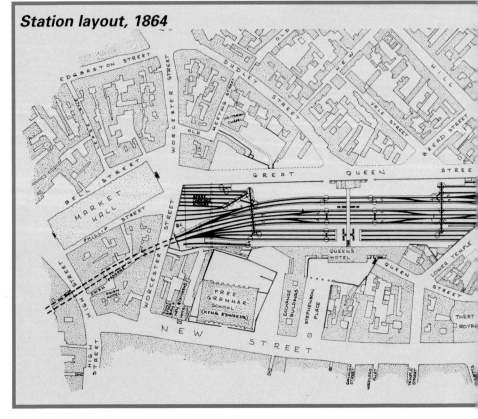

Station layout, 1864

▲Hordes of passengers throng the footbridge over the platforms at New Street in the early days of the century. (The plan, right, shows the exact location of the footbridge.) In 1900, more than 15½ million passengers used the station – this figure had risen to about 20 million by 1914.

ing, which was not completed until 1896.

In the Edwardian age, when wealth was ostentatious and labour cheap, New Street station – spic and span, with its glass roof kept clean – was often the subject of admiring articles in the press. So, too, were the London & North Western Railway steam locomotives, with their coaches in plum and spilt milk, contrasting with the Midland's in crimson lake.

Hard times

A large uniformed staff, including 26 signalmen, worked to the orders of a stationmaster who, in the eloquent words of one admiring writer, was 'the captain in command of all the human and steam forces that aggregate around that little world-microcosm in the railway cosmos called a station'. The highly hierarchical system can be idealised, of course. And not all the trains ran on time.

In World War I the country depended on Birmingham industry, and New Street was central to the massive war effort. The station started to sink into decline. The roof became dirty and the

▲ Its safety valve open to release excess steam, Small Bloomer class 2-2-2 No 1816 stands on one of the centre roads between platforms 1 and 2. In the 1880s, New Street station was in its heyday, the famous glass roof admitting excellent light for an enclosed station of this size.

On the footbridge in the background is the signal cabin which controlled the central part of the station.

▲ Queen's Drive divided New Street into two parts. The roof over the road was removed in 1961 in preparation for the rebuilding work, though this did not start in earnest for another two years.

▼ The sunshine serves only to make the exit to platform nine look even grimier as Baby Scot Class 4-6-0 No 45506 *The Royal Pioneer Corps* waits to leave in the summer of 1959.

companies suffered increasingly from competition. The suburban lines had to compete with the Corporation's tram and expanded bus services, and the national lines became more and more difficult to maintain.

The tonnage of freight carried on British railways per year fell from 343 million in 1923 to 251 million in 1933 and the number of passengers from 1236 million to 799 million. Despite signs of recovery, railway revenue fell by nearly 25% in 1938. World War II increased traffic – and profits – but left a huge backlog of repairs and renewals.

Age of the diesel

World War II was to bring great damage to the fabric of the Victorian station and two years after the end of the war what remained of the great roof was pulled down. Iron disappeared with glass as steel columns were erected and with them – although the danger was not then foreseen – canopies made of asbestos. Steam power itself no longer reigned supreme. The age of the diesel was on the horizon.

In 1947 the Transport Act nationalised British railways, a legislative solution that had been deliberately rejected in the Railways Act of 1921, the prelude to the grouping of 1923. In January 1948, a newly formed British Transport Commission took over management of the railways.

It was not until 1964, however, that Birmingham New Street station began to be rebuilt, in association with the electrification programme, followed by the construction of a shopping mall on a raft over the station.

By then there was a new Birmingham, and a new chapter was starting in the history of the city as well as in the history of railways. In both histories there have been many chapters since.

platforms grey. Gaslight is romantic mainly in retrospect. Now it became tawdry and old-fashioned. The tunnels at either end of the station had always been bottlenecks. Now they began to seem more like barriers.

A landmark date in the interwar years was 1923 when the London & North Western Railway and the Midland Railway amalgamated with other companies to become part of the London Midland & Scottish. There was now one owner and the coaches, like the staff, were in one uniform. Birmingham suffered less from the Depression than most other cities in Britain, but the railway

A day in the life of a signalman

The railway of the 1950s was a world apart, and no inhabitant of that world was more independent than the signalman. Ensconced in his glass-ribbed domain, which not even the stationmaster would enter without permission, he was charged with a burden few would have wished to share.

It is 5.45 on a weekday morning in March 1953, and the daylight is breaking through the mist and low cloud over the Wiltshire countryside as Jack free-wheels his bicycle down the hill along Marlborough Road from the town centre towards Wootton Bassett station. He left home on the other side of town about 10 minutes ago on a journey he has done now for more than a decade.

A local man, he started on the Great Western Railway (GWR) at the age of 15, working as a booking boy in the signalboxes at Swindon. Passing out as a signalman, he worked his way through the grades until now, in his mid-40s, he is a Class 1 signalman, one of three working Wootton Bassett East signalbox.

A short but athletic looking man, with powerful shoulders and forearms gained through years of pulling the signal and point levers, he passes the Beaufort Inn on his right, enters the station yard and pushes his bicycle across the tracks on the public footpath close to East signalbox. Although it is still early in the year, the weather over the past few weeks has been remarkably warm and today promises to be no different.

Propping his bicycle under the signalbox steps, Jack climbs up to the cabin door, which bears an uncompromising black cast-iron sign with the word 'Private' spelled out in white letters. Stepping inside, he is greeted by Fred, the night man. 'The milk empties are just off Swindon,' Fred explains, 'and I'm waiting the out for the Tavistock Junction goods, which was a few minutes early.'

Jack signs the train register to show he is on duty a minute or two before 6.00am and Fred signs off duty at the same time. Although Fred lives at Swindon, it is not easy getting to work at Wootton Bassett by train because the few stopping passenger services do not always accord with the booked shift changes. And it is no good hoping to hitch a lift on a goods train, since it may be cancelled or running late. So Fred travels backwards and forwards on his motorbike, which he parks out of the way on the up platform.

Jack, on his own now, glances at the block indicators to see if there is anything Fred has forgotten to tell him. But, of course, all is in order. There are two indicators to Studley, the next signalbox up

▼ No 5096 *Bridgwater Castle* approaches Wootton Bassett station with a Bristol to Paddington express in 1952. The East signalbox can be seen beyond the bracket signal. The left-hand arm controls entrance to the down goods avoiding line which passes to the rear of the signalbox. Beyond the signalbox is the splitting signal for lines to Bristol and South Wales, with home and distant arms. The GWR prided itself on its signalling and was the first to equip its main lines with automatic train control.

the line – the repeater instrument for up trains and the accepting instrument for down trains.

But to Wootton Bassett West signalbox there are six indicators: the repeater instruments for the down main to Bristol, the down to South Wales and the down goods avoiding line; and the accepting instruments for the up main from Bristol, the up South Wales and the up goods avoiding line. The block instruments are of the typical GWR Spagnoletti type, with a swinging disc which shows half and half for 'line blocked'. It swings one way for 'line clear' and the other for 'train on line'. There is quite a knack in pegging the instruments to one or other of these positions, pressing down the appropriate key and pushing the brass retaining rod across the key to hold it in place – using just one hand.

A promise fulfilled

Glancing at the small stove, which not only heats the signalbox but is the permanent resting place for the kettle and the teapot, Jack sees there is enough coal on the fire for the time being. In fact, the promise of another warm day is being realised and, with the temperature inside the cabin gradually rising, Jack throws open some of the windows.

Two-pause-one rings out on the bell from Studley and the block indicator disc swings to mid position to tell him that the Tavistock Junction goods has cleared the section and is heading towards Swindon. This is followed by two rings from Studley to say that the milk empties have entered the down line section.

Jack replies with two beats and pegs the down line instrument at 'train on line'. Dealing with the milk empties means some shunting to get the tank

wagons into the United Dairies sidings, which are off the up main line at the Swindon end of the station and are controlled from a ground frame released by East signalbox. By the time the York to Swindon and Bristol overnight passenger and mail train passes 10 minutes later, the empties have all been moved off the main line.

A steady stream of trains builds up as the daytime passenger services get under way, interspersed with the odd goods working. All have to be offered and accepted on the block instruments; points levers have to be operated to change points; signal levers have to be pulled to clear; and the times of all block bell signals have to be recorded in the train register.

Jack checks each train as it goes past, making sure that there are no passengers in obvious distress, that there is nothing wrong with the train itself and, above all, that the tail lamp is on the rear to show that the train is complete. Only then does he pass it out of section.

The shunter at the United Dairies ground frame rings to say that the milk engine is ready to come back through the station en route to the down sidings where it will pick up the coaches for the train carrying staff to the Swindon workshops, due to be away at 7.10.

An hour or so later, the pace quickens. At 8.10, West signalbox rings three-pause-one for the

▲ In this GWR signalbox, BR standard block instruments have replaced the GWR Spagnoletti type, but still retained are its rare dial route indicators, only required where there were numerous options. At Wootton Bassett East trains for the South Wales line were billed as 'branch' trains as a route code.

▼ King class 4-6-0 No 6004 *King George III* roars through Wootton Bassett with the eastbound Red Dragon from South Wales in December 1961. It was less than a year before the Kings were withdrawn, and No 6004 is showing signs of poor maintenance, leaking steam from around the piston glands.

Express derailment
In the early hours of 27 June 1946, the 11.50pm express goods from Paddington to Carmarthen was wrecked at Wootton Bassett. Somehow the signalman had managed to get the lever of the facing lock bolt into the locked position, allowing the signals to be cleared. However, the diamond crossing switches were not fully home and locked, with the result that the train was derailed on the switch diamond crossing at the intersection of the down South Wales and up Bristol lines. No lives were lost.

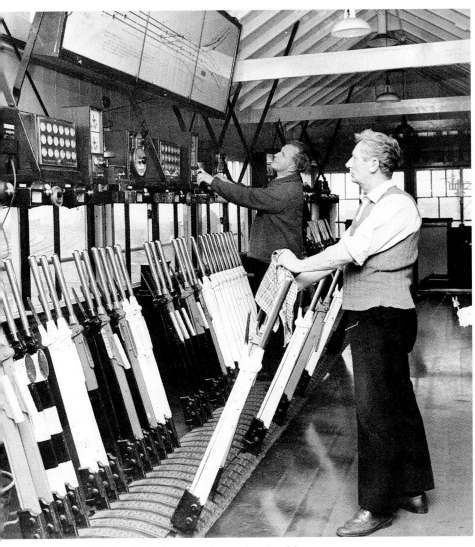

Swindon West to tell them '7 o'clock Weston TL (through line)'.

In a quiet moment, Jack fills a bucket from the cold-water tap at the small sink and starts mopping the lino floor. The signalbox chores are divided between the three regular men. The middle turn man, who takes over from Jack, will clean the windows and the late turn man will polish the brass of the instruments.

All goes well until about 10.15, when the code ring for East signalbox sounds on the omnibus telephone circuit. It is Shrivenham advising that the 8.55 express from Paddington to Pembroke is eight minutes late and could clash through the junction. Jack rings Chippenham. 'How's the 7.50 Taunton? – right time OK.' That means both trains coming together. Better to let the up train run, as it is still on the slight climb to Swindon.

Two 'Is line clear?' bells sound almost simultaneously – one from Studley for the 8.55 and one from West box for the 7.50. Jack offers both trains on, changing the one-three code for the 8.55 train to four beats to West box. Nothing for it but to pull off on the up for the 7.50. This train is going well as Jack dashes backwards and forwards along the frame pulling and resetting levers. The frame is not entirely in sequence, with the main line switch diamond lever separated from its locking levers. As usual, Jack does the work armed with a

▼ GWR 2-6-2T No 5547 pauses during shunting of the up sidings, as seen from the window of Wootton Bassett East signalbox on a gloomy afternoon in the 1950s. The same locomotive was also used to shunt the United Dairies sidings and prepare the early afternoon milk train to London.

6.40am Bristol – Swindon stopping train. As this goes past East signalbox at 8.21, Jack realises he has not had a Stoke Gifford – Hanwell goods off the South Wales line offered up the goods line to make way for a couple of faster trains. 'Just off Brinkworth now' comes the response from a call to West box. 'That's cutting it fine,' says Jack.

The 7.18 stopper from Bristol via Badminton to Swindon is only a section behind the goods, and booked 12 minutes behind the 7.18 towards Swindon is the 7.00am from Weston-super-Mare, the first morning express from the Bristol line to Paddington. This is one train a signalman delays at his peril.

No use holding the local to let the 7.00am run ahead because the 3.55am Fishguard boat train is also coming up the South Wales line, booked only five minutes behind the 7.00am. But it all just about works. Out of section for the 7.18 from Studley, offer four bells for the 7.00am, accepted, pull off, check the repeater for the up distant arms to ensure they have come off.

A few minutes later, the 7.00am speeds through, a Castle class 4-6-0 at its head, whistle shrieking two long blasts and a crow (cock-a-doo-dle-do) to confirm that it is alright for water and does not need to stop at Swindon. Jack checks its special red and white tail lamp on the rear of the last coach, to be slipped at Didcot, then phones

East and West

Wootton Bassett had a remarkably complex layout controlled from two signalboxes, East and West. East box was the larger and more important of the two since it controlled the points of the route split between the South Wales and Bristol lines. West box also controlled both routes, but was concerned mainly with the exit from the down goods loop and down sidings on the Bristol line and the entrance to the up goods loop from the South Wales line.

West box was sometimes switched out, but East box was open continuously. It was worked in three eight hour shifts during the week and two 12 hour shifts on Sunday. The late turn man one week did the early turn the following week, and the night shift the week after that.

▼ GWR 2-8-0 No 3846 hauls an up goods past the East signalbox in September 1955. It was vital for signalmen to keep a careful eye on such trains: an undetected wagon hot box could lead to fire or even derailment and cause chronic delays to following trains. A tell-tale wisp of smoke was the first sign that the axlebox was beginning to overheat.

cloth, which prevents the levers from being corroded by sweat from his palms.

The 8.55 missed the distant, but Jack has the home and starting signals clear, and West box distants are clear as the train coasts through the station. With the 50mph restriction through the junction towards the South Wales line, it has not lost much more time.

Footsteps outside the signalbox herald the daily visit of the Stationmaster, or SM. In spite of his rank, he gives a nominal tap on the door before entering. 'Hello Jack.' 'Morning Guvnor, it's a warm one today.'

'The sunshine's fine,' says the SM, 'but a month without rain has dried my garden up. A bit different to a few weeks ago with all those floods in the east. Now, let's have a look at the book. Bristol wants to know why somebody stopped the Dragon last week.' The SM has just received a memo from the District Operating Superintendent's office in Bristol inquiring about an incident involving the Red Dragon express from Carmarthen.

Someone let a goods out too close in front of the Dragon and it was checked approaching Swindon. The signalman may not have been at fault. The engine of the goods might have been steaming badly. Either way, the register will show the times of the block bell signals.

'And what about the hot box you had last week,' asks the SM. 'Why wasn't it taken off here?'

'Well Guvnor, I had all boards off, and I didn't see the wisp of smoke on a wagon near the middle until after it had gone by the box. But it would have been pushing it to have stopped an unbraked goods in time, so I sent 'Stop and examine' to Studley. It may not have been smoking when it

went by Brinkworth. That's the trouble with the old grease box wagons.'

'Well, we stopped the job for over an hour,' says the SM.

Jack is philosophical: 'We can never win with Bristol.'

A ring on the block bell from West signalbox heralds the four-beat 'Is line clear?' bell signal for the 11.45am Bristol – Paddington off the South Wales line. Soon after, the 9.00am all stations stopping train from Weston-super-Mare to Swindon is offered on the main line, reminding the SM that he has to attend the local train. 'I'm off. Don't worry, I'll square that hot box.'

Between trains, Jack finds time to eat his sandwiches and make tea. He empties about two days' worth of tea leaves out of the pot, but makes no attempt to wash it. That would spoil the taste of traditional signalbox tea, which is produced simply by adding hot water and tea to what is already there. He has brought a container of milk with his lunch box and, after pouring some of this into a clean mug, he tops up with a torrent of dark brown liquid from the pot.

Weighing the balance

The signalbox clock shows 2.00pm and Les, the late turn man, arrives. In the eight hours since he came on duty, Jack has handled about 50 trains, sent a few thousand passengers safely on their way, made sure that London received its milk and passed or shunted thousands of tons of goods. And all for a basic wage of £8 a week, plus overtime if he works a rest day, a Sunday or a night shift. But it is a secure job and, although his wife is not too happy about shift work, the railway is Jack's way of life. He could earn half as much again working in a factory, but money isn't everything.

The development of railway carriages

For all but a small élite, travelling by train used to be a dreary, daunting and even dangerous experience. But after a slow start, the railway companies began to improve conditions, and by the turn of the century even third-class passengers were able to ride in reasonable comfort.

Early rail travel was a bone-shaking experience. The new steam locomotive was able to move people at unprecedented speeds, yet the first railway carriages were hardly different from the horse-drawn mail coaches that had evolved during the previous century. On the Stockton & Darlington Railway, opened in 1825, where passengers came second to coal, the passenger trains were formed of road carriages fitted with flanged wheels and were still drawn by horses.

The Liverpool & Manchester Railway of 1830 was planned right from the start as a steam worked passenger and goods line, but the link with road carriages was still much in evidence. The trains consisted of three mail coach-type compartments mounted on a single four-wheeled underframe. As with the traditional mail coach, the luggage was carried on roof racks and the mail in a boot at one end.

Even the guard was perched high up on a seat so that he could see over the roofs of the other coaches to the engine and respond to any signal from the engine crew to apply or release the handbrake. There was a door to each compartment,

▼ Fresh flowers, armchair seats, and linen napkins and tablecloths are provided for this third-class dining car used on the Anglo-Scottish expresses of the East Coast Joint Stock around the turn of the century. The basket-weave holders below the clerestory roof are intended primarily for top hats.

with a drop window and, in most cases, a window on either side of the door.

The coach bodies were usually built of timber, with ornate mouldings covering the joints between the panels. Seats were padded, perhaps with arm and head rests, and the inside of the doors and bodywork often had upholstered panels. At night, an oil lamp would be suspended from an opening in the roof.

A matter of class

These facilities were for the élite only, however, as right from the start, the railways reflected the British class system. Coaches for the middle class were much less ornate than those for the rich, with box-like wooden bodies, possibly glazed windows or even just an open space in the doors, and a semblance of padded seating. These second-class coaches were sometimes divided by partitions into compartments, like their first-class counterparts.

Thus was born the standard British compartment carriage, which has survived for over a century and a half and is only now finally disappearing as the last of the old Southern Region suburban electric trains are withdrawn from Network SouthEast.

As for the poorest passengers in those early railway days, they often had to ride on slow, lumbering goods wagons, since many railways, fearing that the behaviour of the lower orders would annoy their wealthier patrons, refused to provide third-class carriages. But even where such carriages were provided, they were little more than open boxes, with backless benches and holes in the floor to let out the rainwater.

The Great Western Railway (GWR), with its 7ft broad gauge, introduced some handsome six wheel first-class coaches, 24ft long and 9ft 6in wide, each with four compartments. They were much larger than coaches on standard 4ft 8½in gauge railways, which were often only 6ft and no more than 7ft wide at that time.

In contrast, the GWR third-class coaches were open wagons with sides just 2ft high, so that there was little to prevent passengers from simply falling off. As a parliamentary inquiry was told in 1839, the GWR provided third-class carriages of 'an inferior description at very low speeds' and, like the London & South Western and London & Birmingham railways, 'combined them with cattle, horses and empty wagons'.

Disaster heralds new law

On Christmas Eve 1841, a GWR train, including two third-class carriages, ran into an earth slip in Sonning cutting near Reading and inevitably the

▶The interior of this third-class compartment of a London Midland & Scottish Railway side corridor main line coach built in 1946 reflects standards of comfort that would have astonished third-class rail travellers of a century before. Armrests, here folded back, divided the seats into three on each side when pulled down. Decor was in 'Empire timbers' and over-the-shoulder reading lamps were provided.

▼ These composite corridor coaches of the early 1900s – one of the Great Eastern Railway (below) and one of the Caledonian Railway (bottom) – included both first- and third-class compartments. They also featured two of the most modern amenities – lavatories and electric lighting.

passengers were tipped out, eight being instantly killed and 17 severely hurt.

In 1844, Parliament passed the Regulation of Railways Act, which required the railways to carry third-class passengers in covered carriages, at an average speed of not less than 12mph and at a fare of not more than one penny a mile. It was the beginning of a new deal.

Carriages themselves also improved, gradually becoming longer and wider. By the 1860s, they were often 30ft or so in length and – except on the broad gauge GWR – between 7ft and 8ft wide. The three-class system still prevailed, however, with well-padded and plush interiors in the first class, little padding on seats in the second and bare wooden boards in the third.

Railway revolution

Then in the 1870s came a revolution. The Midland Railway abolished second-class accommodation and improved its third-class carriages, notably by fitting them with upholstered seats and seat backs. It also reduced first-class fares. Other main line railways gradually followed suit, and third-class passengers, at least on express and long distance trains, finally began to be treated as people rather than cattle.

It was also in the 1870s that the Midland's general manager, James Allport, made a tour of American railroads and met entrepreneur George Mortimer Pullman. Pullman, disgusted with the poor standards of American railroad cars, had negotiated to run luxury cars of his own design on certain lines, charging the passengers a Pullman supplementary fare.

The upshot was the introduction of Pullman cars on the Midland Railway, including parlour saloons with end balconies, open interiors and armchair seats for day use, and convertible saloons for night services.

For second- and third-class passengers, upholstered bench-type seats and backs were installed in the parlour saloons, allowing more people to be seated than in their first-class equivalents. Compared to the conventional British coaches of the time, the Pullman cars were massive, measuring 58ft long and 9ft wide, and running on pivoted four wheel bogies at each end.

But the British public was not yet ready for such advances and the Pullman trains were not a

The clerestory roof

One of the most noticeable features of the early British railway carriage was the clerestory roof, in which the centre was raised above the sides and partially glazed to give extra light. It was first seen on a few early Great Western Railway saloons in 1838, but really came to the fore on the Midland Railway in the 1870s.

By the turn of the century, the design had become common on main line coaches, with overall heights from the floor to the highest part of the roof of just over 8ft. The impression was one of great elegance.

The design did have disadvantages, however. It tended to let in the rain and it made a coach liable to break in two in the event of an accident.

Clerestory roofs began to be phased out after World War I, though they appeared on some coaches produced by the London Midland & Scottish Railway in the 1920s, and were used on new London Underground carriages until the mid-1930s.

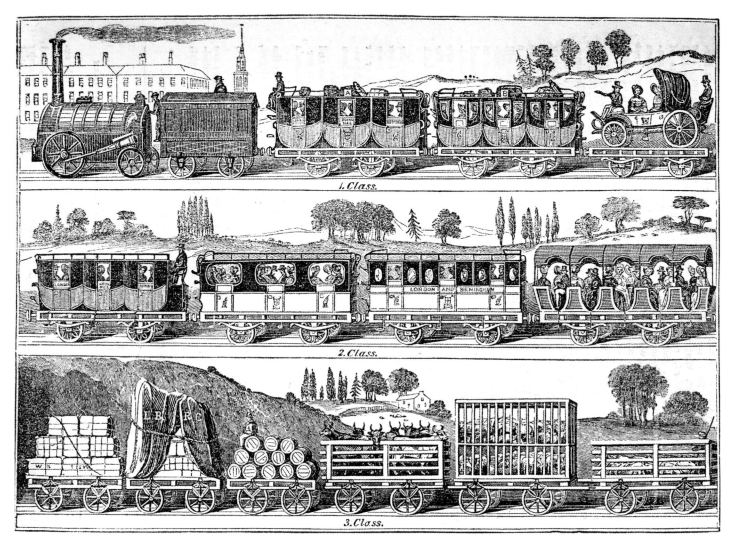

1. Class.

2. Class.

3. Class.

▲This print of rolling stock in use on the London &
Birmingham Railway in the 1840s highlights the
differences between first, second and third class
accommodation. The railways were reluctant to
provide proper carriages for third class passengers,
fearing that this would encourage rail travel among
the 'lower orders' and thereby offend, or even drive
away, higher class patrons.

Special trains
Some of the finest coaches available to the general public, as distinct from royalty, have been those in special trains. Probably the best ever were those built in 1907 for the London & North Western Railway's London – Liverpool trans-Atlantic boat-trains. Their large compartments had ornately decorated ceilings and fine timber panelling, and were furnished with sofas and armchairs, in addition to the normal seating.

Thirty years later, both the London Midland & Scottish Railway and its great rival, the London & North Eastern Railway, produced special sets of coaches for certain routes. Most striking were the first class compartments on the LNER's West Riding and Coronation trains, with their modern interior decor, stainless steel fittings and single armchair seats in alcoves.

success. However, there was a steady improvement in standards. Again, the Midland led the way, building longer coaches and mounting them on bogies, which gave a much smoother ride than the old rigid four and six wheelers.

In 1873, the North British Railway introduced the first sleeping cars in Britain. Six years later, the Great Northern Railway introduced the first restaurant car with on-board cooking facilities. However, apart from Pullmans, there was still no means for passengers to move from one coach to another while the train was moving, which meant they had to join or leave the diner at an intermediate station or remain there throughout the journey.

Improving passenger comfort
It was not until 1892 that the first true corridor train with inter-coach gangways was introduced, on the GWR between Paddington and Birkenhead. Other improvements to passenger comfort came with the provision of better heating and lighting. Oil lamps gradually gave way to compressed gas and this, in turn, was eventually replaced by electric lighting. Radiators fed by steam from the locomotive began to displace rugs and footwarmers, the metal containers filled with hot water and sodium acetate which passengers had been hiring since the earliest days of rail travel.

By the turn of the century, British carriage

design had taken on features which are still familiar to us today. Corridor trains with restaurant cars were becoming standard for long distance services, and non-corridor compartment coaches for short distance and suburban work.

Most new designs were on bogies, and lengths varied from around 50ft to over 70ft on some GWR types where, following the end of the broad gauge in 1892, larger clearances were available than elsewhere. On the South Eastern Railway, for example, between Charing Cross, Hastings and Dover clearances were tight and remedial work was necessary to run larger coaches with more than 8ft wide bodies. Even today work is still needed on a few tight spots to allow free passage of trains to the Channel Tunnel.

Peak period of design
The decade between the death of Queen Victoria and the outbreak of World War I saw British carriage design reach its zenith. Some of the more

►The lavish interior of this first-class dining car on the Manchester, Sheffield & Lincolnshire Railway in the 1890s was typical of the luxury that wealthier rail travellers now regarded as their due. 'They expect not only a seat for themselves,' wrote one contemporary observer, 'but another for their feet.'

opulent sleeping and dining coaches were outstanding examples of the coachbuilder's art, featuring finely panelled ceilings and compartment partitions with wood carvings, mouldings and lining. Externally, timber bodies were panelled with raised mouldings picked out in fine lining to emphasise the main background colour.

And colour was what distinguished one railway from the next, whether it was the crimson lake of the Midland, the varnished teak of the Great Northern or the purple-brown and spilt milk of the London & North Western.

However, from around World War I, materials began to change. Steel instead of timber became more common for coach underframes and a number of railway companies started using steel for coach body construction instead of wood. A few even went as far as steel body framing, though this was a development that did not become really noticeable until after the 1923 Grouping.

With the emergence of the Big Four, economy of production became the order of the day. The London Midland & Scottish Railway (LMS), for example, began mass-producing timber coach bodies, with kits for sides, ends and roofs.

Together with the London & North Eastern Railway (LNER), the LMS was also responsible for another far-reaching innovation – the provision of open accommodation for third-class passengers.

The open saloon with a row of double seats on either side of a central passageway was more comfortable than the traditional side corridor compartment.

The open saloon style later became standard on British Railways for both main line and suburban second class accommodation, and even on some first-class coaches, as well.

World War II brought further design refinements, but little real change, and by 1948, when the Big Four were nationalised, much was as it had been in the 1930s and earlier, although steel body panels had become standard. Further changes would not be made until much later.

▼ Built in the 1860s, this third-class carriage was open internally above wooden bench seats with low backs. Note the circular door handles and the safety chains in addition to the normal coupling. There were no power brakes in those days, only handbrakes on the tender and on selected carriages.

A day in the life of a city stationmaster

The stationmaster of a major London terminus was like the general of a well-drilled army, with each member attending to his own prescribed task. But the man at the top was still responsible for many details, from the smooth operation of the timetable to the greeting of VIPs.

▶ A platform conference precedes the departure of a principal train at Paddington in 1942. Even during wartime, London stationmasters saw off such trains in person, and wearing formal dress.

◀ Clad in the traditional garb of the senior London stationmaster, the man in charge at Waterloo looks out over his kingdom. Stationmasters in the capital were issued with vouchers, which they used to be kitted out at high class tailors and hatters in Savile Row and Jermyn Street.

An outer suburban train draws to a stop at one of the main London terminus stations soon after 8.30am on a raw March morning in 1939. From a first class compartment steps a commanding figure wearing a black overcoat and bowler hat, and carrying a rolled umbrella and briefcase. As he passes the ticket barrier, the ticket inspector raises his hand in salute: 'Good morning, sir, rather chilly today.'

Leaving the inspector to deal with the other early morning arrivals, the bowler-hatted figure strides across the concourse and enters a door marked 'Stationmaster'. His task is to run one of the largest stations on the system, with long-distance trains to many parts of the country, and a thriving local service bringing thousands of commuters daily into the capital.

After exchanging greetings with his clerk, the stationmaster (SM) confers briefly with one of the assistant stationmasters (ASMs), checking that all has gone well during the night and that no problems have arisen at the start of the morning rush hour.

There are three ASMs, each on an eight hour shift, who are involved in the detailed running of the station. The job of the SM is to co-ordinate and delegate, a far cry from the role of the rural stationmaster, who will often get his hands dirty wielding a shunting pole or issuing tickets.

Climbing the ladder

Not that the SM is unfamiliar with life at the sharp end. The son of a Midlands signalman, he joined the railway at the age of 14 as a lad porter and spent the next 40 years making his way up the promotion ladder. In 1931, he was put in charge of one of the railway's major provincial stations, receiving his present posting four years later. Had he been given the posting when he was younger, he might well have moved on to take charge of a district or division. He is now coming up to 62, however, and this job will be his last before retirement.

There is a knock on the office door and the tea lady bustles in with the SM's regular 9.00am cup

about holiday specials and one about the measures to be taken if war comes – an eventuality that seems all too likely with Hitler's recent takeover of Czechoslovakia and Britain's promise to support Poland in the event of a German attack.

There is also an external meeting, with a representative of the GPO to sort out the problems caused by mail bags from one of the morning expresses. Finally, the clerk gives the SM a reminder, if one was needed, that the Royal Train is due later in the day. This is by no means the first time that the SM has greeted members of the Royal Family, but he regards the occasion with a mixture of anticipation and apprehension. All has gone smoothly before, but each time there is the niggling fear that something might go wrong.

It is now 9.45 and the SM gets ready to go out on the platforms. He swops the jacket of his black suit for a morning coat and dons a top hat, the traditional attire of the senior London stationmaster. Like his counterparts at the capital's other main stations, he always oversees the departure of the principal trains of the day.

Passing through the ticket barrier, he casts an appraising eye over the polished brass of the door handles, the shining glass of the windows, the gleaming bodywork of the coaches. He also inspects the shoes, collars, uniforms and haircuts of the train and platform staff.

A minute or two before departure time, the SM checks down the platform to see that the starting signal is clear. He nods to the platform inspector, whistles are blown, doors are closed, more whistles are blown, the guard waves his green flag, a

▼ The stationmaster at King's Cross, Mr Harry Ireland, admires the Order of Leopold II, conferred on him by the King of the Belgians. Mr Ireland was well-known to the monarch, often greeting him on his visits to London.

of sweet brown Typhoo and plate of digestives. His wife is forever lecturing him about the dangers of too much sugar, but he has not had a day's illness since joining the railway and he feels as fit now as he did when he was 20.

At 9.15 there is another knock on the door and his clerk comes in with the morning mail. There is the usual assortment: memos from divisional or headquarters office requiring his personal attention; letters from businesses requesting information about parcels traffic; queries from the General Post Office (GPO) concerning the dispatch of mailbags; complaints about delayed departures or poor travelling conditions; inquiries about large parties travelling on ordinary trains and larger parties travelling on special trains.

The clerk makes notes on the action to be taken, setting aside the items that have to be passed on to either division or headquarters, or to one of the departments within the station itself. Much of the incoming correspondence will already have been filtered and dealt with.

The clerk now goes through the diary. There are three internal meetings: one about the extra trains for the forthcoming Grand National, one

signal passes down to the driver by raised arms from the platform staff and the express is away exactly on time.

At 10.30 the relevant officials assemble in the SM's office to discuss the trains for the Grand National. The overall arrangements for running special trains for sporting events, whether the Grand National, the Cup Final or Cowes Week, are in the hands of the train office. This is located at either headquarters or the divisional office, depending on the railway. The provision of coaches is the responsibility of rolling stock control and the laying on of locomotives that of the motive power department.

But the details of the platforming and the provision of guards and ticket inspectors falls to the SM, who has to liaise with his guards inspector to ensure that enough men are available. He also has to discuss with the ASMs and platform inspectors which specials should run from which platforms and how these can be fitted in between the regular services.

Threat from the air

But for how much longer will it be possible to run sporting specials? That is the question still in everyone's mind at the 11.30 meeting to discuss some of the proposed arrangements in the event of war. Other questions also clamour for answer. Will the railway be able to handle the proposed mass evacuation of mothers and children from London and other big cities to the rural areas? Will it be able to cope with a vastly increased military traffic and still continue to bring thousands of workers in and out of London to keep the commercial life of the nation going? Will the main line stations be able to survive air attacks?

The main item on the agenda is, in fact, Air Raid Precautions, and the meeting discusses proposals for lighting at night consistent with both the blackout regulations and safety on the trains and platforms. It also debates blast protection, calculating the number of sandbags needed to provide cover for doors and windows. But what happens if a bomb shatters the acres of glass in the station roof? That is a contingency not covered by the proposals from headquarters, and the meeting breaks up in considerable gloom.

Mail bag obstruction

But there is no time for introspection. The GPO representative has arrived and is ushered into the SM's office. The problem he is here to discuss arises with the mail arriving on one of the morning expresses. The departure of this train is closely followed by the arrival of a second express and a parcels train, one on either side of the platform, with the result that mail bags still being loaded on to platform trolleys are causing a serious obstruction. They decide to try a platform change, but if that doesn't work, the train office will be asked to get the parcels train retimed.

It is well past 1.00pm now and the SM has a tray of sandwiches and a pot of coffee sent over from the staff canteen. He has less than 40 minutes before the next meeting, called to consider the summer timetable. Some of the peak summer extra trains are to start in May instead of July, but already the platform arrangements have to be made and the rosters of guards and ticket inspectors checked. Again, everyone is contemplating the possibility of war and wondering if there will be any holiday trains this summer.

Soon after the meeting breaks up, the SM's clerk comes in with the letters, typed up from his morning notes, which require the SM's signature. He also brings the afternoon mail, which includes a number of complaints about seat reservations being totally wrong on one service because the

▼ The Euston stationmaster chats to the footplate crew of No 46240 *City of Coventry*, who await a footplate guest – the Rev Eric Treacy. As well as supervising all platform arrangements and train operations, the stationmaster was also responsible for signalboxes and booking, parcels and telegraph offices.

empty train arrived in a back to front formation. This was certainly not the fault of anyone at the station and the SM asks his clerk to forward the complaints to headquarters.

There is just time for a quick tour of the station before the arrival of the Royal Train. The SM's first call is at the main booking office to see the chief clerk. The previous day's figures for ticket sales and the lateness figures were already in his in-tray, but with all the meetings he has not had a chance to digest them. That is a task he will take home with him. Certainly, bookings have been increasing lately, but many of the journeys have been by military personnel using travel warrants instead of tickets, which has meant extra work for the clerks in claiming payment from the authorities.

The SM looks in briefly at the parcels office and the seat reservation office. It is now almost 6.00pm and the SM heads back to his office to meet the duty ASM, the senior station inspector and a superintendent from the railway police.

They confirm that all is in hand for the arrival of the Royal Train. It is due at 7.00pm, by which time the worst of the evening rush hour will be over. The arrangements have been planned for several weeks. This is not a formal occasion, with pomp and ceremony, but a fairly low-key return by the King and Queen from the Midlands, where they have been visiting factories gearing up for war production.

But the formalities are still observed. The plat-form to be used by the Royal Train is closed off to the public and screened by an empty train on an adjoining track with its blinds down. The red carpet is unrolled and the end placed at exactly the spot where the door of the Royal compartment will open. At precisely seven o'clock the Royal Train steams in, four-lamp headcode alight, and eases to a halt. Top hat in hand, the SM moves forward and bows as the Royal couple step off the coach. 'Good evening Your Majesty,' he says to the King. 'I hope you had a good journey.'

Speedy exit

There is a ripple of excitement beyond the ticket barrier and the gathering crowd applauds enthusiastically as the Royal party hurries through to the line of gleaming black Rolls Royces waiting in the station forecourt.

Half an hour later, clad once again in black overcoat and bowler hat, the SM boards the train that will take him back to his caring wife and comfortable suburban villa. If war really does come, perhaps he should send Violet to stay with her sister in Somerset. But it's no good looking on the black side. The worst may never happen.

▼ **A group of London & North Eastern Railway stationmasters tour Liverpool Street station after attending a conference in the capital in 1932. Note the proliferation of bowler hats and brightly polished shoes, an indication of pride in the job.**

Rituals of greeting

The degree of ceremony that went with the greeting of VIPs at the big London stations depended largely on why they were travelling. When the Royal Family was going about its normal duties – opening a new factory or unveiling a public monument, for example – the proceedings were usually low key, with the stationmaster giving the greeting. The same consideration applied when the Royal Family was starting or returning from a holiday at Balmoral or Sandringham.

However, on more formal occasions, such as a Royal tour or civic banquet, the Lord Lieutenant of the county or the Lord Mayor usually made the initial greeting, with the stationmaster in attendance. When a foreign head of state on an official visit arrived in London by train, then the monarch was there to provide an official welcome, with the stationmaster playing only a minor role.

Manual signalboxes

Manual signalboxes, which can still be found on some secondary BR lines and on many preserved lines, originated in the middle of the 19th century when signal and points levers were first grouped together at stations and junctions. Illustrations of signalbox interiors from 1860 show that much would be familiar today.

Signalboxes vary in design according to the company or contractor which built them. Some are mainly timber, others are constructed from brick, with some a combination of both materials. They are usually built on two levels, the operating floor upstairs where the signalman works, and the locking room downstairs. On the upper floor a line of windows at both ends and stretching along the side facing the railway gives the signalman a good view of the trains and signals.

The first thing a visitor notices inside is the row of large, numbered steel levers, each controlling a signal, a set of points or a point lock. They stand about 4ft (1.3m) high, most leaning away from the signalman. Levers are pulled towards the signalman for the reverse position. The rounded top of the lever held by the signalman is usually polished steel rather than painted. The signalman always uses a duster when pulling these, as the steel would soon rust from hand perspiration.

Behind the main lever handle is a second one – the catch handle – which controls a weighted block or spring near the bottom. This holds the lever in either the normal or reverse position. The levers extend through slots below the floor to a pivot in the frame downstairs. An extension at right angles is attached to the signal wires or the point rods. Bars attached to the front of the levers also pass into the interlocking frame. This consists of horizontal and vertical slides which ensure that signals cannot conflict with other signals or points.

The block shelf with its array of instruments is set above the levers. These include bells for operating the block system, the block instruments themselves, and indicators showing whether out-of-sight signal arms have responded to a lever movement or whether signal lamps are alight.

Above the block shelf is a track layout diagram showing the positions of signals and points and the lever numbers. Some diagrams are illuminated by red lights along the tracks to show if a train is occupying a section of line. In some signalboxes this indication is shown on a separate track circuit indicator on the shelf. Finally, there are plungers which must be pressed to release electric locks on levers.

Furniture is sparse – a chair and table for meal breaks, a desk for the train register book where all signalling movements are recorded, and various operating notices and timetables. Depending on location, the lighting is by oil or electricity and inevitably there is a stove, usually fired with solid fuel, on which the kettle is always ready to make tea. The floor lino is washed daily, the brass on instrument cases is polished and all operating equipment is kept clean and tidy.

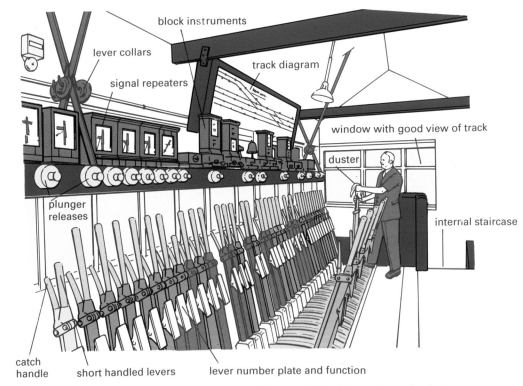

block instruments

lever collars

track diagram

signal repeaters

window with good view of track

duster

plunger releases

internal staircase

catch handle

short handled levers

lever number plate and function

▲ All manual signalboxes have a bank of levers controlling signals, points and point locks. Each lever is painted in a specific colour to identify them: red for stop signals, yellow for distant signals, black for points and blue for facing point locks.

◄ Signalman Rogers waits intently for the 10 o'clock time check in Liverpool Street station box. It was vital that signalmen all worked to the same time. On the LNER two time signals were sent out every day by special code, so signalmen could co-ordinate their clocks.

CHAPTER FOUR

When Things Went Wrong

When an excursion train ran away while being divided, disaster struck (see page 173). Here the wreckage of the coaches is depicted with the overturned locomotive of the 10.35 am train from Armagh to Warrenpoint, 12 June 1889. The very heavy casualties caused a national outrage and resulted in the introduction of continuous brakes on all passenger trains.

Abbots Ripton 1876

**A severe snowstorm and icy temperatures led
to signals freezing in the clear position and to a
collision between an up Scottish express and a goods train.
To make matters worse, a down express ran into
the wreckage and 13 people died.**

Late in the afternoon of 21 January 1876, the weather was bitterly cold with gale force winds. A belt of heavy snow swept in from the Bristol Channel across the south Midlands, disrupting services on the Great Western, London & North Western and Midland railways. It reached the Great Northern (GN) main line at around 6pm. The snowflakes were large – bigger than a two shilling piece, one witness said – and they stuck to pulley wheels, signal arms, track and buildings. Three to four inches (7–10cm) of ice soon clung to telegraph and signal wires.

Abbots Ripton lies on the East Coast main line between Huntingdon and Peterborough, part way along a 1 in 200 hump on otherwise fairly flat country. To the north, in 1876, the next signalboxes were Woodwalton, 1¾ miles (3km) away, then Connington a further two miles (3.25km) on, and Holme almost two miles (3.25km) beyond. To the south of Abbots Ripton was Stukeley signalbox

2½ miles (4km) away and then Huntingdon, two miles (3.25km) beyond.

The rules regarding snow provided for platelayers (permanent way staff) to take up duties at distant and certain stop signals to make sure that the signals were working, to repeat their indication by a hand lamp, and to put down detonators when the signals were at danger. But by the time the snow set in that afternoon, the platelayers had finished for the day and it would have taken some time to call them out again.

The first crash

Until the end of the afternoon the weather had not delayed trains unduly. The 10.30am Edinburgh – King's Cross Scotch Express, known unofficially as the Flying Scotsman, had left York about three minutes late and had lost another three minutes by the time it reached Peterborough. Ahead of it, from Peterborough, was a coal train, which was

▼ A crowd of spectators braved the freezing conditions to gawp at the aftermath of the accident in which Stirling single No 48, the Leeds express (shown in the left foreground), ploughed into the Flying Scotsman, demolishing the third and fourth coaches, and killing 13 people in the process.

booked to leave the East Midlands junction at 5.35pm but actually left at 5.53pm.

Peterborough telegraphed details of the progress of the Flying Scotsman forward to Holme, Abbots Ripton and Huntingdon. Many signalboxes on the GN line were equipped with the electric telegraph, in addition to the block system, for sending general messages, but the intermediate signalboxes at Connington, Woodwalton and Stukeley were not stations and did not have this facility.

The signalman at Holme planned to shunt the coal train off the main line to clear it for the Flying Scotsman. His signals were at danger. But the coal train did not stop, and ran on towards Connington. The Holme signalman could not 'talk' to the Connington signalman on the tele-graph to tell him what had happened, so he merely signalled the train forward on the block instruments. But he was able to telegraph Abbots Ripton to tell them to shunt the coal train there.

From Holme to Abbots Ripton the coal train was signalled on the block instruments in the normal way. When the coal train approached Abbots Ripton all signals were clear, even though the signalman had placed the levers to danger. Fortunately, the coal train driver knew the working and was expecting to be shunted, and the signalman, unaware that his signals were working badly, used a red lamp to stop the train.

The Flying Scotsman was catching up fast and, as far as Woodwalton, was signalled correctly. The Woodwalton signalman had not received the line clear of goods train signal from Abbots Ripton and placed his up line signal levers to danger, but had done nothing more. On the footplate of the Flying Scotsman the driver saw clear white lights on the Woodwalton signals and, a mile or so on, a clear white light on Abbots Ripton distant signal.

The coal train was still backing into a siding when the Flying Scotsman came storming out of the blizzard at about 50mph (80km/h). It hit the sixth, fifth and fourth wagons of the coal train, pushing the front wagons and the coal engine forward, with the engine, tender and some of the coaches from the express thrown across the down line.

The second crash

The Abbots Ripton signalman was in a state of shock, but other staff came to help, including some of the local platelayers, who had turned out again when they realised it was snowing heavily. The signalman tried to telegraph Huntingdon for help, and to tell them to stop down trains. But Huntingdon did not acknowledge the message.

▼ Taken from a sketch by one of the passengers, this illustration shows a working party removing the injured, hampered by the darkness and the falling snow. Behind them, in the centre, can be seen the six-wheeled tender, with a fire iron still firmly wedged into the coal.

Snow stops signals

Signals frozen in the clear position were to blame when the Flying Scotsman crashed into a shunting coal train at Abbots Ripton in the terrible snowstorm of 21 January 1876.

A second collision between a down express and the wreckage of the Flying Scotsman, which caused 13 deaths, could have been avoided if signalmen had been more efficient.

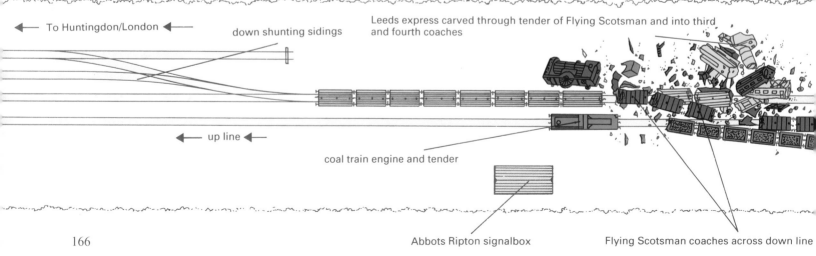

← To Huntingdon/London ←

down shunting sidings

Leeds express carved through tender of Flying Scotsman and into third and fourth coaches

← up line ←

coal train engine and tender

Abbots Ripton signalbox

Flying Scotsman coaches across down line

Signals old and new
Before the Abbots Ripton accident many railways were still using the old three-position slotted post semaphore, which was pivoted from inside the slot. After the accident, the Great Northern adopted the somersault signal instead, in which the arm was balanced. Snow was deemed to be evenly spread along the arm. Other railways evolved signal arms attached to the heavy spectacle casting, which automatically put the signal to danger if a wire or rod broke. The upper quadrant signal was a development of the 20th century, which was even better since any snow on the arm would weigh it down to the danger position.

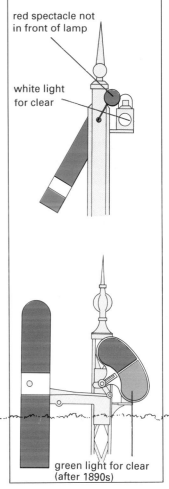

red spectacle not in front of lamp

white light for clear

green light for clear (after 1890s)

▲ Three manually operated winches and a working party armed with levers were required to lift the derailed engine of the Flying Scotsman, 2-2-2 Single No 269, from its side. The lack of a brake on the engine is clearly visible from this angle.

It was obvious that signals were showing clear, even though the levers were at danger in the signalbox, so the fireman of the coal train, armed with detonators, set off in the up direction to stop any trains on the down line. The rest of the crew, finding their engine was still working, started after him towards Huntingdon. It was still snowing hard.

The Abbots Ripton signalman had given up trying to call Huntingdon on the telegraph and, instead, at 6.52pm sent the five beat bell signal 'line blocked' to Stukeley. Just at that moment the 5.30pm King's Cross – Leeds down express was passing Stukeley. Had Abbots Ripton sent that bell signal straight away at 6.45pm, the Leeds train could have been shown a red light at Stukeley.

The fireman had just fixed two detonators close to the Abbots Ripton down distant signal, about 1000 yards (1km) from the crash, when his own engine caught him up. As he climbed aboard, the down express approached. The coal train driver sounded a series of whistles and the crew showed a red light to the express, which was running at over 50mph (80km/h) on the falling gradient.

Its driver responded by sounding an emergency whistle for brakes to be applied – like many trains of the time there was no continuous brake through the train, just the tender hand-brake and hand-brakes operated by guards in three brake vans – and himself put the engine into reverse. But it was no use. The Leeds express was still travelling at about 15mph (24km/h) as it carved through the tender of the Flying Scotsman and demolished the third and fourth coaches of the up train. It was in these coaches that most casualties occurred, with 13 passengers killed and 53 injured.

Acknowledgement from Huntingdon finally came through at 7.05pm, 10 minutes after the second collision.

The GN main line was equipped with what was then thought of as modern signalling, including

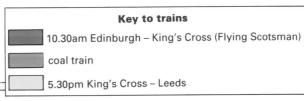

Key to trains

■ 10.30am Edinburgh – King's Cross (Flying Scotsman)

■ coal train

□ 5.30pm King's Cross – Leeds

→ down line →

up shunting siding

→ To Peterborough →

▲ The scene of devastation on the night of Saturday, 21 January 1876, shortly after the crash between the Great Northern Scotch and Leeds expresses. The bottom arm of the Abbots Ripton signal can be seen in the centre of the picture frozen in the caution position.

Human error

Human error was partly to blame for both collisions. The Holme stationmaster, who had been told that the coal train was running against signals, could have made more effort to stop and warn the Flying Scotsman, as could the Holme signalman. He was blamed for not placing detonator signals on the line and failing to display a red lamp in his box. Either man might have prevented the first collision.

With regard to the second collision, the Huntingdon signalman was clearly at fault for not responding quickly to Abbots Ripton's urgent telegraph. The Abbots Ripton signalman was to blame for wasting time trying to contact Huntingdon when he should have sent the five beat 'line blocked' signal to Stukeley immediately. Both measures might have stopped the second crash.

the absolute block system. So how could one, let alone two, collisions occur?

The signals themselves were a legacy from the days of time interval working, when the semaphore arms showed three positions – danger (horizontal), caution (inclined down at 45°) and clear (arm vertical and invisible inside the slotted wooden post). But with the block system, only two indications were needed – danger and clear. The clear position was still with the arm almost vertical inside the slotted post.

Night indications were given by an oil lamp with coloured spectacles linked to the arm mechanism passing in front of the oil lamp. At that time only one colour was needed – red for danger – because the light indication for clear was white. When the signal arm was pulled to the clear position, the red spectacle simply moved away from the lamp and the direct light of the oil lamp was seen as white by a driver.

There were distant signals generally around half a mile (0.75km), or a little more, from the home signals, to give drivers advance warning of whether they had to stop or had a clear run through, but they were little different in style, and at night showed the same red for caution and white light for clear. Drivers were expected to know the line thoroughly – which signals were distants and which were stops.

The main difference in train signalling by the block instruments at that time was that the line

was deemed to be clear unless a train was actually in the block section between two signalboxes. The block indicators showed two out of the three indications of today's instruments – 'line clear' and 'train on line'.

But a prime difference from today was that the block indicator needle was used to send messages in addition to the block bells, by being flicked from the centre to one side or the other. When a train was approaching a signalbox, the signalman called the attention of the signalman at the box ahead by one beat on the bell. When this was acknowledged the dial needle was used to send two beats to the left to show a passenger train was entering the section. The signalman at the far end then firmly pegged the needle pointing at 'train on line', which was displayed in both signalboxes.

When the train passed the signalbox ahead, the signalman there called back with a beat on the bell, and the block indicator needle was flicked twice to the right to mean 'line clear', whether or not another train was due. While the train was actually in the section, the signals at the entry signalbox were placed at danger, but as soon as the train was clear of the signalbox ahead, they were pulled to clear in the same fashion as automatic colour-light signals today.

Therefore the semaphore arms were normally at clear, unless there was a train in the section ahead. They could remain in this position for quite a long time. That day, the snow and ice had led to the arms becoming frozen in the clear position. This was a prime factor in the events leading to the Abbots Ripton disaster.

Recommendations

The Board of Trade inspector, Captain Tyler, made many recommendations after this accident, but the main ones that affected signalling from then on were that the block section should not be regarded as clear until a train was actually due. Therefore, signals would normally be at danger, and if they did stick it would be an error on the side of safety. Also, that signals be redesigned so that they could not be made inefficient by ice and snow and if they failed, this would be indicated in the signalbox. But whatever the failures that night, Capt Tyler remarked on the high standards of signalling which were normal on the Great Northern Railway at that time.

As for the second collision, this would have been prevented if the train had been equipped with continuous brakes and as in many reports he recommended their adoption.

Other recommendations included the use of hand lamps to supplement signals in poor weather; provision of telegraph instruments in all signalboxes; the building of an extra track for slow trains up Connington bank; the stoppage of less important traffic in severe weather and more guidance for and supervision of staff working in fog and snow.

He advised that in severe weather, fogmen with detonators should stand at the signals.

Tay Bridge 1879

As the Dundee train reached the south bank of the Tay a gale was at full fury. The signalman watched the red tail lamps move on to the bridge. Suddenly, after a violent gust, there came a burst of light, then blackness. Where once there had been train lights and high girders there was nothing.

Before 1878 there was no bridge over the Tay estuary. The great Forth and Tay firths cut deeply inland, so travellers needing a direct route north from Edinburgh faced the discomfort of two ferry crossings to link with connecting trains.

In 1871 plans were laid to span the Tay. The designer was engineer Thomas Bouch who planned to build a lattice girder bridge supported by brick piers. After construction had commenced, however, and 14 brick piers had been erected, it was discovered that the bed of the Tay was not composed of the hard rock that had been expected. Bouch amended his plans to replace the proposed brick piers with cast-iron columns filled with concrete and bedded on a circular masonry base.

On 1 June 1878 the great Tay Bridge was opened for rail traffic. It was an impressive structure – at two and a quarter miles (3.5km) it was by far the longest in the world. With the exception of two spans at 227ft (69m), the main spans were 245ft (75m) apart and the girders over the shipping channel were raised to permit a navigable headway of 88ft (27m) above high water level; these were known as the high girders.

Queen Victoria crossed the bridge soon after it was opened and Bouch was knighted for his great achievement. Triumphant with the acclaim, he began work on designs for a bridge to span the Forth estuary.

Towards disaster

On Sunday 28 December 1879, a severe gale was blowing across Scotland. Trees came crashing down, slates and even entire roofs were sent flying. The winds were at their most ferocious over the open expanse of water of the two great firths, the Forth and the Tay. One ship recorded winds up to force 11, with violent gusts well over 70mph (113km/h).

▼ An artist's impression of the rescue operation conducted to search for survivors after the collapse of the Tay Bridge. Steam launches and divers' barges were employed to scour the Tay for any sign of life – none was found.

Passengers on the Sunday afternoon service from Edinburgh must have been thankful when the gale-lashed ferry across the Forth arrived safely on the north shore. They boarded the train at Burntisland secure in the knowledge that it would take them all the way to Dundee without the need for a second ferry across the Tay.

Few trains ran in Scotland on Sundays. The train which left Burntisland at 5.20pm that afternoon was the return working of the afternoon mail train. It had five coaches and a van, all small box-like four wheelers. Normally it was hauled by an 0-4-2 tank locomotive, but on this day the little engine had broken down and the train was worked by a relatively new engine, an inside cylinder 4-4-0, No 224.

As the train from Burntisland reached the south bank of the Tay the driver slowed to take the train staff from the signalman. This baton was his token of authority to enter the single line across the bridge. No 224 then moved slowly on to the bridge.

The signalman saw the red tail lamps recede into the darkness, then he fought his way back to his signalbox – the wind was so strong that he had to crawl on his hands and knees. He sent the 'train entering section' signal to the signalbox at the Dundee end of the bridge.

At full fury the wind tore across the mouth of the Tay, lashing spray into the night air and several people became aware that something was dreadfully wrong. A red flash was seen just as the train reached the high girders. Someone watching from a house on the north shore realised that the train lights could no longer be seen. There was just enough light in the sky to see that instead of high girders there was nothing but space. There was only one explanation. The bridge had fallen.

▶ When No 224 was salvaged, the chimney, cab and dome casing were missing and the footplate was distorted. The engine was repaired and put back to work – although it was nearly 30 years before any driver would take it over the new Tay Bridge.

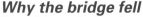

Why the bridge fell

One of the early theories was that the bridge had given way and the train had plunged into the void. This was soon dispelled however when a diver found the train lying within the wreckage of the girders at the bottom of the estuary.

When the fierce wind whistled up the firth it hit the side of the train, exerting an increased pressure on the bridge. It proved too much for the structure and the whole section gave way.

The committee of inquiry concluded that the bracing ties and the cast-iron lugs to which they were secured were not nearly strong enough to resist the maximum pressure that could be exerted by a cross wind. It emerged that the ties had begun to work loose soon after the bridge was opened. Henry Noble, the maintenance manager, had ordered packing to be inserted to regain the tension in the ties. However, he failed to report either the weakening of the ties or the corrective action he had taken.

The reasons given for the weakening of the ties, other than the stress of storms, was the bad workmanship of the lugs and the excessive speed of trains over the bridge – some people refused to travel over the bridge in the southbound direction because they were alarmed by the speed of trains over the steep downhill gradient at the northern end of the bridge.

The construction of the piers was also criticised by the inquiry. The minor alterations to the design following the discovery that the estuary bed was not hard rock was described as 'a very grave mistake'. The bridge should have been redesigned completely.

A new Tay Bridge was designed by W H Barlow, who had been one of the participants in the inquiry into the loss of Bouch's bridge. The second Tay Bridge was opened in 1887. During its construction the remaining parts of the old bridge were used as a guide – the second bridge being built on new piers alongside the original ones.

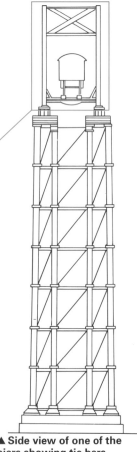

▲ Side view of one of the piers showing tie bars.

Old Tay Bridge Disaster, 1879: The Engine

Up from the depths

The only survivor of the Tay Bridge disaster was the locomotive, No 224.

Salvage work began in April 1880. Some of the high girders, with the remains of coaches, were brought to the surface. The engine was also recovered, though it took three attempts. Twice the locomotive plunged back to the estuary bed after the lifting tackle broke when the engine was near the surface.

At the third attempt No 224 was finally landed on the south shore. It had lost its chimney and cab but was able to be towed on its own wheels to Glasgow for repair. After that it continued on principal express work until displaced by larger, more powerful locomotives in 1907. No 224 survived a further 12 years on humbler duties until it was withdrawn for scrap in 1919.

A sailor on watch aboard a ship in the firth had also seen the train lights move out over the bridge. He looked away, then back – and train and bridge girders had gone. As consternation grew, two brave railwaymen fought their way along the bridge through the storm and returned with the grim news: the Tay Bridge was down.

Final reckoning

Later that evening the Tayport ferry attempted to search the area. No survivors were found. At first light the next morning the full horror of the calamity was apparent. The whole of the high girder section had gone. Later a naval diver found the girders, lying on their side on the river bed with the train sitting between them. Clearly the bridge had been blown over sideways. The engine and first four coaches were not seriously damaged, but the fifth coach and the van at the back were

▶The high girders which surrounded the train as it crashed into the Tay estuary prevented all but the last two carriages from being completely destroyed. The coaches were still sitting within the cage of the girders when they were salvaged.

171

badly smashed up.

At first there was confusion over the number of passengers on the train – tickets had been collected with those from other trains at a previous stop. After a careful check, it was estimated that 80 people died that tragic night.

What went wrong?

Because of the scale of the accident a full court of inquiry was set up. A woeful tale of incompetence unfolded: there was an inadequate survey of the estuary bed, lack of provision by Bouch for wind pressure and, above all, scandalously poor workmanship in the cast-iron of the pier columns, girders and bracing. The cast-iron piers varied in thickness – in places the walls were so thin they could hardly have taken their share of the weight, particularly when the bridge was under attack by the elements.

'We find,' concluded the court's summing up, 'that the bridge was badly designed, badly constructed and badly maintained.' But, according to the inquiry, Bouch bore the burden of responsibility – he was 'mainly to blame' – though seemingly he didn't know of many of the defects during construction nor of the problems in keeping the tie bars rigid afterwards.

It was the end for Bouch. His plans for the Forth Bridge discarded, he died a broken man a year after the accident. A replacement bridge over the Tay was constructed seven years later.

▼ **In the calm after the storm the full extent of the damage could be seen. All three sections of high girders, from pier 28 to pier 41, had fallen into the Tay in a mass of twisted metal, leaving the amputated piers behind.**

Recommendations

Following the Tay disaster, the Board of Trade established rules regarding allowances for wind pressures in railway structures. The engineers' calculations had to allow for the pressure of the wind from the most severe gales and storms, not only on the structures themselves but also on any trains that might be on the bridges. The details varied for each structure depending on whether it was solid, like a masonry arch, latticed, as in some girder bridges, or with rounded or square cornered piers.

Although not specifically criticised in the Tay Bridge inquiry, the use of cast-iron for girders – which had resulted in a number of bridge failures from the early days of railways – was highlighted 12 years after the Tay Bridge disaster by a bridge collapse on the London – Brighton line. It was recommended in the subsequent report by the Board of Trade inspector that bridge girders should be constructed from wrought iron or steel.

Today there are no restrictions on train operation over the Tay and Forth bridges during high winds, since the bridge structures are fully able to withstand anything that the elements can throw at them. On 5 February 1990, however, the Tay Bridge was closed to trains for four days when, after prolonged heavy rain, the river was running high and fast and damage was seen to the southernmost pier. At first it was thought that the foundations might have failed, but after the water subsided the bridge was examined and the damage was found to be superficial.

Armagh 1889

**On 12 June 1889, 10 carriages of a Sunday
school excursion, with over 600 passengers on board, were
unhooked from their locomotive and careered out of control down
a 1 in 75 incline before smashing into an oncoming train.
It was Ireland's worst ever rail accident.**

Old operating methods dating back 50 years to the pioneering days of railways, an inadequate braking system, an engine not powerful enough to work a heavy train, and a staff argument led to Ireland's worst ever railway accident at Armagh in 1889. Parliament was shocked into making new rail safety measures compulsory by law.

The branch railway from Armagh to Warrenpoint on the east coast of Ireland was steeply graded as it climbed out of Armagh on the northern slopes of the ridge of high ground which further east became the Mourne Mountains. The line had been built in 1864 by an independent company, but in 1879 had been taken over by the Great Northern Railway of Ireland (GNRI). It was of single track, worked on the staff and ticket system in conjunction with time-interval operation, a method of working railways which had been in use since the 1830s.

On 11 June 1889, the GNRI traffic department in Dundalk had arranged for an excursion train to run from Armagh to Warrenpoint at 10.00am the next day. Around 800 passengers were expected and a 13-coach train was planned, including two brake vans, for which the locomotive department had booked a small 2-4-0 tender engine, No 86.

Even before the empty train arrived at Armagh, two more coaches had been added, and by the time loading began there were so many passengers that the stationmaster proposed to add two more. The driver of No 86 protested, and even threatened to take only the original 13. The stationmaster made some caustic comments but the driver, who was not very familiar with the line, insisted and said that he ought to have been provided with a more powerful 0-6-0.

A suggestion was made to transfer some of the coaches to the following regular train at 10.35am, which was a much lighter formation. Its engine could also have been used to assist the excursion up the 1 in 75 gradient to the summit just over three miles (5km) from Armagh. However, by

▼ **The shattered remains of the last three vehicles litter the 70ft (22m) high embankment about 1¹/₂ miles (2.5km) east of Armagh. The coaches on the runaway were all light, wooden six-wheelers and two were smashed to matchwood on impact, as well as the rear brake van. The train behind the overturned 0-4-2 became uncoupled and ran down the incline before being brought under control with hand brakes.**

◀ The 0-4-2 locomotive of the 10.35 train lies overturned on the top of the embankment after the crash. It was travelling at about 5mph when the runaway coaches smashed into it. The force of the collision dislodged it from the tender and train.

Thomas McGrath, and Elliot conferred on what best to do. They could have kept the train where it was, held on the vacuum brake and sent a man back down the line to warn the following train. This could then have been brought slowly up behind and used to push the stalled train.

Alternatively they could split the excursion so that No 86 could take the first part forward and park the coaches in the siding at Hamilton's Bawn (the first station, about two miles beyond the summit). The front guard told Elliot that the siding there already contained some wagons but that they should be able to get five coaches in. No 86 could then return for the rest of the train.

A fatal mistake

Elliot made the fatal decision to divide the train. He went back and told the rear guard to apply his handbrake and place stones under the wheels. The front guard also put a single stone under a wheel of the sixth coach while he unwound the screw coupling to lift the link from the coupling hook of the fifth coach.

Tragically, just as he did so the engine driver eased back and did just what the rest of the staff were trying to avoid – moving the rear ten coaches. The front portion moved back no more than a

Uncoupling the train

As the excursion did not have automatic continuous brakes, safety chains connected adjoining coaches on each side of the central screw coupling. The screw coupling allowed the buffers, which were sprung, to be held just in contact with each other.

As the train was stopped on the vacuum brake, some of the buffers may have been slightly compressed; the screw couplings were not absolutely tight because mixed lengths of buffer shanks made this impossible. The side safety chains were slack to allow passage round curves.

The guard said he undid the safety chains and vacuum pipe between the two coaches. This released the brakes, but, with the hand brakes applied and stones under the wheels, nothing moved. He was then able to undo the screw coupling without the need for the engine to set back to ease the couplings.

Tragically, just as he lifted the link from the hook of the fifth coach, the engine came back slightly and compressed the buffers. This pushed the rear coaches and started them back towards disaster.

now the excursion driver was sufficiently annoyed at suggestions that he couldn't get his train to the summit to refuse any offers of help. He decided to take the 15 coaches.

Even so it was 10.15 before the train got away, with around 940 passengers on board, two-thirds of them children from a Sunday school. Many were standing, not only in the passenger coaches, but in the brake vans as well. As was customary at the time the passenger coach doors were locked to prevent 'unauthorised access'.

The engine was not short of steam and at first climbed the gradient well. Gradually it began to lose speed until, just short of the summit, it could make no further progress and stalled.

The train was equipped with the Smith's pattern non-automatic vacuum brake in which the brakes were applied by the creation of a vacuum in the system and released by letting in air. In addition there were screw handbrakes which operated only on their own wheels in the two brake vans. The essential feature of the simple vacuum brake was that if the continuous brake pipe through the train was either uncoupled or broken there was, in effect, no brake at all. Naturally the staff on the train knew this.

In charge of the train was the line superintendent's chief clerk, James Elliot. The driver,

A preventable disaster

The utter helplessness of the victims locked into the flimsy coaches and the preventability of the accident were what spurred Parliament to such sweeping actions with the Regulation of Railways Act 1889. The ten runaway coaches had quickly picked up speed from the summit of the 1 in 75 incline reaching 40mph (64km/h) by the point of impact. The collision was so powerful that the rear brake van and rear two coaches were completely destroyed. The engine of the oncoming train was thrown on to its side and the tender and vehicles behind became uncoupled to form another runaway. Only fate and the courage of the staff saved these coaches from a further accident. Automatic brakes, the absolute block system and interlocking controls, all of which survive to this day, were all made compulsory within 12 months.

To Armagh (1½ miles)

detached vans and passenger coaches

detached tender and horsebox

point of impact

overturned 0-4-2 tender locomotive

foot or so (half a metre), but it was enough. The stone under the sixth coach was crushed to powder so there was nothing to stop the coaches rolling back, buffering up against the rear brake van and pushing it over its little pile of stones.

The driver tried to set back properly to catch up the slowly moving rear coaches while one of the staff tried desperately to get the coupling link over the hook again. But it was no use. On the 1 in 75 gradient the weight of coaches, crammed full of passengers, was too much for the handbrake and gradually the 10 runaway coaches speeded up.

At Armagh station the 10.35 train was ready to leave with no one aware of the drama developing three miles (5km) up the line. Behind the 0-4-2 tender locomotive was a horse box, two vans and three passenger coaches – a lightweight train. Under the time-interval rules the minimum 10 minute gap between following passenger trains had more than elapsed, the driver of the 10.35 had the wooden staff for the section (the excursion driver had been given a ticket authorising him to occupy the single line) and, about four minutes late, he was given the right away.

The 0-4-2 was soon climbing the 1 in 75 gradient and was about one and a half miles (2.5km) from the summit when the fireman saw the runaway coaches hurtling towards him. The driver quickly applied the simple vacuum brake but he had not quite stopped when the runaways smashed into his train at over 40mph (64km/h).

The coaches were all small, light, wooden six-wheelers. The brake van and first two coaches leading the runaways were destroyed, while the rest piled high up on the track and down the steep embankment. All those in the brake van (including 15 passengers) had managed to jump out, but in the other coaches the passengers were locked in.

And now there was another runaway train. The 0-4-2 engine had been knocked on its side by the force of the collision and the coupling bar to the tender had broken. The tender and the horse box began to run back. Meanwhile the two vans and three passenger coaches had also broken free from the horse box and they too were running back. Luckily the driver had been flung on to the tender and, despite being injured, he was able to screw on the tender hand brake, stopping that part. The guard also managed to apply his hand brake on the rear part of the train and stopped it about a quarter of a mile (0.5km) down the line.

Inevitably there were many casualties. Of the 600 passengers in the runaway coaches of the

▼ A dramatic artist's impression of the immediate aftermath of the accident shows bodies strewn down the side of the embankment beneath the splintered remains of the rear three vehicles. Most of the fatalities occurred in the rear two coaches which were locked shut. Passengers and staff on the brake van had already jumped clear.

N

To Hamilton's Bawn/Goraghwood/Warrenpoint

to first five coaches and locomotive No 86 (1 mile)

surviving runaway coaches

...bris of rear brake van and rear two coaches

embankment (70ft high)

Key to trains

10.00 excursion
Armagh – Warrenpoint

10.35 regular
Armagh – Warrenpoint

Absolute block

To operate this system the line is divided into block sections with a signalbox at the boundaries of each section. Each signalbox has single stroke bells and single needle block telegraph instruments. Each line has two block instruments, one for the section to the rear and one for the section ahead. There is one bell for each pair of up and down lines towards the next signalbox ahead and another towards the signalbox in the other direction. If the signalbox controls a junction there will be another bell and two block instruments for the branch, and for any additional running lines.

With a complicated series of bell codes, something like the morse system, each signalman was able to ensure that the block ahead of his box was clear before allowing a train into it. This system had to be employed by law from 1889 and survives today where old-style mechanical signalling is still used.

▼A large crowd gathered on the embankment after the crash. The tender on the right became dislodged from the locomotive of the 10.35, threatening to become a second runaway. However, the driver was thrown from the footplate on to the tender, and managed to apply the hand brake.

excursion, 80 were killed or died later, including 22 children. A further 262 were injured.

The inquiry

In the inquiry into the immediate causes of the accident, the inspecting officer, Major General Hutchinson found, after trials, that engine No 86 was able to take a 15 coach train to the summit in the hands of an experienced driver. He also found that a brake van similar to the one at the back of the uncoupled 10 coaches should have been able to hold a train of that size on the 1 in 75 gradient.

He could find no reason why the excursion was unable to get to the summit, despite the engine working near to its limit. As for the brake in the rear van, was it in full working order or had it been tampered with? There were 15 passengers crammed into the van and there were suggestions that some of them might have interfered with it.

Although Hutchinson concluded that the driver of the excursion should not have been rostered for the job as he knew so little about the line, he placed most of the responsibility on Elliot for authorising the train to be uncoupled.

But Hutchinson's findings provoked much more. Even though only eight passengers were killed in other rail accidents in the British Isles in 1889, and fatalities had averaged no more than 28 a year over the previous 20 years (including the 80 lost in the Tay Bridge disaster 10 years before), Parliament decided it had had enough.

For years the Board of Trade (which supervised railways until the formation of the Ministry of Transport in 1919) had been urging the railway companies, through its railway inspecting officers, to adopt better safety standards.

Had the absolute block system been in force, which would have allowed only one train at a time on to the section, the 10.35 train could not have left Armagh with the excursion train already stalled. And if automatic vacuum brakes had been in use, the brake blocks would have been hard on the wheels of all the coaches when the train was divided. Given the horrific nature of the accident these issues were tackled by Parliament with uncharacteristic speed and decisiveness.

The Railways Act

The 1889 Regulation of Railways Act made automatic continuous brakes on all passenger trains compulsory. The absolute block system on all passenger lines was also enforced, with strict controls and only a few special exemptions. This meant that lines had to be equipped with the block telegraphs to operate the absolute block system. Now it was the law, directors of railway companies could no longer plead poverty or that their lines ran quite well without using the block system.

Interlocking between levers was also made compulsory for passenger lines so that signals could not give conflicting indications,

and signals leading through points could not be pulled to clear unless the points were correctly set.

The Act did not specify which type of automatic brake was to be used. By 1889 two variations were popular: the vacuum system in which a vacuum kept the brakes off, and the Westinghouse which used compressed air to do so. The vacuum system became more or less standard after 1923 while BR changed to more powerful compressed air brakes in the late 1960s.

The 1889 Act gave rail safety the force of law and set the standards which, in their basic form, survive today.

Abermule 1921

**Single line railways operate under strict
safety regulations, making it impossible for two trains
to be on the same section at the same time. At Abermule in
1921 a catalogue of human errors caused the impossible to
happen, resulting in a head-on collision and 17 deaths.**

On 26 January 1921 the 10.25am up express from Aberystwyth to Manchester left Newtown on time, heading the four miles (6.5km) north-east towards Abermule in rural mid-Wales. Driver Prichard Jones was in possession of a Newtown – Abermule tablet, which meant that no other train could legitimately be on that section of line at the same time. His Cambrian 4-4-0 No 95 hauled a train consisting of a six-wheeled van behind the tender and six wooden-bodied bogie coaches.

As he accelerated down the falling gradient he reached 50mph (80km/h). About one and a half miles (0.75km) before Abermule, the gradient steepened to 1 in 123 and the driver shut off steam ready to slow to about 10mph (16km/h) through Abermule for the hand exchange of the tablet pouches.

Suddenly, to his horror, he saw the smoke of another train coming towards him no more than 300yd (274m) away. He immediately made a full application of the vacuum brake and sounded the whistle. Then he and his fireman climbed out on to the steps ready to jump.

The two engines met head-on at a combined speed of about 60mph (97km/h). The other train was the 10.05am down slow from Whitchurch to Aberystwyth, composed of six coaches hauled by Cambrian 4-4-0 No 82. Both engines and tenders were wrecked in the collision, together with the first four coaches of the up express train and the leading coach of the down slow train.

Fourteen passengers were killed in the accident and so too were the driver and fireman of No 82 and the guard of the express. Over 30 passengers were injured, including two railwaymen travelling as passengers. The driver and fireman of No 95, who managed to jump off just before the collision, were also seriously injured, as was the guard of the slow train.

▼ The disaster at Abermule was the only major single line head-on collision in Britain this century. Seventeen died in the accident, most of the fatalities occurring in the fourth coach of the express train, pictured below. The third coach telescoped right through it, sweeping the entire contents of the fourth coach – including the passengers – into a mass of wreckage at the rear end.

Single line safety

The Cambrian Railways' principal route from Oswestry to Pwllheli/Aberystwyth was a typical rural main line, with many features in common with similar routes elsewhere in the more remote parts of Britain. Largely single tracked with passing loops at stations, it ran across mid-Wales, through the mountains, linking the English West Midlands and north-west areas to the coastal resorts of Cardigan Bay, chief of them being Aberystwyth. As an independent backwater, time tended to pass the line by and railway operating methods had changed little for decades.

During the latter part of the 19th century a number of pioneering signal engineers had developed various forms of electrically interlocked instruments for working on single lines, using a variety of different shaped tokens. Cambrian Railways adopted Tyer's No 6 electric tablet system: two instruments were provided for every single line section – one at each end – each with about ten metal discs, called tablets, which were given to drivers as their authority to be on a single-line section of track.

Each tablet, with the names of the stations between which it applied engraved on it, was kept in a vertical stack in the electrically interlocked tablet machines. When a tablet was drawn from one instrument, both would become locked so that no

Head-on collision

The 10.05am down stopping train from Whitchurch to Aberystwyth and the 10.25am up express from Aberystwyth to Manchester were booked to cross at Abermule station.

During the stationmaster's lunch break – but contrary to regulations – the junior porter at Abermule accepted the express train from Newtown on the tablet instrument.

When the down slow train arrived at Abermule, the driver handed his tablet to a junior clerk, who in turn gave it to the stationmaster. The stationmaster did not know that the junior porter had accepted the up express and, thinking that he had been given the tablet for the single-line section to Newtown, he handed the pouch containing the tablet back to the driver.

The two trains sharing the single line crashed head-on into one another at a combined speed of about 60mph. Fourteen passengers were killed, as were the driver and fireman of the down train and the guard of the up express.

more tablets could be removed until the first was reinserted into either machine. Both instruments showed if a tablet had been drawn out and whether it was for an up or down train. Thus at all stations with a passing loop there were two tablet instruments – one for the section on one side and one for the section on the other. It was a safe and reliable system, but unfortunately not one that was impervious to incompetence.

Abermule station

The layout and operation at Abermule station had remained unchanged for many years. The next station to the north-east was Montgomery, three and a half miles (5.5km) away. To the south-west was Newtown, four miles (6.5km) distant.

The signalbox was at the Montgomery end of Abermule station and controlled a level crossing. Because of an old limitation by the Board of Trade

▲ The first coach of the slow train was totally destroyed and the two leading compartments of the second coach (pictured above) were also wrecked, with the bogies knocked away backwards.

Key to trains

10.05 Whitchurch – Aberystwyth

10.25 Aberystwyth – Manchester

underframe of first carriage of up express train

boiler of locomotive No 82

wheels and motion of locomotive No 95

4 sets of bogie wheels

up direction

from Newtown

second carriage of up express train

part of roof of third carriage of up express train

tender of locomotive No 95

boiler of locomotive No 95

tender of locomotive No

on the distance at which points could be worked from the signalbox, the points at the Newtown end of the station, leading to the single line, were worked from a ground frame released from the signalbox.

The signalbox had a lever controlling the platform starting signal towards Newtown, but there was also a slot on the signal worked by a lever in the ground frame to make sure that the points were correctly set before the signal arm could be cleared. The tablet instruments were not in the signalbox – which was the usual position – but in a room in the station building near to the stationmaster's office, so that the stationmaster could personally oversee operations.

On 26 January 1921, a relief stationmaster was on duty at Abermule who knew the working well (the regular stationmaster was on holiday). Also on duty were one of the two regular signalmen, a young porter, and a junior clerk who did booking office work and collected tickets. Only the signalmen and the stationmaster were allowed to work the tablet instruments, and instructions had been issued to say that stationmasters had to watch over the signalling, particularly when express trains were involved.

The 10.05 from Whitchurch and the 10.25 from Aberystwyth were booked to cross at Abermule at about midday. The relief stationmaster was away from the station having lunch when Montgomery offered to Abermule the 10.05 train from Whitchurch on the tablet instrument bell. The signalman was in the office where the tablet instruments were located and correctly accepted the 10.05 train by working plungers on the machine to a prescribed routine, which gave Montgomery a release to draw out a tablet from the instrument there for the section to Abermule. The Abermule instrument then showed that a tablet was out for a down train.

The signalman telephoned to Moat Lane Junction beyond Newtown to find out how the express was running and was told that it was on time. The signalman passed on the details to the two juniors and went back to the signalbox to open the level-crossing gates and clear the signals for the stopping train to enter the station.

At about the same time the relief stationmaster came back, but nobody told him about the stopping train or of the whereabouts of the express, so he went to the goods yard to check on some wagon

movements. While he was gone, Newtown sent the 'Is line clear?' bell signal to Abermule for the express; as nobody else was near, the junior porter – who knew how to work the tablet instruments – accepted, allowing Newtown to draw a tablet for the Newtown – Abermule section to give to the express driver.

The junior porter went to the ground frame at the Newtown end to set the points for the express to run in, but he would have needed a release from the signalbox. At that moment the 10.05 train arrived at the down platform.

The junior clerk on the up platform crossed the line and collected the tablet in its pouch from the 10.05's driver and intended taking it to the tablet instrument to clear the section back to Montgomery. Instead, the relief stationmaster returned from the goods yard, saw the youngster with the tablet in his hands and asked where the express was. Whether the young clerk had realised what the porter had done or not, he replied that it was just past Moat Lane. Only the porter at the ground frame at the far end of the platform knew

Gaslit coaches
Five out of six coaches of the down slow train were gaslit, as were four out of seven coaches of the up express train. Fortunately the head-on collision between the two trains did not result in a fire – the consequences of a gas explosion in the wooden-bodied coaches would have been even more horrific.

▼ The combined length of both trains was reduced by about a quarter in the collision. The two engines and tenders and five coaches (four of the express, one of the slow train), which would have covered about 115yd (105m) of track before the crash, were reduced to a 50yd (46m) mass of tangled wreckage.

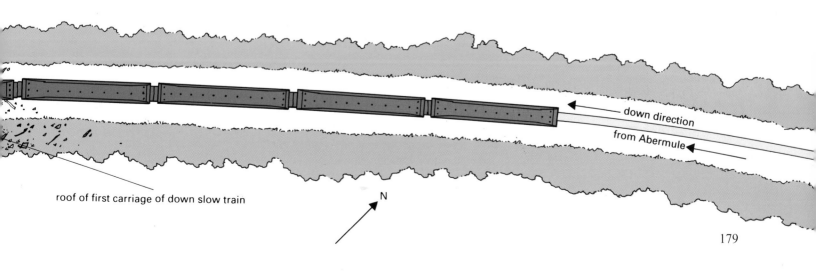

roof of first carriage of down slow train

down direction

from Abermule

N

▲ An engine driver at Abermule station receives a leather pouch containing a tablet for the single line ahead, just as the driver of the fateful 10.05am down slow from Whitchurch to Aberystwyth did on 26 January 1921 – only he was mistakenly given the tablet for the line he had just covered. The hoop attached to the pouch allowed exchange on the move up to 10mph (16km/h), the recipient putting his arm through the hoop to collect it.

that the express was actually in the section from Newtown.

What conversation then passed between the junior clerk and the stationmaster was never really discovered. The boy said he asked the stationmaster to change the tablet while he collected tickets from the stopping train. The stationmaster thought the boy had said the tablet had been changed and that the 10.05 train was going on.

Whatever was said, the stationmaster did not check the tablet he now held in his hands. Had he looked he would have seen 'Montgomery – Abermule'. Had he gone to the tablet instruments near his office he would have seen the instrument for the Newtown section showing tablet out for an up train – the express. He did neither. He handed the tablet in its pouch to the driver of the 10.05.

The porter correctly at his duties working the ground frame was trying to set the points for the express to enter but he did not have the lock on the ground frame released from the signalbox. Instead, he saw the stationmaster giving the right away to the 10.05 train. He thought that Newtown must have cancelled the express and that the stopping train was going on to cross the express at Newtown. The signalman had cleared his down starting lever and the porter cleared his signal lever, releasing the slot on the signal arm which went to clear. It was the signal to disaster.

There was just one last hope. As the stationmaster handed the tablet to the 10.05's driver, the driver should have checked it – as required by the rules – to see that he had been issued with the proper one for the section. He had actually been given the one he had recently surrendered to the junior clerk; had he looked at it the accident would not have happened. As it was, within five minutes both he and his fireman lay dead, together with fourteen passengers and the guard of the other train.

What went wrong?

Colonel Sir John Pringle, the railway inspecting officer who chaired the inquiry, found that the accident occurred from a combination of failures to adhere to working instructions and the rule book.

The juniors should never have been allowed to work the tablet instruments, nor to handle the tablets in collecting them and delivering them to the drivers. There was a lack of supervision by the stationmaster – and he himself had failed to ensure that he was being given the correct tablet.

Any one of the people involved, from the two juniors, the signalman, the stationmaster and the 10.05's driver, could have saved the situation had they either looked at the equipment or told those who should have known what they had done. It was a complete failure of communication.

Colonel Pringle criticised the fact that the tablet instruments were away from the signalbox, and that a separate ground frame was needed to control the west end of the layout.

Recommendations

Colonel Pringle recommended that the tablet instruments should be in the signalbox under the direct control of the signalman. He also suggested that the instruments should be interlocked with the starting signal leading into the single line section, so that the starting signal could be cleared only when the correct tablet (or key token or staff) had been drawn out. This would prevent clear signals from being displayed to a train which did not have the correct tablet for the single line ahead.

Had this form of interlocking been provided at Abermule, it would have prevented the signal for the 10.05 down slow train to proceed to Newtown from being pulled to clear.

Sevenoaks 1927

A large 2-6-4 tank engine, hauling a Cannon Street to Deal express in August 1927, started to roll at 60 mph (97kph) as it approached Sevenoaks. The engine was derailed and the train piled up against a bridge, killing 13 passengers.

The summer of 1927 had been wet like many English summers, and 24 August was little different. Indeed, it had been the wettest summer on record in the south of England and that morning there had been three heavy thunderstorms over the Weald of Kent. The ground was waterlogged and the chalk and clay of the area would have lost some of its firmness in very wet conditions.

The former South Eastern Railway main line from Charing Cross and Cannon Street ran through London Bridge and soon after passing New Cross, five miles (8km) from the start, began the 12 mile (19km) climb to the summit of the North Downs at Knockholt. The gradients were largely at 1 in 120 but were a little easier at 1 in 310 through Orpington. Once over the top it was downhill to Dunton Green, four miles (6.5km) ahead, but trains were swallowed up almost at once into the 2610yd (2387m) Polhill Tunnel.

Emerging from the tunnel, trains were either in shallow cuttings or on low embankments until the dip at Dunton Green from where there was a two mile (3.25km) rise to Sevenoaks. Approaching Sevenoaks the line was in a cutting which was crossed by a road overbridge. This was unusual because it had separate arches for each of the two tracks, so there was a bridge pier between the up and down lines.

The 5pm express from Cannon Street to Deal via Ashford and Folkestone on that August afternoon was booked to run non-stop to Ashford and cover the 56 miles (90km) in 65 minutes. This was a tight schedule because of the slow start caused by the tortuous track between Cannon Street and London Bridge. Two of the Southern Railway's constituent companies, the London Brighton & South Coast Railway (LBSCR) and the South Eastern & Chatham Railway (SECR) had built large tank engines for working their coastal expresses. These ran comparatively short distances of 50 to 70 miles (82–113km), unlike those of other main line railways, which normally used tender engines for their longer distance expresses.

Even though tank engines were designed to

▼ The leading coupled wheels of the locomotive were the first to derail, although originally it was thought that the pony truck, which ended up under the driving wheels, was to blame. Other damage to the engine included the destruction of most of the motion, the left cylinder, piston, piston valve and the buffer beam. The tanks, cab, bunker and steps were damaged too.

▲ **With recovery operations under way, this coach has just been lifted upright. Of the eight coaches in the train only four were of any further use, as the steel clad timber-framed bodies did not fare well in the crash. The locomotive can be seen against the side of the cutting on the left.**

to Dunton Green and, although the driver said afterwards that the engine had been running steadily, some passengers thought that the coaches had been rolling sideways between Polhill and Dunton Green. As the engine passed over trailing points in Dunton Green station, the driver felt the engine roll quite badly, dipping and rising with a side-to-side movement. He had applied steam for the climb to Sevenoaks and suddenly noticed a knocking noise at the front. Sometimes there can be knocking in the valve gear and the rods connecting the wheels to the pistons because of wear, but after the driver had shut off steam he could still hear the knocking. He thought that the leading pony truck wheels were derailed and applied the brake. Before it could take effect, the engine reached a set of trailing catch points where the whole locomotive and the train were derailed.

The impetus carried the train forward on the ballast and the engine and first two coaches passed through the left-hand arch of the road overbridge. The majority of the coaches became uncoupled and the fourth became jammed under the bridge where it was crushed. The fifth was a Pullman car, *Carmen*, which slewed round against the approach face of both arches across the down and up lines. Its heavy construction helped to save it from destruction and it remained largely intact, although badly damaged, as the last three coaches pushed it violently against the bridge.

By then the momentum of the rest of the train had been exhausted and despite being derailed, the following carriages were not extensively damaged. The front four coaches were either badly damaged or destroyed, and inevitably the casualties in them were high. There were 13 fatalities and 21 passengers were seriously hurt; 40 more had lesser injuries.

How did such an accident happen? Was it the state of the track, a fault on the engine, the design

work in both directions to save turning, the Southern enginemen preferred to run the engine chimney first, so they were usually turned at each end of the journey. The 5pm train was booked for Class K 2-6-4T, No A800 *River Cray*.

Like all the engines on the SECR designed by Maunsell, the River class had a modern look about them. They had outside Walschaerts valve gear with the footplate raised up over the cylinders and driving wheels and dropped down to a lower level for the cab and bunker. This meant that the water tanks were carried on the higher part of the footplate.

Rolling motion
The train had made the steady climb to Knockholt and accelerated to between 55 and 60mph (88–97km/h) through Polhill Tunnel. It continued

---

Rolling to disaster
A combination of factors meant that the Sevenoaks disaster was waiting to happen. Initially the crash was blamed on the design of the River class 2-6-4T, and they were withdrawn from service at once. There had already been three derailments involving the class, at Bearsted, Maidstone East and Wrotham, and the high centre of gravity caused by the high pitched water tanks was thought to be a factor. However, the locomotives rode without problems on the well-maintained LNER line between St Neots and Huntingdon.

The lightly ballasted track of the SR was not firm enough for heavy modern trains travelling at high speed – the ballast also drained poorly and the summer of 1927 had been the wettest on record. The flimsy sodden track-bed and the high centre of gravity of *River Cray* combined to set up a rolling motion which derailed the train.

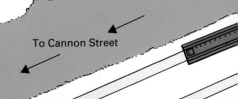

To Cannon Street

of the engine, or the weather? In the subsequent inquiry it emerged that all these factors played a part, yet no single one in itself was responsible. The wide-ranging inquiry was held by inspecting officer Sir John Pringle.

What went wrong?

Early in the inquiry it emerged that the River class 2-6-4Ts had a reputation on former SECR routes for poor riding. Alterations had been made to the spring adjustment of the leading pony truck and the rear bogie, yet there had been three previous derailments of the class, all on the Swanley to Ashford line. Some members of the class were used on the London – Brighton line and on that route there had been no reported problems.

After one of the London Brighton & South Coast Railway's large tank engines had derailed, it was suggested that water had surged around the tanks adding to any sideways movement and making the engine unstable. Had the same thing happened to No 800 at Dunton Green? Sir Herbert Walker, the Southern Railway's general manager, was unhappy about using the River class engines and as an immediate measure took them out of service until checks could be made on their riding. However, Sir John Pringle had suspicions that the fault did not lie entirely with the engine design.

He contacted Nigel Gresley, chief mechanical engineer of the London & North Eastern Railway, and arranged to run a series of trials on the former Great Northern Railway main line between St Neots and Huntingdon, which included the reverse curves alongside the River Ouse at Offord. Two River class 2-6-4Ts were used; one, No A803, was a two-cylinder engine and the other, No A890, was the sole three-cylinder example. A King Arthur class 4-6-0 tender locomotive (No E782) was also tested for comparison. The River class engines ran both chimney first and bunker first at speeds of up to 80mph (129km/h) and all the reports showed them to ride steadily and smoothly without any hint of rolling.

Walker then wanted some trials on another of his main lines, the former London & South Western Railway route between Walton on Thames and Woking, where express trains regularly ran at up to 80mph (129km/h). But here the story was very different. The 2-6-4Ts were

all over the place with severe rolling even on straight track. The independent engineers who supervised the runs thought that the engines could be in danger of derailing. Even the King Arthur 4-6-0, a class which was used on the route regularly rode just as badly as the 2-6-4Ts.

Sir John Pringle decided that the Southern's track standards needed to be looked at more closely. The embankment near Dunton Green was formed from chalk and the lower ballast consisted of part stone and part pebble, with earth or ash binding to hold it together. Pebble or shingle ballast from the seashore does not hold track as firmly as

▲ The stoutly built Pullman car *Carmen* withstood the accident well. It had been constructed in 1891 and was still in SECR maroon livery. Even the next day the lamp in the damaged end vestibule was still lit. The carriage was cut up on site.

To Ashford and Deal

third coach badly damaged

Shoreham Lane overbridge

locomotive No A800 *River Cray* on its side

first and second coaches derailed and badly damaged

fourth coach crushed against overbridge

Pullman car *Carmen* slewed across the tracks

▲The large water tanks of the River class were set above a high footplate which gave these locomotives a high centre of gravity. Before the accident it had already been decided to build no more of these locomotives as heavier trains were making their water capacity inadequate.

Express tank engines

Both the SECR and LBSCR used large tank engines on certain express services. Having seen how the LBSCR handled much of its coastal traffic with 4-4-2Ts, 4-6-2Ts and 4-6-4Ts, the SECR introduced its K class 2-6-4Ts after World War I. The big LBSCR 4-6-4Ts had not been without their problems, which included rolling caused by water surges in the tanks. Baffles fitted inside the tanks cured the problem.

But like the SECR Class 2-6-4Ts, the Brighton 4-6-4Ts were eventually rebuilt as tender locomotives of the Remembrance class. The smaller LBSCR tank engines remained as such until withdrawal.

The tanks and bogies removed from the River class when they were rebuilt were stored at Ashford and fitted to the 15 W class 2-6-4T's, built for freight working round London.

crushed quarried stone with rough edges, because it is rounded and the individual pebbles can move in relation to each other; hence the need for binding. That in itself provided little drainage. Pebbles were also used as top ballast, again with binding.

The bottoms of the sleepers were level with the cess, which is a drainage trench to take surface water away from the track. In fact the rainwater could not easily drain away from the ballast, and with the heavy rainfall of that summer there were undoubtedly soft spots in the chalk bank and the ballast supporting the sleepers. With the weight of trains passing at speed, the sleepers had gradually been pushed into the ballast, which in turn had been forced into the chalk bed. There were thus uneven dips in the track which set up the rolling of the engine at speed.

Sub-standard track

Sir John Pringle concluded that the track at Dunton Green was not up to the standards required for heavy fast-moving trains. Not only were the track bed and the ballast deficient in places, without proper drainage, but the track itself had not been adequately maintained. It was not at the correct levels with proper cant (the raising of the outer rails on curves) or of accurate gauge. Sir John Pringle was convinced that the very heavy rain in the morning on the day of the accident had contributed to the track defects.

He recommended that the SR should undertake strengthening of the road bed on some sections of its main lines, which meant improving the formation under the track and providing a good depth of clean stone ballast under and around the sleepers. The permanent way staff on the ground had not maintained the track to the standards required, particularly in the evenness of the cant on curves.

To be fair to the Southern, the company had been in existence for less than four years and had inherited the track from its pre-Grouping constituents. Much of the track bed between Orpington and Sevenoaks went back to the days when the line was built in the 1860s. The South Eastern Railway used pebble or shingle ballast which came from the Dungeness area. While being cheap and plentiful and adequate for the light loads and speeds of the Victorian years, it was quite unsuitable for the fast heavy traffic which developed after World War I. As a result of Sir John Pringle's comments the Southern set about improving the standards of its principal routes with proper ballasting. From the London & South Western Railway it had inherited Meldon quarry on the northern slopes of Dartmoor. The granite stone ballast and fine chippings it provided were ideal as track ballast and for the fine levelling needed for the cant on curves. Meldon ballast was soon used all over the Southern system.

As for the River class locomotives, Sir John Pringle's report, based on the trials, made it clear that the spring arrangements and the hard riding, the high centre of gravity and the surging of water in the tanks if a roll started, all helped to increase the rolling tendency on poor track, which in some instances could be dangerous. That was enough for Sir Herbert Walker. He withdrew the River class tank engines and had them rebuilt with the side tanks and rear bunker removed to reappear as 2-6-0 tender engines known as Class U or, in the case of the three-cylinder engine, as Class U1.

Sevenoaks was probably a disaster waiting to happen. But it shocked the Southern management, and the implementation of recommendations following it brought the railway right up to the modern standards of the 1930s.

Recommendations

Sir John Pringle found that the derailment of the train approaching Sevenoaks had several causes.

The track standards were poor. Pebble ballast compacted with ash and earth was not suitable for holding the track under fast and heavy trains. The drainage was bad and the sleepers were sometimes below the level of the drain meaning that water could not run off the track freely.

The top levels of the track were outside the limits so that cant (or superelevation) on curves was uneven and the maintenance gangs had not corrected dips in the rail which started the rolling of locomotives. The wet weather had undoubtedly created soft spots so that sleepers and ballast had sunk into the chalk below.

The River class locomotives had shown that they were unstable on indifferent track but rode very well on the better maintained Great Northern main line during special trials.

Sir John recommended that track strengthening should be undertaken and that local permanent way staff should be given more assistance with tools and equipment to keep the track in good order, especially cant on curves.

Charfield 1928

A few seconds was all that was needed for a goods train to clear the main line at Charfield before the arrival of an express travelling at full speed. It was a few seconds too many however, as the express thundered directly into it.

Charfield was a small country station on the Birmingham – Bristol line of the Midland Railway, which, following the 1923 Grouping, had become part of the LMS. It was the company's West of England line carrying traffic from the north and Midlands to the south-west through what was largely Great Western territory.

Yet though the GWR had lines around Birmingham and was the master of the Bristol area, it had no direct through route all the way from Birmingham to Bristol. Its goods trains had either to go the long way round via Didcot, or use the cross-country route through Cheltenham before travelling over the LMS line from Gloucester to Bristol.

As a result, the LMS Bristol line was usually busy and, just before dawn on 13 October 1928, several trains were heading south-west from Gloucester. Of a group of four, the first two were slow goods trains on their way to Bristol: the previous evening's LMS 10.35pm from Washwood Heath (on the Birmingham – Derby line), and the GWR 9.15pm from Oxley Sidings at Wolverhampton.

Not far behind the GWR goods train was the LMS 12.45am parcels train from Leicester to Bristol, which, being faster, was gradually closing up. The last of the group, the LMS 10.00pm overnight mail and passenger express from Leeds to Bristol, was the most important. This was the one that no signalman would delay without very good reason. The parcels train also had a certain priority and slow-running goods trains had to get out of its way.

Train regulation on former Midland routes was bound up in the control system. While signalmen had limited freedom to run trains, shunting one out of the way of another, known as out of course working, was often a matter for line controllers. They not only kept an eye on train regulation, but also on engine and train crew workings, and on goods train loadings. In this case the controller was based in an office at Fishponds, Bristol.

In order not to delay the parcels train, the controller had decided to shunt the two goods trains out of the way. The LMS was shunted off at Charfield and the GWR goods a little further behind at

▼ An aerial view taken from above the goods shed, south of the bridge, clearly shows the devastation. The overturned mail locomotive is visible through the smoke on the left, while the GWR goods locomotive is seen under the bridge. Debris from the second express coach which reared up on to the bridge is littered along the roadside.

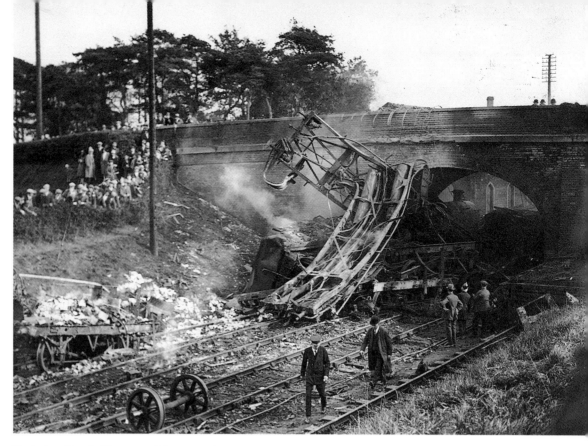

▶ The mangled carcasses of the express coaches rest against the northern end of the bridge. Amazingly, one passenger was thrown clear of the second coach as it rode up over the bridge parapet.

Berkeley Road. The two sidings used were dead ends trailing into the main line, so they could only be reached by running the train beyond the points and backing it into the sidings.

In the normal direction of running, points were trailing. Facing points had been frowned upon (unless absolutely necessary – as at route junctions) right from the dawn of railways, because of the danger of a fast train being accidentally diverted into a siding if the points were set incorrectly. If the points were trailing this was impossible, but it did mean that a goods train being shunted in had first to draw past the points and then reverse in – a time-consuming process.

With both goods trains safely shunted, the line was clear for the parcels train to overtake, which it duly did. As soon as the parcels train had cleared the section from Berkeley Road to Charfield, the GWR goods was let out of the siding to resume its journey. The controller also told the Charfield signalman to let the LMS goods out as soon as he had received 'train out of section' from the next signal-box to the south, Wickwar, for the parcels train. Given a clear line both goods trains could have

been shunted out of the way further south for the express mail train.

An unscheduled stop

Then came the first complication. Once out on the main line the LMS goods stopped at the platform to take water. Its driver had not told the signalman or even asked beforehand whether he could. This took about five minutes. Meanwhile the GWR goods was approaching Charfield from Berkeley Road. The LMS goods restarted and continued south, but with the delay it was clear that the mail was going to be checked by the GWR goods. The Charfield signalman had no alternative but to stop the GWR goods beyond the siding points and set it back into the refuge out of the way of the mail train.

It was still dark and, with a clear sky, mist was beginning to rise. It wasn't thick, and although the signalman thought about fog working he could still see his fog object, a landmark a certain distance away, and decided he was justified in continuing normal block working without fog signalmen. With the GWR goods setting back into the sidings, he was able, in accordance with the regulations, to

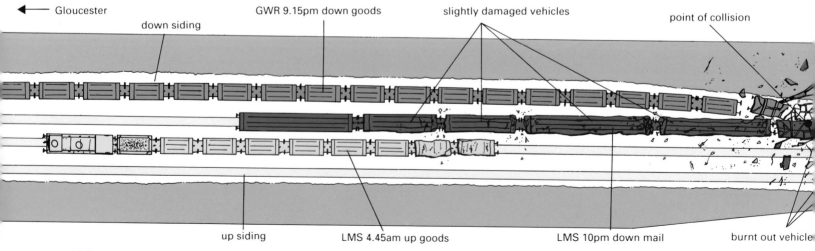

← Gloucester　　　　GWR 9.15pm down goods　　　slightly damaged vehicles　　　point of collision

down siding

up siding　　　LMS 4.45am up goods　　　LMS 10pm down mail　　　burnt out vehicle clear the rear block section by giving 'train out of section' to Berkeley Road and accepting the express.

All his signals were at danger for the mail, and the distant signal lever was set to normal in the lever frame, meaning that the signal should have been at caution. He could not clear his signals with the front of the GWR goods still on the main line moving backwards. The LMS goods train had also not cleared the section to Wickwar.

It was about 5.16am. The slow-moving GWR goods engine was still a few wagon lengths from the points backing into the siding. On the adjoining up line another goods train heading for Gloucester was approaching. The signalman saw his track circuit indicator for the down home signal go from clear to occupied. The mail had arrived.

But to his horror the indicator went back to clear again. The mail had run by his home signal. In seconds, the Class 3 4-4-0 No 714 appeared out of the darkness and at over 60mph (97km/h) hit the eighth wagon of the GWR goods. No 714 was sandwiched between this and the LMS goods train coming the other way. The goods wagons were reduced to matchwood. The eight wooden-bodied coaches of the mail fared little better as they broke up and rode over the wagons. One coach was thrown over the bridge which crossed the line. Worse was to follow however. All the coaches were gaslit. Fire broke out and escaping gas soon ignited the wreckage.

Amazingly, the driver and fireman of No 714 survived. The driver helped as best as he could and tried to rescue passengers before the fire spread through the wreckage and forced him back. He then went to the signalbox to ask in forceful terms what had gone wrong, since he said he had seen a clear green distant signal light.

With the interlocking through the block instruments and with the trailing points set for the sidings, this should have been impossible, yet when the signalman looked at the distant signal repeater it was showing clear. It was found however that wreckage was pressing down on the signal wire and when removed the distant signal arm went back to caution.

Both driver and fireman remained adamant that they had seen a green light at the signal. No 714,

▼ A crane carries out salvage operations next to the overturned remains of the Class 3 4-4-0 No 714, which was hauling the express mail towards Bristol at nearly 60mph (97km/h).

Out of a grey mist

Charfield arose from an unfortunate combination of circumstances. Had the driver of the LMS goods told the signalman beforehand that he needed water, the signalman would have kept him in the siding and let the GWR goods and the mail overtake him. But the cruellest irony was the fact that it only needed a few seconds more for the GWR goods to have shunted clear of the main line before the mail train burst out of the mist. Only a few wagons and the engine remained to be shunted on to the refuge siding when it arrived. According to the findings of the inquiry, the driver of the express had passed the distant signal at caution and the home signal at danger. The accident was compounded by the arrival of the up goods train which sandwiched the express and forced the coaches to pile on top of one another as they reached the bridge. Exploding gas tanks and the ensuing fire made the tragedy complete. Fifteen passengers died.

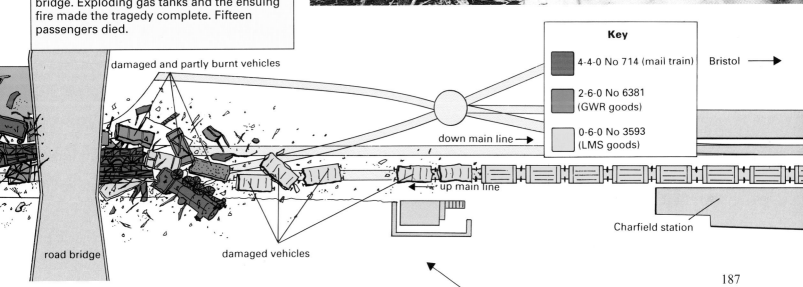

damaged and partly burnt vehicles

Key
■ 4-4-0 No 714 (mail train)
■ 2-6-0 No 6381 (GWR goods)
□ 0-6-0 No 3593 (LMS goods)

Bristol →

down main line →

up main line

Charfield station

road bridge

damaged vehicles

N

like most Midland engines, was driven from the right of the cab so the fireman normally worked on the left side from where he could see the distant signal. How did the signal show green? Had someone deliberately tampered with the wire? We shall never know, for the mystery was never solved.

The mail train fortunately had few passengers, but with the wreckage compressed against the bridge and partly over it as well, and then catching fire, it was inevitable that there would be casualties; fifteen passengers lost their lives. The driver of the mail train was blamed by the inquest for negligence in passing signals at danger. He was then charged with manslaughter at the assize court, but was found not guilty.

The inquiry

The inspecting officer chairing the inquiry, Sir John Pringle, was given conflicting evidence and had a difficult job in establishing what had happened. On the one hand was evidence that the GWR goods was still partly on the main line with the points set for the siding. Through the interlocking, that alone would have held the home signal lever at danger.

On top of this, however, the section to Wickwar was still occupied by the LMS goods so that, with the indicator for that section still at 'train on line', the Charfield signalman could not have cleared his signals even if the GWR goods was fully in the siding. Still the driver and fireman insisted on seeing a green distant light, not with a casual glance but by positive identification.

Nothing was found to show that the distant signal wire or the signal itself had been tampered with, other than by the wreckage of the accident.

Even if in the cold dawn the signal wire to the

▲ The charred remains of one of the four burnt-out coaches from the express mail is lifted away from the scene. Four bodies were extricated from the shell.

lower quadrant distant had contracted and tightened so that the arm drooped slightly, bringing the green spectacle partly in front of the lamp, the signal repeater in the signalbox would have gone to a halfway position showing 'wrong', meaning that the arm was neither at caution nor fully at clear. Yet immediately after the accident the arm and repeater were working normally. The inquiry concluded that the mail train had passed the signals at danger.

Recommendations

Because of the importance of the distant signal in this accident, Sir John Pringle recommended that the GWR automatic train control system be adopted. This used a steel, humped ramp between the rails on the approach to distant signals. A shoe under the locomotive was lifted as it passed over the ramp.

If the signal was at caution, an electrical connection to the ramp was disconnected and the rising shoe sounded a horn warning in the locomotive cab. If this was not acknowledged by the driver, the brakes were applied automatically.

If the signal was clear, an electric current to the ramp was switched on and was picked up in the cab via the shoe. This sounded a bell in the cab and suppressed the brake application. If the driver heard the bell he knew the signal was clear.

Finally, if the distant signal lever in the signalbox was normal, meaning that the signal arm should be at caution, the warning horn was sounded to the driver regardless of the position of the signal arm. There was no doubt that the lever was in the normal position in the Charfield signalbox when the express came through.

Because of this final point, even if the arm

had been partly or fully at clear for some reason at Charfield, the driver would have received a warning because of the normal indication of the lever at the signalbox.

Despite one or two trials, however, none of the other railways adopted the GWR system. Not until the LMS introduced the Hudd magnetic system on the London, Tilbury & Southend line 20 years later (developed soon after by BR into the AWS system) did drivers have a cab warning system outside the GWR.

As for the fire, Sir John was critical of the slow progress in eliminating gaslit coaches, particularly after the recommendations following two previous collisions and fires involving Midland gaslit coaches at Hawes Junction in 1910 and Ais Gill in 1913. Some of the coaches in the Charfield disaster were 40 years old, all with wooden bodies and all gaslit.

As an additional safety feature he also suggested the provision of all-steel guards and parcels vans at the front and back of express trains. However, although the LMS had already built some all-steel coaches in the 1920s, their general introduction was delayed until the BR standard stock of the 1950s.

Whose children?

Apart from the conflicting evidence about the distant signal, there was a second mystery in this accident. Among the dead were two children, badly burnt in the fire – so badly burnt in fact that it was impossible to identify them. Yet nothing emerged linking them with the other passengers. Nobody afterwards reported them missing or was able to provide any clue as to who they were with, or whether they were travelling on their own. How did two young children come to be on the train seemingly unaccompanied? It was just another mystery of the Charfield disaster which has never been resolved.

Shrivenham 1936

A guard remained blissfully unaware as the van and rear five wagons of his coal train detached themselves and coasted to a halt on the Paddington – Bristol main line. Too late he realised the peril he was in, with no time to warn an oncoming express.

The Great Western Railway had a safety record second to none among British railways. This was due partly to the high standards of its staff and the pride they took in the job, and partly to the installation of what was then called automatic train control (ATC) and which we know today as the automatic warning system (AWS). This equipment gave drivers an audible warning in the cab of the indications of distant signals. Thus a major accident on the GWR was a rarity, but when it happened it was news.

While drivers had the beginnings of automation with ATC (if they didn't acknowledge the warning of a distant signal at caution, the brakes were applied automatically), there was little automation for signalmen. True, there was a modicum of safety in that, at some signalboxes, the block indicator for the section ahead had to be at 'line clear' before the signalman could clear his most advanced starting signal into the block section ahead. And if a train was occupying a track circuit at the home signal of the next signalbox, the block indicator could not show 'line clear'. Otherwise though, the correct signalling of trains relied almost entirely on the signalmen carrying out laid down procedures, including watching every train to see that all was in order and that each one was complete.

Stray wagons

January 15, 1936 was one of those days when the GWR made news. Soon after 5am at Shrivenham, on the Paddington – Bristol main line, the overnight 9pm Penzance – Paddington sleeping car train was wrecked when it hit some wagons standing on the up main line. The locomotive, a mighty King class 4-6-0 No 6007 *King William III*, turned over on its side across the down line, and the two leading coaches broke up as they were hurled down the low embankment on the right. The bodies were torn from the underframes, and parts of roofs and interiors were strewn around like matchwood. Though derailed, the rest of the train was not badly damaged. Casualties included one passenger and the driver killed, and ten passengers injured.

But with the GWR ATC system, how

▼ The first coach, a third-class corridor with a heavy steel underframe, lies in bits beside the line. The body was thrown off the frame and rolled over down the bank, coming to rest almost upside down, with the remarkable result that the first five doors could still be opened. The rear five compartments, however, were destroyed.

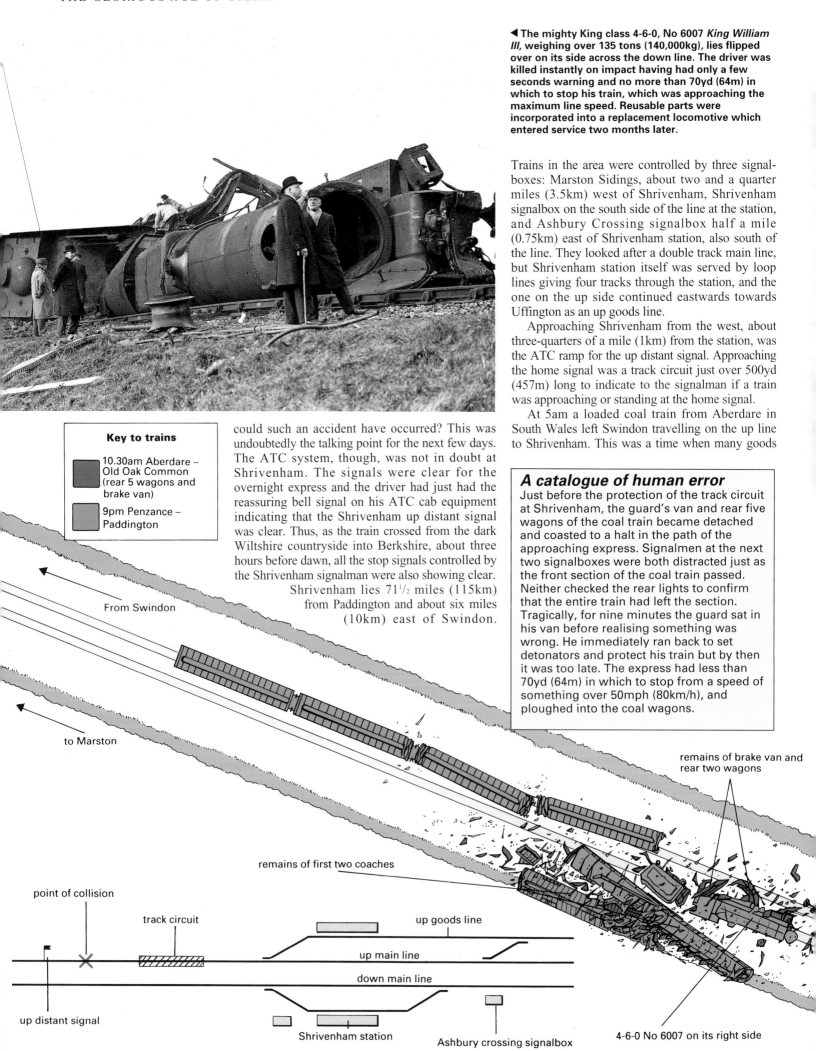

◀ **The mighty King class 4-6-0, No 6007** *King William III*, **weighing over 135 tons (140,000kg), lies flipped over on its side across the down line. The driver was killed instantly on impact having had only a few seconds warning and no more than 70yd (64m) in which to stop his train, which was approaching the maximum line speed. Reusable parts were incorporated into a replacement locomotive which entered service two months later.**

Trains in the area were controlled by three signal-boxes: Marston Sidings, about two and a quarter miles (3.5km) west of Shrivenham, Shrivenham signalbox on the south side of the line at the station, and Ashbury Crossing signalbox half a mile (0.75km) east of Shrivenham station, also south of the line. They looked after a double track main line, but Shrivenham station itself was served by loop lines giving four tracks through the station, and the one on the up side continued eastwards towards Uffington as an up goods line.

Approaching Shrivenham from the west, about three-quarters of a mile (1km) from the station, was the ATC ramp for the up distant signal. Approaching the home signal was a track circuit just over 500yd (457m) long to indicate to the signalman if a train was approaching or standing at the home signal.

At 5am a loaded coal train from Aberdare in South Wales left Swindon travelling on the up line to Shrivenham. This was a time when many goods

Key to trains

10.30am Aberdare – Old Oak Common (rear 5 wagons and brake van)

9pm Penzance – Paddington

could such an accident have occurred? This was undoubtedly the talking point for the next few days. The ATC system, though, was not in doubt at Shrivenham. The signals were clear for the overnight express and the driver had just had the reassuring bell signal on his ATC cab equipment indicating that the Shrivenham up distant signal was clear. Thus, as the train crossed from the dark Wiltshire countryside into Berkshire, about three hours before dawn, all the stop signals controlled by the Shrivenham signalman were also showing clear.

Shrivenham lies 71½ miles (115km) from Paddington and about six miles (10km) east of Swindon.

A catalogue of human error

Just before the protection of the track circuit at Shrivenham, the guard's van and rear five wagons of the coal train became detached and coasted to a halt in the path of the approaching express. Signalmen at the next two signalboxes were both distracted just as the front section of the coal train passed. Neither checked the rear lights to confirm that the entire train had left the section. Tragically, for nine minutes the guard sat in his van before realising something was wrong. He immediately ran back to set detonators and protect his train but by then it was too late. The express had less than 70yd (64m) in which to stop from a speed of something over 50mph (80km/h), and ploughed into the coal wagons.

From Swindon

to Marston

remains of brake van and rear two wagons

remains of first two coaches

point of collision

track circuit

up goods line

up main line

down main line

up distant signal

Shrivenham station

Ashbury crossing signalbox

4-6-0 No 6007 on its right side

trains had no continuous brakes and relied solely on the locomotive steam brake and the hand brake on the guards van at the back. The wagons were loose coupled with a three-link coupling between each one held on the coupling hook of its neighbour. The coal train was scheduled not far ahead of the express, but it was booked to turn off the main line on to the loop at Shrivenham and continue on the goods line so that the express could overtake it unhindered.

The coal train, comprising 53 small, four-wheel wagons, was hauled by a standard 28XX 2-8-0 goods engine and, as usual for such trains, was travelling at around 25mph (40km/h). With an unbraked train of loose coupled wagons relying only on the steam brakes on the locomotive and the hand brake of the guards van, the train crew had to be very careful not to snatch the couplings when starting or stopping or at gradient changes when wagons could buffer up to each other. Otherwise there was a risk that a coupling would break or a coupling link jump off the hook, dividing the train into two parts.

As the coal train approached Shrivenham the distant signal was at caution. This was because it was being turned on to the goods line a little further beyond at Ashbury

▲On the express most of the impact was absorbed by the two leading coaches which broke up as they were hurled down the low embankment. The coach bodies were torn from the underframes, and roofs and interiors were strewn around. In contrast, the third coach had a much more massive steel underframe and withstood the impact far better.

Crossing, rather than at Shrivenham station itself. Whether there was a snatch as the train approached Shrivenham distant signal and the driver began to slow down is not clear, but the last five wagons and the guards van became uncoupled from the rest of the train.

As the main part continued on towards the station these wagons gradually rolled to a stop partway between Shrivenham distant signal and the track circuit approaching the home signal. Thus they were undetected by the signalman. However the signalman should have been looking for the tail lamps as the main part of the train passed Shrivenham signalbox.

Disastrous distractions
It was essential for signalmen to watch each train as it passed and to see the tail lamps to ensure that the train was complete. Just as the Aberdare coal train passed Shrivenham signalbox, a train of empty milk tanks passed on the down line obscuring the signalman's view of the coal train for a few seconds.

He saw the tail lamp on the milk tank train and gave 'train out of section' for it to Ashbury Crossing signalbox. He thought he saw the

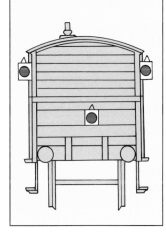

point of collision

To London
Paddington

to Shrivenham and
Ashbury crossing

▲ A crane is used to remove the debris which completely blocked the main Paddington – Bristol line for 20 hours after the collision. Some 220yd (200m) of permanent way in both directions had to be relaid. The axles on the right are all that remains of the guard's van and rear three wagons of the coal train.

diately made an emergency brake application he might have stopped the train before hitting the wagons, or at least hit them at low speed.

As it was, by the time the goods train guard looked out and realised what had happened he had time only to run back about 70yd (64m) waving his red lamp towards the express. It was too late. The express had hardly begun to slow down when *King William III* hit the guards van and toppled over on to its side in a mound of timber and metal.

Someone to blame

It was inevitable that the two signalmen were blamed for not positively seeing the tail lamps of the coal train. Thinking that they had seen the lamps was not good enough. The Shrivenham signalman was held responsible for the collision for it was he who had given 'train out of section' to Marston Sidings and accepted the express.

No less responsible was the guard of the coal train. He was the second line of defence in that if others made an error there was still a chance that he could have saved the situation. But he failed to look out for nine minutes to see why his end of the train had stopped. By then it was too late.

This accident demonstrates the total reliance then placed on human action and the need strictly to observe rules and regulations. Certainly there was a track circuit on the up main line for 500yd (457m) just before the home signal, but since the breakaway wagons had stopped short of the track-circuited part of the line they were undetected. If they had rolled on a little further on to the track circuit, Shrivenham could not have accepted the express. As for the ATC system, it was not at fault. The signals were clear for the express and the ATC duly gave a clear bell indication to the driver. Unfortunately, there were two human errors with no automated back-up to rectify them.

tail lamps on the coal train and gave 'train out of section' to Marston Sidings box and accepted the Penzance sleeper at 5.18am.

Just up the line at Ashbury Crossing the telephone took the attention of the signalman there as the coal train crossed from the main to the goods line. He looked up the line at the receding coal train and saw what he took to be the white light on the guards van. He assumed this had just been changed from red to indicate it had passed from the main line on to the goods line. He was unsure though. Had he seen the red lights? Before giving 'train out of section' he looked through the darkness towards Shrivenham which he could see and the line appeared to be clear. He gave 'train out of section' to Shrivenham and also accepted the sleeper. This allowed the Shrivenham signalman to clear his signals for the Penzance train.

Meanwhile, the guard of the coal train was blissfully unaware that his van and five wagons had been left behind. He thought the train had stopped at the Shrivenham home signal. He did nothing for about nine minutes; nine minutes in which he could have done something to avoid the collision.

In the circumstances, the rules required him to protect the breakaway wagons. This meant going back, walking, even running, with a red lamp, putting down detonators on the rail at a quarter, half, and three-quarters of a mile (0.5, 0.75, 1km) to warn any following train. In nine minutes he might have got back half a mile (0.75km). If the Penzance train driver had seen the red hand signal and imme-

Recommendations

There was very little that could be recommended to avoid a repetition, other than re-emphasising that signalmen had to follow the rules for train signalling and that guards had to carry out protection speedily in the event of an emergency.

Even the Welwyn control system (recommended after the 1935 Welwyn collision), which could prove, through block interlocking, that a train had passed through a section and the signals returned to danger behind it before a second train could be signalled, would not have stopped this collision. This is because it couldn't detect a breakaway which wasn't on a track circuited section – the signalmen were still obliged to see the tail lamps.

The only effective recommendations would have been the elimination of freight trains without continuous brakes, which wasn't achieved for another 40 years, or the adoption of continuous track circuiting, which only became widespread in the 1960s. Both of these developments were held back because of the huge expense involved.

Penmaenmawr 1950

**A light engine on the main line was waiting
to cross into a goods yard. Misunderstandings between
the driver, fireman and guard, and a misheard whistle signal,
led a signalman to clear the signals wrongly. An express
struck the light engine and six people were killed.**

Penmaenmawr station is on the North Wales coastal main line, about five and a half miles (9km) west of Llandudno Junction and 35 miles (56km) from the end of the line at Holyhead.

On the landward side of the station the ground rose to the Penmaenmawr mountain and all the sidings were on the up side (towards London).

None of the points leading to the sidings had any shunt signals, which meant that any move from the main line into the sidings, or over the crossover between the up and down lines, had to be authorised by the signalman giving a hand signal. At night this would be an oil lamp showing a white light.

Light engine confusion

There had already been some confusion in the early hours of Sunday 27 August 1950 on the working of the light engine. When its driver booked on at Llandudno Junction shed at 1.20am, fully expecting to go and pick up the 3am goods train from Penmaenmawr as booked, he was told by the shed foreman that it had been cancelled. Instead he was to run east towards Chester to pick up a train from Mold Junction.

As he topped up the tender water tank on his engine, Crab 2-6-0 No 42885, before leaving the shed, the rostered guard came up and said that Control had changed the instructions and the 3am train from Penmaenmawr would run after all since it included a special load which could not be delayed. The light engine ran the five and a half miles (9km) to Penmaenmawr and stopped in the down platform just short of the signalbox.

There were two ways of getting into the sidings on the up side. The usual way was by stopping the engine on the up line and then setting back through the points. This was what the Penmaenmawr signalman decided to do early on that Sunday morning as the other way was blocked by some goods trucks.

The signalman set the points to cross the engine from the down to the up line and gave the driver a hand signal to make the move. When the engine had cleared the crossover points on the up line, the driver stopped it and gave a pop whistle to let the signalman know where he was.

The driver looked towards the box waiting for

▶ The light engine, which was standing on the up main line, should have run into the sidings and through the crossover out of sight at the bottom left of the picture. But the points to the sidings were reset before the engine had moved.

▲ A crane with a spreader beam works to clear the wreckage of the Irish Mail express. In the background to the left is Penmaenmawr mountain, round which the line to Holyhead ran. Anglesey can be seen on the horizon. The jetty was used for loading granite from the nearby quarry into ships.

Key to trains

Irish Mail

light engine No 42885

down goods train

the oil lamp hand signal. The signalman heard the whistle and restored the crossover points to normal and immediately set the points from the up main line into the up sidings. He took his oil lamp and went outside the signalbox on the steps and gave the hand signal towards the engine by waving the lamp once from side to side.

He had to go on to the signalbox steps since the footbridge girders could have obscured his hand signal. Equally, the bridge meant that he could not automatically see the lights of the engine 275 yards (252m) away, unless he looked under the girders.

Just before the light engine first arrived at Penmaenmawr, the signalman had been offered the second portion of the London-bound Irish Mail express by the next box, Aber, which he accepted. But as he was crossing the light engine he obviously could not clear the signals for it.

At 2.55am the light engine was standing on the up line waiting for the signal to go into the goods yard. At 2.56am Aber sent the 'train entering section' signal to Penmaenmawr for the Irish Mail,

and Penmaenmawr immediately offered it forward to the Llandudno Junction signalman who accepted it.

The driver of No 42885 still had not seen any hand signal after three or four minutes but then saw the guard giving a hand signal by waving his lamp from side to side. The driver opened the regulator to move the light engine but found he was still going on the main line rather than over the points into the sidings. He stopped just as the guard came up to ask what was happening.

The fireman had also been told to change the lamps on the engine from front to back as they were still showing red towards Llandudno Junction and the signals had just been cleared for a down goods train to pass through.

Signals cleared

As the guard reached the engine, the up line signals were cleared. The driver thought that their goods train had again been cancelled and that the engine was going to return to Llandudno Junction, but the guard told him to go forward clear of the points and give a crow (cock-a-doodle-do) whistle.

Almost at once the guard heard and saw the Irish Mail approaching on the up line – the line on which the light engine was standing. The fireman had just got the red light on to the lamp bracket on the back of the tender of No 42885. 'Go forward' shouted the guard to the driver and the driver

Ignoring Rule 55

The inspecting officer blamed the signalman for relying only on a whistle signal to ascertain that the main line was clear. The evidence of the light engine crew was contradictory, but the engine had been on the main line for five minutes or so and they should have told the signalman at once if the move was delayed, under Rule 55. The driver may not have seen the signalman's hand signal. He might have blown the whistle without realising it when he moved towards the sidings. He was wrong to think that his train had been cancelled again when the up line running signals were cleared for the Irish Mail. He had to share some blame. So too did the guard, who did nothing when the engine failed to come into the sidings because the points had been reset for the up Irish Mail.

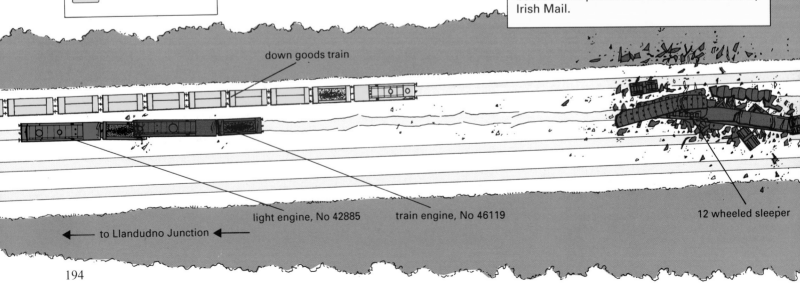

down goods train

light engine, No 42885   train engine, No 46119   12 wheeled sleeper

← to Llandudno Junction ←

opened the regulator to get the engine started, but it was too late.

The big Royal Scot class 4-6-0, No 46119 *Lancashire Fusilier*, hauling the Irish Mail, sparks streaming from the brake blocks clasped tightly on its wheels, was still travelling at between 45 and 50mph (72–80km/h) as it hit the tender of No 42885. The sudden impact broke the coupling between No 46119's tender and its train and the two engines locked together ran forward for 240yd (220m) beyond the point of the collision.

Only the tender of No 42885 was damaged, and partly derailed, but the 4-6-0 had its cylinders smashed, front bogie torn off and was entirely derailed, but in line. The drivers of both engines and one of the firemen were injured but survived.

It dawned on the engine crews almost straight away that a train was signalled on the down line. No 46119's driver, who had been thrown against the back of the boiler, injuring his arm, called to his fireman to go forward and put detonators down to try to stop the goods train from Llandudno Junction.

Nearly 70yd (64m) behind the two damaged engines, the coaches of the Irish Mail lay partly in a pile of wreckage, and partly spreadeagled across the tracks. It was a heavy train of sixteen coaches and only the last six were not derailed. Most of the coaches were standard LMS vehicles built in the 1930s or in the 1940s after the end of World War II, and had steel underframes and timber-framed bodies with steel outer panels.

But two were different: a twelve-wheeled first-class sleeping car, built in 1928 and marshalled second behind the leading full brake and parcels van, which had an all-timber body; and a corridor brake first with an all-steel body dating from 1930. The leading full brake and the first-class sleeper telescoped into each other and the sleeper body was destroyed completely, accounting for five of the six deaths.

The third and fourth coaches (this was the all-steel coach) were derailed, but not seriously damaged except for the bogies and undergear. The following three coaches jack-knifed on to their sides and were damaged, particularly at the body ends.

Inevitably casualties were heavy. Apart from the six dead, one of whom was a sleeping car attendant, 31 passengers and four crew, including both men on No 46119 and the driver of the light engine, were injured.

No track circuits

What had happened in the signalbox to lead the signalman to clear the signals for the Irish Mail, with the light engine standing in its path? It was a dark night and there were no track circuits to help the signalman know where trains were standing.

After the signalman had switched the light engine from the down to the up line and set the points for it to go into the sidings, he had gone on

▲ Considering the damage wrought to the Irish Mail train, the standing engine got off lightly. It remained on the rails and even the back coupling remained intact. Heavy cloud on the night of the accident had meant that the signalman couldn't see where the light engine was standing in the darkness.

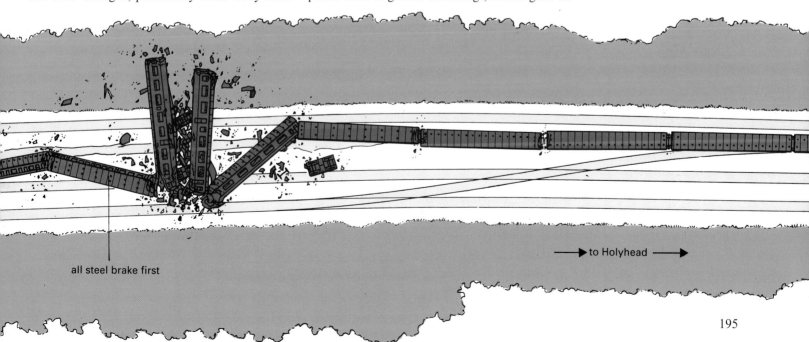

all steel brake first

→ to Holyhead →

▲ Royal Scot No 46119 is still leaking steam from its damaged smokebox as the breakdown crane lifts it with a wire rope sling. To the right were eight sidings, with two more towards Llandudno Junction, which were called the down refuge sidings, although they were on the up (seaward) side of the running lines.

On the footplate of the express, both driver and fireman had seen the clear distant signal and the home signal at green as they approached. But the home signal went back to red. The driver shut the regulator immediately and made a full brake application from 60mph (97km/h), but could not stop before hitting the light engine. After the accident, the driver of No 46119 managed to get off the engine and went back to meet the signalman. He met him on the platform and told him to get the signals back to danger for the down goods.

This too had passed the down distant signal at green, but its driver saw the home signal at danger and heard the detonators put down by No 46119's fireman. He was found collapsed on the lineside afterwards and was taken to hospital. The goods train could not avoid scraping the side of the derailed No 46119 but it was brought to a halt before hitting the wreckage of the Irish Mail coaches. It had been a near thing and a second collision was only just avoided.

As for the cause of the collision, it was never established precisely. It was a tale of claim and counter claim. The signalman told Lt Col G R S Wilson, the inspecting officer at the inquiry, that he had given a clear hand signal with his oil lamp towards the light engine and that he had heard a second pop whistle which to him meant that the engine was clear of the main line.

The driver of No 42885 said he had been looking for a hand signal and never saw one. He denied absolutely that he had given a second whistle. When the engine eventually moved towards the sidings and remained on the main line, points No 11 must already have been put back to normal by the signalman, who thought the move had already been completed.

The inspecting officer held the signalman and the crew of the light engine, and its guard, responsible for their failure to appreciate their obligations. Also, the enginemen had not reminded the signalman of where they were as required under Rule 55. He felt that Rule 69 covering shunting moves like this was ambiguous and that coded whistle signals should be used in future.

to the signalbox steps to show an oil lamp hand signal for it to move. At the same time he gave two rings on an electric bell in the sidings to indicate to the light engine crew that the main line should be cleared promptly for a through train.

About two minutes later he heard a second pop whistle which he naturally assumed was an indication that the engine was inside the yard clear of the main line.

Having received 'line clear' for the Irish Mail from Llandudno Junction he had no hesitation in clearing the signals for it through Penmaenmawr station. At the same time he had a goods train coming from Llandudno Junction and signalled it through to Aber. He had not actually seen the light engine move in the darkness nor could he see a light on it.

Full brake application

But suddenly he saw a red light from the Llandudno Junction end of the station. He immediately threw back the signal levers against the Irish Mail but it was too late – the express was approaching the up home signal a quarter of a mile (0.5km) from the station.

Recommendations

As Penmaenmawr signalbox was to be renewed, the inspecting officer had no recommendation about the limited sighting obscured by the footbridge, the lack of track circuits and the lack of shunting signals on the main lines. The new signalbox, to the east of the station, would have a much better view of the siding connections and of the up/down crossover and it was to be equipped with shunting signals. He recommended a review of Rule 69 regarding shunting moves and suggested the use of coded whistle signals for engines when shunting, with different whistle signals having specific meanings, instead of the short pop whistle being used for a variety of meanings. Following the accident, specific whistle patterns were given particular meanings.

Chapel-en-le-Frith 1957

The heroism of driver John Axon is legendary. He tried desperately to regain control of his runaway freight train as it careered towards the rear of another train, but was unable to prevent the collision. Axon was killed in the crash and was posthumously awarded the George Cross for bravery.

In early 1957 there were two routes between Buxton and Manchester: one on the old Midland Railway line through Chinley and the other – the one on which this accident occurred – the former London & North Western (LNWR) line from Stockport. Both routes had stations at Chapel-en-le-Frith: Central station serving the Midland line and South station serving the LNWR line.

The LNWR route from Buxton climbed steeply through the hills on the western flank of the High Peak area of Derbyshire, to a summit nearly two miles from Buxton at Bibbington's Sidings. The signalbox here controlled the entrance to a goods loop which ran alongside the down main line for nearly half a mile (0.75km), falling at a 1 in 70 gradient to Dove Holes station. The track then ran steeply downhill at 1 in 58 for two and a quarter miles (3.5km) to Chapel-en-le-Frith South station.

At that time signs of the new BR modernisation plan were just beginning to be seen on these lines, with some of the passenger services comprising new diesel multiple unit trains. The freight trains however remained steam hauled.

Freight trains from Buxton normally had a banking engine at the back to help push the trains up the incline, but they were not coupled to the back of the train they were assisting. Just at the summit – and still on the main line – there were stop boards, one for the train engine at the front and another for the banking engine at the back. These were the markers for goods trains to stop and then slowly draw forward. The guard would then pin down enough of the wagon brakes to ensure that the train had sufficient braking power to hold it in check on the steep falling gradient which followed. The steam brake on the engine and tender and the guard's brake at the back were held in reserve to stop the train if necessary. The banking engine, once its task was complete, would head back to Buxton.

▼ The scene after the crash at Chapel-en-le-Frith station was one of complete devastation. The impact of the crash created a mountain of twisted wreckage 25ft (7.5m) high, with over 150 tons (153,000kg) of loose coal strewn across the tracks. It was nearly three days before traffic could be restored through the station.

Approach to Chapel-en-le-Frith

At 10.47 on the morning of 9 February 1957, the signalman at Bibbington's Sidings accepted the 8.45am Rowsley to Edgeley (Stockport) freight train. Hauled by a Class 8F Stanier 2-8-0 freight locomotive, the train comprised 37 wagons – all but three loaded – plus a brake van. After pinning down the wagon brakes at the hill summit the train drew forward into the down goods loop, where it stopped again while a diesel passenger train overtook it on the main line.

As soon as the diesel train had cleared Chapel-en-le-Frith, the Rowsley goods train was signalled out on to the main line at Dove Holes and gradually gathered speed to about 20mph (32km/h) on the downhill run to Chapel-en-le-Frith South station.

Meanwhile, the following 11.05am Buxton to Arpley (Warrington) freight was signalled into the loop at Bibbington's Sidings. The train was hauled by Stanier 2-8-0 No 48188, with 33 wagons – all but two loaded and 24 of them carrying coal – with a brake van at the back and a banker behind.

At the hill summit, instead of stopping at the stop board to pin down the wagon brakes, the train continued on, seemingly with power still applied and with clouds of steam billowing out from the cab. It passed the signalbox and entered the loop much faster than normal. The banker had halted at the stop board, unaware of the major drama which was taking place in the cab of No 48188.

Build up to disaster

When the pipe leading to the driver's brake valve burst open, discharging a jet of scalding high pressure steam into the cab of Class 8F No 48188, driver John Axon struggled to close the regulator. His freight train was just approaching the summit of a steep hill leading down to Chapel-en-le-Frith South station.

Driver Axon instructed his fireman to jump out and apply the wagon brakes, and although he managed to drop six or seven handles, the train was travelling too fast for him to pin them down. The guard applied the handbrake in his van, but it had no effect on the train's speed.

Driver Axon remained at his post in the hope that he would be able to regain control. Tragically, his runaway train smashed into the back of another freight train at Chapel-en-le-Frith, killing Axon and the guard of the train in front.

A two-coach diesel passenger train, which was standing on the up platform at the time of the collision, was also struck by the derailed engine.

▲ After the collision the huge Stanier 2-8-0 finally came to rest after striking the front of the 10.20am Manchester to Buxton diesel passenger train. The front coach of the diesel train sustained only slight damage – mainly broken windows. It is seen here, left of picture, after it had been withdrawn from the wreckage.

Key to trains

11.05am Buxton – Arpley freight train

8.45am Rowsley – Edgeley freight train

10.20am Manchester – Buxton diesel passenger train

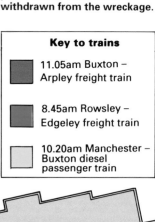

To Stockport ←

up line →

down line ←

Chapel-en-le-Frith South station

Steam leak

The problem had started back at Buxton while the engine was still in the shed. Driver John Axon had noticed a wisp of steam being emitted from the union nut between the steam pipe and the driver's brake valve. Leaks of this kind were not unusual as the pipe entering the brake valve had steam inside it at full boiler pressure and the vibration on the footplate sometimes loosened the union nut so that steam escaped through the join.

The driver reported the steam leak to the fitter at the shed who tightened the union nut holding the pipe end collar hard against the brake valve port face. That stopped the leak and the driver was satisfied. But as the locomotive was on the climb to Bibbington's Sidings the steam leak reappeared. It soon got worse and the driver and fireman tried wrapping rags round the blowing joint. They thought they could get to Bibbington's Sidings where they could stop for assistance, but just as they reached Bibbington's Sidings' distant signal, around 600yd (549m) or so from the summit, there was an explosion of steam as the copper pipe broke free from the joint.

Scalding high pressure steam quickly filled the cab – but what was worse, the jet of steam from the broken pipe was aimed straight at the regulator handle controlling the steam to the cylinders. Going uphill the regulator was hard open and the engine was working flat out – with less than 600yd (549m) to go to the change of gradient and the steep downhill section.

Driver John Axon and Fireman Scanlon tried desperately to get the regulator shut, but they were beaten back by the fierce jet of steam mixed with scalding water. The situation had suddenly

Wagon brakes

In 1957 goods wagons were equipped only with handbrakes. Freight trains always had guards' brake vans at the back, but they too were usually fitted only with handbrakes – although these were controlled from screw handbrake wheels.

The wagon brake handles were on the wagon sides and consisted of a lever which, when the brakes were off, normally rested on a ledge at the top of a vertical frame. To apply the wagon brakes, the lever had to be lifted over the lip and dropped between the sides of the frame and pressed down hard. A pin attached to a chain was inserted in holes through the frame above the lever to prevent it from lifting.

Just dropping the handle without pinning it was not effective; the wagon wheels rubbing against the brake blocks could jerk the brake lever up and down without any braking effect.

◀ With steam still venting from the overturned locomotive, rescuers assess the extent of the damage. Remarkably, No 48188 was repaired and returned to traffic. It was finally withdrawn in 1966.

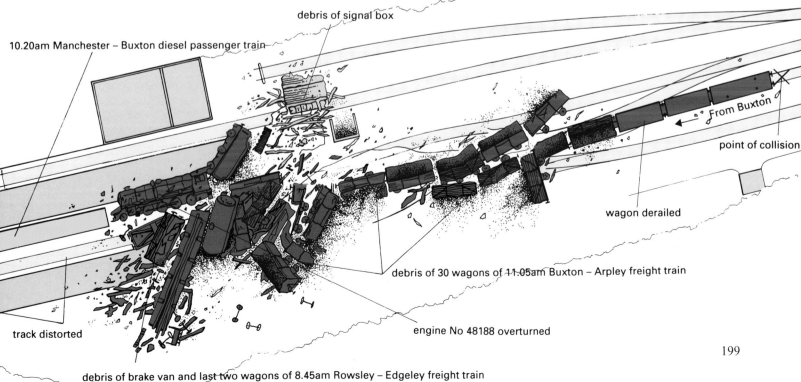

debris of signal box

10.20am Manchester – Buxton diesel passenger train

From Buxton

point of collision

wagon derailed

debris of 30 wagons of 11.05am Buxton – Arpley freight train

track distorted

engine No 48188 overturned

debris of brake van and last two wagons of 8.45am Rowsley – Edgeley freight train become one of survival.

The fireman wrapped his driver's coat around him and both tried repeatedly to get to the regulator handle. They were driven back against the tender by the sheer force of the steam. They managed to wind on the tender handbrake – although it had little effect – and get hold of one of the fire irons. With that they were able to close the regulator partly, but they could not close it fully, so the engine was still under power as it reached the hill summit.

Runaway freight train

Driver Axon told his fireman to jump off and try to pin down some wagon brakes. Fireman Scanlon jumped from the moving engine. He managed to drop the brake levers on about six or seven wagons, but the train was travelling too fast for him to get any pressure on the levers to pin them down. As the train gathered speed on the falling gradient he called to the guard in the brake van to apply his handbrake, but it was no use. The train just went on, getting faster as the heavy, unbraked load pushed the engine downhill towards disaster.

The signalman at Dove Holes was dealing with a freight train entering the up loop when he suddenly became aware of the runaway freight train in the down loop. It should have been stopping at the down loop home signal, but the driver was waving frantically from the right-hand side of the cab which was surrounded by steam. The signalman realised the train was not going to stop and quickly set the points from the loop out on to the main line to give the driver a chance of regaining

Into legend
At Euston station in 1981, Class 86 locomotive No 86261 was named *Driver John Axon G.C.* in honour of his bravery and courage on the footplate of his Stanier 8F.

Axon's heroism also passed into legend with a folksong written about his courage, called *The Ballad of John Axon.*

Steam pipe joint

The connection to the driver's brake valve from the combined ejector and steam valve was made by a 1¹⁄₈in (28mm) copper pipe. The screwed end of the brake valve was butted to a collar brazed on to the end of the steam pipe. The joint was packed with impregnated asbestos and secured with a union nut.

When it was examined after the accident it was discovered that the collar had been badly brazed on to the pipe and with repeated tightening the brazing eventually failed until it became so loose that the pipe blew out.

stop valve to ejector steam valves

main steam stop valve

steam manifold

whistle handle

small ejector steam valve

large ejector steam valve

driver's brake valve

live steam from boiler inside this pipe

driver's seat

reversing screw handle

regulator handle

Cab interior of a Stanier 2-8-0

union nut

impregnated asbestos packing

crack

copper pipe

live steam at full pressure in this pipe

brazing metal

nut deformed

pipe broke away from brazing

brake valve steam entry port

bronze collar

▲ **A cloud of lime and coal dust from the wagons filled the sky after the crash and showered down, covering the surrounding area in a strange monochromatic blanket.**

control. Had he not changed the points the engine would have run off the end of the loop, through the signalbox and into the platform end.

Even though the Rowsley freight had not cleared the section to Chapel-en-le-Frith, there was a chance that the Buxton freight might be able to stop in time. The Dove Holes signalman telephoned through to Chapel-en-le-Frith to tell the signalman there what had happened. A diesel train had just arrived there at the up platform and staff quickly called on passengers to get off the train and clear the platform.

The Rowsley freight was running into the station on the down line at about 20mph (32km/h) when the Buxton freight emerged from Eaves Tunnel, about a mile (1km) from the station, travelling fast in a cloud of steam. The crew of the diesel train tried to attract the attention of the enginemen on the Rowsley train, but it was too late.

Collision

The Buxton freight was travelling at about 55mph (88km/h) when it rammed the back of the Rowsley train, killing the guard. The big Stanier 2-8-0 overturned to its right on to the up line, demolishing the signalbox and throwing the signalman out on to the sidings below. Around and behind was the debris of the last two wagons and the brake van of the Rowsley freight and nearly all the wagons of the Buxton train which, with around 150 tons (153,000kg) of loose coal, formed a pile of wreck-

age 25ft (7.5m) high across both tracks. The overturned engine stopped against the front of the diesel train on the up line.

The Rowsley freight was pushed 300yd (274m) forwards by the impact and although much of the train was undamaged and remained on the track, the shock wave reverberated through the train and three wagons near the front were derailed.

The guard of the Buxton train had remained in his van holding the brake hard on with his brake stick. This was not enough to slow down the runaway, but he could have done no more.

Tragically, driver Axon was killed in the cab of No 48188. He had stuck to his post to the last – though he must have realised that even if he could shut off the regulator completely he would still be without any brake control. Even if he had been able to get to the reversing wheel to try to reverse the engine, the unbraked wagons would have overwhelmed the engine completely. Driver Axon was posthumously awarded the George Cross for his outstanding example of devotion to duty.

What went wrong?

The inspecting officer, Brigadier C A Langley, praised the actions of all the staff. He concluded that the accident had happened because of the bad brazing between the pipe and the collar on the steam pipe to the driver's brake valve. The joint had been leaking before and had been reported on 10 occasions during the previous 15 months. In each case the fitter had tightened the union nut and had stopped the leak. None of the fitters had undone the union to examine the collar and the brazing, for in all cases the leak had been stopped so poor brazing had not been suspected. In fact by tightening the nut, the nut itself had been distorted and had gradually damaged the collar until the brazed joint broke and the copper pipe was blown out by the force of the steam.

A different form of joint with a coned collar had already been introduced. It made a better steam-tight joint into the fitting to which the pipe was attached, and the brazing could be seen instead of being hidden under the union nut. Ironically, a coned collar had been used to join the other end of the steam pipe on No 48188.

Recommendations

The inspecting officer, Brigadier Langley, recommended that with any steam leak like the one on No 48188 the fitter had to take down the pipe and check the joints. The new type of coned joints were to be adopted for the future, but existing butt joints were to be examined regularly.

Primarily though, the inspecting officer recommended the adoption of full automatic braking throughout the wagons of freight trains – an ideal not achieved until more than 25 years later. This recommendation referred to vacuum brakes, but by the time automatic braking was generally introduced on freight trains the more powerful compressed air brake system had been adopted.

Telegraph instruments

In 1837, the London & Birmingham Railway experimented with an electric telegraph between Euston and Camden. The first public use of the system, however, was on the Great Western (GWR) between Paddington and West Drayton in 1838. The electric telegraph quickly proved its worth, particularly in the field of safety, and other railways soon followed suit. By the 1880s all the major lines were equipped with electric telegraph circuits.

Variations and developments led to quite sophisticated train signalling arrangements, which controlled the traffic with a remarkable degree of safety at even the busiest stations and junctions. The basic telegraph system, however, provided merely a means of communicating messages between two or more locations by the transmission of electrical impulses along a wire between them.

For the most part, the instruments were contained in a polished hardwood case about 18in (457mm) high by 9in (229mm) wide. Near the top in the front face was a round dial with an upright indicator, or needle, which was pivoted in its centre. On receipt of an electrical impulse, the top of the needle moved left or right a few degrees. The Morse code was used, movement to the left representing a dot, to the right a dash.

Two small sounders were fixed to the dial, one each side, so that the operator would hear the needle tap out the message and be able to write it down without looking away from the paper. On the front of many telegraph instruments, just below the dial, was a sloping wooden writing surface about 11in (279mm) wide by 9in (229mm) deep, with a metal spike or hook at the top for securing the message paper.

The transmitter was usually a turned wooden handle fixed vertically to the front of the instrument beneath the writing surface. Experienced telegraph operators could send and receive messages almost as quickly as they could speak.

Although the development of the telephone brought much greater flexibility to railway operations, many telegraph circuits remained in use well into the 20th century. Indeed, they survived on the Eastern Region of British Railways until the mid-1960s.

A minority of railways, particularly those of the Cheshire Lines Committee, used Bright's telegraph instruments. These machines still used the Morse code, but through separate transmitting and receiving instruments. The transmitter was 3in (76mm) high and was mounted on a 6in (152mm) square wooden base.

The receiver was 15in (381mm) high, 12in (305mm) wide and 8in (203mm) deep, with a wooden base and sides, and a curved metal back, forming an open-fronted sounding box. Fixed to the sides within this box were two electric sounders with different tones, giving the operator a distinctly audible message.

Collecting telegraph instruments

Although telegraph instruments are in rather shorter supply than block instruments, they are usually cheaper. This is because, unlike the latter, they are seldom marked with the owning company's name or initials. A single-needle telegraph instrument in good working condition will cost around £60 to £90, while one requiring some restoration or mechanical repair should be obtainable for a good deal less than that.

Bright's telegraph instruments, although still without railway company markings, are much rarer and you should expect to pay in the region of £150 to £200 for a transmitter and receiver set. Instruments appear from time to time at most of the railway auctions and in railway collectors' magazines.

◄▲ The fine workmanship of this rare Midland Railway Spagnoletti telegraph instrument (left) can be appreciated with its top removed. The most common type is the Great Northern Railway example (above, left), with a scarce double-sided instrument for teaching purposes (above, right).

CHAPTER FIVE

LIVING STEAM

The National Railway Museum

Occupying a 17 acre site near York station, the National Railway Museum is the largest museum of its kind in the world. Its exhibits span almost two centuries and range from a full-size working replica of Stephenson's *Rocket* to a section of the Channel Tunnel.

▼ Resplendent in its green and black livery, the first of the large Atlantics, No 251, built for the Great Northern Railway in 1902, is one of the locomotives displayed around the turntable in the Great Hall. Also pictured, right, is the London & South Western Railway Adams 4-4-0 No 563, dating from 1893.

Previous page: A winter's scene on the Bluebell Railway. Locomotive 0-6-0T No 58850, originally belonging to the North London Railway, is over 100 years old.

'It is nothing short of a national disgrace', an indignant reader wrote to the *Railway Magazine* in 1917, 'that no All-British Railway Museum exists for preserving in chronological sequence the inception and progress of our national railway. It is high time that this was remedied and the Government should provide the necessary funds.'

The government, however, had other priorities – it was still desperately searching for a way to beat the Kaiser – and almost 60 years were to elapse before the opening of the National Railway Museum (NRM) in York in 1975. That year saw two separate collections – one from the Museum of British Transport in Clapham, London, and the

other from the London & North Eastern Railway (LNER) Museum in York – combined under one roof.

The new Museum was housed in the former 19th century York engine shed, now named the Great Hall. However, despite extensive rebuilding work, it was discovered in 1988 that the roof was structurally unsound. The repair work was included in a £6 million renovation and improvement scheme, and the new-look NRM opened in April 1992.

It is now the largest museum of its kind in the world. The public display area has doubled in size, and visitors can see more of Britain's railway heritage than ever before.

▲ **Standing side by side are three of the NRM's oldest locomotives: North Eastern Railway 0-6-0 No 1275 of 1874; London & North Western Railway 2-2-2 No 1868** *Columbine* **of 1845; and Furness Railway 0-4-0 No 3 of 1846, nicknamed Coppernob.**

The visitors' car park is close to the north entrance, which leads directly into the Great Hall. If you have come by train, a 10 minute walk from York station will take you to the main entrance, a new steel and glass building that gives access both to the South Hall and, via a subway under the busy Leeman Road, to the Great Hall.

The South Hall, once the North Eastern Railway's goods depot in the city, was originally used by the NRM for storage purposes. However, during the redevelopment of the Great Hall, it served as an exhibition centre, and this function continues.

Displays in the South Hall are devoted to Travelling by Train, a theme which applies to both passengers and freight. There is a rich variety of rolling stock – freight, express, suburban and royal – some displayed with appropriate locomotives. One of the couplings is between a 1905 Great Western Railway (GWR) 2-8-0 freight locomotive, No 2818, and a train of open wagons and enclosed vans.

Freight lines during the steam age had extensive cartage services, so alongside the train are horse-drawn and motor vehicles, to remind visitors that door-to-door transit involved railway-operated road services.

Passenger trains on display

Passenger travel between the turn of the century and World War I is illustrated by three trains. The East Coast Express comprises the North Eastern Railway (NER) M class 4-4-0, No 1621, built in 1893, and two carriages, one from the Great Northern Railway and the other from the East Coast Joint Stock. The latter, a third-class corridor carriage of 1897, is often open to visitors, with Museum staff in railway porters' uniform opening the doors for you.

The Branch Line Train is represented by a London & South Western Railway carriage and tank locomotive. The carriage, a prize specimen from 1903, is a tri-composite brake, with six compartments – two for each of the three classes – and is a complete train in itself.

If you have a taste for opulence, then you need look no further than the 1913 first-class Pullman

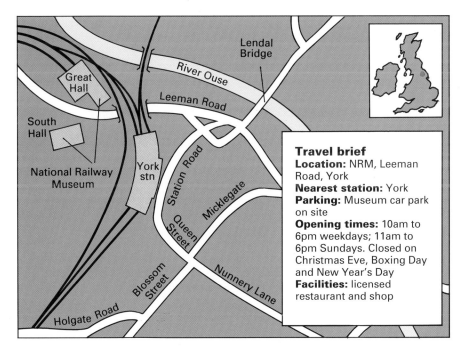

Travel brief
Location: NRM, Leeman Road, York
Nearest station: York
Parking: Museum car park on site
Opening times: 10am to 6pm weekdays; 11am to 6pm Sundays. Closed on Christmas Eve, Boxing Day and New Year's Day
Facilities: licensed restaurant and shop

▲ The NRM's working replica of *Rocket* has become almost as famous as Robert Stephenson's original. Commissioned by the Museum for the 150th anniversary celebrations of the Liverpool & Manchester Railway in 1979, the reproduction *Rocket* has travelled to many countries, including Japan and the United States.

◄ Located in the South Hall, the Treasure Trove features items from the NRM's vast collection of railway memorabilia. These range from luggage labels and presentation watches to an imposing candelabra once owned by Robert Stephenson.

parlour car *Topaz*. Paired with the elaborately decorated South Eastern & Chatham Railway (SECR) Wainwright 4-4-0, No 737, dating from 1901, *Topaz* epitomises the grand epoch of railway travel. The car, with its red velvet chairs, fine wood veneers and polished brass table lamps, ran originally on the SECR. It later served on the Southern Railway (SR) and on British Railways, often in Boat Trains for the Continent.

Breaking with tradition

Equally impressive, though in a rather different way, is the 1885 Midland Railway (MR) six-wheel compartment carriage, No 901, which is coupled to an 1899 Midland 4-2-2, No 673. At the end of the 19th century, the company abolished second class, upgrading its third class facilities and providing them on all trains. The reforms represented a drastic break with tradition, but they soon achieved their aim of attracting more passengers, many of whom travelled in the new and better carriages exemplified by No 901.

Soft upholstery is provided in both first and third class compartments, the only real difference between them being the latter's lack of arm rests and slightly smaller dimensions.

Next to No 901 is another MR vehicle, a superbly restored 1914 third class dining car, complete with kitchen facilities. The tables are elegantly laid with glasses, china and silverware, and life-like figures in period dress occupy some of the seats.

One of the NRM's most popular attractions is its collection of royal rolling stock, which ranges from Queen Adelaide's coach of 1842 to a 1941 LMS saloon built for HM Queen Elizabeth, the Queen Mother, and later used by HM Queen Elizabeth II until her Silver Jubilee year in 1977.

Among the displays is the London & North Western Royal Train, made up of two saloons and a dining car and headed by a 1935 London Midland & Scottish (LMS) 4-6-0, No 5000. The three vehicles were built in the early 1900s for King Edward VII and Queen Alexandra, and the dining car continued to be used on royal journeys until 1956.

Another crowd-puller is Wagons-Lits No 3792, which is paired with a 1934 SR Schools class 4-4-0, No 925 *Cheltenham*. No 3792 is one of the sleeping cars that made up the famous London to Paris Night Ferry service introduced by the Southern in 1936. Unlike many Wagons-Lits cars, which were given a traditional wood veneer, No 3792 was constructed entirely of metal, thus enabling it to comply with shipboard fire regulations.

Riding behind *Rocket*

Outside, in the South Yard, there are special weekend rides behind the NRM's two full-size working replicas – one of the 4ft 8½in gauge *Rocket* and the other of the 7ft gauge *Iron Duke*. Main line steam and diesel locomotives are also operated, as well as a 7¼in gauge miniature railway.

This version of *Rocket* – there is an earlier model in the Great Hall – was built in 1979, since when it has visited many countries. Weighing only eight tons, it can be transported easily and holds the distinction of being the first full-sized steam locomotive to have flown the Atlantic – by wide-bodied jet.

Large-scale exhibits

The theme of the Great Hall is the Technology of Railways, and the displays reflect not only the past, but also the present and the future. Thus visitors entering from the subway are immediately confronted by a huge concrete ring as used in the running tunnels of the Channel Tunnel.

No less overwhelming is the scale of some of the earlier engineering projects on show here, whether it be the gantry of eight GWR lower-quadrant signals from Northolt in Middlesex or the 19th century NER footbridge from Percy Main in Northumberland.

Locomotive enthusiasts will be impressed by a line-up spanning a period of 150 years, with steam, diesel and electric traction all represented. The engines are grouped round turntable A – turntable B disappeared during the redevelopment – and range from the tall-chimneyed *Agenoria* of 1829 to the prototype High Speed Train power car of 1972.

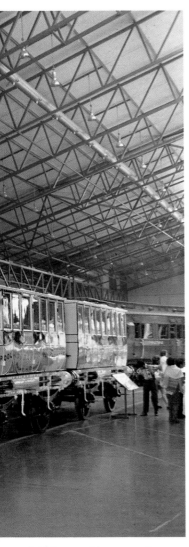

▶ This superbly restored Midland Railway third-class dining car, with kitchen facilities and passenger accommodation, dates from 1914. A few years earlier, the Midland had shocked the other railway companies by abolishing second class on its trains and upgrading the third-class facilities.

◄Part of the NRM's collection of royal carriages is East Coast Joint Stock saloon No 395, built in 1908 for King Edward VII. The vehicle, made of varnished teak and decorated in Louis XVI style, was later used by Queen Mary and Queen Elizabeth, the Queen Mother.

dynamometer car in recollection of the famous run of 1938, when the blue-painted Pacific became the world's fastest steam locomotive.

For sheer size, the prize must go to the 192-ton 4-8-4 built by the Vulcan Foundry in Newton-le-Willows in Lancashire in 1935 for Chinese National Railways. Locomotives, rolling stock and signalling equipment have been exported by British manufacturers all over the world, and the 4-8-4 is on show with many other examples.

Presiding over the north end of the hall, and wearing a suitably contemplative expression, is a statue of George Stephenson. It stood originally in the Great Hall of Euston station, but survived the drastic redevelopment that destroyed Euston's famed Doric Arch in the 1960s. The ornamental gates that once graced the station also survived and they are displayed near the great Stephenson.

▼ North Eastern Railway (NER) 2-2-4T No 66 *Aerolite* stands beneath the NER footbridge from Percy Main station in Northumberland. Built in 1869 at Gateshead, *Aerolite* is the only NER two-cylinder compound to survive.

If you are interested in the internal workings of a steam engine, look out for *Rocket* and *Ellerman Lines*. *Rocket* was built in 1829 and this replica of 1935 has been sectioned to show how the original was designed. No 35029 *Ellerman Lines*, an SR 4-6-2 of 1949 vintage, has also been sectioned. An electrically powered drive rig enables its motion and driving wheels to be turned.

Another exhibit of special interest to steam enthusiasts is the London & North Eastern Railway 4-6-2 *Mallard*, which is paired with a

Another famous railway pioneer, George Hudson, known to his contemporaries as the Railway King, declared that his intention was to make all the railways come to York, the city of which he was Lord Mayor. This financial rogue never realised his ambition, but almost a century and a half after his downfall, York is enjoying its own kind of railway glory.

The Talyllyn Railway

**Opened in 1866, the narrow gauge
Talyllyn Railway became one of the most neglected and
poverty-stricken lines in Britain. By 1951, closure seemed
inevitable. But then a group of enthusiasts stepped
in – and helped to make railway history.**

In Britain today, more than 50 preserved railways provide the welcome opportunity to ride behind a steam locomotive. New schemes are regularly proposed and this enthusiasm for recreating the past – aptly described as a second Railway Mania – is not confined to British shores. From Slovakia to New Zealand, from Switzerland to Brazil, volunteer-run railways ensure that the age of steam lives on.

Yet the first railway to be preserved and the inspiration for all that followed was one of Britain's most obscure and neglected lines. The 7¼ mile (12km) Talyllyn Railway (TR) opened in 1866 to transport slate from the Bryn Eglwys Quarry, near Abergynolwyn, to the Cambrian Railways' main line at Tywyn, then known as Towyn. The gauge

was 2ft 3in, unusual for Britain, but shared by the Corris Railway at nearby Machynlleth.

Two locomotives were supplied by Fletcher Jennings of Whitehaven. No 1 *Talyllyn*, built in 1864 as an 0-4-0ST, was soon reconstructed as an 0-4-2ST to improve its rough ride. An 0-4-0WT, No 2 *Dolgoch*, followed in 1866. Four coaches and a brake van – all four-wheelers – along with an assortment of slate and general goods wagons, completed the TR's stock.

For 85 years, the TR led an unremarkable existence. As slate traffic declined, passenger loadings increased from the growing number of tourists in mid-Wales. In 1911, both railway and quarry were bought by local MP and landowner Henry Haydn Jones. The quarry closed in 1947, but Haydn Jones

▼ The sylvan setting of the TR makes spring or winter an ideal season for photography, enabling the light to penetrate areas shaded by foliage in the summer. Here 0-4-2ST No 3 *Sir Haydn* hauls a train near Dolgoch. Built in 1878, the locomotive came from the neighbouring Corris Railway that ran to the slate quarries of Aberllefenni.

▲ 0-4-0WT No 6 *Douglas* stands at Tywyn station. A 1918 product of Andrew Barclay Sons & Co in Kilmarnock, *Douglas* spent most of its pre-TR existence working the 2ft gauge railway at RAF Calshot, near Southampton.

kept the railway running. Subsidising it out of his own pocket, he operated trains three days a week in summer until his death in 1950.

By this time, the TR was almost moribund. Virtually no maintenance had been undertaken for many years. *Talyllyn* had not worked since the mid-1940s. The entire operable stock of the railway consisted of *Dolgoch* and a handful of coaches, all over 80 years old and in poor repair.

It is surprising that anyone noticed the imminent demise of this remote line. However, three enthusiasts, Bill Trinder, Tom Rolt and Jim Russell, who knew and loved the little railway, were not prepared to see it die. They called a public meeting in October 1950, which led to the formation of the Talyllyn Railway Preservation Society (TRPS).

Handover to amateurs

At the time, the idea of a railway run by amateurs with volunteer support was completely unprecedented. None the less, Lady Haydn Jones handed the line over to effective TRPS control and in May 1951 the railway ran trains to Rhydyronen. The usual summer service to Abergynolwyn followed, with record passenger loadings. The tribulations of operating the delightful, if life-expired, railway are entertainingly described in Rolt's book, *Railway Adventure*.

More rolling stock was urgently required. Fortunately, the closed Corris Railway's last two locomotives survived at Machynlleth in British Railways' ownership. BR generously sold them to the Talyllyn for £25 each (plus another £25 for transport) and in March 1951 they became Nos 3 and 4 of the TR, the same numbers they had carried under Corris, Great Western and BR auspices.

The Talyllyn named No 3, an 1878 0-4-2ST from Hughes of Loughborough, *Sir Haydn*, after

the line's late owner. No 4, a 1921 Kerr Stuart 0-4-2ST, became *Edward Thomas*, after the TR's long-serving manager.

Work to make the track safer was also put in hand immediately, although the last of the old rails was only replaced in 1992. Developments and improvements continued, with more locomotives obtained, new carriages built, passing loops installed and a train control system introduced. In 1976, the TRPS extended passenger services from Abergynolwyn to Nant Gwernol along track which had carried only slate trains previously.

The TR's Tywyn Wharf terminus is a short walk from the main-line station on the scenic Cambrian Coast route. Originally, Wharf – then known as King's – was only a freight yard, where slate was transhipped on to the Cambrian.

The red brick goods office forms the core of the present enlarged station building. Further down the platform is the Narrow Gauge Railway Museum, with fascinating displays about lines throughout the British Isles.

Every TR train is steam-hauled and all the original rolling stock is regularly used. If you are lucky, *Dolgoch*, now well into its second century

The Corris Railway

The Corris Railway (CR) had much in common with its westerly neighbour, the Talyllyn. From 1859, it transported slate from Aberllefenni and Corris down to the main line at Machynlleth, and to wharves on the River Dyfi beyond. Passenger services operated between the 1880s and 1931. It was possible in summer to undertake a grand tour from Tywyn, travelling on the TR to Abergynolwyn, taking a connecting road service via Tal-y-llyn Lake to Corris, using the CR down to Machynlleth and finally boarding the main line train back to Tywyn. The CR closed in 1948, but in recent years a preservation society has opened a museum at Corris and rebuilt a short section of track there.

▶ One of the original locomotives of the Talyllyn Railway, No 2 *Dolgoch*, an 0-4-0WT, is seen near Nant Gwernol. Now returned to its original state, the locomotive often heads restored coaches from the closed Glyn Valley and Corris lines.

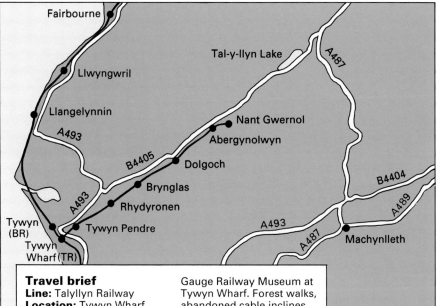

Faster by foot
On an August Saturday
every year, the TR hosts its
Race the Train event, one of
the most relaxed events in
the Welsh Amateur Athletics
Association's calendar. A
special return train operates
between Tywyn and
Abergynolwyn while several
hundred runners race it over
a cross-country course
closely following the railway
line.

As the train usually takes
about 1¾ hours for the
return journey, many of the
athletes qualify for the
special certificate presented
to those who manage to
outpace it. Everyone taking
part receives a medal and all
proceeds go to charity.

▶ **The TR's two original
locomotives – 0-4-0WT No 2
Dolgoch and 0-4-2ST No 1
Talyllyn – double-head a train
west of Dolgoch. Both
locomotives were built by
Fletcher Jennings & Co of
Whitehaven and remained the
sole motive power on the line
for more than 80 years.**

nerve centre of the line. Carriage sheds on both
sides of the track allow the TR to keep its entire
stock under cover here. Inside the locomotive
shed, on the right, is 0-4-0WT No 6 *Douglas*, built
by Barclay for an Admiralty 2ft gauge line in
1918. Named after its donor, *Douglas* was given
to the TR in 1953 and regauged. The railway's
three small diesels can often be seen in Pendre
yards.

Leaving Pendre behind, the train is soon skirting the foot of the hills that rise to the south. To
the north is the flood plain of the River Dysynni,
with more low mountains beyond.

Climbing between hedges, the train passes
three tiny halts before reaching Rhydyronen's
slate-built station. Efforts were once made to promote a mineral water source here, but there is little
traffic nowadays.

From Rhydyronen the railway continues along
the valley of the River Fathew, a tributary of the
Dysynni, with hills closing in on both sides. A
long straight section gives fine views ahead of the
mountain range leading up to the 2930ft (893m)
Cader Idris.

Exchange of tokens

At Brynglas, the first passing loop since Pendre,
Sir Haydn, the older of the Corris engines, is waiting with a train for Tywyn. Tokens for the single
line are exchanged before your own train pulls
away again.

The valley narrows now, and the line begins to
climb on to the hillside. At several places along
the route the TR is enclosed by slate fences. The
railway's lack of funds meant that everything was
done at minimum cost and waste slate was the
cheapest building material available.

Shortly after entering a pleasant wood, the line
emerges on to the dramatic three-arch Dolgoch
Viaduct, with the gorge of the Nant Dolgoch
glimpsed through the trees 50ft (15m) below.
Almost immediately, Dolgoch station is reached –

of service, will be working your train. Restored
coaches from the closed Glyn Valley and Corris
lines are often marshalled along with modern
bogie vehicles, built in traditional style. Because
of tight clearances under bridges, carriage doors
are on the left-hand side only.

The train runs through a cutting from Wharf to
Pendre, the original passenger terminus and the

a charming halt delightfully set amid banks of rhododendron bushes. The open hillside rises steeply from the trackside opposite the platform.

All trains take water at Dolgoch. Sadly, the original tank on its picturesque slate plinth has been disused since 1961. Its replacement is an unattractive metal structure, located to accommodate longer trains.

It is worth breaking your journey here to visit the waterfalls in the wooded ravine. On a June weekend in 1990, the gorge became an open-air theatre for a performance of Shakespeare's *A Midsummer Night's Dream*. Transport was provided by hourly trains throughout the night, marketed as a Midsummer Night's Steam.

From Dolgoch you continue along an ever more scenic hillside ledge, passing Quarry Siding loop by the TR's old ballast quarry. Craggy mountains, with patches of yellow gorse, rise sharply above the railway. Just before Abergynolwyn, the train passes through more woods.

Original passenger terminus

For over a century, Abergynolwyn was the TR's passenger terminus, though the present building dates from 1969. The long platform holds two trains simultaneously. Workings from Nant Gwernol, the upper terminus opened in 1976, arrive first, stopping at the western end, where a loop allows trains from Tywyn to pass them and halt further east. Because there are no facilities at Nant Gwernol, downhill trains stop at Abergynolwyn long enough for passengers to visit the café and shop.

Heading the Tywyn train today is 0-4-2T No 7 *Tom Rolt*. Built by Barclay in 1948 as a 3ft gauge 0-4-0WT for Bord na Mona, the Irish Turf Board, it was regauged and completely rebuilt at Pendre, entering service in 1991.

▲ No 1 *Talyllyn* stands at Brynglas with the three bow-sided carriages and brake van supplied by Brown Marshalls & Co of Birmingham for the opening of the TR in 1866. Delivered as an 0-4-0ST, *Talyllyn* was rebuilt with a trailing axle in 1867.

Your train is drawn out of Abergynolwyn on to the old mineral extension, running along a precipitous ledge through dense woodland. The winding route required considerable work to make it safe for passenger trains. Above Abergynolwyn village, the line curves south into the Nant Gwernol ravine to reach the simple terminus.

A recent footbridge across the gorge provides access to a network of forest walks. You can also climb the abandoned inclines to see the remains of the Bryn Eglwys Quarry at the head of the valley.

But what of the railway's namesake? The lake of Tal-y-llyn, spectacularly situated at the foot of Cader Idris, lies three miles (5km) beyond Abergynolwyn station. The TR never reached it and was never intended to. The Act of Parliament authorising the railway merely specified a line 'towards Talyllyn', bestowing a name on the TR almost by default.

Delivery to the door

Although Abergynolwyn lies about half a mile (0.8km) from its station, there was once a much closer link between the TR and the village. At a point on the mineral extension where the line is 150ft (46m) above Abergynolwyn, a cable-operated incline allowed goods wagons to be lowered to the village.

From storage sidings at the bottom, two branches ran along the streets so that deliveries could be made by rail to the back doors of many houses and waste removed in the same way. Wagons could be pushed manually, hauled by horses or rolled along by gravity.

◄ The TR's newest locomotive, 0-4-2T No 7 *Tom Rolt*, crosses the three-arch Dolgoch Viaduct. Outshopped by Andrew Barclay in 1948, it began life as a 3ft gauge 0-4-0WT with the Irish Turf Board. It joined the TR in the early 1970s as 'Irish Pete' and was given its present name in memory of the well-known writer, and one of the founders of the TR Preservation Society.

The Ffestiniog Railway

**Deep within Snowdonia National Park lies the
Ffestiniog Railway. Opened more than 150 years ago to
carry slate from mountain quarries to the ships at Portmadoc,
it is a fine example of a working narrow gauge railway.**

The Festiniog Railway (FR) was opened in 1836 to transport roofing slates from the quarries of Blaenau Ffestiniog, some 700 feet (200m) above sea level, to Portmadoc (now known as Porthmadog), 13½ miles (20km) away on the coast. For more than a quarter of a century the line was worked by gravity, the wagons rumbling down laden from the quarries and being hauled back empty by horses.

However, with the introduction of steam in 1863, the Ffestiniog Railway – it now uses the Welsh form of two Fs in its title – began to carry passengers. After years of decline, it has become a mecca for tourists attracted by the prospect of an exciting journey through the mountains and forests of Snowdonia. Excursions usually begin at Porthmadog, and to get there you pass through some of the best scenery in Wales.

In high summer, the crowds throng the booking hall, shop and platform of Porthmadog Harbour station, while alongside stands a rake of red and cream coaches, some newly built in the FR's own workshops, others restored originals dating back to 1873, when the Ffestiniog became the first British railway to use bogie coaches.

You can travel first or third class. Although first class is obviously more expensive, it entitles you to travel either in the observation car or near the engine in one of the old non-corridor coaches – a treat in itself, though the disadvantage is that you get no on-train refreshment services.

True to the original

At the head end stands a unique and remarkable locomotive, the brass plate on its tank sides proclaiming it as *Merddin Emrys*, a double-ended 0-4-4-0 built by the Ffestiniog Railway in 1879 to the patent of Robert Fairlie. It is painted a glorious deep red and, though rebuilt, captures the spirit of the original. An articulated machine, with twin boilers and a central cab, its double bogie is a forerunner of the arrangement now standard for diesel

▼ Dwarfed by the slopes and slate tips of the Moelwyn Mountains, the Fairlie double engine 0-4-4-0 *Merddin Emrys* hauls a down train from the terminus of Blaenau Ffestiniog past the waters of Llyn Ystradau. The engine, built by the Ffestiniog Railway in 1879 and recently restored to its Victorian splendour, was one of the pioneering double bogie units. During the 1870s, such locomotives went into operation on a number of other railways.

and electric locomotives.

Just before the start of the hour-long journey, a deep whistle echoes along the platform and *Merddin Emrys* moves its train on to the Cob, the great 19th century sea wall which lies round the curve from the station exit. On the left are magnificent views of Snowdonia, with a toll road immediately below and the open sea to the right.

At the end of the Cob are the Boston Lodge Works, which not only overhaul but also build engines for the Ffestiniog Railway. And what a fascinating variety there is.

The roster includes a modern double Fairlie, *Earl of Merioneth*, completed at Boston Lodge in 1979; two 2-4-0 saddle tanks, *Linda* and *Blanche*, which both started life on the old Penrhyn Quarry Railway and have been modified to cope with the

arduous hauls on the FR; an American Locomotive Company 2-6-2 tank, *Mountaineer*, built for use on military supply lines in France during World War I; and the 0-4-0 saddle tank, *Prince*, one of the pioneer engines used by the FR when it converted to steam in 1863, and the oldest steam locomotive in the world still running on its original line.

Converting to oil

Today all the FR's steam locomotives are fired by oil instead of coal – a change forced because the sparks of the coal burners were a serious threat to lineside forestry. Although the engines can burn a mixture of waste oil and diesel oil, the FR's fuel bill is formidable. It has reduced costs by using its more economical diesel locomotives for off-peak

▶ The FR's latter-day version of a Fairlie double engine, *Earl of Merioneth*, steams across the Cob, the great 19th century sea wall linking Porthmadog and the railway workshops at Boston Lodge. Completed at the workshops in 1979, the *Earl* was the first Fairlie to be built for 68 years.

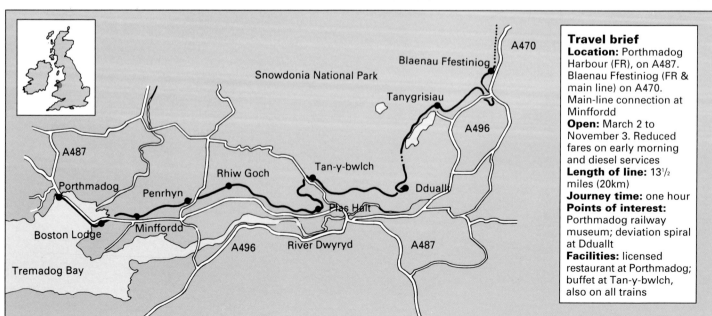

▶ One of the first four steam engines brought into service on the FR in 1863, 0-4-0 *Prince*, makes its way through the lush woodland between Penrhyn and Tan-y-bwlch. Such tracts were often set on fire by flying sparks from coal burners, so in the 1970s the company decided to convert its fleet from coal to oil firing.

▼ A lone motorist gives way to a summer season train hauled by *Earl of Merioneth*. The *Earl* and its vintage stable companion, *Merddin Emrys*, completed 100 years earlier, take on the bulk of the FR traffic at busy times since each one is in essence two engines back to back and so has the power to handle the heaviest trains.

working.

The first stop on the way from Porthmadog is Minffordd, which is an interchange station with the Cambrian Coast line. A mile or so away is the famous Italianate village of Portmeirion, and well worth a visit in itself. Created by Sir Clough Williams-Ellis, it was used as a setting for the 1960s television series, *The Prisoner*.

Climbing the foothills beyond Penrhyn, *Merddin Emrys* rattles and hisses into the platform at Tan-y-bwlch, the halfway point of the journey, and draws up alongside the water tower. In the 1930s and '50s, passengers would be greeted by the station mistress, the late Bessie Jones, dressed in Welsh national costume and handing out tea from the station house.

Although there is no longer free refreshment, Tan-y-bwlch remains a popular tourist attraction.

A nature trail starts from the station car park and runs by Llyn Mair, a picturesque lake with picnic areas from which you can watch the many types of water fowl.

To the east, the Moelwyn Mountains look down on the Vale of Ffestiniog and far to the south the skyline is marked by the silvery shape of the nuclear power station at Trawsfynydd – an incongruous symbol of the present in a world that has remained largely unchanged since the whistle of the steam engine first shrilled through the woods across Llyn Mair.

After the deluge

From Tan-y-bwlch the train crawls up towards Dduallt. Here prior to World War I the station master was a famous Welsh bard whose writing lamented the effects of working in such isolation. The line used to pass through a long tunnel beyond the station, but this was blocked up in the 1950s, when the Llyn Ystradau reservoir was built for a hydro-electric power station at Tanygrisiau, and the far entrance now lies below the normal water level.

The revised route makes a 220° turn around a huge deviation spiral – the only one of its kind in Britain – crosses over the original track by a new bridge and enters the 300yd (274m) long Moelwyn tunnel, which was carved out by volunteer miners working for the FR in 1975-76.

Beyond the tunnel, the line runs by the side of Llyn Ystradau, its waters almost lapping the low carriage steps as *Merddin Emrys* steams past to regain the old track formation at Tanygrisiau. Passengers alighting here can go on a guided tour

End of the line

Not every exhibit in Porthmadog station museum has seen the end of its useful life. One item that was recently resurrected was the FR's funeral car. Built in 1875 as a quarrymen's coach and converted 10 years later into a hearse, the vehicle had taken its place among the FR's collection of railway memorabilia in 1954.

Its recall into service was triggered by the death of one of the FR's volunteer workers, Maggie Warner. As a fitting tribute to Maggie, it was decided to scatter her ashes on the FR, and the funeral car was recommissioned to take part in the ceremony. Several of Maggie's colleagues have been inspired to ask for a similar send off when the time comes.

of the nearby power station. Or they can take the path that leads to a secluded lake and the ruins of a once thriving slate mining community.

Within a couple of minutes, the train pulls into Blaenau Ffestiniog. This final section of the old line was reopened in 1982; and the new terminus, incorporating a souvenir shop and travel and tourist centres, was built jointly by the FR and British Rail. The terminus connects with the Conwy Valley branch line, enabling tourists to continue on to the north Wales coast.

But there is plenty to see around Blaenau Ffestiniog itself, including the old slate mines of Llechwedd and Gloddfa Ganol, which are both open to visitors. A special battery electric train will take you into the heart of Llechwedd.

Attempt at revival

The attempt to revive the Ffestiniog Railway began in 1951, with the formation of the Festiniog Railway Society. (Somewhat confusingly, the society has stuck with the English form of only one F.) The line had lain derelict since 1946 – a state of affairs which the Ffestiniog Railway Company, heavily in debt and with neither income nor prospects, could do little to change.

But in 1954 the company was taken over by a wealthy benefactor of the society – his shares were subsequently transferred to a charitable trust – and from then on the two organisations worked hand in hand to relaunch the railway. After eight years of total neglect, the line was so overgrown with

▲ A crowded passenger train pulled by *Earl of Merioneth* brushes past the front gardens of cottages at Tanygrisiau. The remains of the temporary terminus can be seen to the left of the train; the run-round loop and sidings were lifted after the line was finally reopened to Blaenau Ffestiniog.

In the wake of 'Little Wonder'

The first Fairlie locomotive, *Little Wonder*, appeared on the FR in 1870. Designed by Robert Fairlie, it had two boilers back to back, a firebox and a central cab – an arrangement that gave it more than double the power of its predecessors. Moreover, by mounting each boiler on a power bogie, Fairlie ensured that his engine could negotiate sharp curves and steep gradients.

Other Fairlies soon followed, including *Merddin Emrys* (below), still in use after more than a century. A number of foreign railways also took up the engine and the Russians even used some broad gauge versions, but its main effect was to increase the efficiency of narrow gauge lines.

brambles, bushes and even small trees that for much of its length it was impossible even to walk along it.

Thanks to the efforts of volunteers from the society, the line was gradually cleared, and in 1955 the 0-4-0 *Prince*, fitted with a new boiler, travelled the first section to be reopened – the one mile from Porthmadog to Boston Lodge.

By 1968, the line had been made operational as far as Dduallt. But beyond there the volunteers faced the toughest obstacle of all – the Llyn Ystradau reservoir. The electricity authorities had obtained permission to go ahead with this scheme before the FR's revival and it was only after a prolonged legal battle that they were forced to pay compensation to the FR.

This helped to fund the deviation spiral, but again much of the work was carried out by volunteers. In 1978, their efforts were rewarded with the reopening of the 2³/₄ mile (4km) section from Dduallt to Tanygrisiau. Four years later, with the line clear once again all the way to Blaenau, the rebirth of the FR was complete.

The Bluebell Railway

Named after the swathes of bluebells in the adjoining woods, the Bluebell Railway in Sussex is one of the few independent lines to rely exclusively on steam. Its fleet of some 30 locomotives spans five generations and ranges from tiny Terrier tank engines to a giant 2-10-0.

Of nearly 100 independent steam railways operating in the UK today, the Bluebell Railway, in the heart of rural Sussex, is one of the best known. The original line was opened in 1882 by the London, Brighton & South Coast Railway (LBSCR) and ran for 18 miles (29km) between Lewes and East Grinstead. The line was finally closed by BR in 1958, but the section known as the Bluebell was resurrected in 1960.

It is not the biggest or scenically the most spectacular of the preserved railways – but it has a great deal of charm and was the first to prove that railway enthusiasts could successfully run a line which BR had abandoned. The single track line, which leads northwards from the Bluebell's Sheffield Park headquarters, runs for five miles (8km) through a pastoral backdrop of farms, fields and woodland to Horsted Keynes, which until 1990 was the limit of train operations.

Since then, however, the Bluebell has extended operations to Kingscote a further four miles (6.5km) towards East Grinstead; the continuing section of track is being steadily relaid to connect the Bluebell Railway with the main line.

Crossing the Ouse

Sheffield Park is easily accessible by road and it is from here that most passengers begin their journey. Pulling gently away from the platform, the train crosses the River Ouse and rumbles past the trackside marker denoting the Greenwich Meridian. The river looks innocuous enough now, but in times of spate it has been known to flood the valley floor away to the left.

The total travelling time of 35 minutes for the round trip between Sheffield Park and Horsted

▼ The Bluebell's insistence on authenticity is reflected in every aspect of its operations – from the provision of fire buckets outside the porters' room at Horsted Keynes station to the restoration of locomotives such as the 1875 veteran *Stepney*, seen below working in tandem with 0-6-0WT *Bellerophon*, a visiting engine from the Keighley & Worth Valley Railway in West Yorkshire.

▲The crew of BR Standard 4MT 2-6-4T No 80064, an engine dating from 1953, wait the right away at Sheffield Park. The Bluebell employs six full-time railway staff and is served by around 100 regular volunteers, and many others who help out occasionally.

Blooming Bluebell
British Railways was still building steam locomotives when it axed the 18 mile stretch of money-losing line between Lewes and East Grinstead in 1958.

A year later, the Bluebell Railway Preservation Society was launched. Its first objective was to buy the five mile middle section between Sheffield Park and Horsted Keynes.

BR's asking price of £34,000 was too high, but pursuing the option of a five-year lease, the society was able to run its first service on 7 August, 1960. The Bluebell was about to bloom again.

Keynes is governed partly by the Department of Transport's 25mph (40km/h) upper speed limit, which applies to almost all steam railways on the standard gauge, and partly by the demands of the two 1 in 75 gradients on the line.

The first of these extends for one and a half miles (2km) up Freshfield Bank and begins almost immediately after the train has left Sheffield Park. It is by no means the most severe in the world of steam railways – but it is still a stiff test for a small engine and crew with five fully laden coaches weighing 200 tons or more.

Having crested Freshfield Bank, the train pushes through the open farmland of the Sussex Weald. To the right, the land becomes noticeably more hilly as, for the next two miles (3km), the railway flirts with the edges of Lindfield Wood.

It is not long before the train is digging in for the second major climb of the journey, which leads to Horsted Keynes. The exhaust note of the engine echoes back off the big red-brick Three Arch Bridge at the start of a long curve to the right, and it is here that the train crew usually whistle up to let the Horsted Keynes signalman and station staff know of their approach.

Passing the Bluebell's carriage and wagon

▶ No 928 *Stowe*, a Southern Railway Schools class locomotive of 1934, the most powerful 4-4-0 in the country, heads a rake of matching green Bulleid and Maunsell coaches. The Bluebell is famed for its ability to run pre-nationalisation engines with the appropriate rolling stock.

shops on the right and the abandoned Haywards Heath line junction on the left, the train eases into the impressively spacious Horsted Keynes station, its grandiose buildings, four platforms and passenger subway a legacy of its days as an important link in the Southern Railway network.

All-steam policy

Almost alone among Britain's independent lines, the Bluebell is still a 100% steam operated railway, having resisted for 30 years the temptation to run a diesel. Even for yard shunting and works trains, the staff and volunteers still turn out at dawn to light up in the traditional way. And although back in 1965 the railway was presented with a tiny petrol engined shunter, it serves no active role, existing merely as a relic.

The all-steam policy is part of the Bluebell's obsession with authenticity – the accurate portrayal of stations, booking offices, waiting rooms, signalboxes, locomotives and coaches just as they used to be.

Historically, the line had three different operators before the preservationists took over. From 1882 to 1922 it belonged to the LBSCR. With the grouping of the railway companies in 1923, it was run by the Southern Railway. And with nationalisation in 1948, it became a part of the British Railways empire.

Each of the railway companies had its own individual livery and house style – and the railway today reflects them all. So, while Sheffield Park is

restored as an LBSCR station of the turn of the century, Horsted Keynes is the very image of a busy Southern Railway country junction of the 1930s; and Kingscote, the second station on the East Grinstead extension, commands the appearance of a BR station of the early 1950s.

Matchless collection

The Bluebell Railway today boasts a matchless collection of classic locomotives and coaching stock from the Victorian and Edwardian eras – thanks to the foresight of its first volunteers, who in the winter of 1960 drew up a shopping list of vintage locomotives still in BR service, but in imminent danger of being scrapped.

In those early days, however, cash was scarce, and many engines on the Bluebell list did go to the breaker's yard. Nevertheless, the fleet now stands

▲ **Beribboned for a Bluebell Railway gala day, an LSWR Adams Radial 4-4-2T No 488, built in 1885, stands amid the suitably Victorian surroundings of Sheffield Park station. The locomotive, bought by the Bluebell from BR in 1961, was given a major overhaul 10 years later. It has had several changes of livery since arriving at Sheffield Park, but is shown here decked in its original colours.**

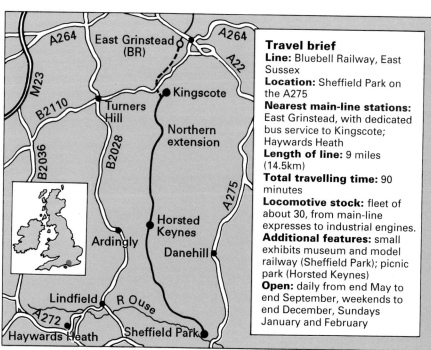

Travel brief
Line: Bluebell Railway, East Sussex
Location: Sheffield Park on the A275
Nearest main-line stations: East Grinstead, with dedicated bus service to Kingscote; Haywards Heath
Length of line: 9 miles (14.5km)
Total travelling time: 90 minutes
Locomotive stock: fleet of about 30, from main-line expresses to industrial engines.
Additional features: small exhibits museum and model railway (Sheffield Park); picnic park (Horsted Keynes)
Open: daily from end May to end September, weekends to end December, Sundays January and February

at around 30 (15 of them privately owned) and ranges from main-line express locomotives to humble industrial engines.

Sheffield Park loco shed boasts no fewer than five centenarian engines, as well as representatives from each of the three principal pre-grouping railway companies in the south – the LBSCR, the South Eastern & Chatham Railway (SECR) and the London & South Western Railway (LSWR).

The first locomotive to be bought from British Railways, in May 1960, was the diminutive LBSCR Terrier Class A1X 0-6-0T No 55 *Stepney*, dating from 1875. It was the inspiration for the Reverend W Awdry's children's book, *Stepney the Bluebell Engine*. Restored to its original mustard coloured livery, and carrying a face mask on the smokebox, it is the undoubted celebrity of the line.

Oldest member of the fleet is another A1X engine, No 72 *Fenchurch*, now in its 120th year and the first of its class to enter service. Both *Fenchurch* and *Stepney* worked the Havant-Hayling Island branch at different stages in their careers.

The aesthetic favourite of the fleet is probably the LSWR Adams Radial 4-4-2T No 488, dating from 1885. It was designed for suburban passenger work but ended its days with British Railways on the Axminster – Lyme Regis run. Recently restored, it remains the elegant epitome of Victorian locomotive design.

At the other end of the spectrum for both size and power is BR Class 9 2-10-0 express freight engine No 92240, totally rebuilt after 13 years in a South Wales scrapyard.

However, the Bluebell Railway's collection of more than 60 historic passenger coaches, based at Horsted Keynes carriage depot, is not there simply for show. For despite a throughput of more than 200,000 passengers a year, the Bluebell

prides itself on running 50- and 60-year-old coaches on its normal service trains, matched wherever possible with historically appropriate locomotives.

Some of the carriages date from the 1920s, and were designed by the SECR chief mechanical engineer, Richard Maunsell, with later stock from the 1940s and '50s, produced by Southern Railway Chief Mechanical Engineer Oliver Bulleid. All of these are the envy of other independent steam railways, which started out too late to acquire much more than redundant ex-BR coaches of the 1950s and '60s.

▲ A North London Railway 0-6-0T of 1880, No 58850, its smokebox door hung with a wreath of Remembrance Day poppies, waits to couple up to a brake coach at the southern end of Horsted Keynes. The water crane, semaphore signal and platform barrow recall the rural charm of bygone days.

◄ Empty stock headed by a Southern Railway 4-6-2, No 35027 *Port Line*, of 1948 vintage, waits for No 55 *Stepney* to clear its path. In its guise as the Bluebell Engine featured in the Rev Wilbert Awdry's children's stories, *Stepney* has helped to impress many youngsters with the attractions of steam.

▶ Bluebells border the line as No 80064 steams through Lindfield Wood. It was not far from here that a trackman named Pope was supposedly murdered by a gamekeeper. The facts are lost in time, but in the early 1960s trains carrying school parties would sometimes spot 'Pope's ghost' – a part acted out by some long-suffering member of the Bluebell staff wearing a white sheet.

ACKNOWLEDGEMENTS

Photographs: 2, 3 Eaglemoss Publications, 5 Eaglemoss Publications/John Suett, 6,7 Science Museum, 8 Millbrook House/Hugh Ballantyne, 9 Science Museum, 10 Millbrook House, 11 Millbrook House/L.Good, 12 Millbrook House, 13 Roger Bastin, 14 Graham Wiltshire, 15 National Railway Museum, 16 Millbrook House/E.Treacy, 17 Millbrook House, 18 National Railway Museum, 19 Millbrook House, 20 Brian Stephenson, 21 Rail Archive Stephenson, 22 Millbrook House/L.Good, 24,25 Millbrook House, 26 Loco Publishing Co., 27 J.A.Coiley, 28 Geoff Rixon, 29 Millbrook House, 30 National Railway Museum, 31 Colour-Rail, 32 David Rodgers, 33 Millbrook House, 34(t) David Rodgers, (b) Millbrook House/P.M.Alexander, 35 Lawrence Waters, 37 Spectrum, 38 Hulton-Getty, 39 Millbrook House/E.Treacy, 40(t) National Railway Museum, (b) David Rodgers, 41 Colin Garratt, 42 Millbrook House/Colour-Rail/J.T.Inglis, 43 Hulton-Getty, 44 Millbrook House/Colour-Rail/Kenneth Leach, 45 Millbrook House/Gavin Morrison, 46,47 Millbrook House/Colour-Rail, 48 Millbrook House/Hugh Ballantyne, 49 Hulton-Getty, 50 A.E Hooker, 51,52 Colour-Rail, 52-53(b) Dr. L.A. Nixon, 54 Millbrook House/Patrick Whitehouse, 55 Millbrook House/Hugh Ballantyne, 56 Millbrook House/Patrick Whitehouse, 57,58 Millbrook House/Hugh Ballantyne, 60 Harold Edmonson, 61 Union Pacific, 62,63 Harold Edmonson, 65,66 Millbrook House/Hugh Ballantyne, 67 State Railway Authority of New South Wales, 68 Millbrook House/Hugh Ballantyne, 69 David Rodgers, 70 Millbrook House/G.W. Morrison, 71,72 Millbrook House/Colour-Rail, 73 Chris Kapolka, 74-75(l) Peter Cavalier, 75(r) Chris Kapolka, 76 Colin Garratt, 77 David J. Holman, 78 Anthony Lambert, 79 Dennis Hardley, 80(t) Collections/Alain le Garsmeur, 80-81(b) Millbrook House/K. Sanders, 81(t) Collections/Alain le Garsmeur, (b) David Rodgers, 82(t) Millbrook House/Peter J. Robinson, (b) Dennis Hardley, 83-85 Millbrook House/Patrick Whitehouse, 86(t) Millbrook House/Patrick Whitehouse, (b) Millbrook House/Chemins de Fer de Provence, 87 David Rodgers, 88 Colin Garratt, 89(t) Terry Hanson, (b) Peter W. Robinson, 90(tl) Terry Hanson, 90-91(b) Colin Garratt, 91(tr) David Rodgers, 92 Donald Brooks, 93,94 Paul Stratford, 95(t) Donald Brooks, (b) Paul Stratford, 96 Eaglemoss Publications/John Suett, 97,98 Chris Kapolka, 99(tr) Robert Harding Picture Library, (bl) David Rodgers, 100 Chris Kapolka, 101 John Hunt, 102 Millbrook House, 103,104,105 Anthony Lambert, 106 David Eatwell, 107(t) P.C.Riley, (b) Anthony Lambert, 108-109 Anthony Lambert, 110 Les Nixon, 111,112 Anthony Lambert, 112-113 Millbrook House/Gavin Morrison, 113(b) Les Nixon, 114(b) Millbrook House/Gavin Morrison, 114-115(t) Anthony Lambert, 116 John Hunt, 118 Millbrook House/J.S.Whiteley, 119(t) Robert Harding Picture Library, (b) Millbrook House/Patrick Whitehouse, 120 Peter Skelton, 121 Millbrook House/Hugh Ballantyne, 122 Robert Harding Picture Library, 123 Mary Evans Picture Library, 124 David J. Holman, 125 Anthony Lambert, 126(t) David J. Holman, 126-127(c) Anthony Lambert, 127,128 David Rodgers, 129 Hulton-Getty, 130 Millbrook House/Patrick Whitehouse, 131, 132-3 Millbrook House, 133(t) Hulton-Getty, (bl) Popperfoto, (br) Hulton-Getty, 134(tl) Hulton-Getty, (bl) Millbrook House/Hugh Ballantyne, 134-5 Hulton-Getty, 136 Hulton-Getty, 137(t) Hulton-Getty, (b) Illustrated London News, 138 Hulton-Getty, 138-9(t) Jim Winkley, 139(b) Millbrook House, 140 National Railway Museum, 140-141(t) National Railway Museum, 141(br) Anthony Lambert Collection, 142(t) Illustrated London News, 142-143(b) Millbrook House, 143(tr) National Railway Museum, 145 Aerofilms, 146 Millbrook House, 146-147 National Railway Museum, 148 Michael Mensing, 149-151 Millbrook House, 151(b) Geoffrey Kichenside, 152 R.C. Riley, 153,154 Mary Evans Picture Library, 155 Millbrook House, 156 Hulton-Getty, 157(t) Hulton-Getty, (b) Millbrook House, 158,159 Hulton-Getty, 160 Millbrook House, 161,162,163 Hulton-Getty, 164 Millbrook House, 165-169 Hulton-Getty, 170 City of Dundee Art Galleries and Museums, 171(t) City of Dundee Art Galleries and Museums, (b) Scottish Records Office, 172 City of Dundee Art Galleries and Museums, 173,174 Illustrated London News, 175 Hulton-Getty, 176 Illustrated London News, 177 Mirror Syndication, 178-180 Illustrated London News, 181-184 Hulton-Getty, 185 Mirror Syndication, 186 Hulton-Getty, 187 Illustrated London News, 188-192 Hulton-Getty, 193 Popperfoto, 194-199 Topham, 200-201 Press Association, 202(l) Jeremy Corbett, (r) Anthony Lambert, 203 Mike Esau, 204,205 Jim Winkley, 206(t) Sylvia Cordaiy Picture Library/P.S.Linfoot, (b) National Railway Museum, 207 Sylvia Cordaiy Picture Library/Monika Smith, 208(t) National Railway Museum, (b) Jim Winkley, 209 Derek Huntriss, 210 David Rodgers, 211 Eddie Castellan, 212(t) Anthony Lambert, (b) Eddie Castellan, 213 Peter Johnson, 214 David Rodgers, 215 Peter Johnson, 216 Millbrook House, 217(inset) Peter J.Stone, (b) Mike Esau, 218(t) Collections/Alain le Garsmeur, (b) Millbrook House/John Whiteley, 219(t) Peter J. Stone, 220(t) Mike Esau, (b) Collections/Alain le Garsmeur, 221 Mike Esau.

Illustrations: 7 Geoffrey Wheeler, 10-11 Salamander, 16-17 Maltings Partnership, 20-21 Geoffrey Wheeler, 23 Paul Kellett, 25-26 Geoffrey Wheeler, 28-29 Stuart Black, 30 Paul Kellett, 31 National Railway Museum, 32-33 Stuart Black, 35 National Railway Museum, 36 Kevin Jones Associates, 38-39, 42-43 Stuart Black, 44 National Railway Museum, 46-47 Stuart Black, 48 National Railway Museum, 50-51 Stuart Black, 52 National Railway Museum, 56-57 Salamander, 58 Greater Manchester Museum of Science and Industry, 60-61 Salamander/Stuart Black, 63 National Railway Museum, 64(t) Kevin Jones Associates, (b) Eaglemoss Publications, 66-67 John Holroyd, 68 State Railway Authority of New South Wales, 70-71 Stuart Black, 72 National Railway Museum, 80(bl), 82(tl) Ron Mardle, 85, 88, 93 Mick Gillah, 98(tl) Ron Mardle, (b) Mick Gillah, 100 Ron Mardle, 102,109,115 Mick Gillah, 117 Graham Dorsett, 120-121 Mick Gillah, 122 Ron Mardle, 126 Mick Gillah, 144(l) Paul Kellett, (r) Kevin Jones Associates, 146-147 Richard Foster, 162 Graham Dorsett, 170-171, 174-175, 178-179, 182-183, 186-187, 190-191 Paul Kellett, 194-195 © HMSO, 1997, 198-199 Paul Kellett, 211 Duncan Kitson, 214 Mick Gillah, 219 Paul Kellett.